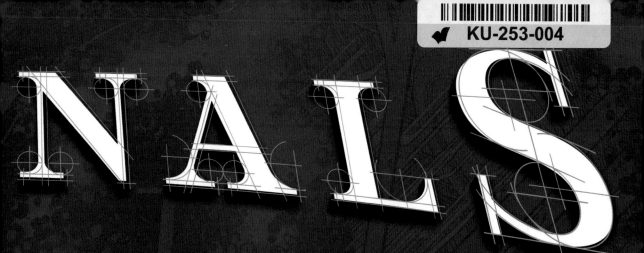

NALS

Created by Jack Kirby

WRITER: Neil Gaiman

PENCILS: John Romita Jr.

INKS: **Danny Miki and Tom Palmer**
with Tim Townsend, Jesse Delperdang and Klaus Janson

COLORS: **Matt Hollingsworth**
with Paul Mounts and Dean White

LETTERS: **Todd Klein**
COVER ART: **Rick Berry**
ASSISTANT EDITOR: **Sean Ryan**
EDITOR: **Nick Lowe**

COLLECTION EDITOR: **Jennifer Grünwald**
ASSISTANT EDITORS: **Michael Short & Cory Levine**
ASSOCIATE EDITOR: **Mark D. Beazley**
SENIOR EDITOR, SPECIAL PROJECTS: **Jeff Youngquist**
SENIOR VICE PRESIDENT OF SALES: **David Gabriel**
BOOK DESIGNER: **Patrick McGrath**
VICE PRESIDENT OF CREATIVE: **Tom Marvelli**

EDITOR IN CHIEF: **Joe Quesada**
PUBLISHER: **Dan Buckley**

ERNALS BY NEIL GAIMAN. Contains material originally published in magazine form as ETERNALS #1-7. First printing 2007. ISBN# 0-7851-2176-5. Published by MARVEL PUBLISHING, INC., a subsidiary of MARVEL ENTERTAINMENT, INC. OFFICE OF PUBLICATION: 417
h Avenue, New York, NY 10016. Copyright © 2006 and 2007 Marvel Characters, Inc. All rights reserved. $29.99 per copy in the U.S. and $48.00 in Canada (GST #R127032852); Canadian Agreement #40668537. All characters featured in this issue and the distinctive
ames and likenesses thereof, and all related indicia are trademarks of Marvel Characters, Inc. No similarity between any of the names, characters, persons, and/or institutions in this magazine with those of any living or dead person or institution is intended, and
y such similarity which may exist is purely coincidental. Printed in the U.S.A. ALAN FINE, President & CEO Of Marvel Toys and Marvel Publishing, Inc.; DAVID BOGART, VP Of Publishing Operations; DAN CARR, Executive Director of Publishing Technology; JUSTIN F.
ABRIE, Managing Editor; STAN LEE, Chairman Emeritus. For information regarding advertising in Marvel Comics or on Marvel.com, please contact Joe Maimone, Advertising Director, at jmaimone@marvel.com or 212-576-8534.
9 8 7 6 5 4 3 2 1

INTRODUCTION

Some history.

In 1968, an author named Erich Von Däniken published a book called *Chariots of the Gods?* The question mark was the most interesting part of the title and our first hint that what the man was offering was conjecture and theory, not cold 'n' hard fact.

Hint #2: The book was subtitled "Unsolved Mysteries of the Past." That kind of mystery often remains unsolved, forever and even after that. One can come up with possible solutions, logical deductions and maybe even a pat scenario that seem to explain a mystery of the past…but let's be honest here. Can you prove beyond a reasonable doubt — or even an unreasonable one — that ancient civilizations *weren't* visited by space travellers and heralded as gods? Huh, can you? No, of course you can't.

The alien visitation was Von Däniken's thesis, but it was not his invention. Truth to tell, no one seems to know who came up with it…perhaps some Martian gave it to the great-great-great-great-etc.-grandfather of the caveman in those Geico commercials. But it dates back to at least the turn of the century…and not the current one. The one before. Sometime in the forties, a fellow named Jack Kirby read about it in some magazine, and it intrigued him.

Mr. Kirby drew and sometimes wrote comic books. You probably already knew that. The whole notion of gods visiting this planet had always intrigued him, dating back at least to 1940 and the very first story he ever did for Marvel, "Mercury in the 20th Century."

Jack didn't necessarily believe that aliens had visited Earth and impacted the development of *homo sapiens*, but that was okay. He also didn't believe a runt could be injected with a super-soldier formula and turn into Captain America, and that hadn't stopped him from co-creating that character's adventures. Ideas to Jack were these malleable, amorphous blobs, as valuable as whatever you could make out of them. You could use one as a good starting point for your imagination and then roam freely from there, perhaps even to some higher, more persistent truth.

Prehistoric interplanetary tourists? Well, maybe. Jack thought it was an intriguing concept…and it sure could explain a great many things that weren't explainable via more prosaic history. Those statues on Easter Island, for instance — where the hell did they come from? It was a riddle that fascinated Kirby all his life, and those statues turn up in a half-dozen comic stories he drew over the years. They even came to life and greeted another god on Earth — the Mighty Thor — in his debut story in 1962.

Maybe the huge, stone images were left by aliens…or more likely, carved by Earthlings to commemorate the arrival of people who looked like that. To Kirby, it was as good an explantion as any -- and a great starting point for something or other.

The publication of *Chariots of the Gods?* in '68 redoubled his interest in the concept. By 1972, the book was an unconfined best-seller, and there were a dozen others covering the same turf, expanding on or rebutting Von Däniken's premise. Kirby bought and read every one he could find. He never quite believed the hypothesis met any reasonable standard of proof, but he sure believed there was a comic book in it. In 1975, he got his chance to prove the latter.

In '75, Jack Kirby created, wrote and drew *The Eternals* for Marvel. He didn't call it that at first. His original name was *The Celestials*.

Someone at Marvel didn't like that title. Someone else got the idea to call the series *Return of the Gods* and to emulate the title lettering from Von Däniken's best-selling paperback. For a while, it was going to be that, but Jack objected. Then DC Comics objected. (They were bringing back Jack's *New Gods* series but without him, and they were calling it *Return of the New Gods*.) Then someone gct worried that Mr. Von Däniken might have a thing or three to say about it…

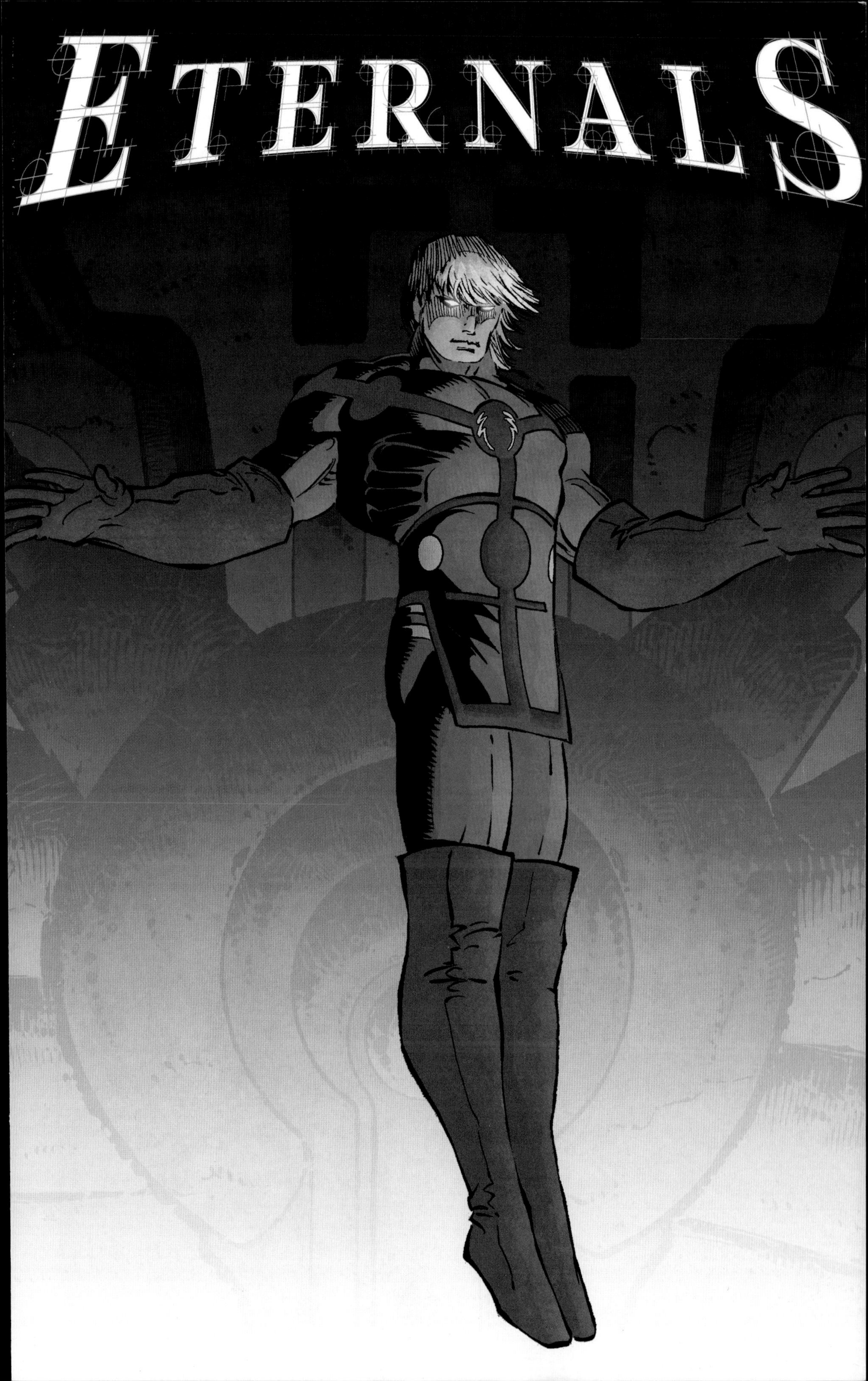
ETERNALS

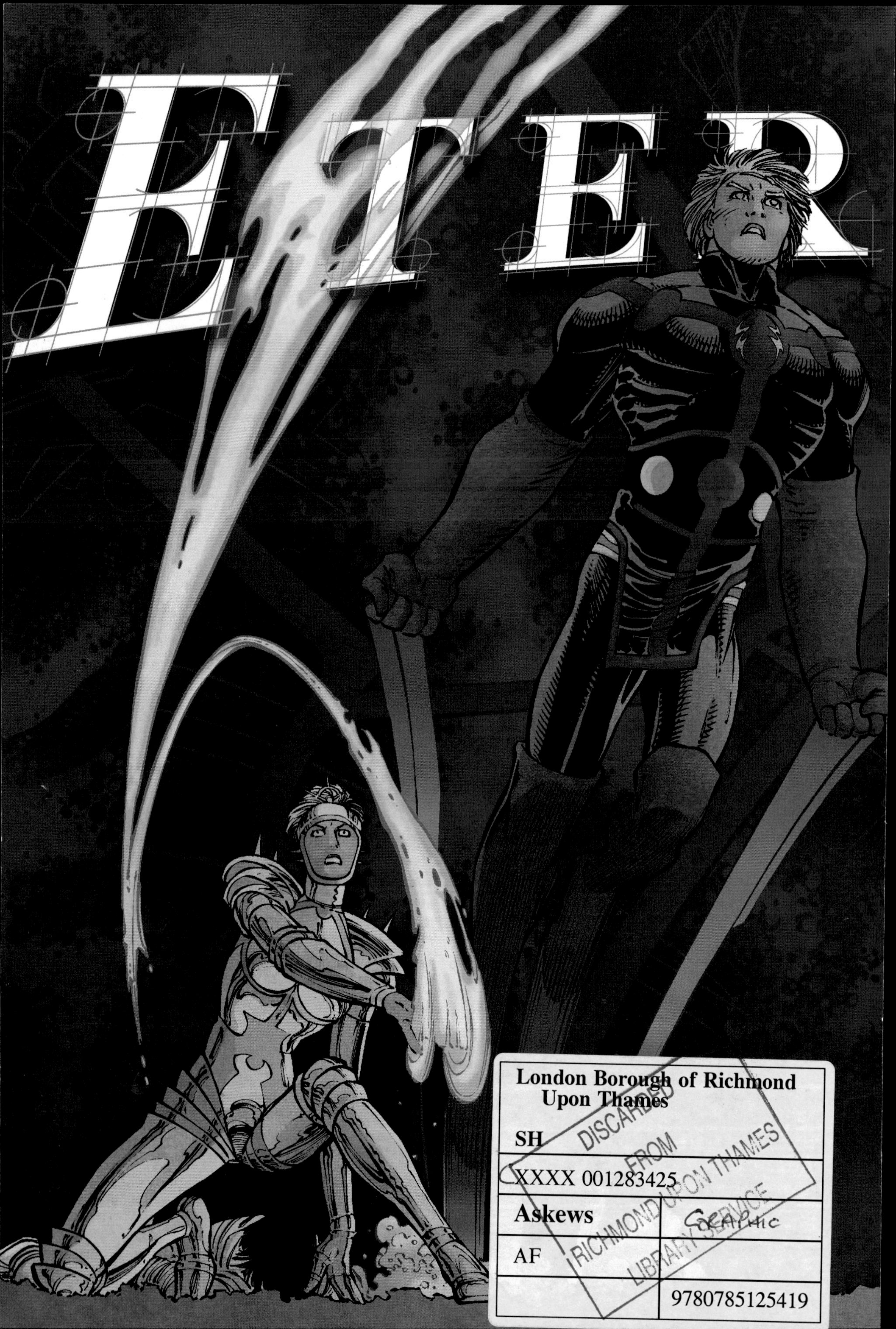
ETER

...so Jack's book became *The Eternals*, as good a name as any. He did nineteen issues and an Annual. In one of them, he wrote the following...

"I feel that playing around with this sort of conjecture is highly entertaining, and that we should aim our gunsights at this giant puzzle we've inherited more often. We can't leave it all to the professors, pundits, and paperback prophets. The puzzle belongs to you and me as well. And beneath the Royal Aegis of Marvel Comics, you and I can get together and — carefully provisioned with all the junk food we can carry — just have ourselves a ball with the grand discussion of all the ideas and characters which spring from the yarns in pages such as these."

Jack didn't know it at the time, but he was writing to Neil Gaiman...and maybe to others who have had or will someday have their own spin on this franchise.

Just as you probably know who Jack was, you probably know who Neil is. If not, just know that he is, like Kirby, a writer of extraordinary imagination and an even more extraordinary grasp of who people are, how they act and how they relate to the world around them, even when that world isn't the one on which some of us dwell. The story you're about to read will back me up on that.

Neil "got it" at once. He recognized that Kirby had provided that fertile starting point on which to build. He did not ape Jack, nor did he go too far in the opposite direction, razing the building and starting anew. Rather, he returned to Square One and built a new narrative, employing as much of Jack's as seemed to fit.

A lot of things must have because they're still there, but the end product is in no way Refried Kirby. It's a Neil Gaiman comic, and there's no better guarantee these days than that. Even better, it's a Neil Gaiman comic expertly illustrated by John Romita Jr., who matches every note of power in the story but still catches every ounce of humanity, even when it's super-humanity. Fittingly, he does not ape Jack except maybe to achieve the same energy and compelling involvement.

Don't worry if you never read what Kirby did. Neil and John are too good to leave you stranded in the book you already purchased. Their story is self-contained and expertly told, and the less I tell you about it up front, the better.

Except to address this question: Did those aliens alight on this planet eons ago and plant the underlying seeds of our civilization? Beats the heck outta me, My cynical side says you're nuts to think that... but then, my cynical side orders a pizza and expects it to arrive late and cold, and that's not always correct. You may enjoy the following more if you tell your cynical side to shut up for the next however-many-pages-there-are-in-this-book.

Leave it at the door, stock up on all the junk food you can carry, and allow Gaiman and Romita to lead you through a glorious speculation. You're in good hands...and so is Jack's creation.

— *MARK EVANIER*

Mark Evanier writes TV shows and cartoons and comics, but may well be proudest of his time working with the late Jack Kirby. He is the author of Kirby: King of Comics, *which will be published in October 2007 by Harry N. Abrams Publishing Co.*

CHAPTER ONE: INTELLIGENT DESIGN

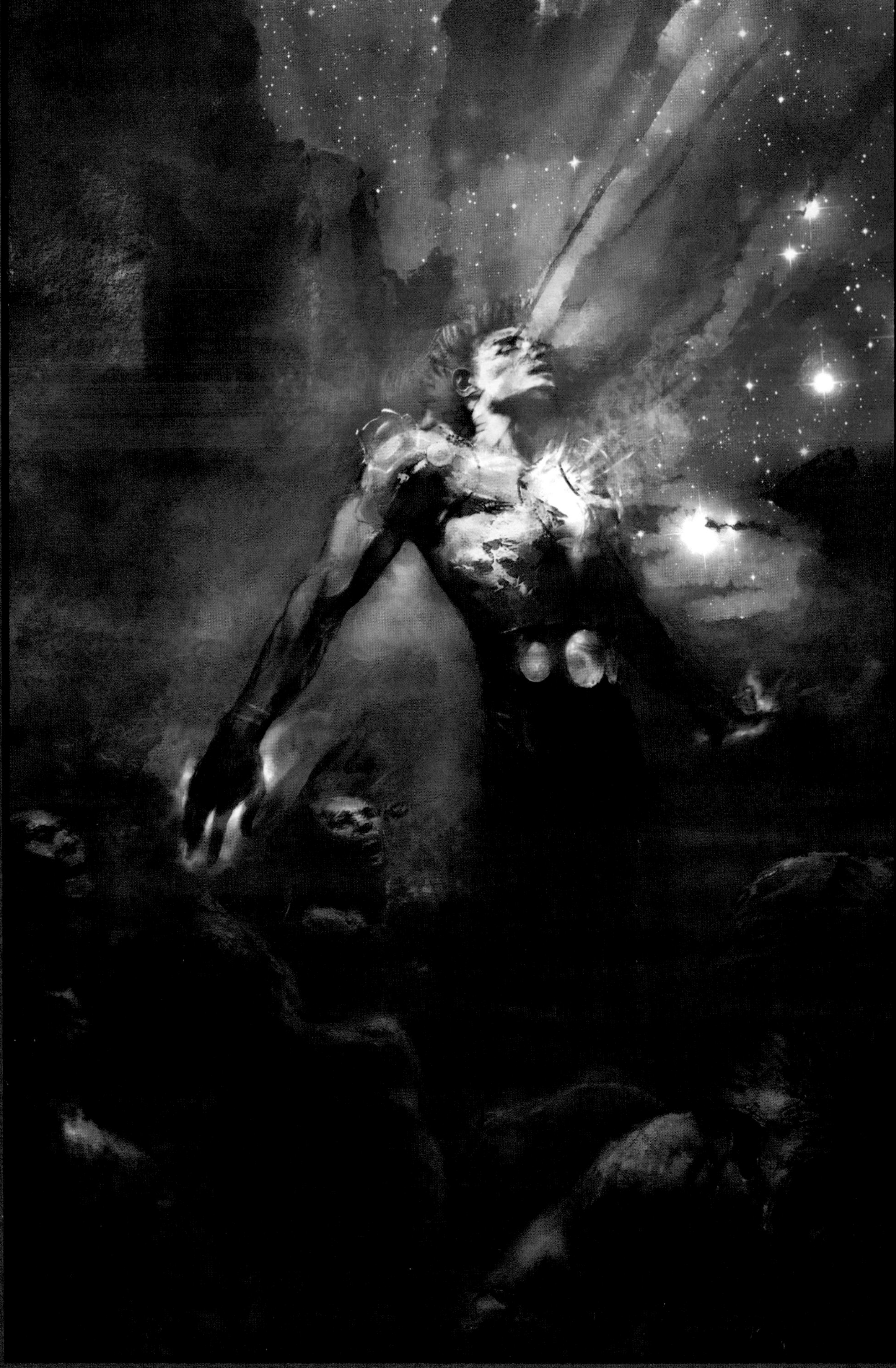

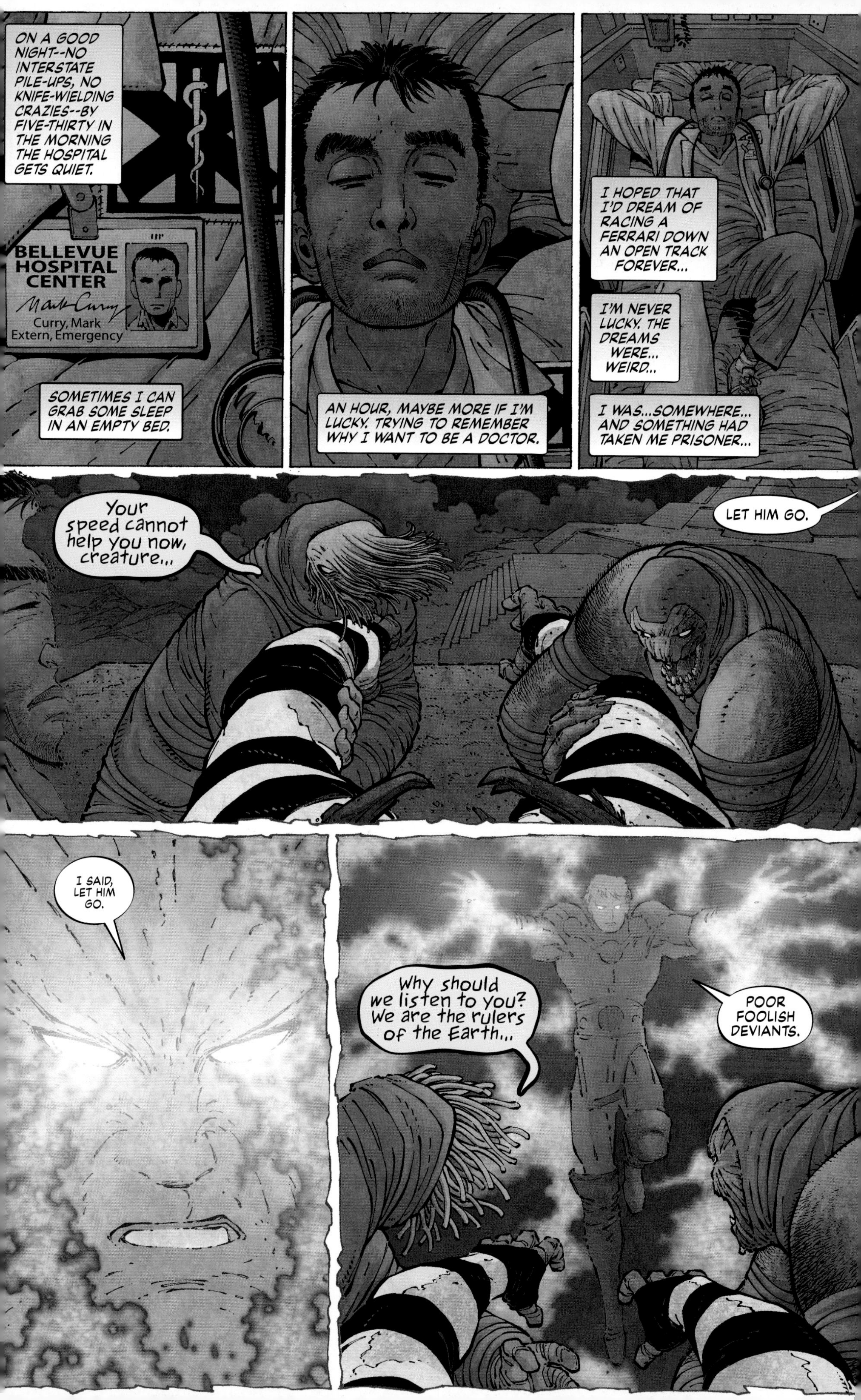
ON A GOOD NIGHT--NO INTERSTATE PILE-UPS, NO KNIFE-WIELDING CRAZIES--BY FIVE-THIRTY IN THE MORNING THE HOSPITAL GETS QUIET.
BELLEVUE HOSPITAL CENTER
Curry, Mark
Extern, Emergency
SOMETIMES I CAN GRAB SOME SLEEP IN AN EMPTY BED.
AN HOUR, MAYBE MORE IF I'M LUCKY. TRYING TO REMEMBER WHY I WANT TO BE A DOCTOR.
I HOPED THAT I'D DREAM OF RACING A FERRARI DOWN AN OPEN TRACK FOREVER...
I'M NEVER LUCKY. THE DREAMS WERE... WEIRD...
I WAS...SOMEWHERE... AND SOMETHING HAD TAKEN ME PRISONER...
Your speed cannot help you now, creature...
LET HIM GO.
I SAID, LET HIM GO.
Why should we listen to you? We are the rulers of the Earth...
POOR FOOLISH DEVIANTS.

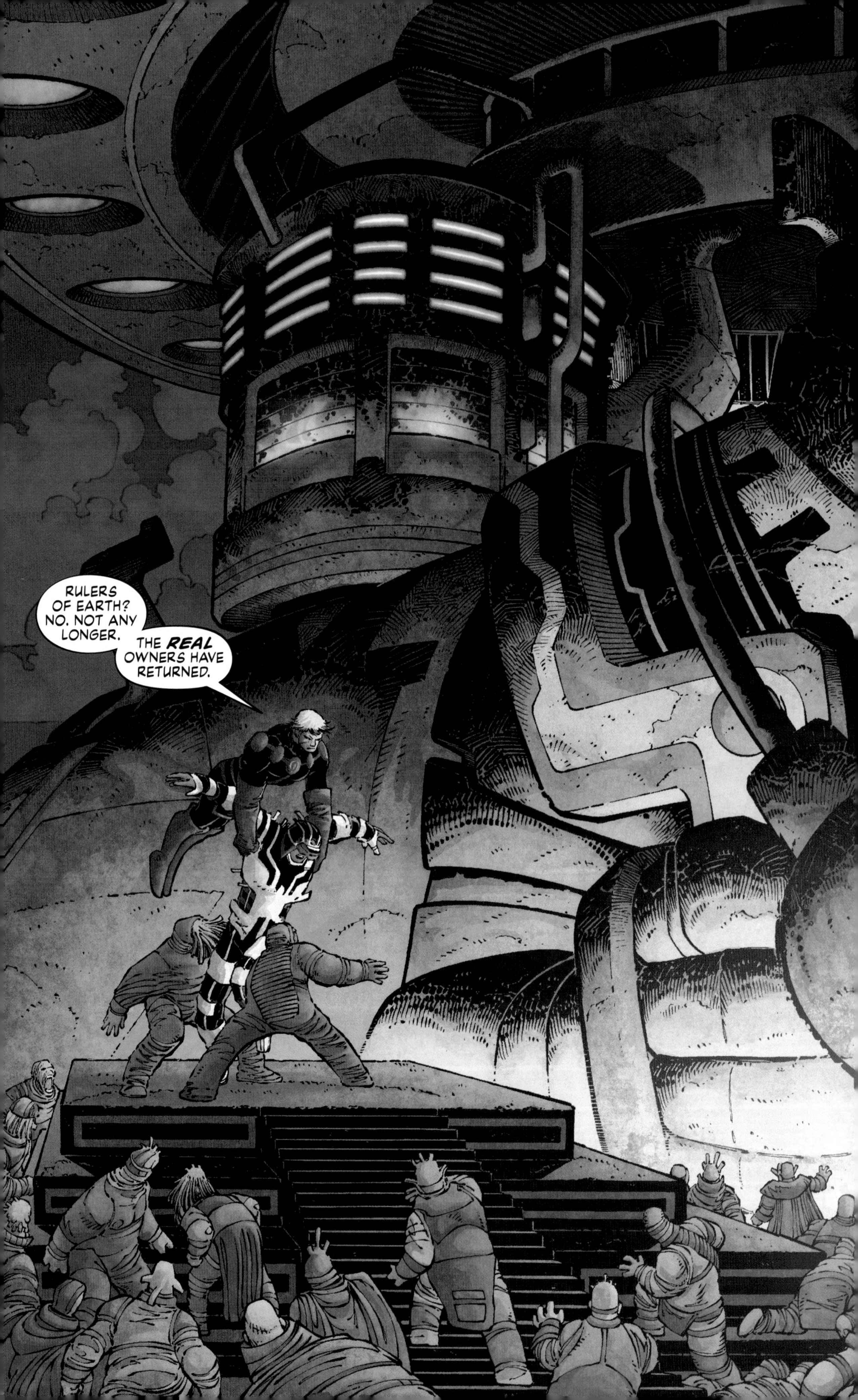
RULERS OF EARTH? NO. NOT ANY LONGER.
THE REAL OWNERS HAVE RETURNED.

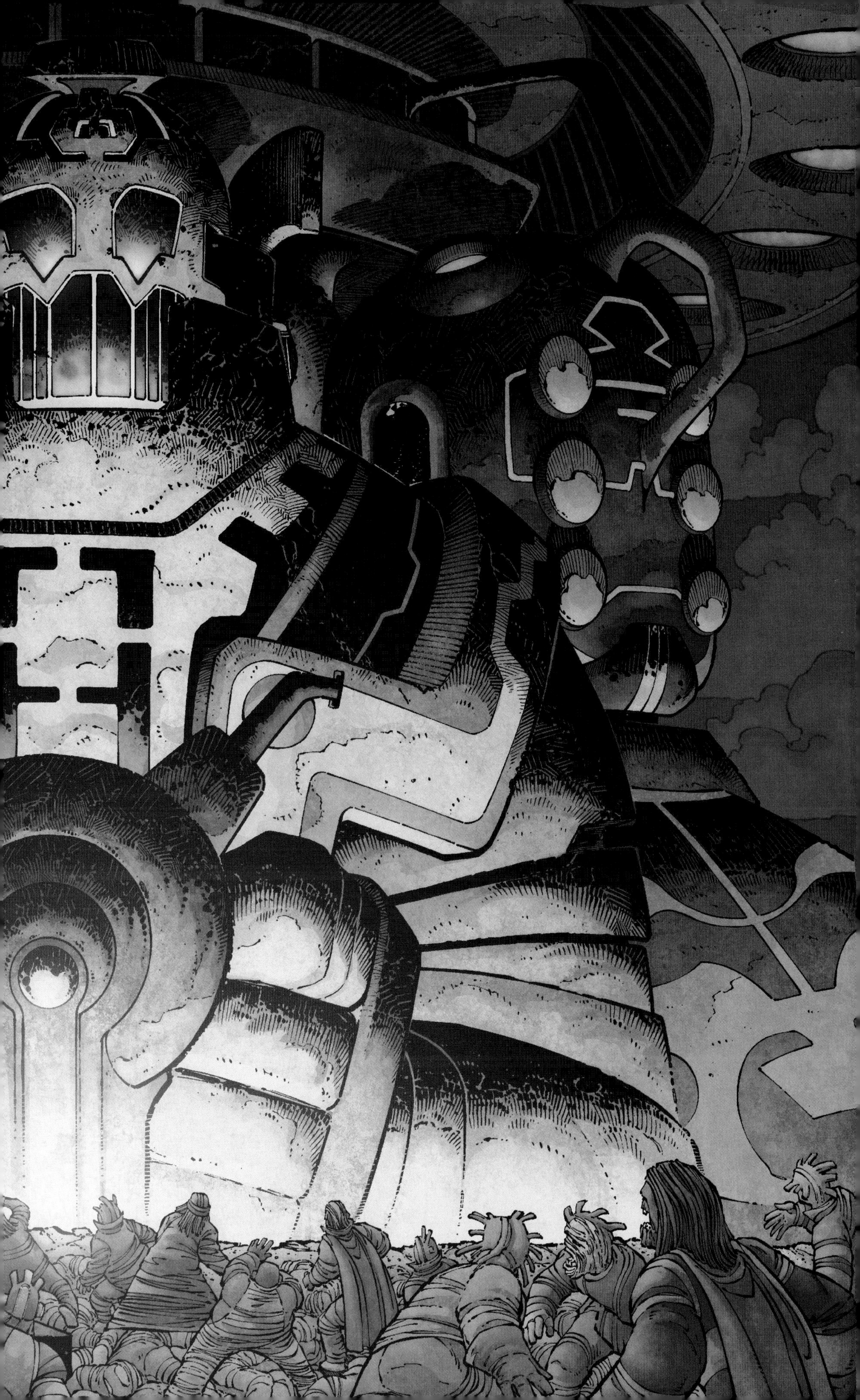

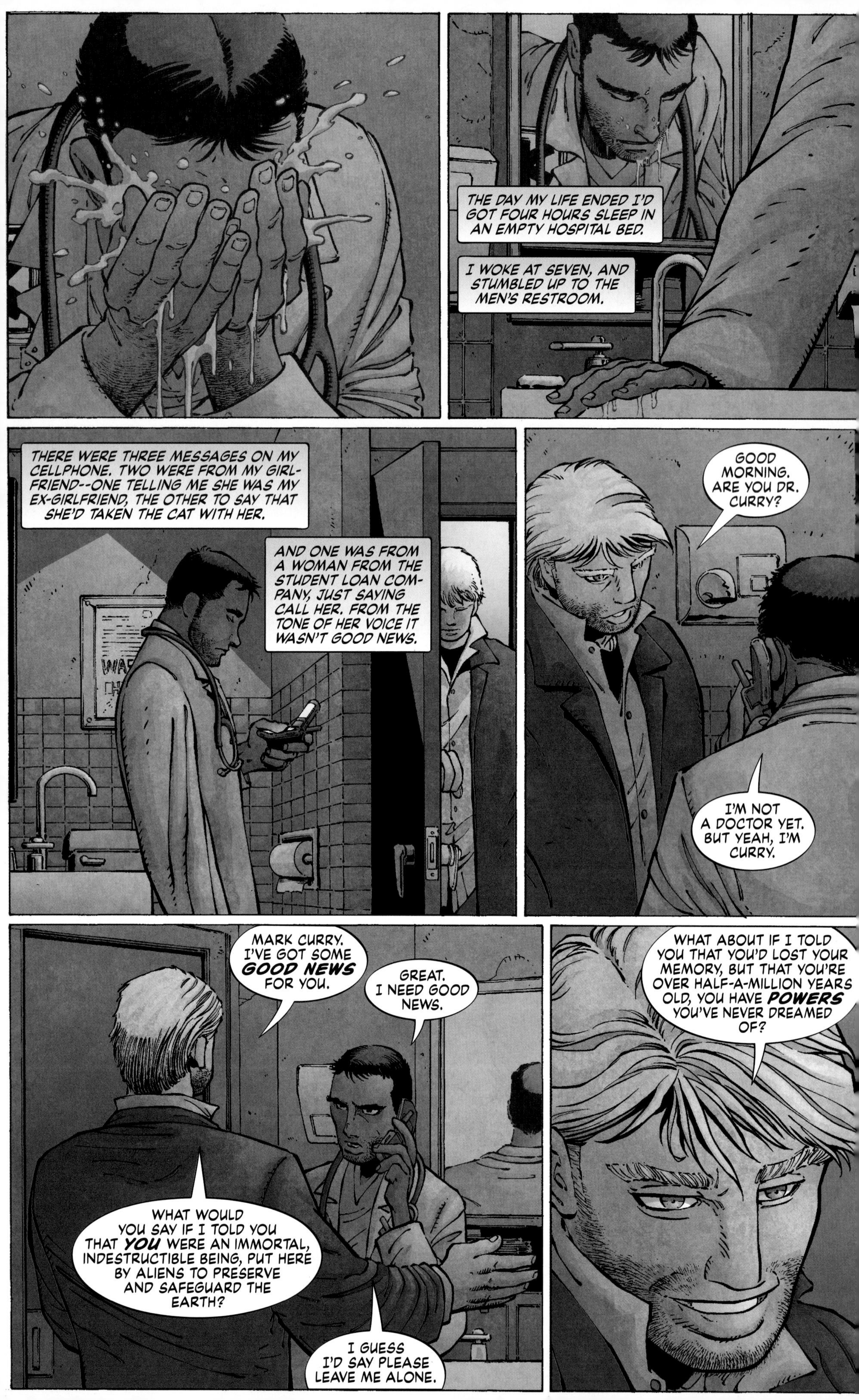
THE DAY MY LIFE ENDED I'D GOT FOUR HOURS SLEEP IN AN EMPTY HOSPITAL BED.
I WOKE AT SEVEN, AND STUMBLED UP TO THE MEN'S RESTROOM.
THERE WERE THREE MESSAGES ON MY CELLPHONE. TWO WERE FROM MY GIRL-FRIEND--ONE TELLING ME SHE WAS MY EX-GIRLFRIEND, THE OTHER TO SAY THAT SHE'D TAKEN THE CAT WITH HER.
AND ONE WAS FROM A WOMAN FROM THE STUDENT LOAN COMPANY, JUST SAYING CALL HER. FROM THE TONE OF HER VOICE IT WASN'T GOOD NEWS.
GOOD MORNING. ARE YOU DR. CURRY?
I'M NOT A DOCTOR YET. BUT YEAH, I'M CURRY.
MARK CURRY. I'VE GOT SOME GOOD NEWS FOR YOU.
GREAT. I NEED GOOD NEWS.
WHAT WOULD YOU SAY IF I TOLD YOU THAT YOU WERE AN IMMORTAL, INDESTRUCTIBLE BEING, PUT HERE BY ALIENS TO PRESERVE AND SAFEGUARD THE EARTH?
I GUESS I'D SAY PLEASE LEAVE ME ALONE.
WHAT ABOUT IF I TOLD YOU THAT YOU'D LOST YOUR MEMORY, BUT THAT YOU'RE OVER HALF-A-MILLION YEARS OLD, YOU HAVE POWERS YOU'VE NEVER DREAMED OF?

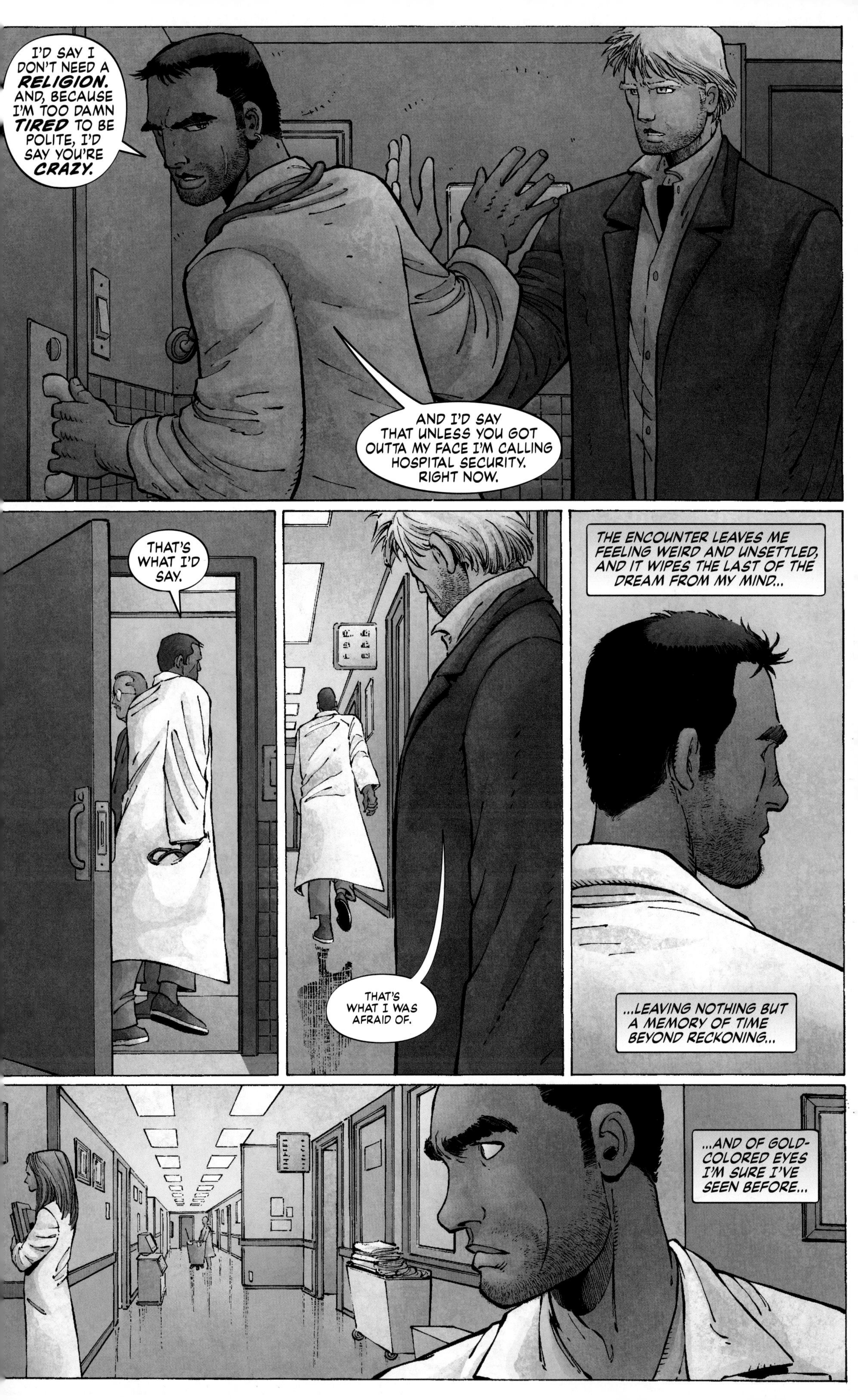
I'D SAY I DON'T NEED A RELIGION. AND, BECAUSE I'M TOO DAMN TIRED TO BE POLITE, I'D SAY YOU'RE CRAZY.
AND I'D SAY THAT UNLESS YOU GOT OUTTA MY FACE I'M CALLING HOSPITAL SECURITY. RIGHT NOW.
THAT'S WHAT I'D SAY.
THAT'S WHAT I WAS AFRAID OF.
THE ENCOUNTER LEAVES ME FEELING WEIRD AND UNSETTLED, AND IT WIPES THE LAST OF THE DREAM FROM MY MIND...
...LEAVING NOTHING BUT A MEMORY OF TIME BEYOND RECKONING...
...AND OF GOLD-COLORED EYES I'M SURE I'VE SEEN BEFORE...

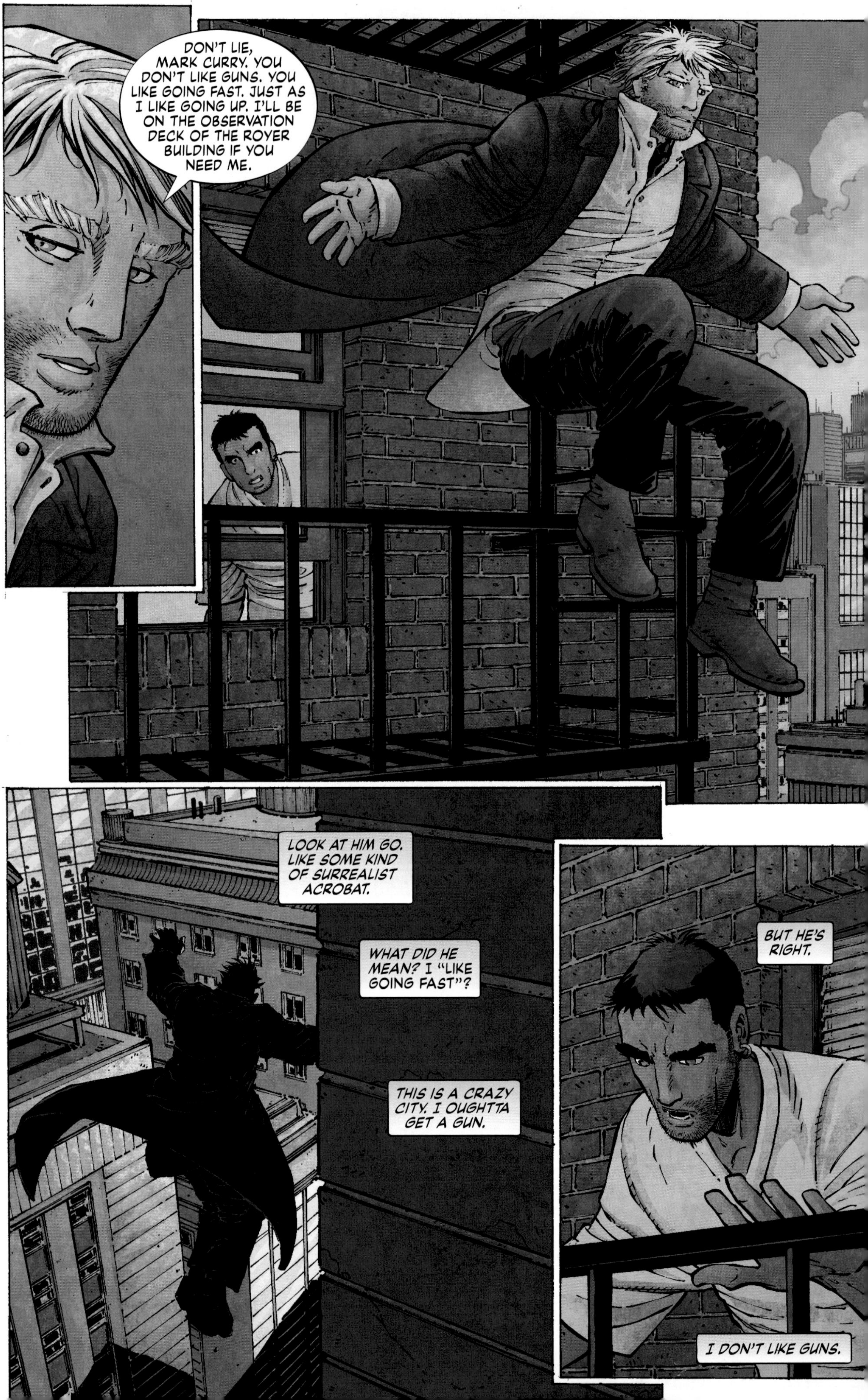
DON'T LIE, MARK CURRY. YOU DON'T LIKE GUNS. YOU LIKE GOING FAST. JUST AS I LIKE GOING UP. I'LL BE ON THE OBSERVATION DECK OF THE ROYER BUILDING IF YOU NEED ME.
LOOK AT HIM GO. LIKE SOME KIND OF SURREALIST ACROBAT.
WHAT DID HE MEAN? I "LIKE GOING FAST"?
THIS IS A CRAZY CITY. I OUGHTTA GET A GUN.
BUT HE'S RIGHT.
I DON'T LIKE GUNS.

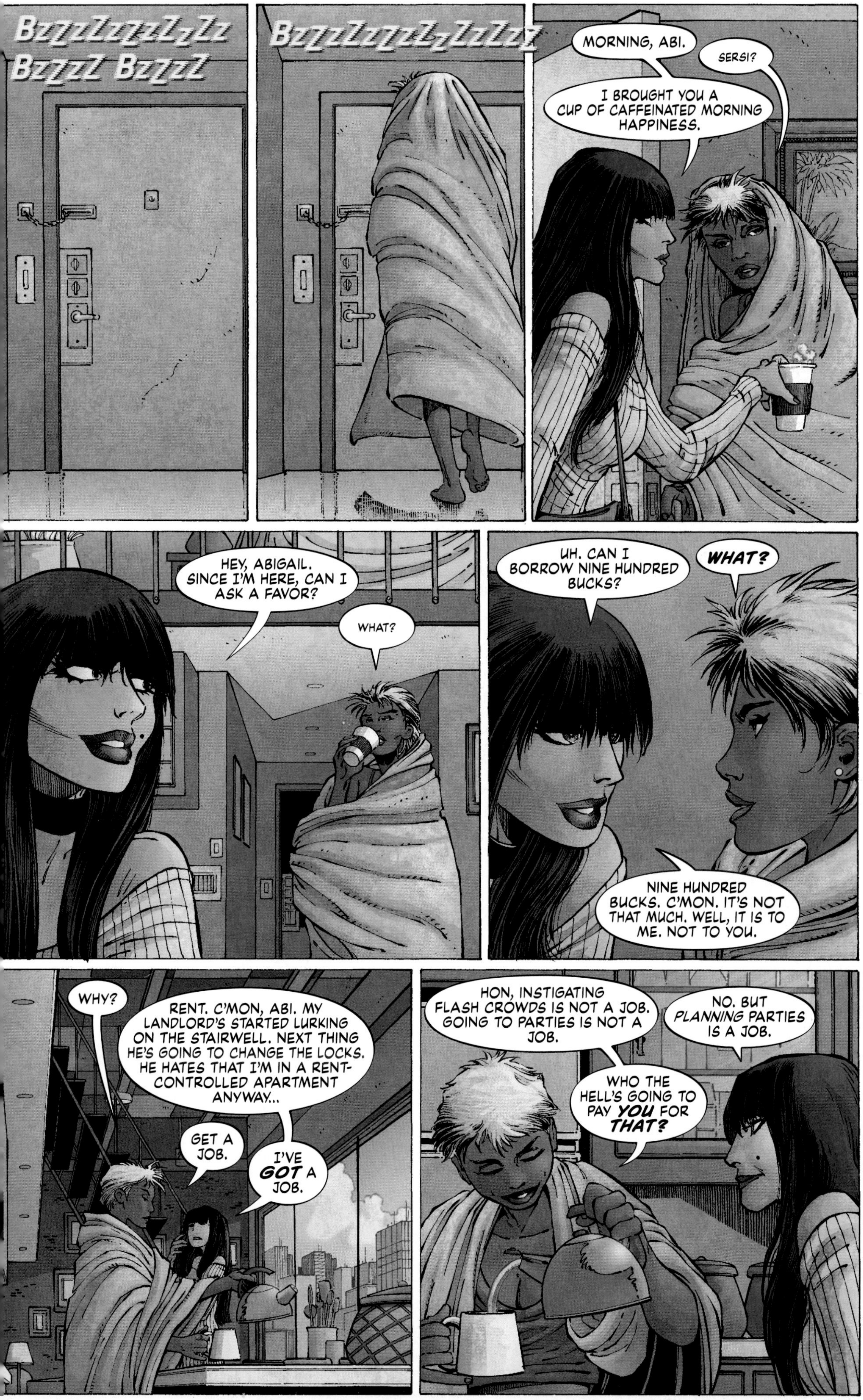
BzzzZzzzZzZz
BzzzZ BzzzZ
BzzzZzzzZzZzZzZ
MORNING, ABI.
SERSI?
I BROUGHT YOU A CUP OF CAFFEINATED MORNING HAPPINESS.
HEY, ABIGAIL. SINCE I'M HERE, CAN I ASK A FAVOR?
WHAT?
UH. CAN I BORROW NINE HUNDRED BUCKS?
WHAT?
NINE HUNDRED BUCKS. C'MON. IT'S NOT THAT MUCH. WELL, IT IS TO ME. NOT TO YOU.
WHY?
RENT. C'MON, ABI. MY LANDLORD'S STARTED LURKING ON THE STAIRWELL. NEXT THING HE'S GOING TO CHANGE THE LOCKS. HE HATES THAT I'M IN A RENT-CONTROLLED APARTMENT ANYWAY...
GET A JOB.
I'VE GOT A JOB.
HON, INSTIGATING FLASH CROWDS IS NOT A JOB. GOING TO PARTIES IS NOT A JOB.
NO. BUT PLANNING PARTIES IS A JOB.
WHO THE HELL'S GOING TO PAY YOU FOR THAT?

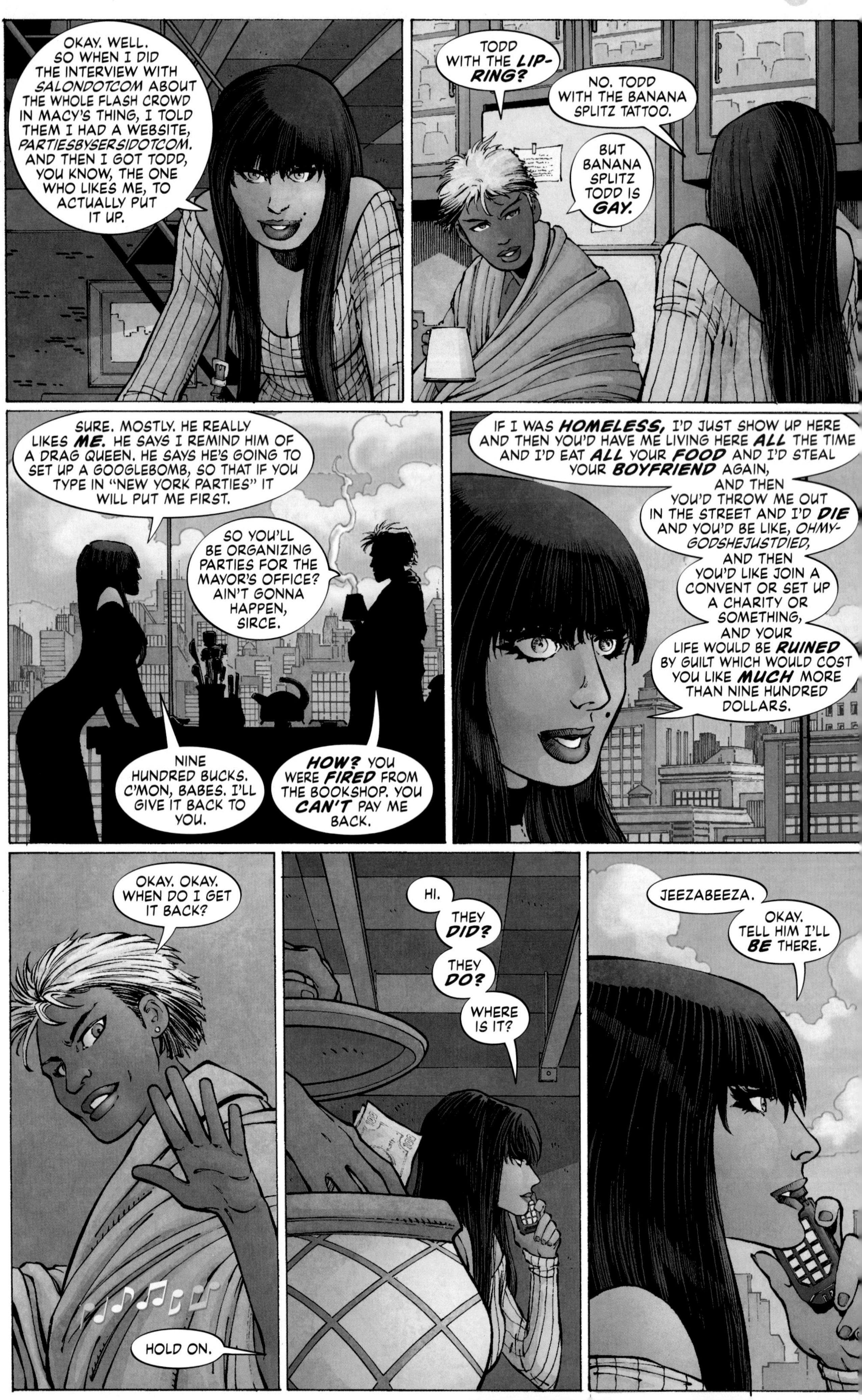

OKAY. WELL. SO WHEN I DID THE INTERVIEW WITH *SALONDOTCOM* ABOUT THE WHOLE FLASH CROWD IN MACY'S THING, I TOLD THEM I HAD A WEBSITE, *PARTIESBYSERSIDOTCOM*. AND THEN I GOT TODD, YOU KNOW, THE ONE WHO LIKES ME, TO ACTUALLY PUT IT UP.
TODD WITH THE ***LIP-RING?***
NO. TODD WITH THE BANANA SPLITZ TATTOO.
BUT BANANA SPLITZ TODD IS ***GAY.***
SURE. MOSTLY. HE REALLY LIKES ***ME.*** HE SAYS I REMIND HIM OF A DRAG QUEEN. HE SAYS HE'S GOING TO SET UP A GOOGLEBOMB, SO THAT IF YOU TYPE IN "NEW YORK PARTIES" IT WILL PUT ME FIRST.
SO YOU'LL BE ORGANIZING PARTIES FOR THE MAYOR'S OFFICE? AIN'T GONNA HAPPEN, SIRCE.
NINE HUNDRED BUCKS. C'MON, BABES. I'LL GIVE IT BACK TO YOU.
HOW? YOU WERE ***FIRED*** FROM THE BOOKSHOP. YOU ***CAN'T*** PAY ME BACK.
IF I WAS ***HOMELESS,*** I'D JUST SHOW UP HERE AND THEN YOU'D HAVE ME LIVING HERE ***ALL*** THE TIME AND I'D EAT ***ALL*** YOUR ***FOOD*** AND I'D STEAL YOUR ***BOYFRIEND*** AGAIN, AND THEN YOU'D THROW ME OUT IN THE STREET AND I'D ***DIE*** AND YOU'D BE LIKE, *OHMYGODSHEJUSTDIED,* AND THEN YOU'D LIKE JOIN A CONVENT OR SET UP A CHARITY OR SOMETHING, AND YOUR LIFE WOULD BE ***RUINED*** BY GUILT WHICH WOULD COST YOU LIKE ***MUCH*** MORE THAN NINE HUNDRED DOLLARS.
OKAY. OKAY. WHEN DO I GET IT BACK?
HOLD ON.
HI.
THEY ***DID?***
THEY ***DO?***
WHERE IS IT?
JEEZABEEZA.
OKAY. TELL HIM I'LL ***BE*** THERE.

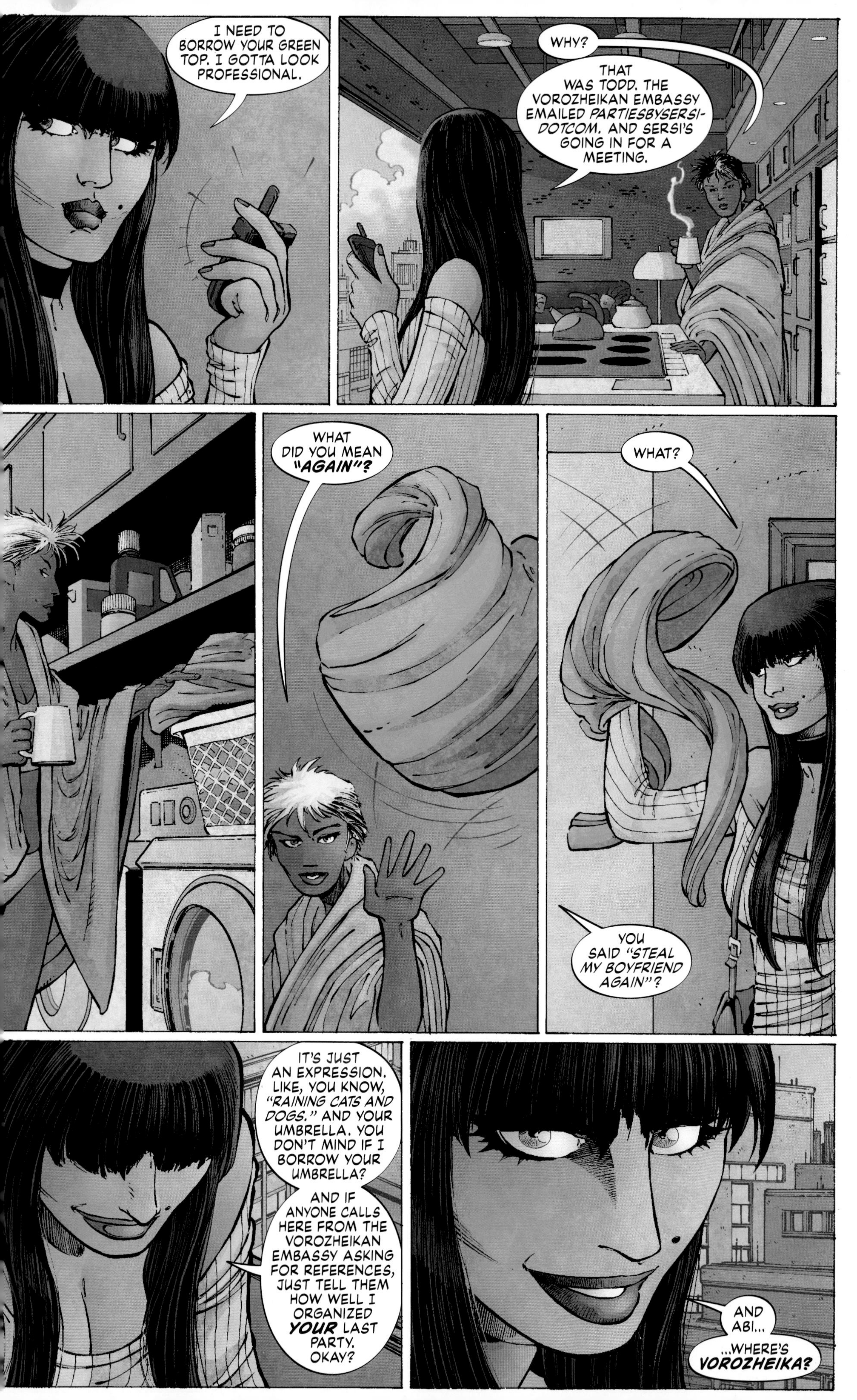
I NEED TO BORROW YOUR GREEN TOP. I GOTTA LOOK PROFESSIONAL.
WHY?
THAT WAS TODD. THE VOROZHEIKAN EMBASSY EMAILED *PARTIESBYSERSI-DOTCOM*. AND SERSI'S GOING IN FOR A MEETING.
WHAT DID YOU MEAN *"AGAIN"*?
WHAT?
YOU SAID "STEAL MY BOYFRIEND AGAIN"?
IT'S JUST AN EXPRESSION. LIKE, YOU KNOW, *"RAINING CATS AND DOGS."* AND YOUR UMBRELLA. YOU DON'T MIND IF I BORROW YOUR UMBRELLA?
AND IF ANYONE CALLS HERE FROM THE VOROZHEIKAN EMBASSY ASKING FOR REFERENCES, JUST TELL THEM HOW WELL I ORGANIZED ***YOUR*** LAST PARTY. OKAY?
AND ABI...
...WHERE'S ***VOROZHEIKA?***

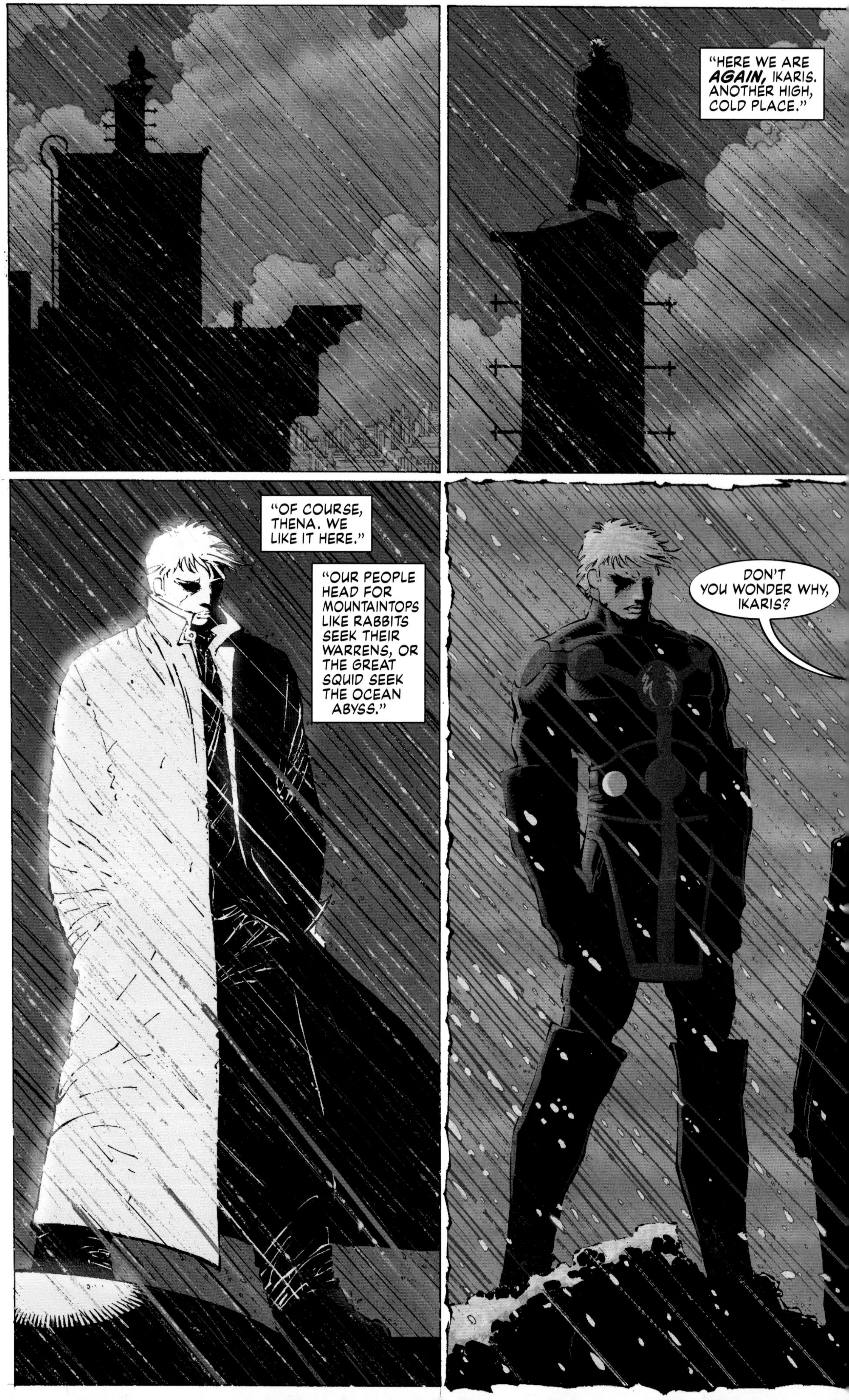
"HERE WE ARE AGAIN, IKARIS. ANOTHER HIGH, COLD PLACE."
"OF COURSE, THENA. WE LIKE IT HERE."
"OUR PEOPLE HEAD FOR MOUNTAINTOPS LIKE RABBITS SEEK THEIR WARRENS, OR THE GREAT SQUID SEEK THE OCEAN ABYSS."
DON'T YOU WONDER WHY, IKARIS?

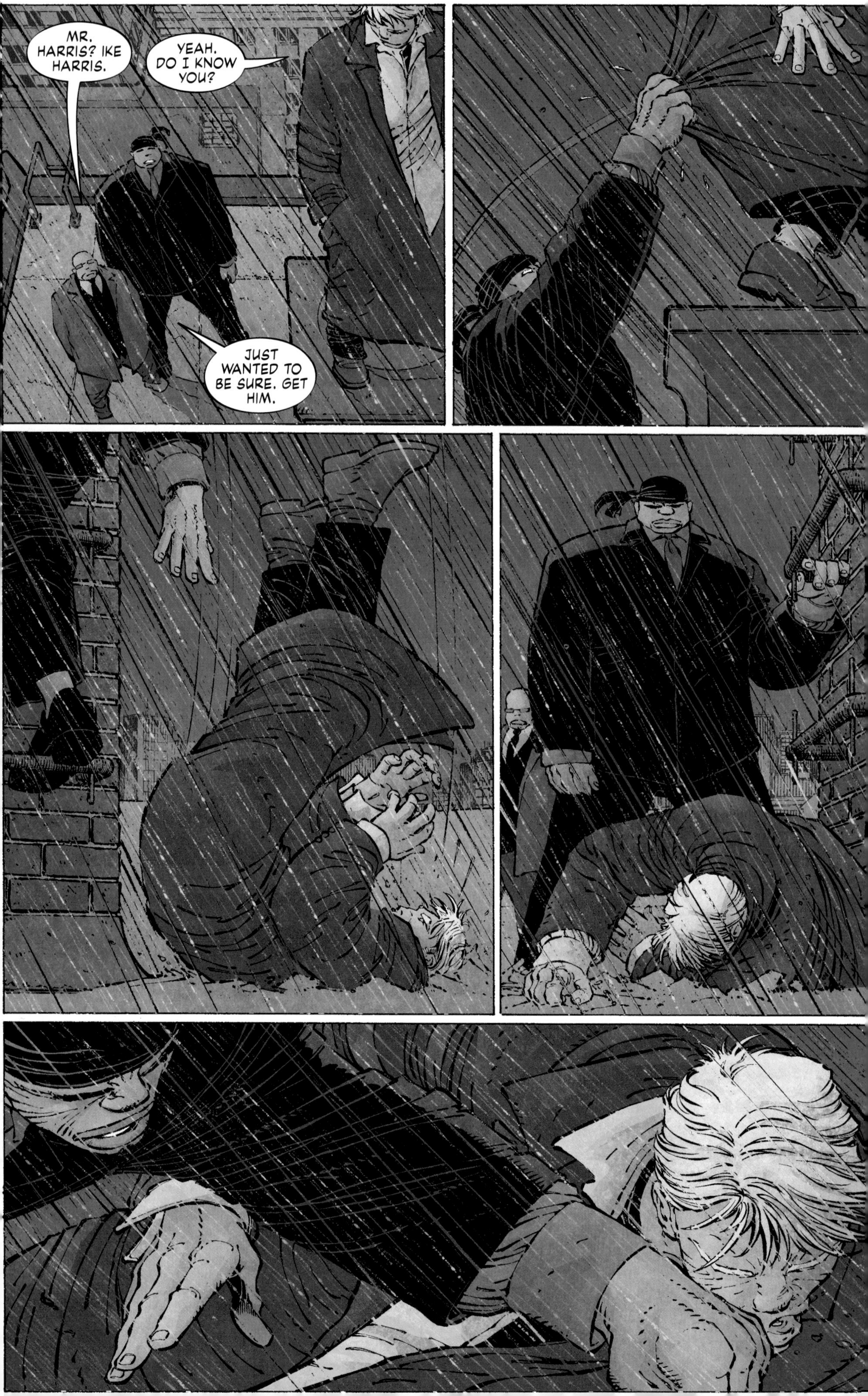
MR. HARRIS? IKE HARRIS.
YEAH. DO I KNOW YOU?
JUST WANTED TO BE SURE. GET HIM.

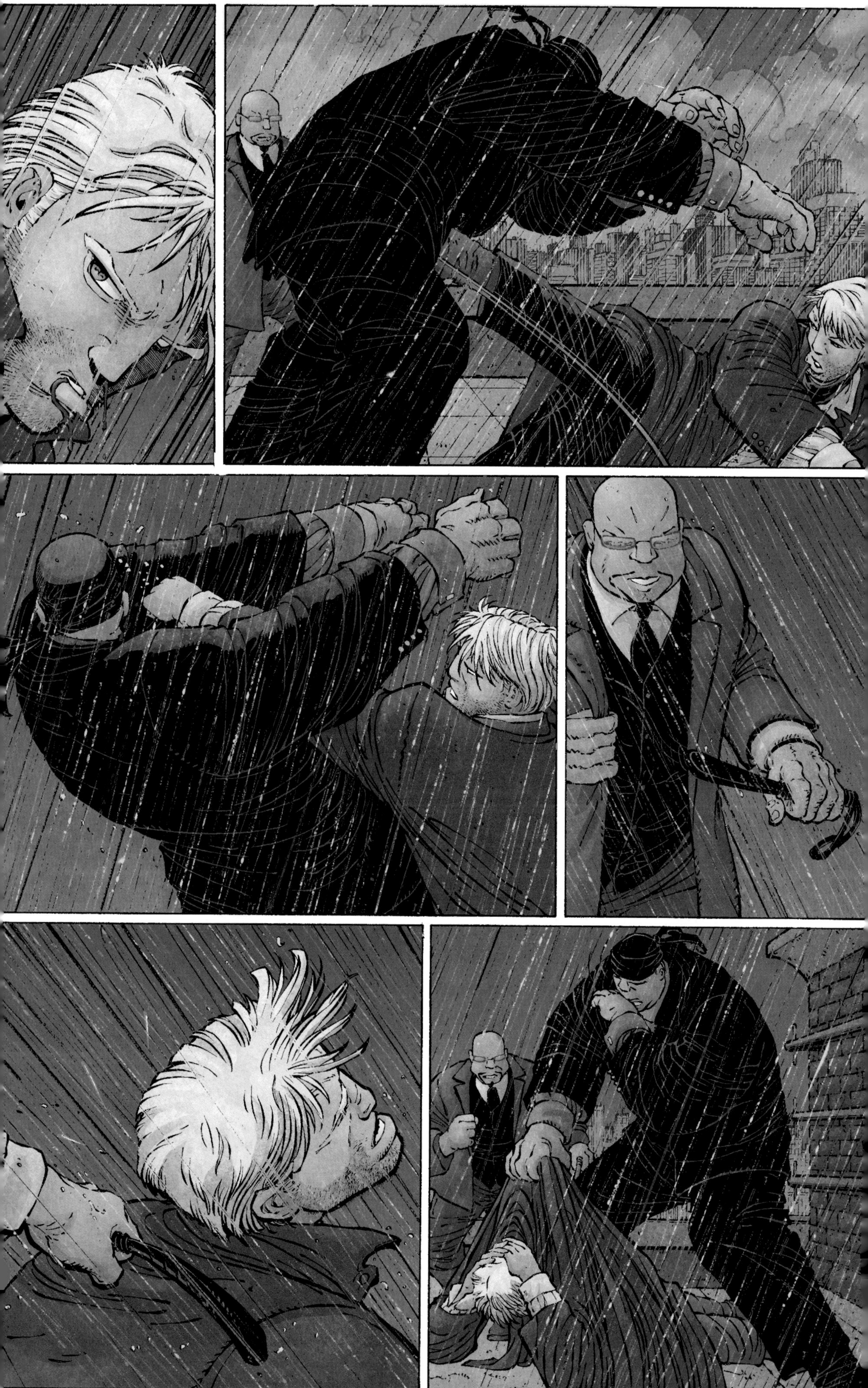

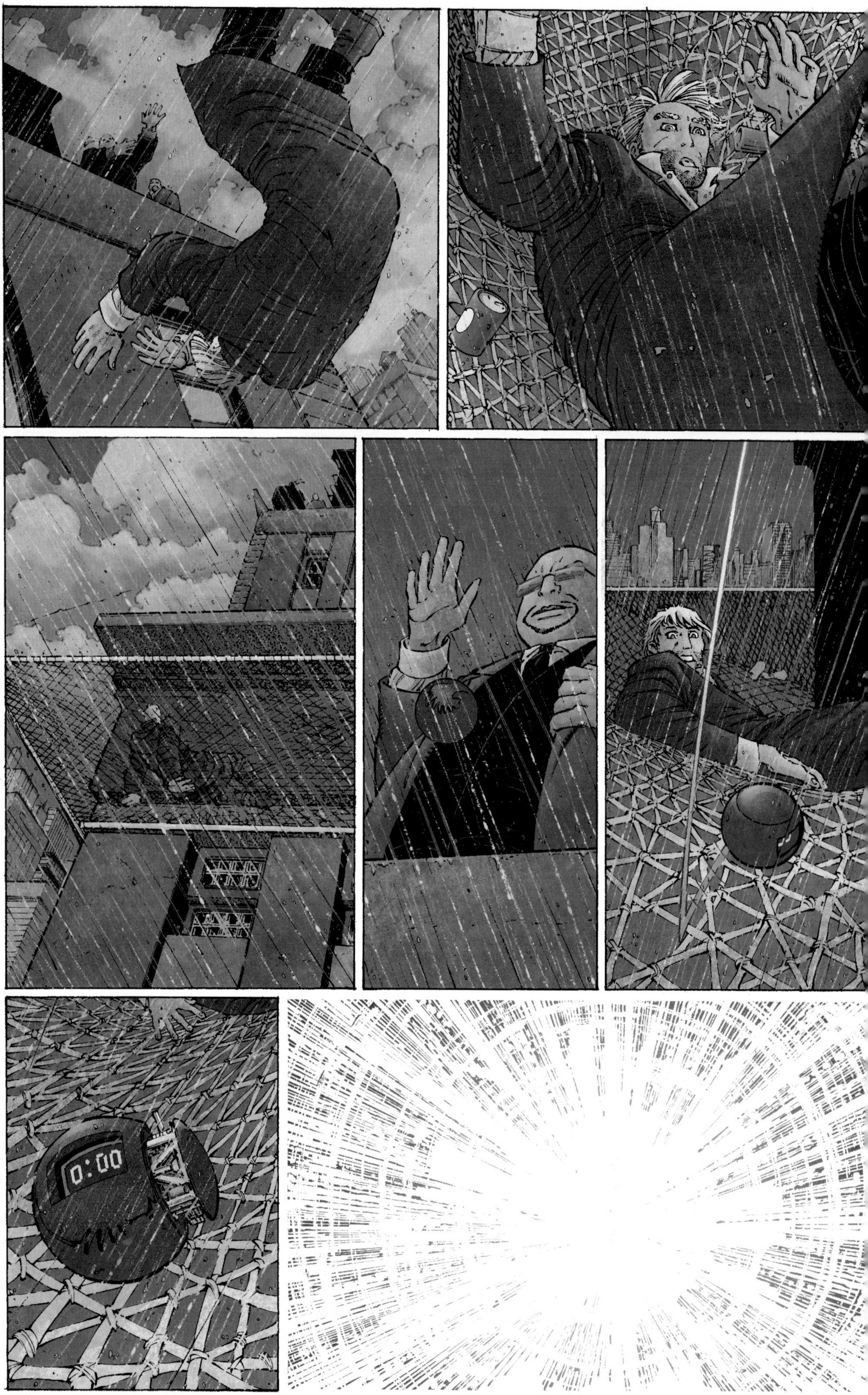
0:00

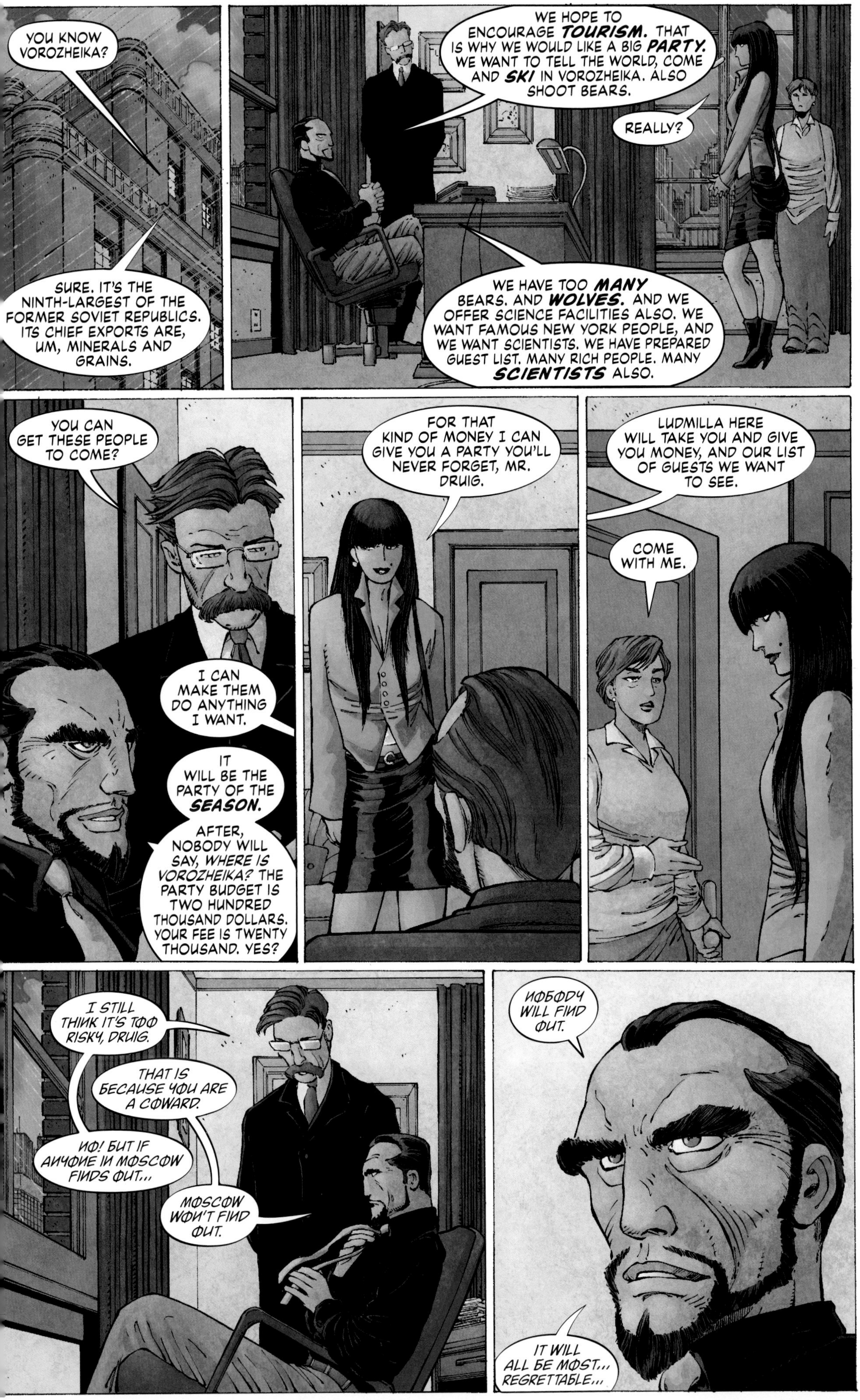
YOU KNOW VOROZHEIKA?
SURE. IT'S THE NINTH-LARGEST OF THE FORMER SOVIET REPUBLICS. ITS CHIEF EXPORTS ARE, UM, MINERALS AND GRAINS.
WE HOPE TO ENCOURAGE TOURISM. THAT IS WHY WE WOULD LIKE A BIG PARTY. WE WANT TO TELL THE WORLD, COME AND SKI IN VOROZHEIKA. ALSO SHOOT BEARS.
REALLY?
WE HAVE TOO MANY BEARS. AND WOLVES. AND WE OFFER SCIENCE FACILITIES ALSO. WE WANT FAMOUS NEW YORK PEOPLE, AND WE WANT SCIENTISTS. WE HAVE PREPARED GUEST LIST. MANY RICH PEOPLE. MANY SCIENTISTS ALSO.
YOU CAN GET THESE PEOPLE TO COME?
I CAN MAKE THEM DO ANYTHING I WANT.
IT WILL BE THE PARTY OF THE SEASON.
AFTER, NOBODY WILL SAY, WHERE IS VOROZHEIKA? THE PARTY BUDGET IS TWO HUNDRED THOUSAND DOLLARS. YOUR FEE IS TWENTY THOUSAND. YES?
FOR THAT KIND OF MONEY I CAN GIVE YOU A PARTY YOU'LL NEVER FORGET, MR. DRUIG.
LUDMILLA HERE WILL TAKE YOU AND GIVE YOU MONEY, AND OUR LIST OF GUESTS WE WANT TO SEE.
COME WITH ME.
I STILL THINK IT'S TOO RISKY, DRUIG.
THAT IS BECAUSE YOU ARE A COWARD.
NO! BUT IF ANYONE IN MOSCOW FINDS OUT...
MOSCOW WON'T FIND OUT.
NOBODY WILL FIND OUT.
IT WILL ALL BE MOST... REGRETTABLE...

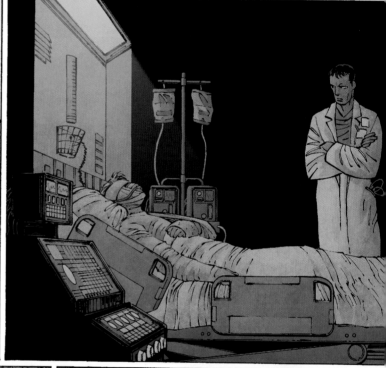

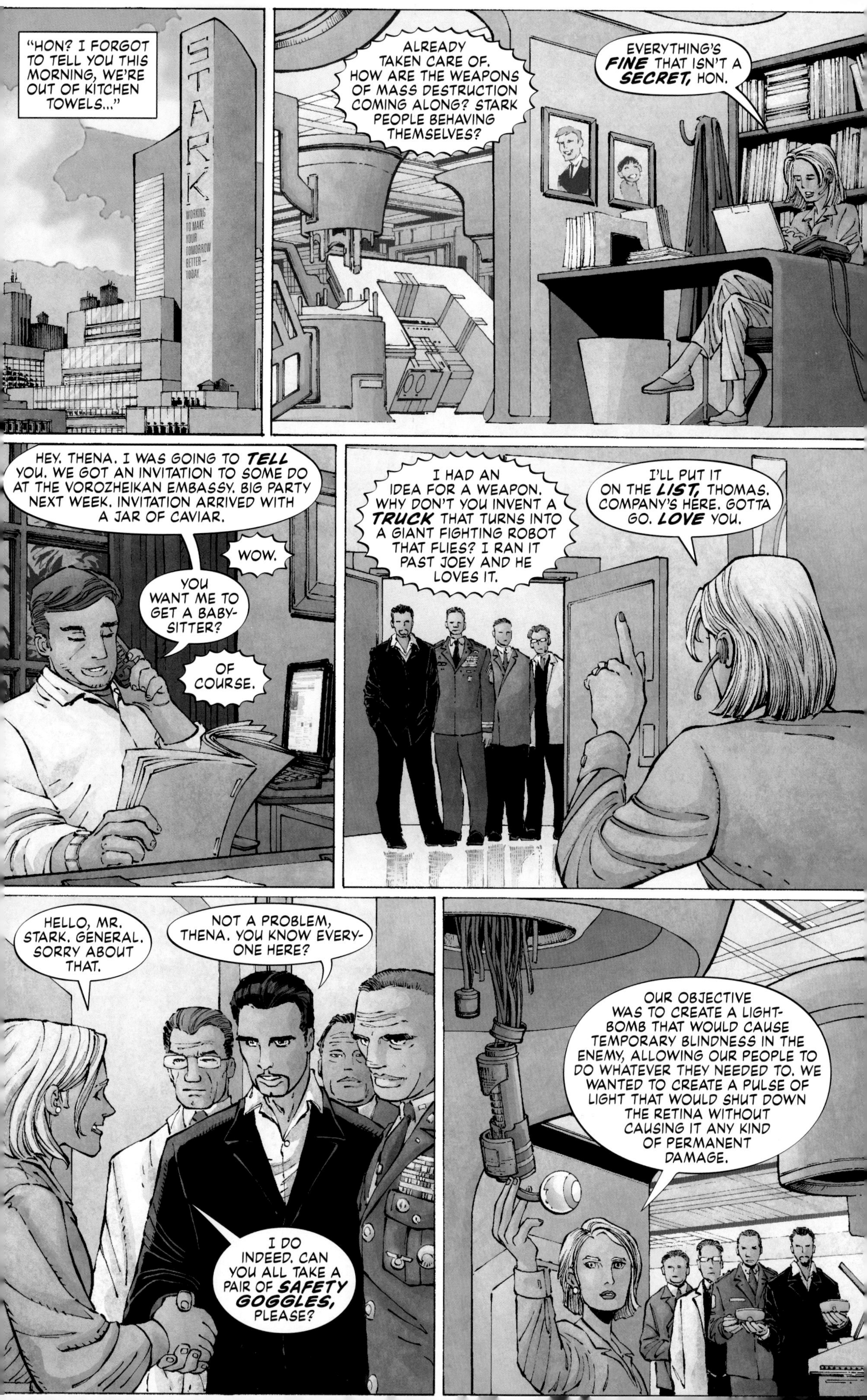
"HON? I FORGOT TO TELL YOU THIS MORNING, WE'RE OUT OF KITCHEN TOWELS..."
STARK
WORKING TO MAKE YOUR TOMORROW BETTER—TODAY
ALREADY TAKEN CARE OF. HOW ARE THE WEAPONS OF MASS DESTRUCTION COMING ALONG? STARK PEOPLE BEHAVING THEMSELVES?
EVERYTHING'S **FINE** THAT ISN'T A **SECRET,** HON.
HEY. THENA. I WAS GOING TO **TELL** YOU. WE GOT AN INVITATION TO SOME DO AT THE VOROZHEIKAN EMBASSY. BIG PARTY NEXT WEEK. INVITATION ARRIVED WITH A JAR OF CAVIAR.
WOW.
YOU WANT ME TO GET A BABY-SITTER?
OF COURSE.
I HAD AN IDEA FOR A WEAPON. WHY DON'T YOU INVENT A **TRUCK** THAT TURNS INTO A GIANT FIGHTING ROBOT THAT FLIES? I RAN IT PAST JOEY AND HE LOVES IT.
I'LL PUT IT ON THE **LIST,** THOMAS. COMPANY'S HERE. GOTTA GO. **LOVE** YOU.
HELLO, MR. STARK. GENERAL. SORRY ABOUT THAT.
NOT A PROBLEM, THENA. YOU KNOW EVERY-ONE HERE?
I DO INDEED. CAN YOU ALL TAKE A PAIR OF **SAFETY GOGGLES,** PLEASE?
OUR OBJECTIVE WAS TO CREATE A LIGHT-BOMB THAT WOULD CAUSE TEMPORARY BLINDNESS IN THE ENEMY, ALLOWING OUR PEOPLE TO DO WHATEVER THEY NEEDED TO. WE WANTED TO CREATE A PULSE OF LIGHT THAT WOULD SHUT DOWN THE RETINA WITHOUT CAUSING IT ANY KIND OF PERMANENT DAMAGE.

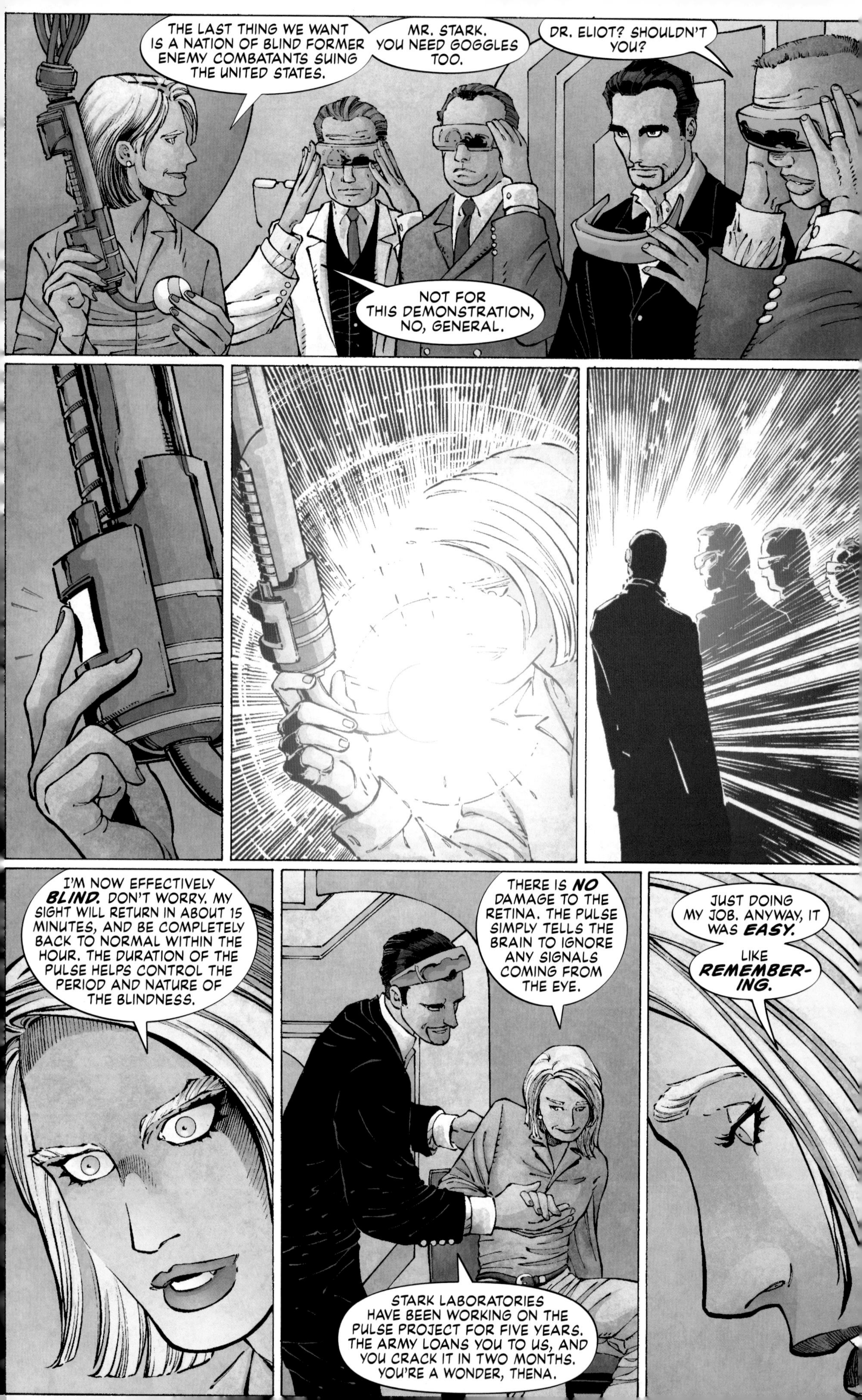

THE LAST THING WE WANT IS A NATION OF BLIND FORMER ENEMY COMBATANTS SUING THE UNITED STATES.
MR. STARK. YOU NEED GOGGLES TOO.
DR. ELIOT? SHOULDN'T YOU?
NOT FOR THIS DEMONSTRATION, NO, GENERAL.
I'M NOW EFFECTIVELY **BLIND.** DON'T WORRY. MY SIGHT WILL RETURN IN ABOUT 15 MINUTES, AND BE COMPLETELY BACK TO NORMAL WITHIN THE HOUR. THE DURATION OF THE PULSE HELPS CONTROL THE PERIOD AND NATURE OF THE BLINDNESS.
THERE IS **NO** DAMAGE TO THE RETINA. THE PULSE SIMPLY TELLS THE BRAIN TO IGNORE ANY SIGNALS COMING FROM THE EYE.
STARK LABORATORIES HAVE BEEN WORKING ON THE PULSE PROJECT FOR FIVE YEARS. THE ARMY LOANS YOU TO US, AND YOU CRACK IT IN TWO MONTHS. YOU'RE A WONDER, THENA.
JUST DOING MY JOB. ANYWAY, IT WAS **EASY.**
LIKE **REMEMBER-ING.**

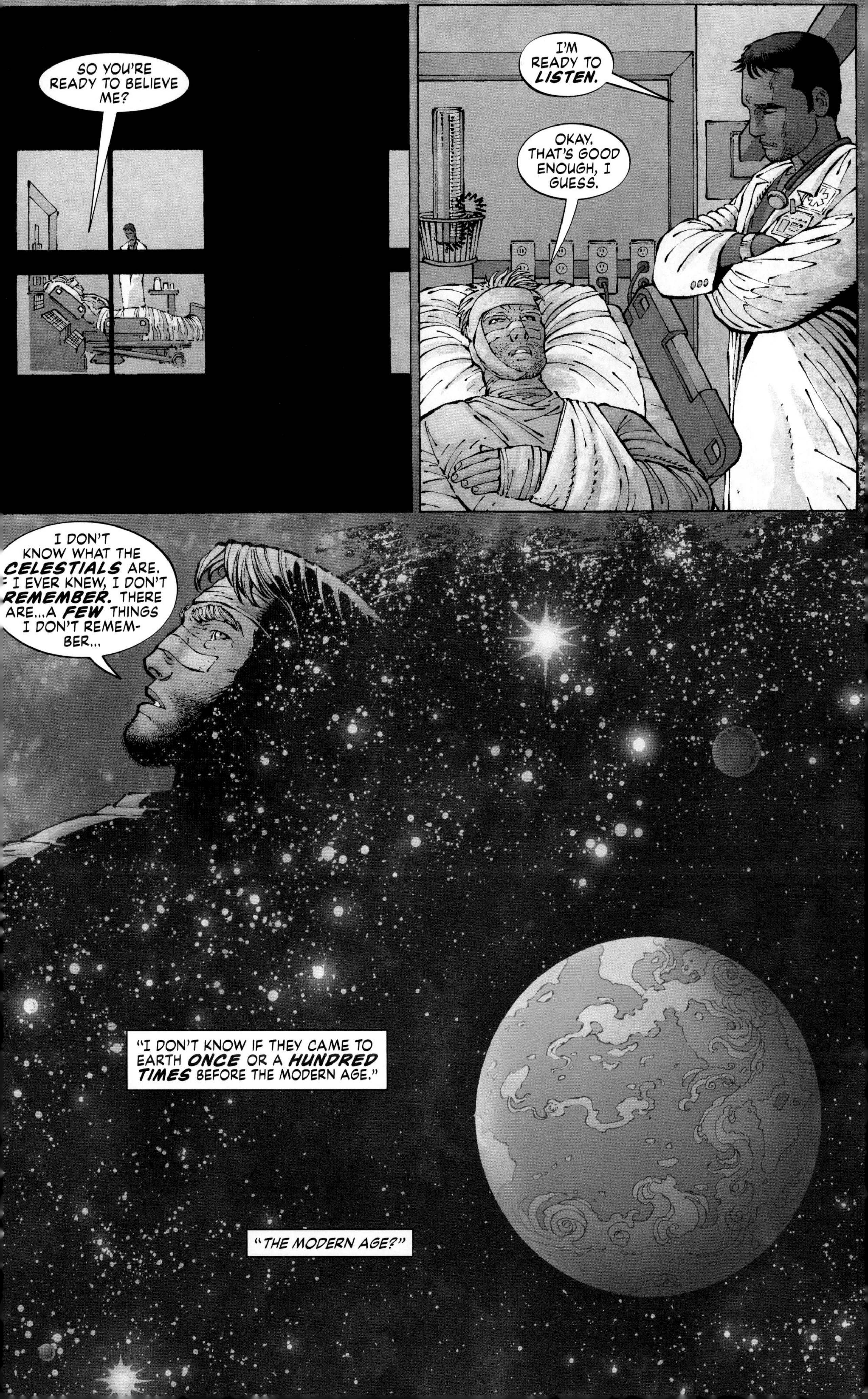

SO YOU'RE READY TO BELIEVE ME?
I'M READY TO LISTEN.
OKAY. THAT'S GOOD ENOUGH, I GUESS.
I DON'T KNOW WHAT THE CELESTIALS ARE. IF I EVER KNEW, I DON'T REMEMBER. THERE ARE...A FEW THINGS I DON'T REMEMBER...
"I DON'T KNOW IF THEY CAME TO EARTH ONCE OR A HUNDRED TIMES BEFORE THE MODERN AGE."
"THE MODERN AGE?"

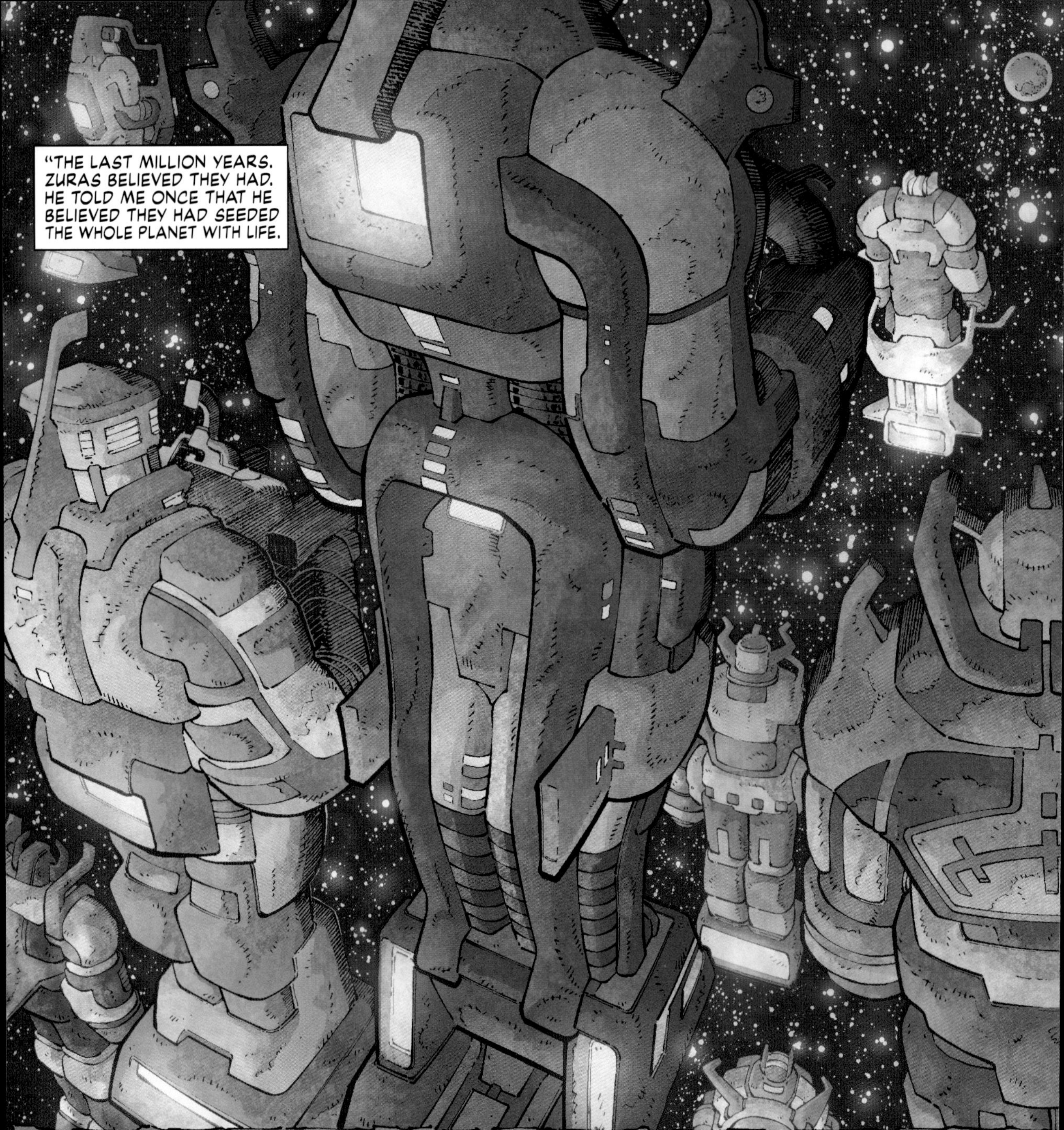
"THE LAST MILLION YEARS. ZURAS BELIEVED THEY HAD. HE TOLD ME ONCE THAT HE BELIEVED THEY HAD SEEDED THE WHOLE PLANET WITH LIFE.
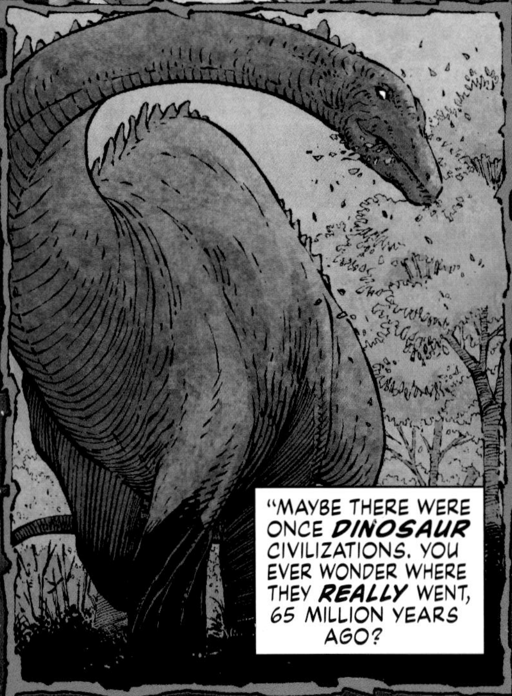
"MAYBE THERE WERE ONCE ***DINOSAUR*** CIVILIZATIONS. YOU EVER WONDER WHERE THEY ***REALLY*** WENT, 65 MILLION YEARS AGO?
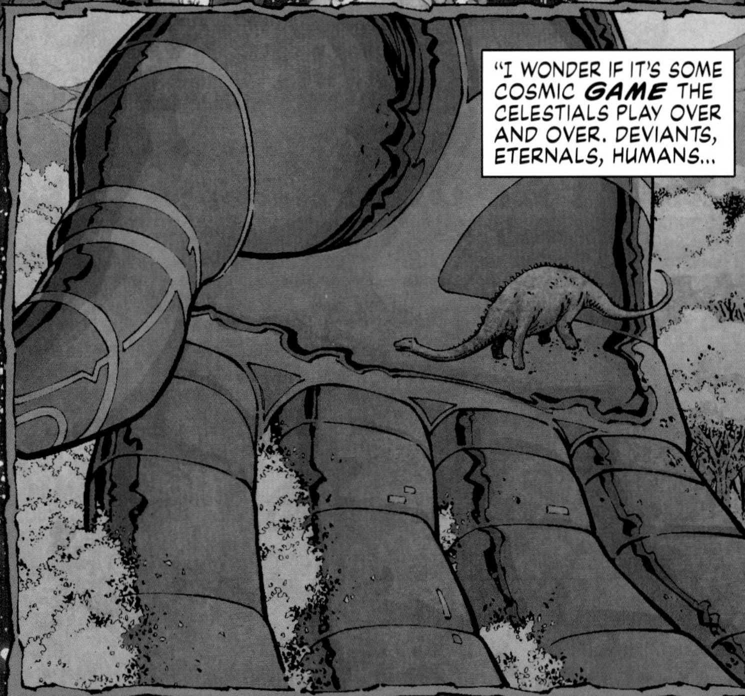
"I WONDER IF IT'S SOME COSMIC ***GAME*** THE CELESTIALS PLAY OVER AND OVER. DEVIANTS, ETERNALS, HUMANS...

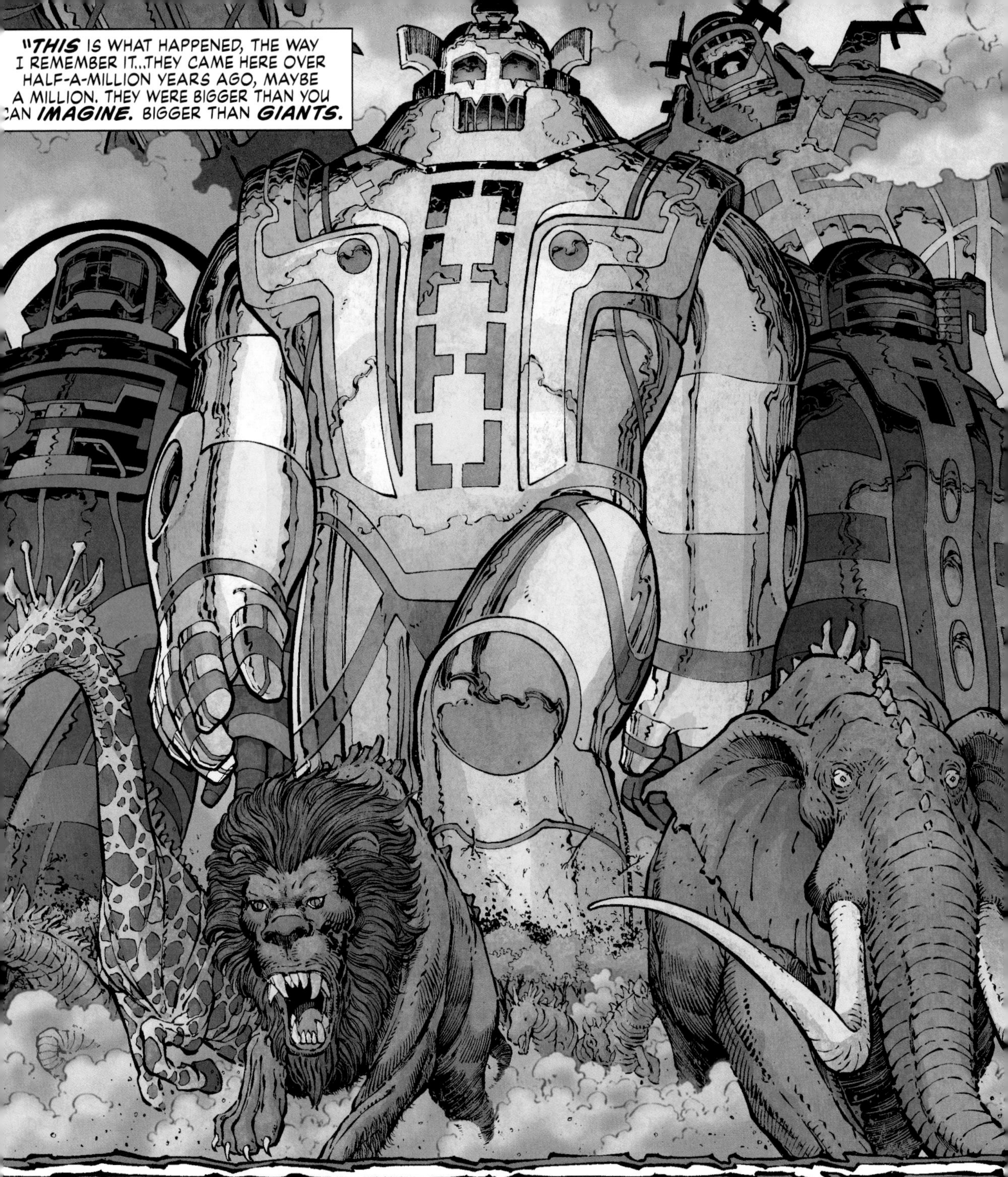
"THIS IS WHAT HAPPENED, THE WAY I REMEMBER IT...THEY CAME HERE OVER HALF-A-MILLION YEARS AGO, MAYBE A MILLION. THEY WERE BIGGER THAN YOU CAN IMAGINE. BIGGER THAN GIANTS.

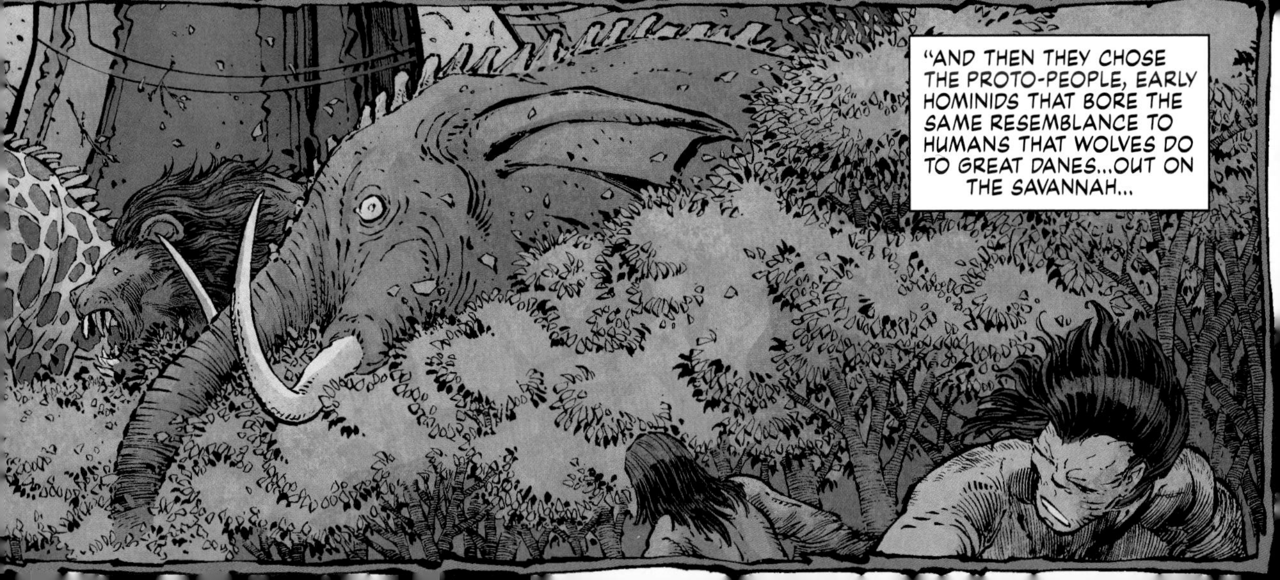
"AND THEN THEY CHOSE THE PROTO-PEOPLE, EARLY HOMINIDS THAT BORE THE SAME RESEMBLANCE TO HUMANS THAT WOLVES DO TO GREAT DANES...OUT ON THE SAVANNAH...

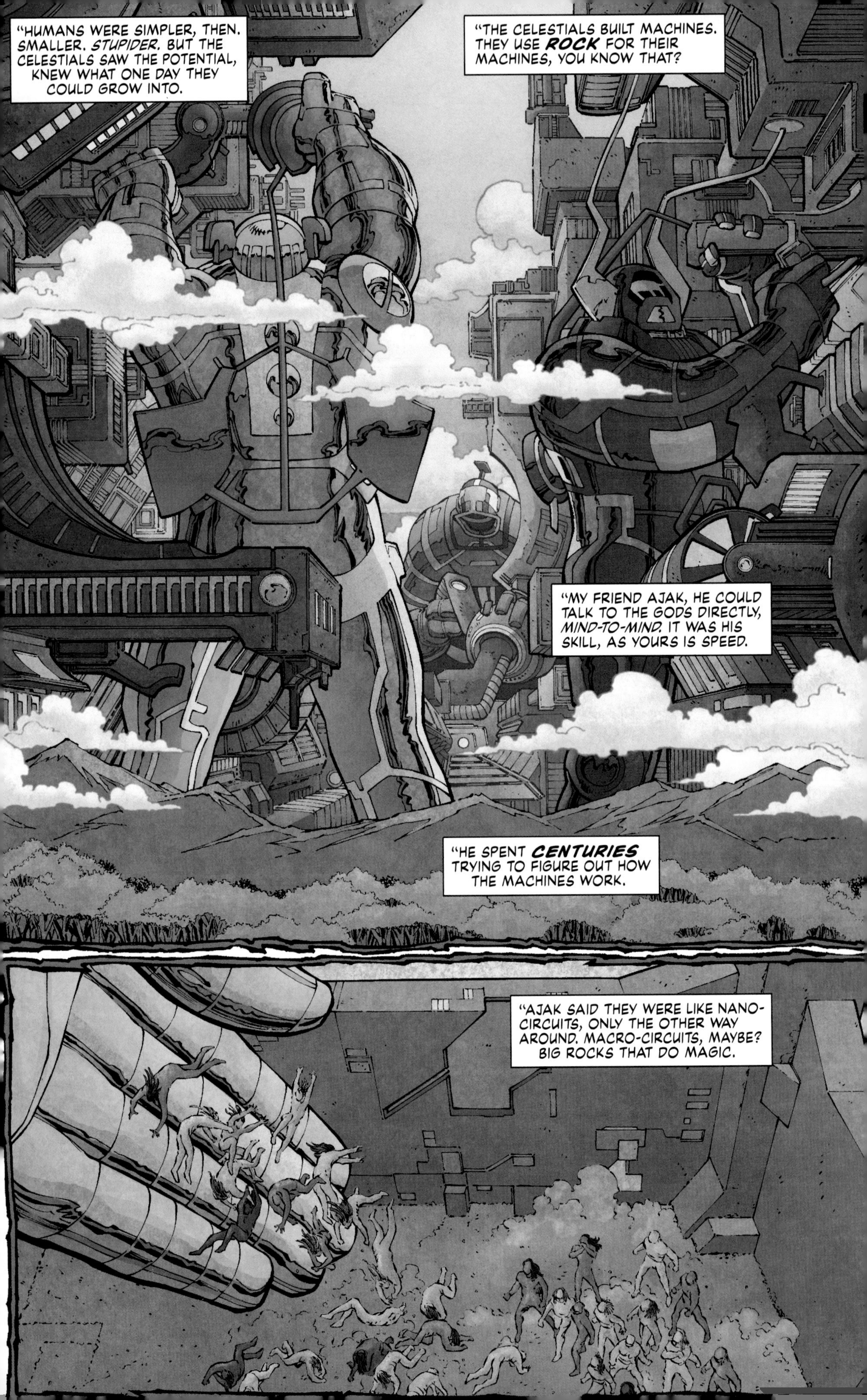
"HUMANS WERE SIMPLER, THEN. SMALLER. *STUPIDER.* BUT THE CELESTIALS SAW THE POTENTIAL, KNEW WHAT ONE DAY THEY COULD GROW INTO.
"THE CELESTIALS BUILT MACHINES. THEY USE **ROCK** FOR THEIR MACHINES, YOU KNOW THAT?
"MY FRIEND AJAK, HE COULD TALK TO THE GODS DIRECTLY, *MIND-TO-MIND.* IT WAS HIS SKILL, AS YOURS IS SPEED.
"HE SPENT **CENTURIES** TRYING TO FIGURE OUT HOW THE MACHINES WORK.
"AJAK SAID THEY WERE LIKE NANO-CIRCUITS, ONLY THE OTHER WAY AROUND. MACRO-CIRCUITS, MAYBE? BIG ROCKS THAT DO MAGIC.

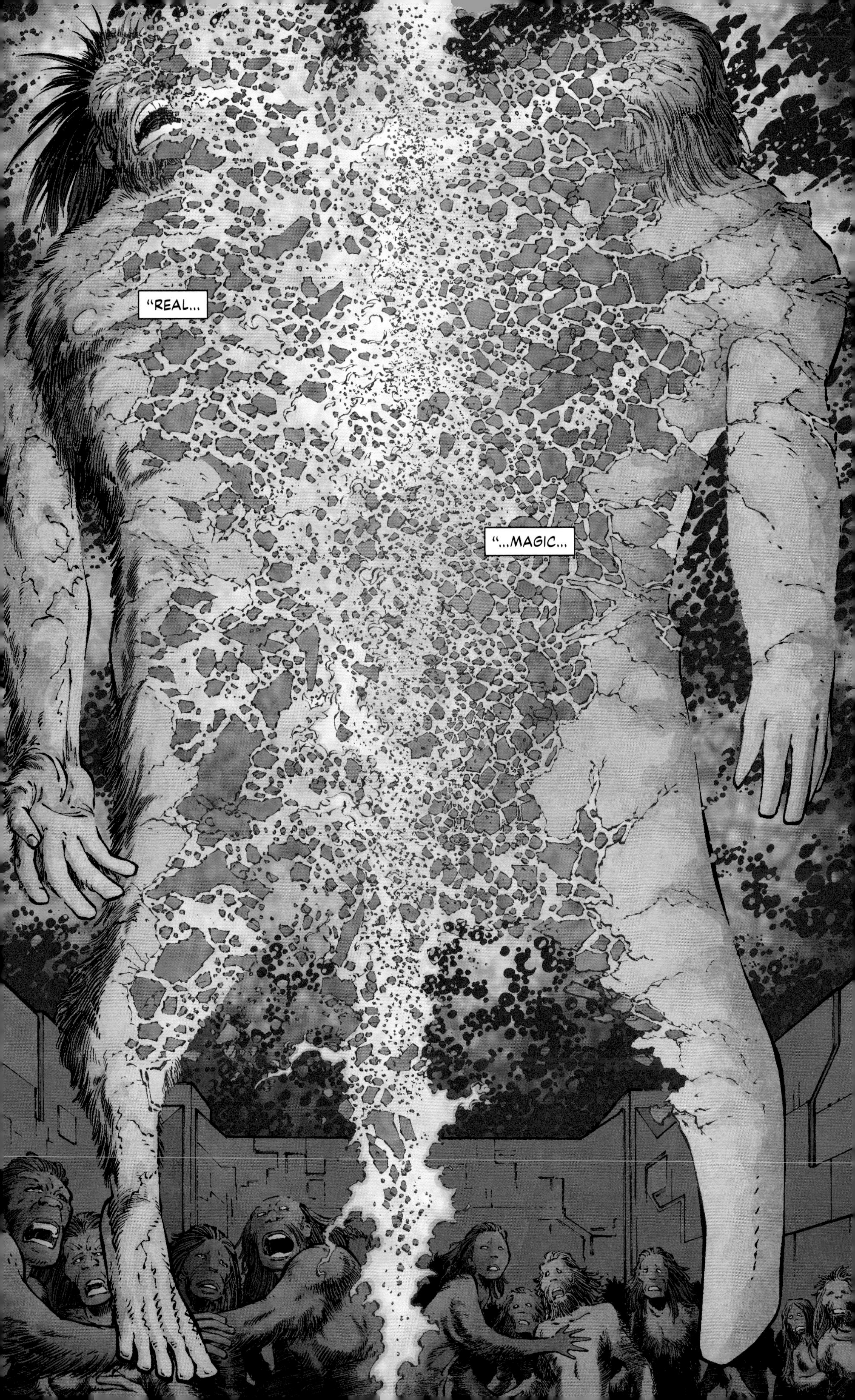
"REAL...
"...MAGIC...

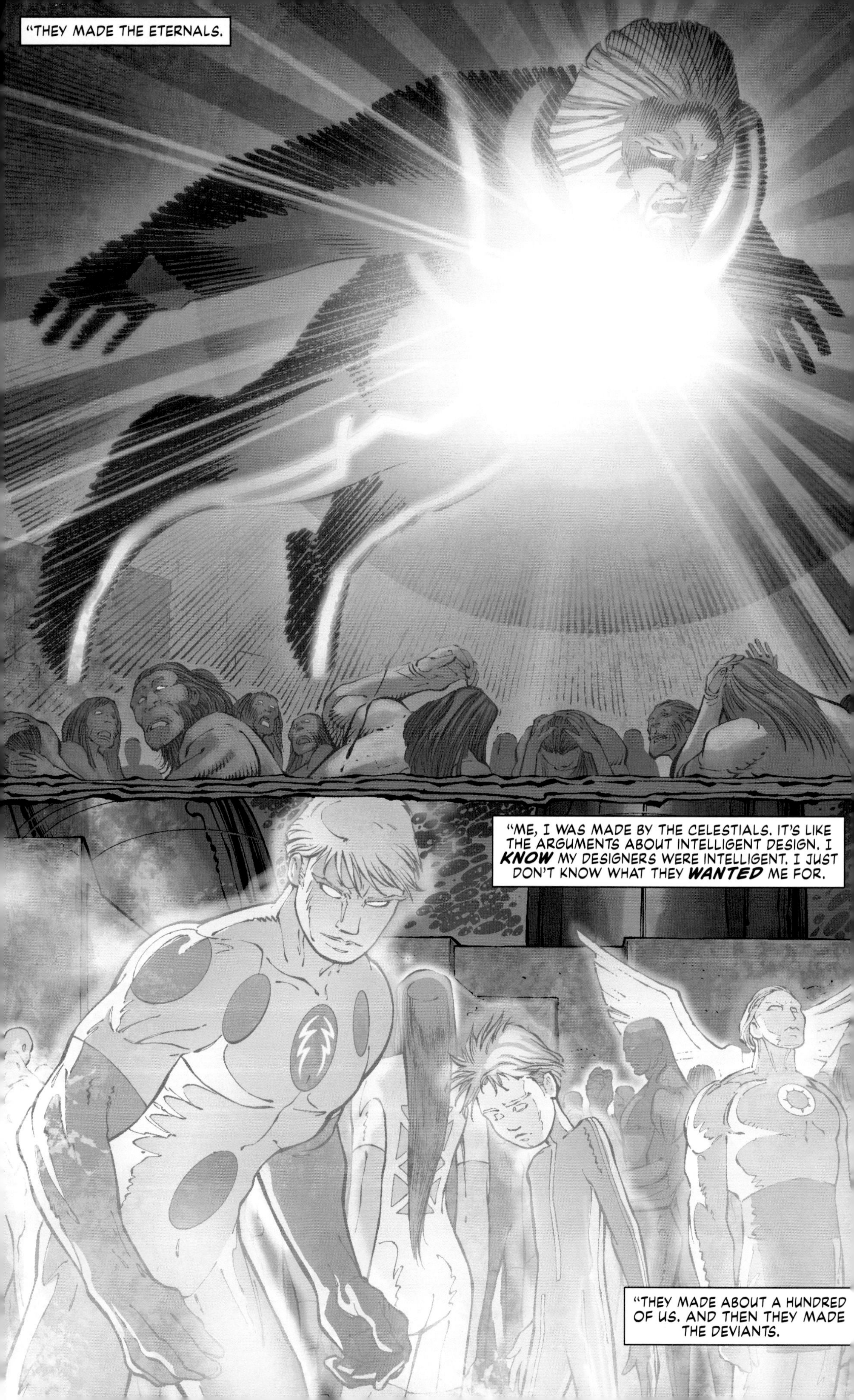
"THEY MADE THE ETERNALS.
"ME, I WAS MADE BY THE CELESTIALS. IT'S LIKE THE ARGUMENTS ABOUT INTELLIGENT DESIGN. I KNOW MY DESIGNERS WERE INTELLIGENT. I JUST DON'T KNOW WHAT THEY WANTED ME FOR.
"THEY MADE ABOUT A HUNDRED OF US. AND THEN THEY MADE THE DEVIANTS.

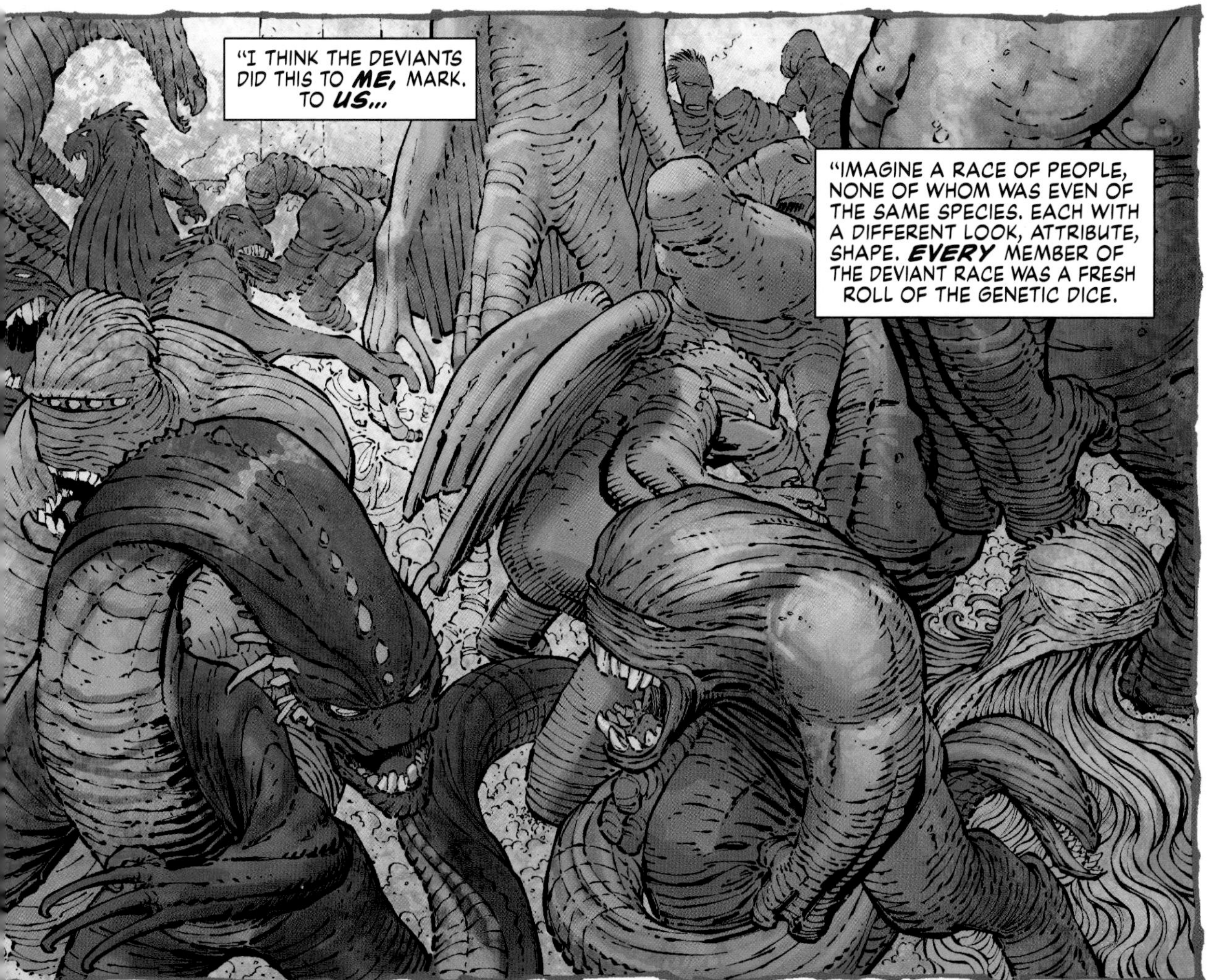
"I THINK THE DEVIANTS DID THIS TO *ME,* MARK. TO *US*...
"IMAGINE A RACE OF PEOPLE, NONE OF WHOM WAS EVEN OF THE SAME SPECIES. EACH WITH A DIFFERENT LOOK, ATTRIBUTE, SHAPE. *EVERY* MEMBER OF THE DEVIANT RACE WAS A FRESH ROLL OF THE GENETIC DICE.
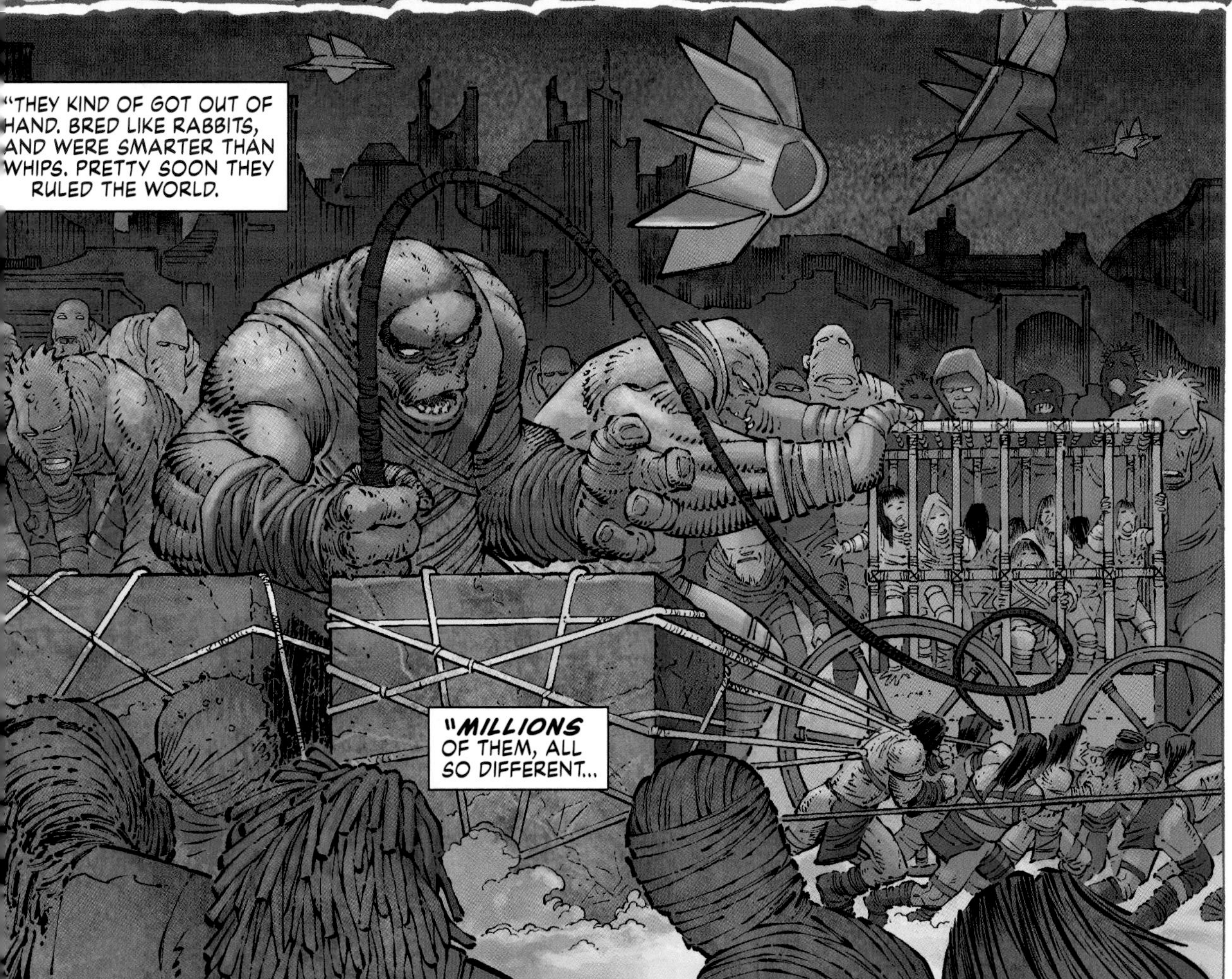
"THEY KIND OF GOT OUT OF HAND. BRED LIKE RABBITS, AND WERE SMARTER THAN WHIPS. PRETTY SOON THEY RULED THE WORLD.
"*MILLIONS* OF THEM, ALL SO DIFFERENT...

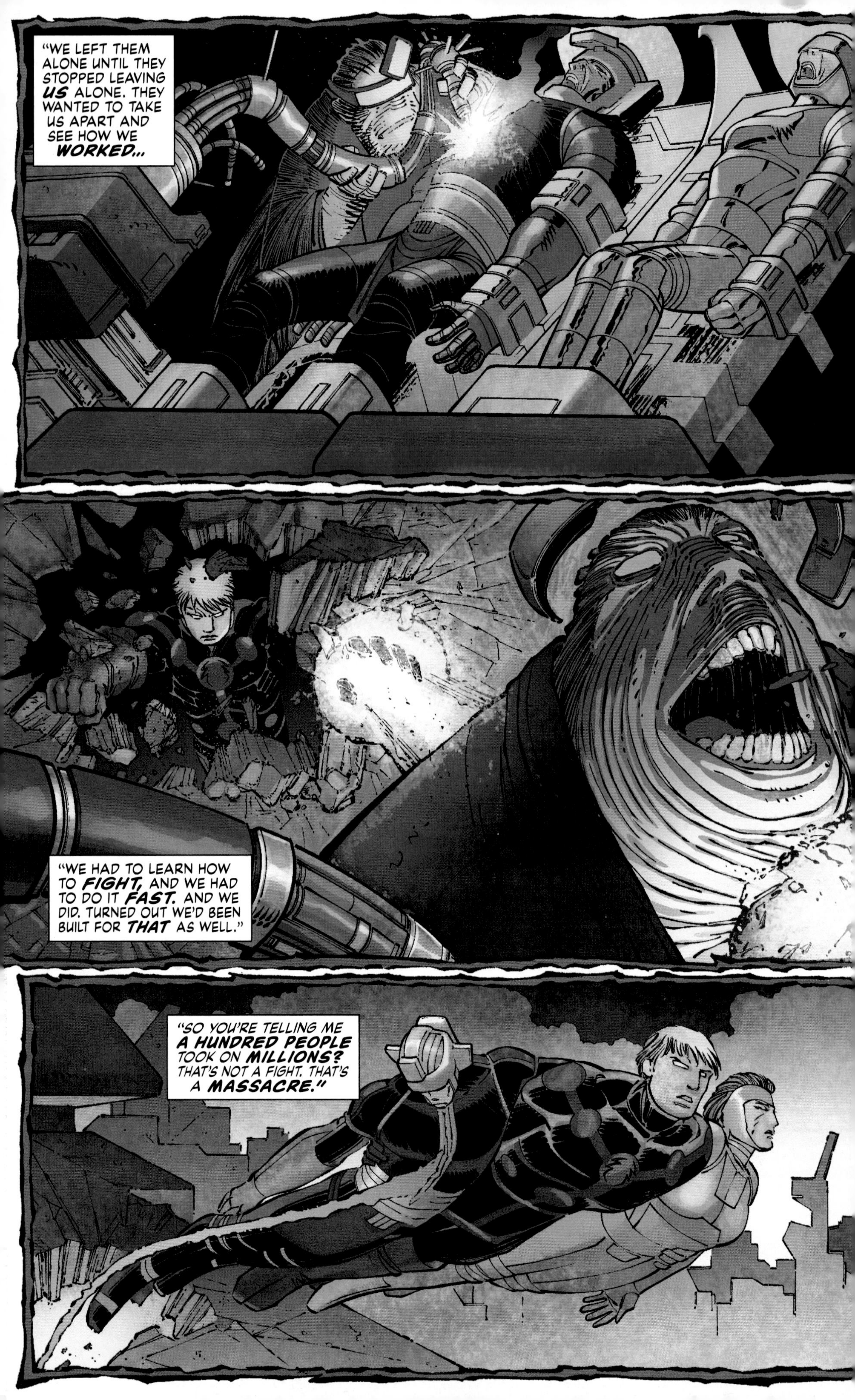
"WE LEFT THEM ALONE UNTIL THEY STOPPED LEAVING *US* ALONE. THEY WANTED TO TAKE US APART AND SEE HOW WE *WORKED...*
"WE HAD TO LEARN HOW TO *FIGHT,* AND WE HAD TO DO IT *FAST.* AND WE DID. TURNED OUT WE'D BEEN BUILT FOR *THAT* AS WELL."
"SO YOU'RE TELLING ME *A HUNDRED PEOPLE* TOOK ON *MILLIONS?* THAT'S NOT A FIGHT. THAT'S A *MASSACRE."*

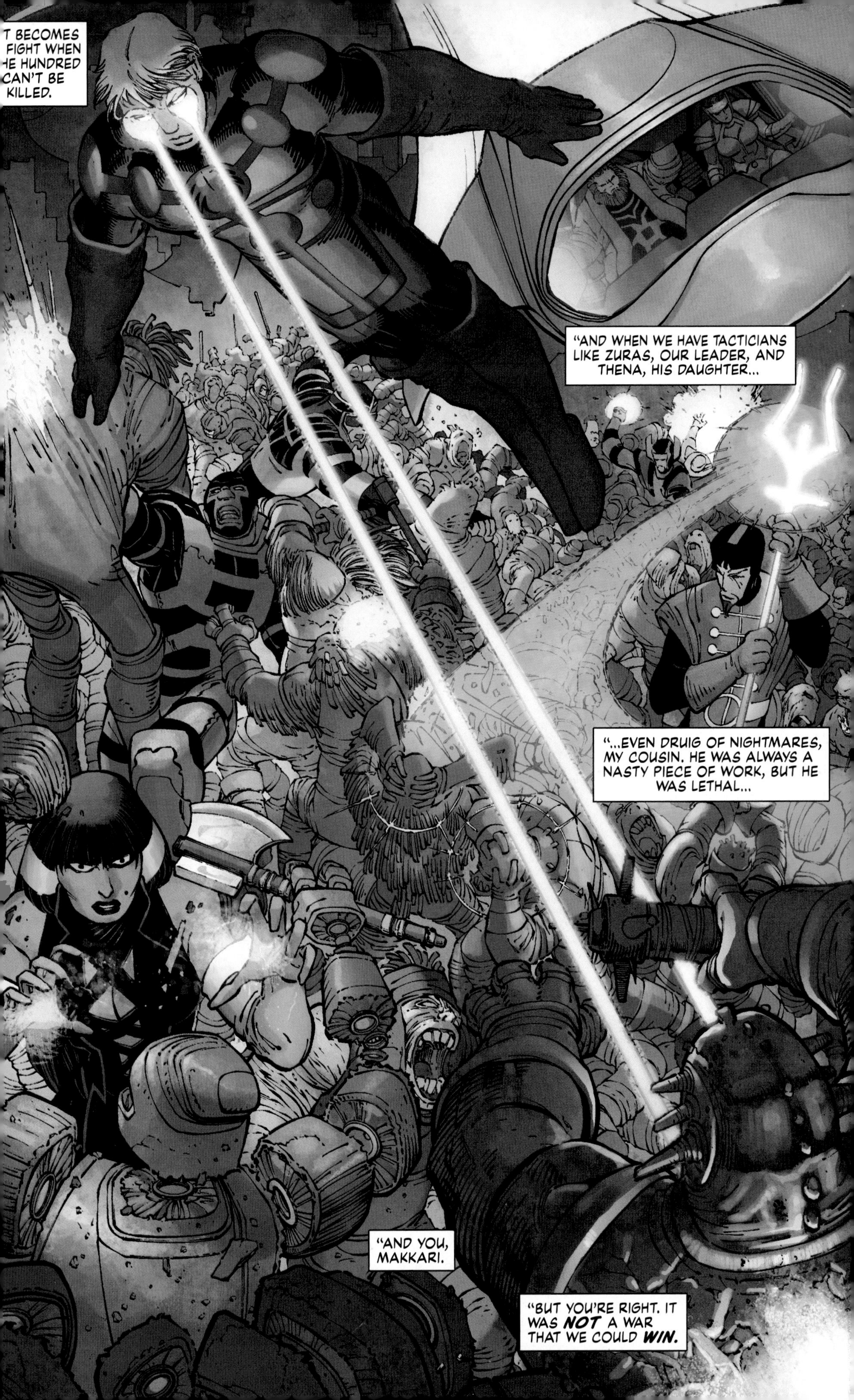
T BECOMES FIGHT WHEN HE HUNDRED CAN'T BE KILLED.
"AND WHEN WE HAVE TACTICIANS LIKE ZURAS, OUR LEADER, AND THENA, HIS DAUGHTER...
"...EVEN DRUIG OF NIGHTMARES, MY COUSIN. HE WAS ALWAYS A NASTY PIECE OF WORK, BUT HE WAS LETHAL...
"AND YOU, MAKKARI.
"BUT YOU'RE RIGHT. IT WAS NOT A WAR THAT WE COULD WIN.

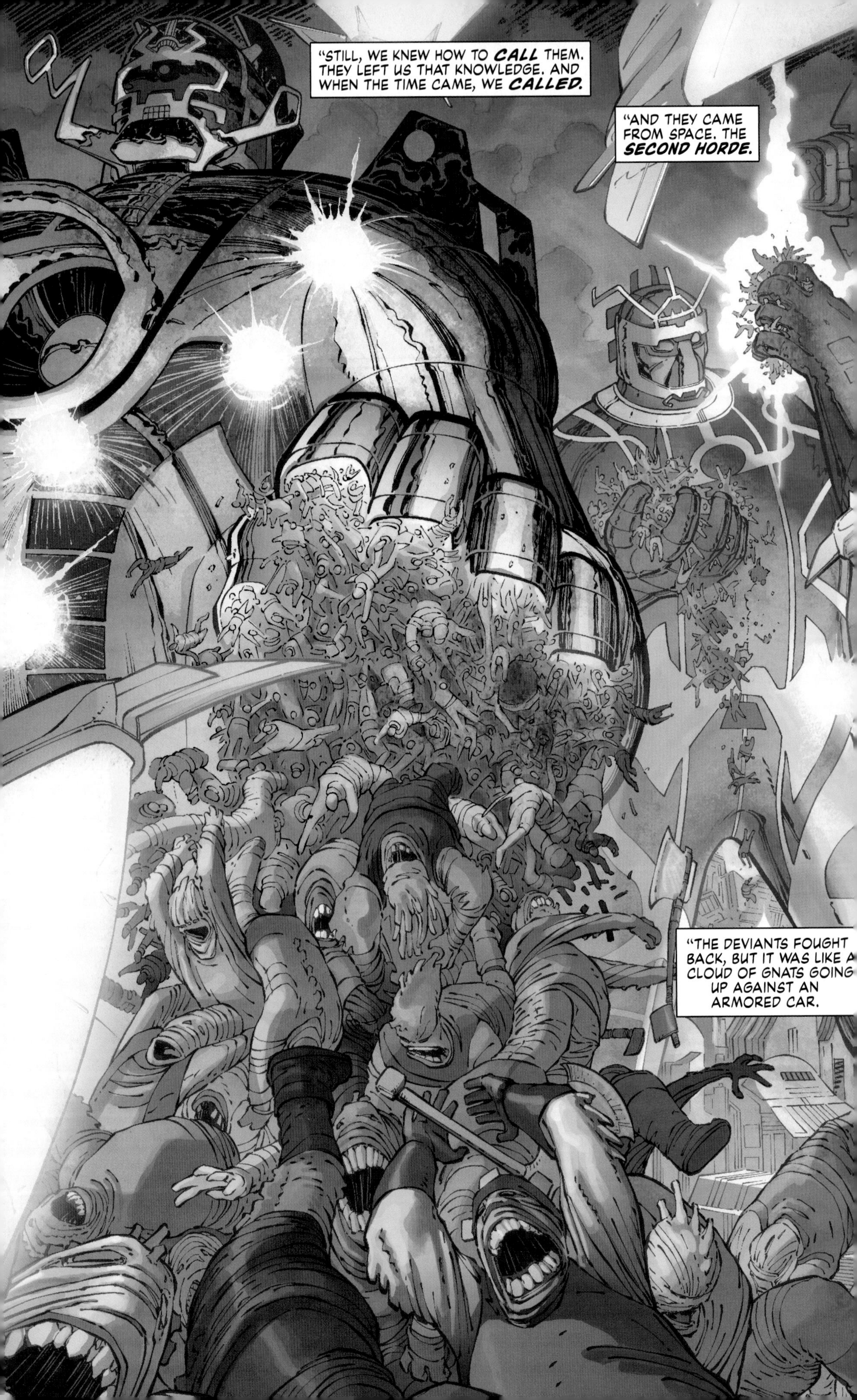
"STILL, WE KNEW HOW TO **CALL** THEM. THEY LEFT US THAT KNOWLEDGE. AND WHEN THE TIME CAME, WE **CALLED**.
"AND THEY CAME FROM SPACE. THE **SECOND HORDE**.
"THE DEVIANTS FOUGHT BACK, BUT IT WAS LIKE A CLOUD OF GNATS GOING UP AGAINST AN ARMORED CAR.

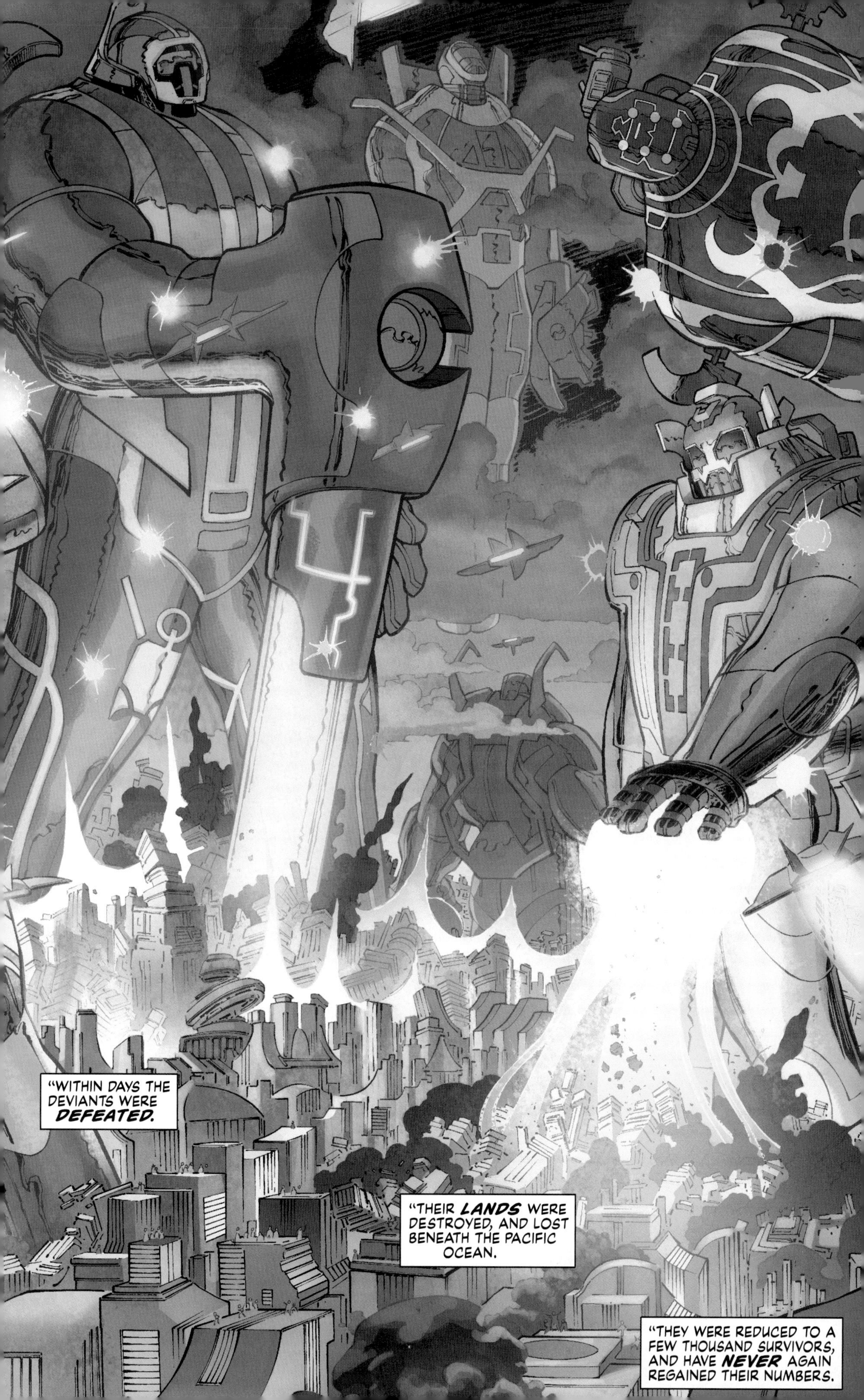
"WITHIN DAYS THE DEVIANTS WERE **DEFEATED.**
"THEIR **LANDS** WERE DESTROYED, AND LOST BENEATH THE PACIFIC OCEAN.
"THEY WERE REDUCED TO A FEW THOUSAND SURVIVORS, AND HAVE **NEVER** AGAIN REGAINED THEIR NUMBERS.

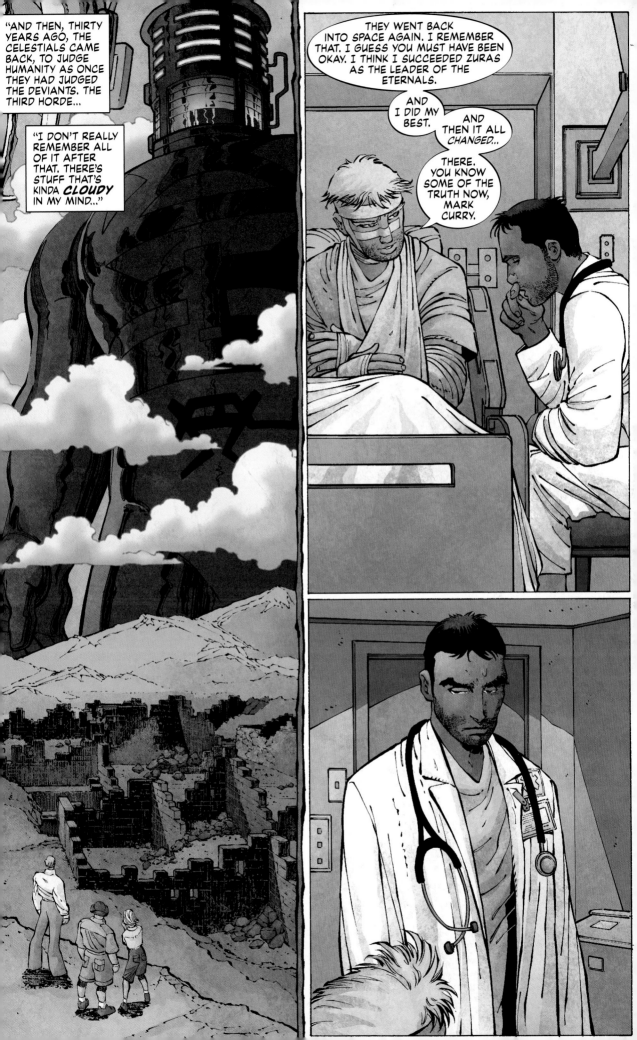

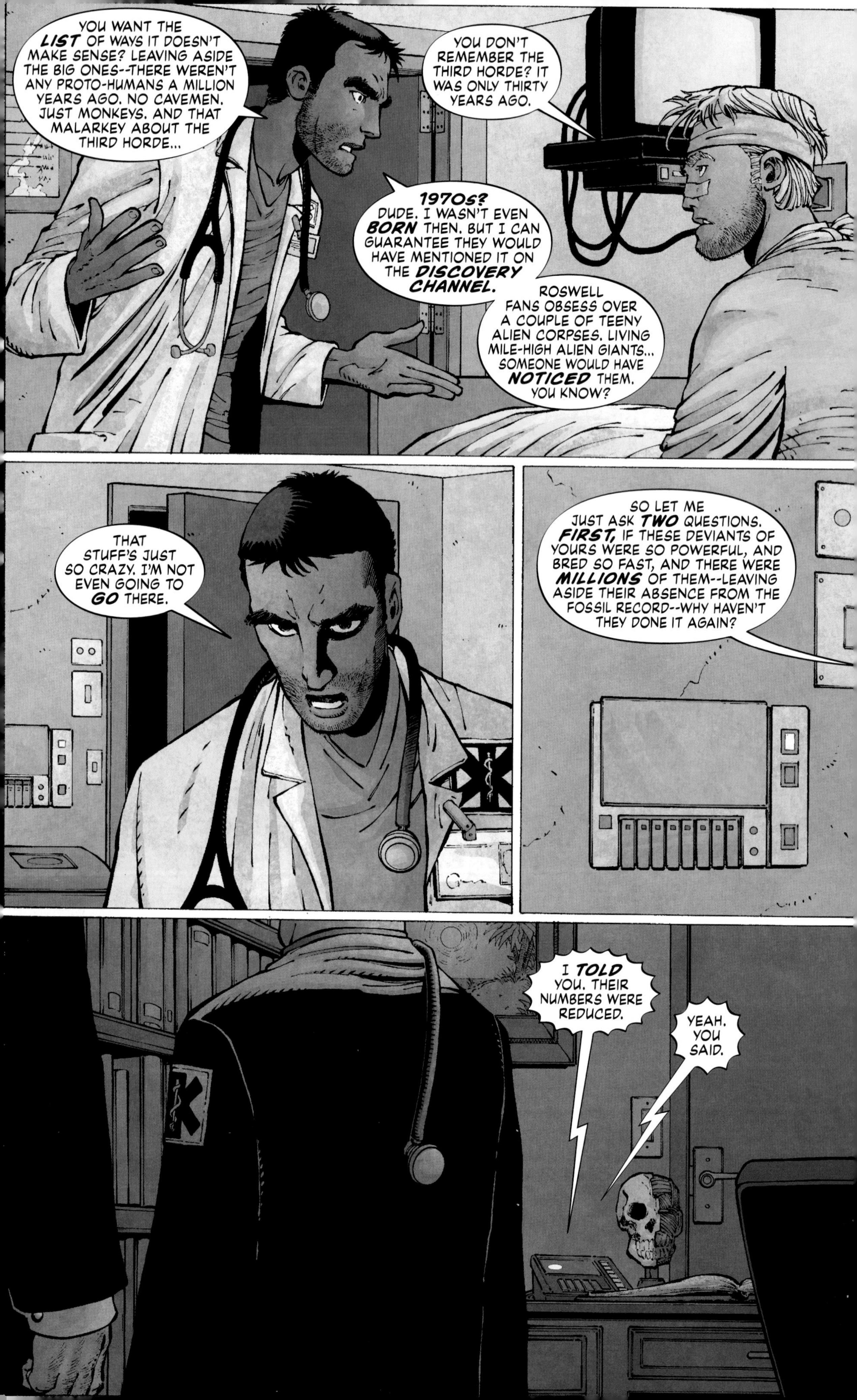
YOU WANT THE LIST OF WAYS IT DOESN'T MAKE SENSE? LEAVING ASIDE THE BIG ONES--THERE WEREN'T ANY PROTO-HUMANS A MILLION YEARS AGO. NO CAVEMEN. JUST MONKEYS. AND THAT MALARKEY ABOUT THE THIRD HORDE...
YOU DON'T REMEMBER THE THIRD HORDE? IT WAS ONLY THIRTY YEARS AGO.
1970s? DUDE. I WASN'T EVEN BORN THEN. BUT I CAN GUARANTEE THEY WOULD HAVE MENTIONED IT ON THE DISCOVERY CHANNEL.
ROSWELL FANS OBSESS OVER A COUPLE OF TEENY ALIEN CORPSES. LIVING MILE-HIGH ALIEN GIANTS... SOMEONE WOULD HAVE NOTICED THEM. YOU KNOW?
THAT STUFF'S JUST SO CRAZY. I'M NOT EVEN GOING TO GO THERE.
SO LET ME JUST ASK TWO QUESTIONS. FIRST, IF THESE DEVIANTS OF YOURS WERE SO POWERFUL, AND BRED SO FAST, AND THERE WERE MILLIONS OF THEM--LEAVING ASIDE THEIR ABSENCE FROM THE FOSSIL RECORD--WHY HAVEN'T THEY DONE IT AGAIN?
I TOLD YOU. THEIR NUMBERS WERE REDUCED.
YEAH. YOU SAID.

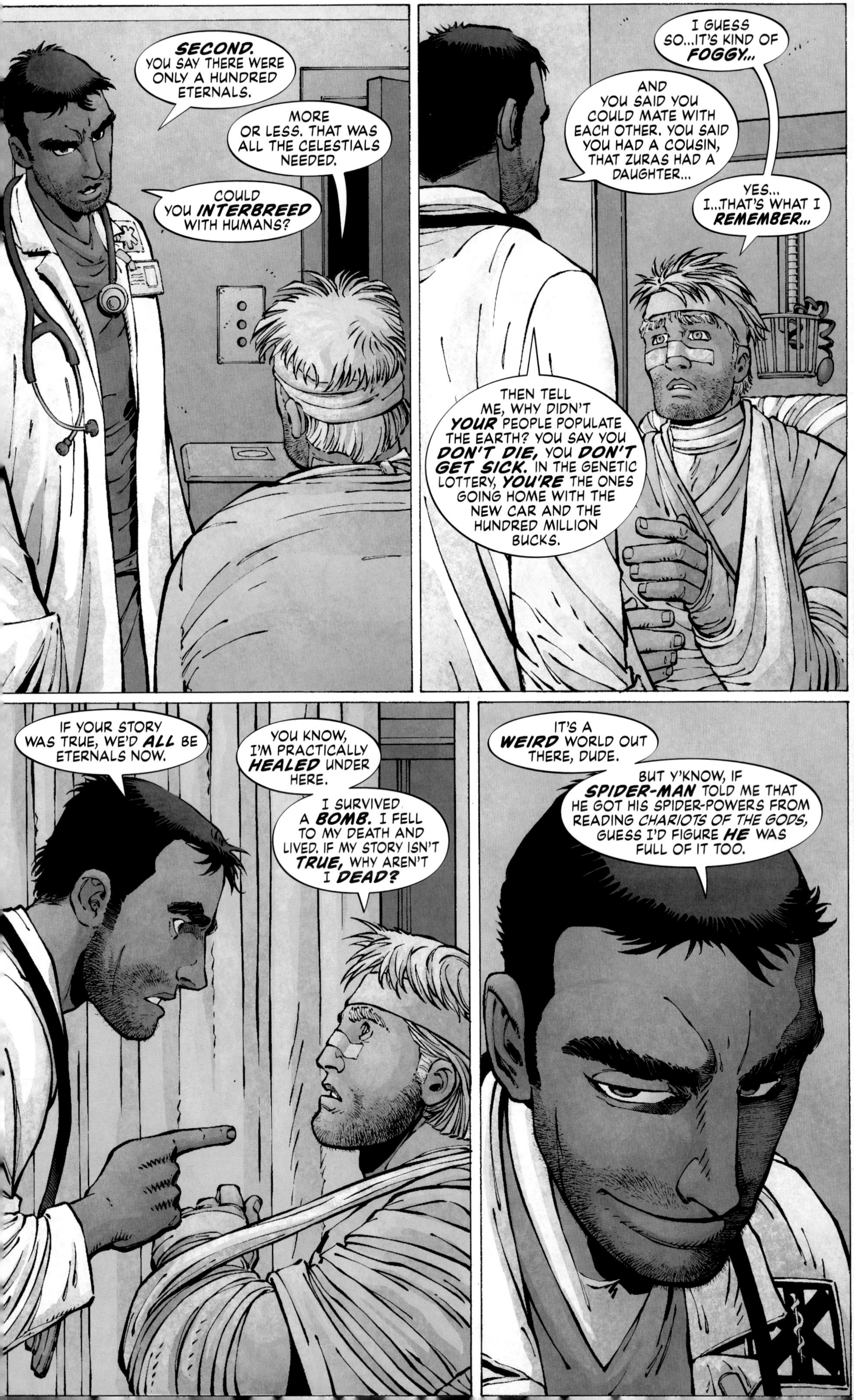

SECOND. YOU SAY THERE WERE ONLY A HUNDRED ETERNALS.
MORE OR LESS. THAT WAS ALL THE CELESTIALS NEEDED.
COULD YOU INTERBREED WITH HUMANS?
I GUESS SO...IT'S KIND OF FOGGY...
AND YOU SAID YOU COULD MATE WITH EACH OTHER. YOU SAID YOU HAD A COUSIN, THAT ZURAS HAD A DAUGHTER...
YES... I...THAT'S WHAT I REMEMBER...
THEN TELL ME, WHY DIDN'T YOUR PEOPLE POPULATE THE EARTH? YOU SAY YOU DON'T DIE, YOU DON'T GET SICK. IN THE GENETIC LOTTERY, YOU'RE THE ONES GOING HOME WITH THE NEW CAR AND THE HUNDRED MILLION BUCKS.
IF YOUR STORY WAS TRUE, WE'D ALL BE ETERNALS NOW.
YOU KNOW, I'M PRACTICALLY HEALED UNDER HERE.
I SURVIVED A BOMB. I FELL TO MY DEATH AND LIVED. IF MY STORY ISN'T TRUE, WHY AREN'T I DEAD?
IT'S A WEIRD WORLD OUT THERE, DUDE.
BUT Y'KNOW, IF SPIDER-MAN TOLD ME THAT HE GOT HIS SPIDER-POWERS FROM READING CHARIOTS OF THE GODS, GUESS I'D FIGURE HE WAS FULL OF IT TOO.

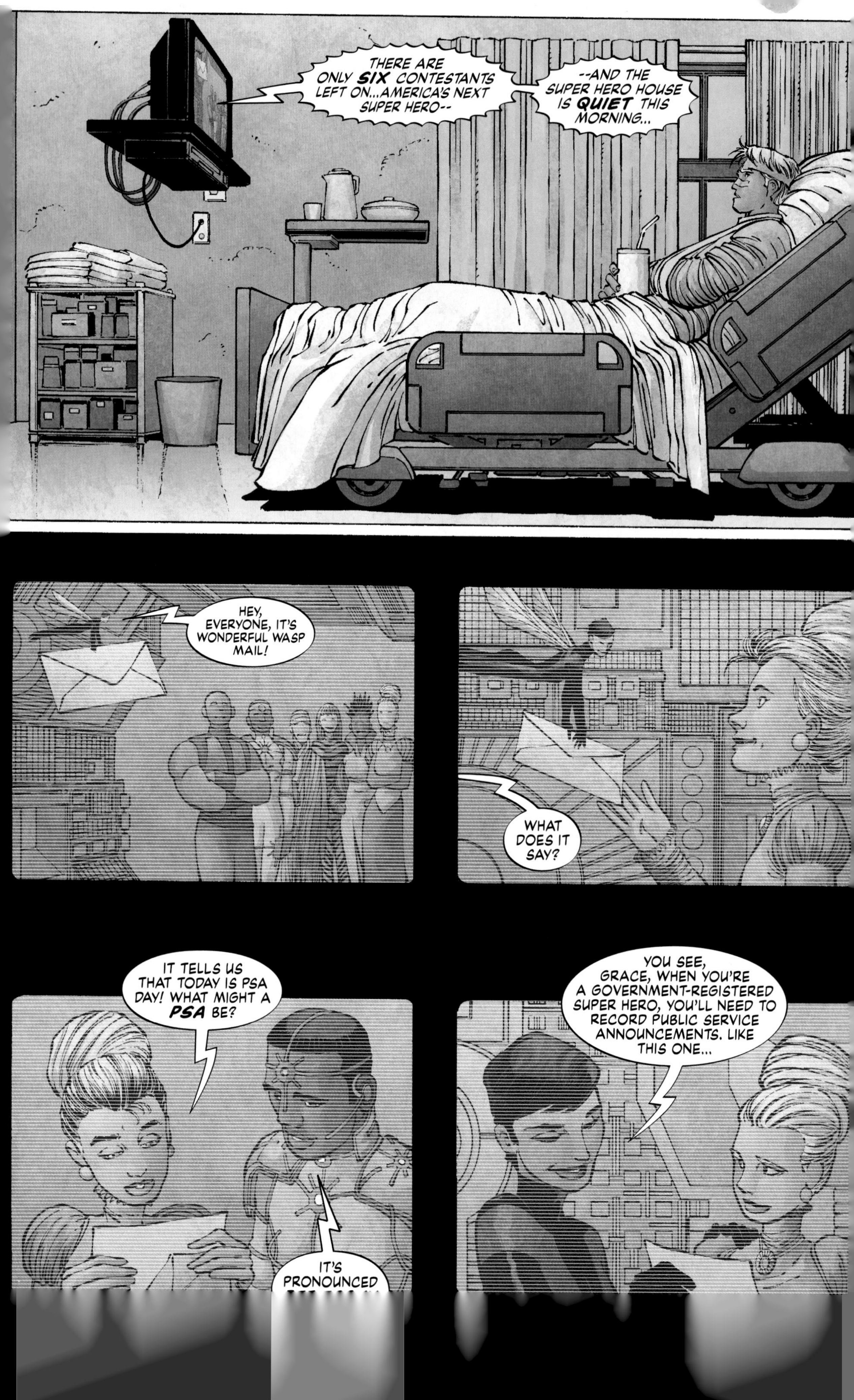
THERE ARE ONLY SIX CONTESTANTS LEFT ON...AMERICA'S NEXT SUPER HERO--
--AND THE SUPER HERO HOUSE IS QUIET THIS MORNING...
HEY, EVERYONE, IT'S WONDERFUL WASP MAIL!
WHAT DOES IT SAY?
IT TELLS US THAT TODAY IS PSA DAY! WHAT MIGHT A PSA BE?
IT'S PRONOUNCED
YOU SEE, GRACE, WHEN YOU'RE A GOVERNMENT-REGISTERED SUPER HERO, YOU'LL NEED TO RECORD PUBLIC SERVICE ANNOUNCEMENTS. LIKE THIS ONE...

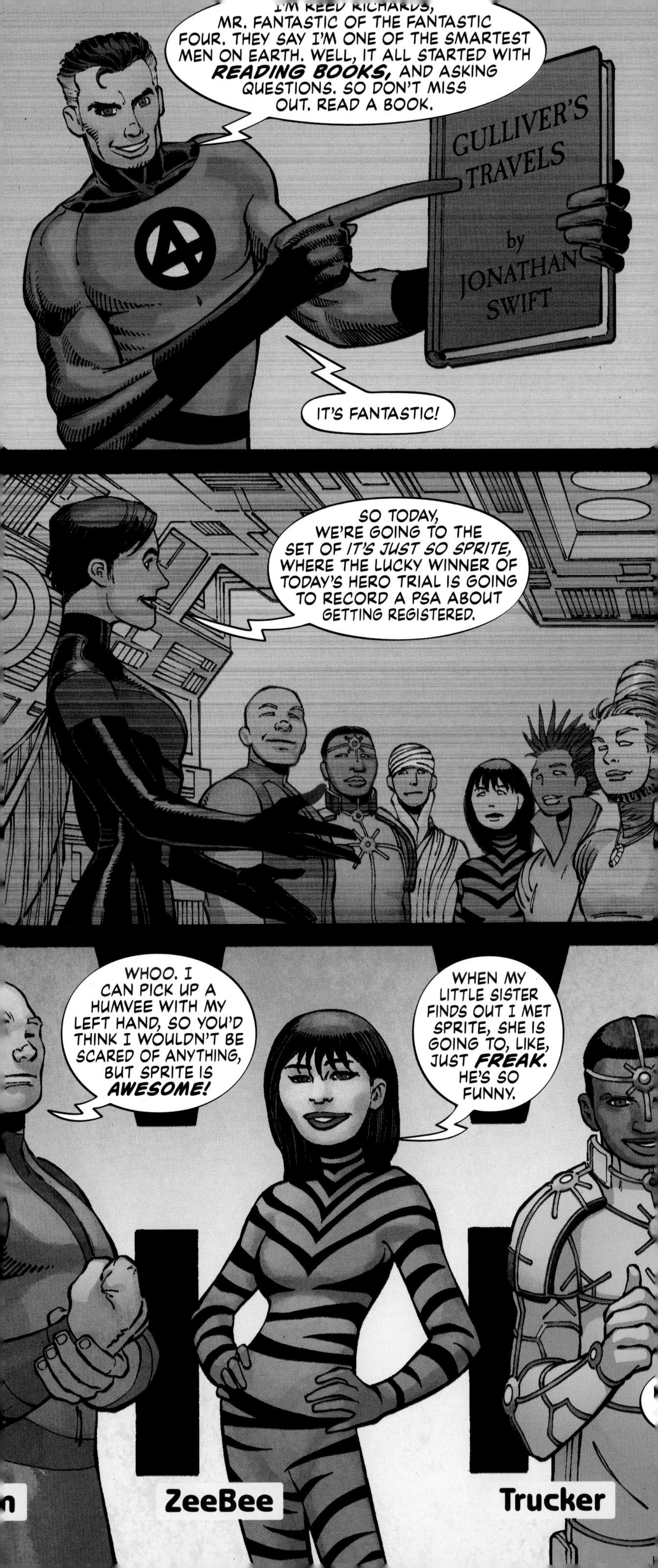
I'M REED RICHARDS, MR. FANTASTIC OF THE FANTASTIC FOUR. THEY SAY I'M ONE OF THE SMARTEST MEN ON EARTH. WELL, IT ALL STARTED WITH **READING BOOKS,** AND ASKING QUESTIONS. SO DON'T MISS OUT. READ A BOOK.
GULLIVER'S TRAVELS by JONATHAN SWIFT
IT'S FANTASTIC!
SO TODAY, WE'RE GOING TO THE SET OF *IT'S JUST SO SPRITE,* WHERE THE LUCKY WINNER OF TODAY'S HERO TRIAL IS GOING TO RECORD A PSA ABOUT GETTING REGISTERED.
WHOO. I CAN PICK UP A HUMVEE WITH MY LEFT HAND, SO YOU'D THINK I WOULDN'T BE SCARED OF ANYTHING, BUT SPRITE IS **AWESOME!**
WHEN MY LITTLE SISTER FINDS OUT I MET SPRITE, SHE IS GOING TO, LIKE, JUST **FREAK.** HE'S SO FUNNY.
ZeeBee
Trucker

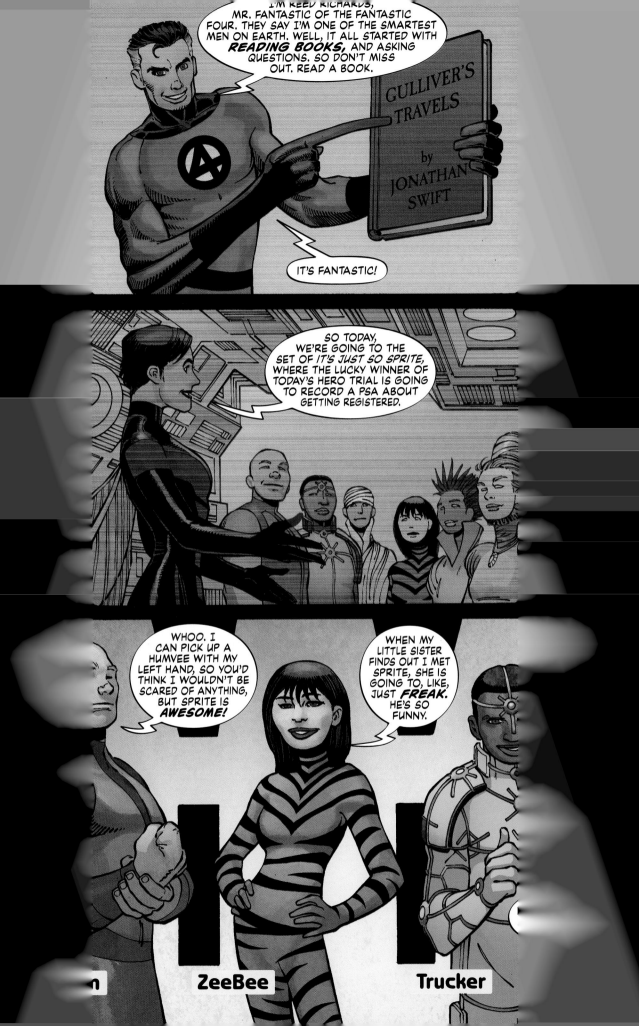

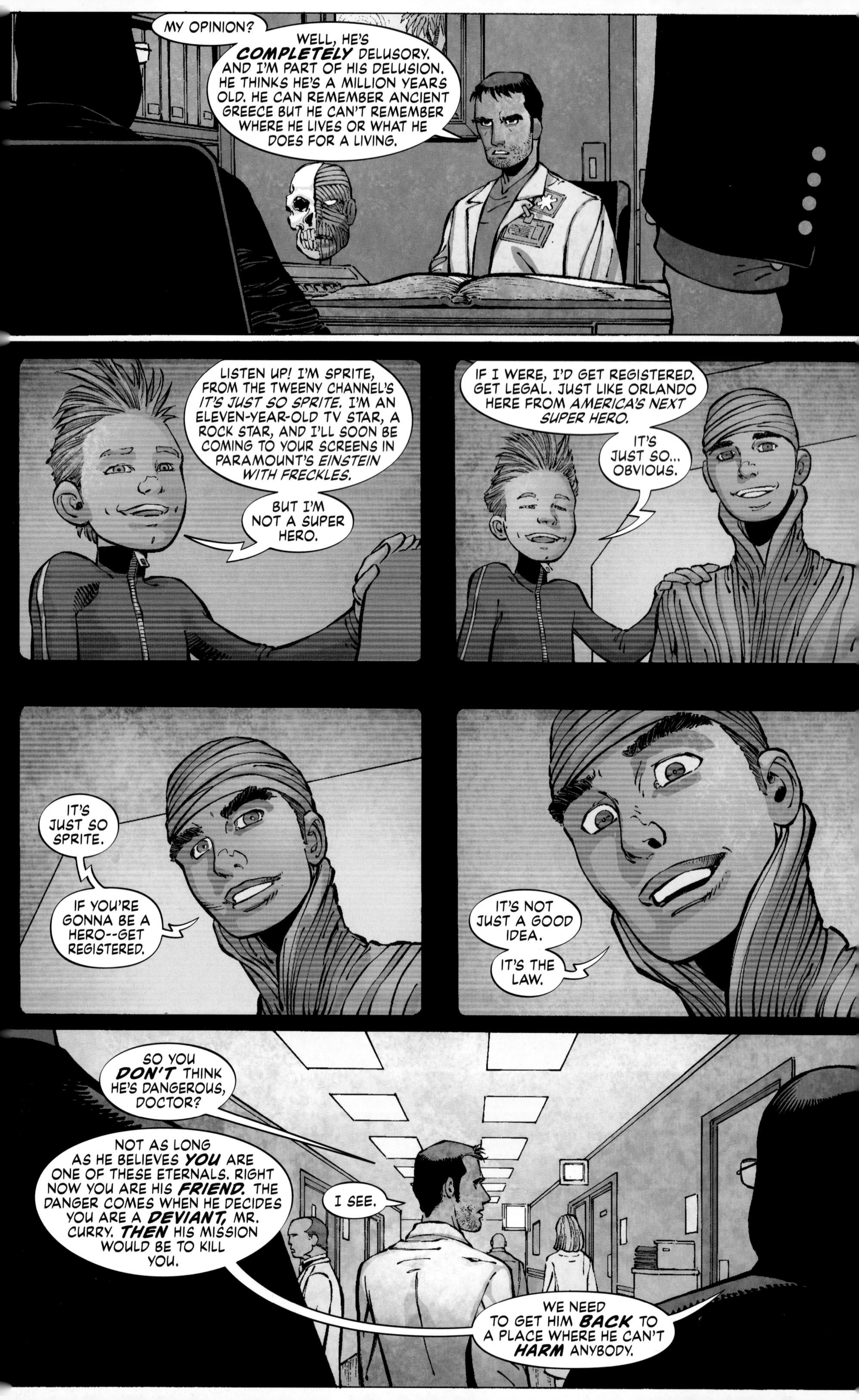
MY OPINION?
WELL, HE'S COMPLETELY DELUSORY. AND I'M PART OF HIS DELUSION. HE THINKS HE'S A MILLION YEARS OLD. HE CAN REMEMBER ANCIENT GREECE BUT HE CAN'T REMEMBER WHERE HE LIVES OR WHAT HE DOES FOR A LIVING.
LISTEN UP! I'M SPRITE, FROM THE TWEENY CHANNEL'S IT'S JUST SO SPRITE. I'M AN ELEVEN-YEAR-OLD TV STAR, A ROCK STAR, AND I'LL SOON BE COMING TO YOUR SCREENS IN PARAMOUNT'S EINSTEIN WITH FRECKLES.
BUT I'M NOT A SUPER HERO.
IF I WERE, I'D GET REGISTERED. GET LEGAL. JUST LIKE ORLANDO HERE FROM AMERICA'S NEXT SUPER HERO.
IT'S JUST SO... OBVIOUS.
IT'S JUST SO SPRITE.
IF YOU'RE GONNA BE A HERO--GET REGISTERED.
IT'S NOT JUST A GOOD IDEA.
IT'S THE LAW.
SO YOU DON'T THINK HE'S DANGEROUS, DOCTOR?
NOT AS LONG AS HE BELIEVES YOU ARE ONE OF THESE ETERNALS. RIGHT NOW YOU ARE HIS FRIEND. THE DANGER COMES WHEN HE DECIDES YOU ARE A DEVIANT, MR. CURRY. THEN HIS MISSION WOULD BE TO KILL YOU.
I SEE.
WE NEED TO GET HIM BACK TO A PLACE WHERE HE CAN'T HARM ANYBODY.

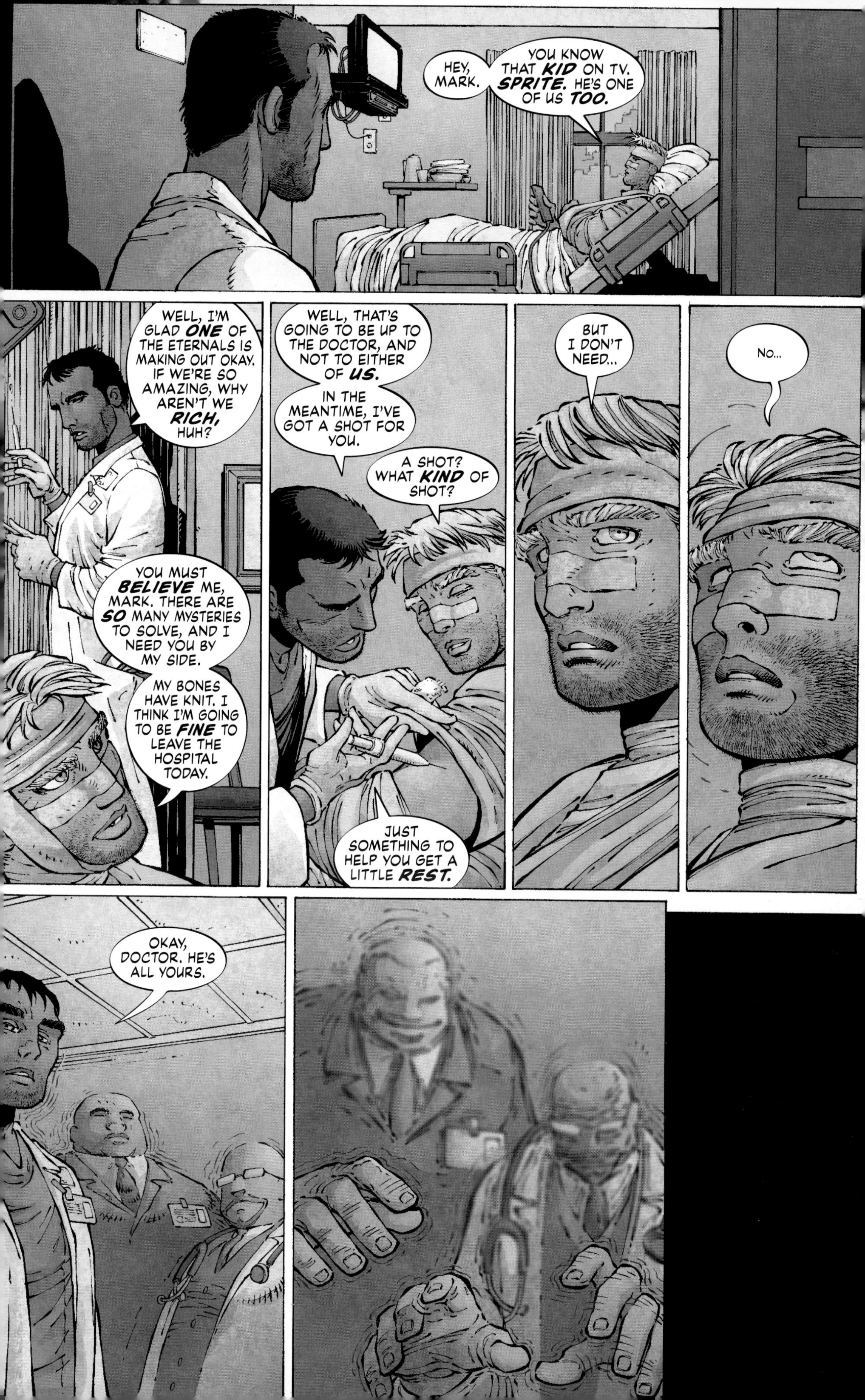
HEY, MARK.
YOU KNOW THAT KID ON TV. SPRITE. HE'S ONE OF US TOO.
WELL, I'M GLAD ONE OF THE ETERNALS IS MAKING OUT OKAY. IF WE'RE SO AMAZING, WHY AREN'T WE RICH, HUH?
YOU MUST BELIEVE ME, MARK. THERE ARE SO MANY MYSTERIES TO SOLVE, AND I NEED YOU BY MY SIDE.
MY BONES HAVE KNIT. I THINK I'M GOING TO BE FINE TO LEAVE THE HOSPITAL TODAY.
WELL, THAT'S GOING TO BE UP TO THE DOCTOR, AND NOT TO EITHER OF US.
IN THE MEANTIME, I'VE GOT A SHOT FOR YOU.
A SHOT? WHAT KIND OF SHOT?
JUST SOMETHING TO HELP YOU GET A LITTLE REST.
BUT I DON'T NEED...
NO...
OKAY, DOCTOR. HE'S ALL YOURS.

CHAPTER TWO: IDENTITY CRISIS

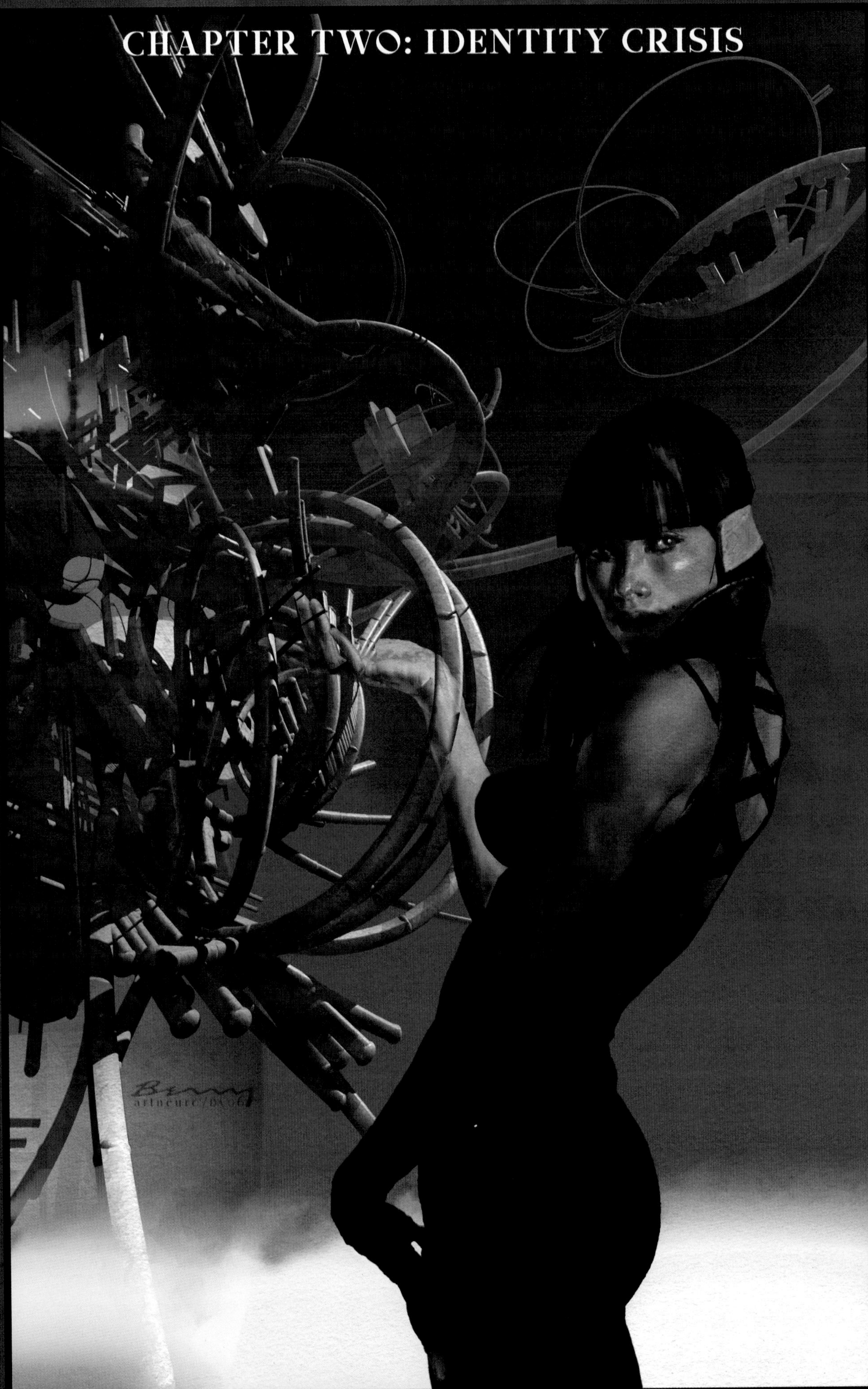

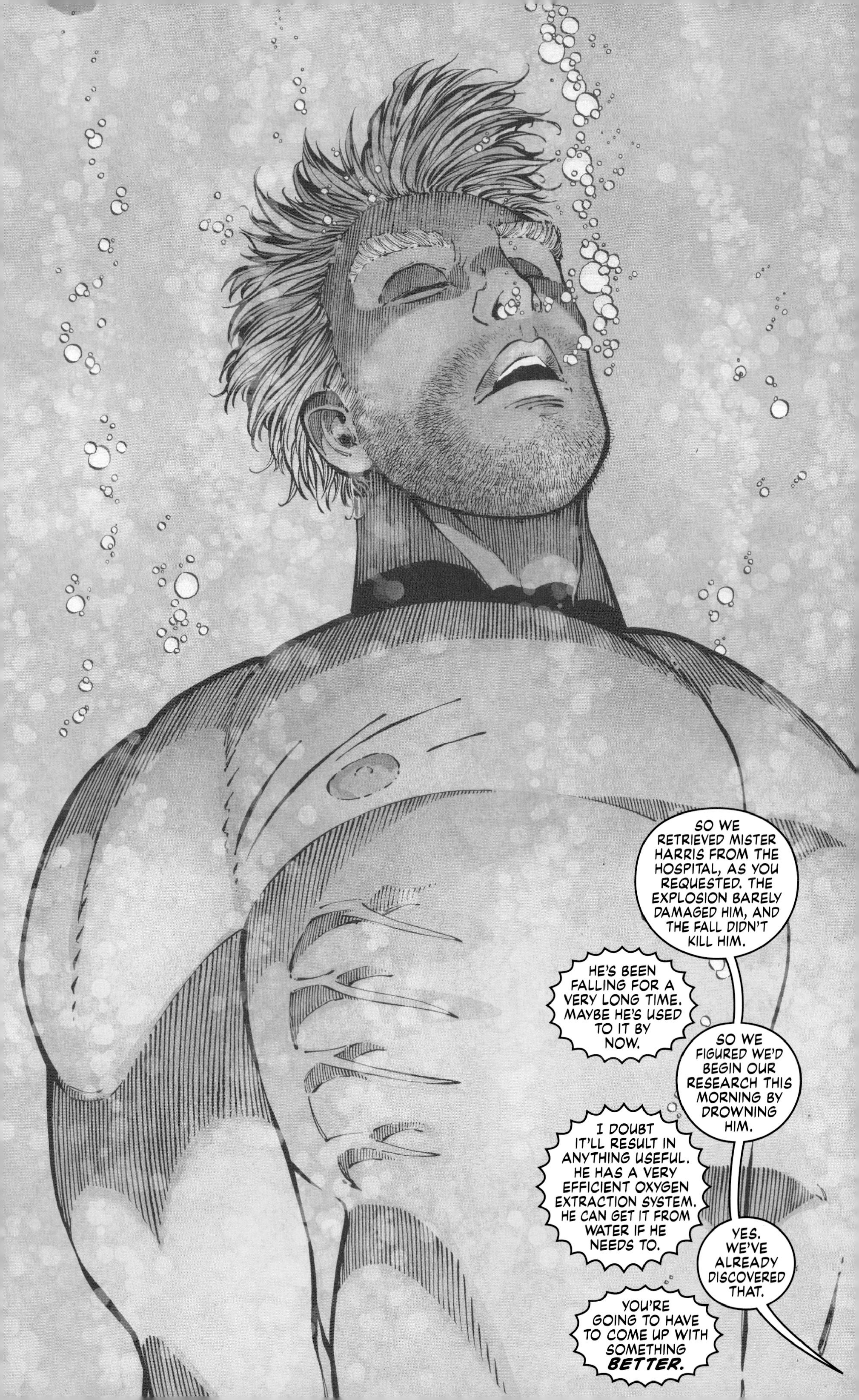
SO WE RETRIEVED MISTER HARRIS FROM THE HOSPITAL, AS YOU REQUESTED. THE EXPLOSION BARELY DAMAGED HIM, AND THE FALL DIDN'T KILL HIM.
HE'S BEEN FALLING FOR A VERY LONG TIME. MAYBE HE'S USED TO IT BY NOW.
SO WE FIGURED WE'D BEGIN OUR RESEARCH THIS MORNING BY DROWNING HIM.
I DOUBT IT'LL RESULT IN ANYTHING USEFUL. HE HAS A VERY EFFICIENT OXYGEN EXTRACTION SYSTEM. HE CAN GET IT FROM WATER IF HE NEEDS TO.
YES. WE'VE ALREADY DISCOVERED THAT.
YOU'RE GOING TO HAVE TO COME UP WITH SOMETHING ***BETTER.***

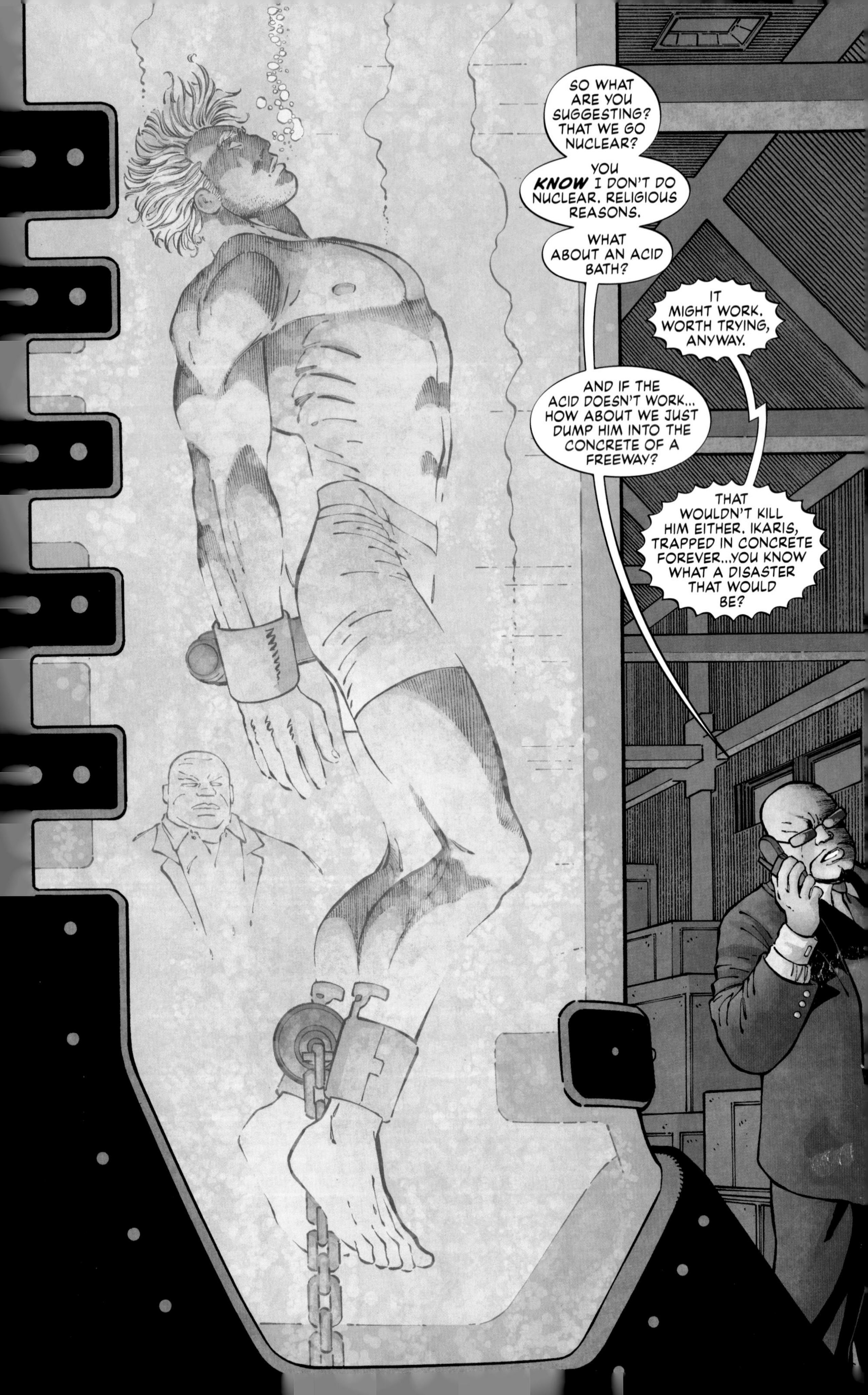
SO WHAT ARE YOU SUGGESTING? THAT WE GO NUCLEAR?
YOU **KNOW** I DON'T DO NUCLEAR. RELIGIOUS REASONS.
WHAT ABOUT AN ACID BATH?
IT MIGHT WORK. WORTH TRYING, ANYWAY.
AND IF THE ACID DOESN'T WORK... HOW ABOUT WE JUST DUMP HIM INTO THE CONCRETE OF A FREEWAY?
THAT WOULDN'T KILL HIM EITHER. IKARIS, TRAPPED IN CONCRETE FOREVER...YOU KNOW WHAT A DISASTER THAT WOULD BE?

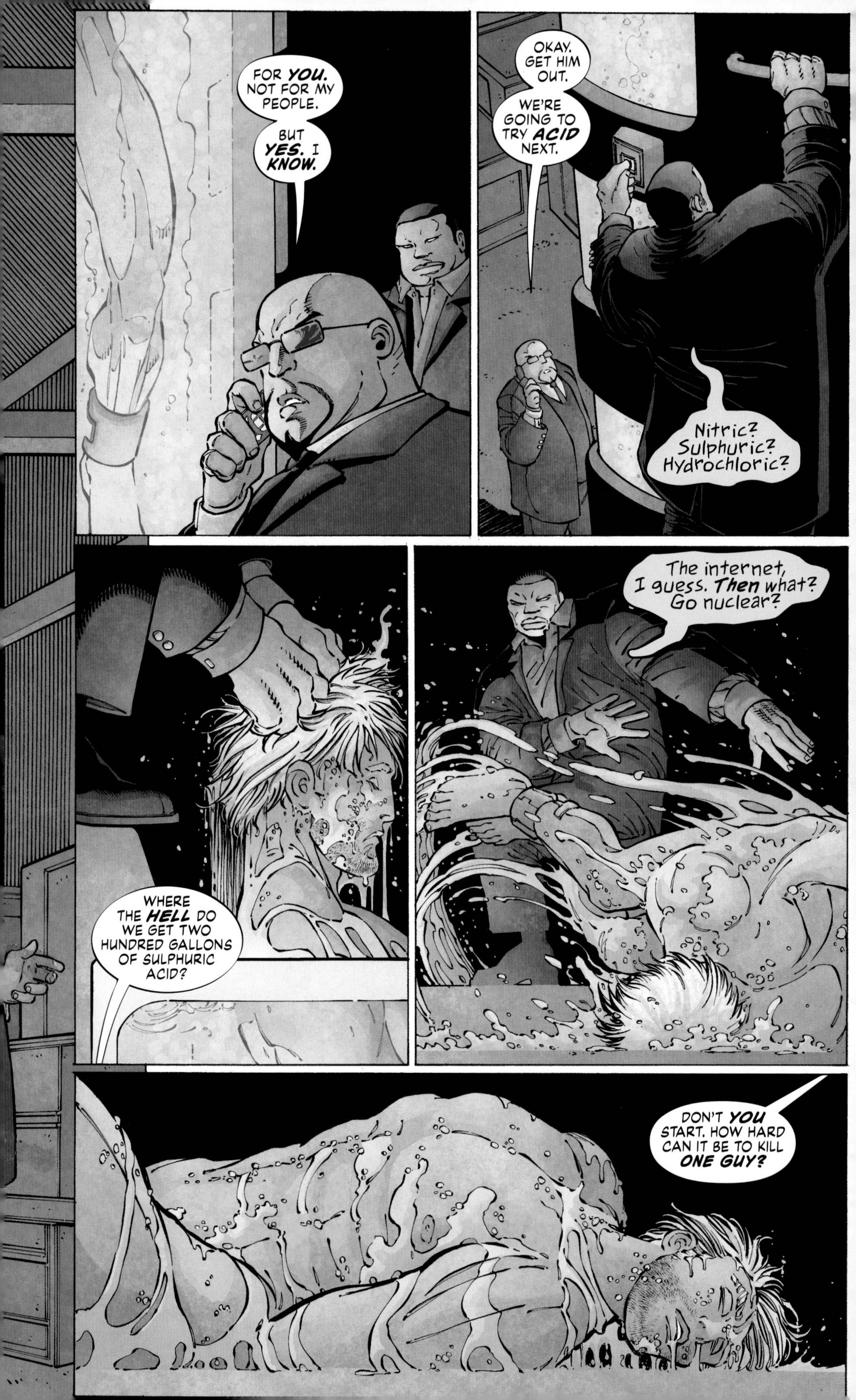
FOR **YOU.** NOT FOR MY PEOPLE.
BUT ***YES.*** I ***KNOW.***
OKAY. GET HIM OUT.
WE'RE GOING TO TRY ***ACID*** NEXT.
Nitric? Sulphuric? Hydrochloric?
WHERE THE ***HELL*** DO WE GET TWO HUNDRED GALLONS OF SULPHURIC ACID?
The internet, I guess. ***Then*** what? Go nuclear?
DON'T ***YOU*** START. HOW HARD CAN IT BE TO KILL ***ONE GUY?***

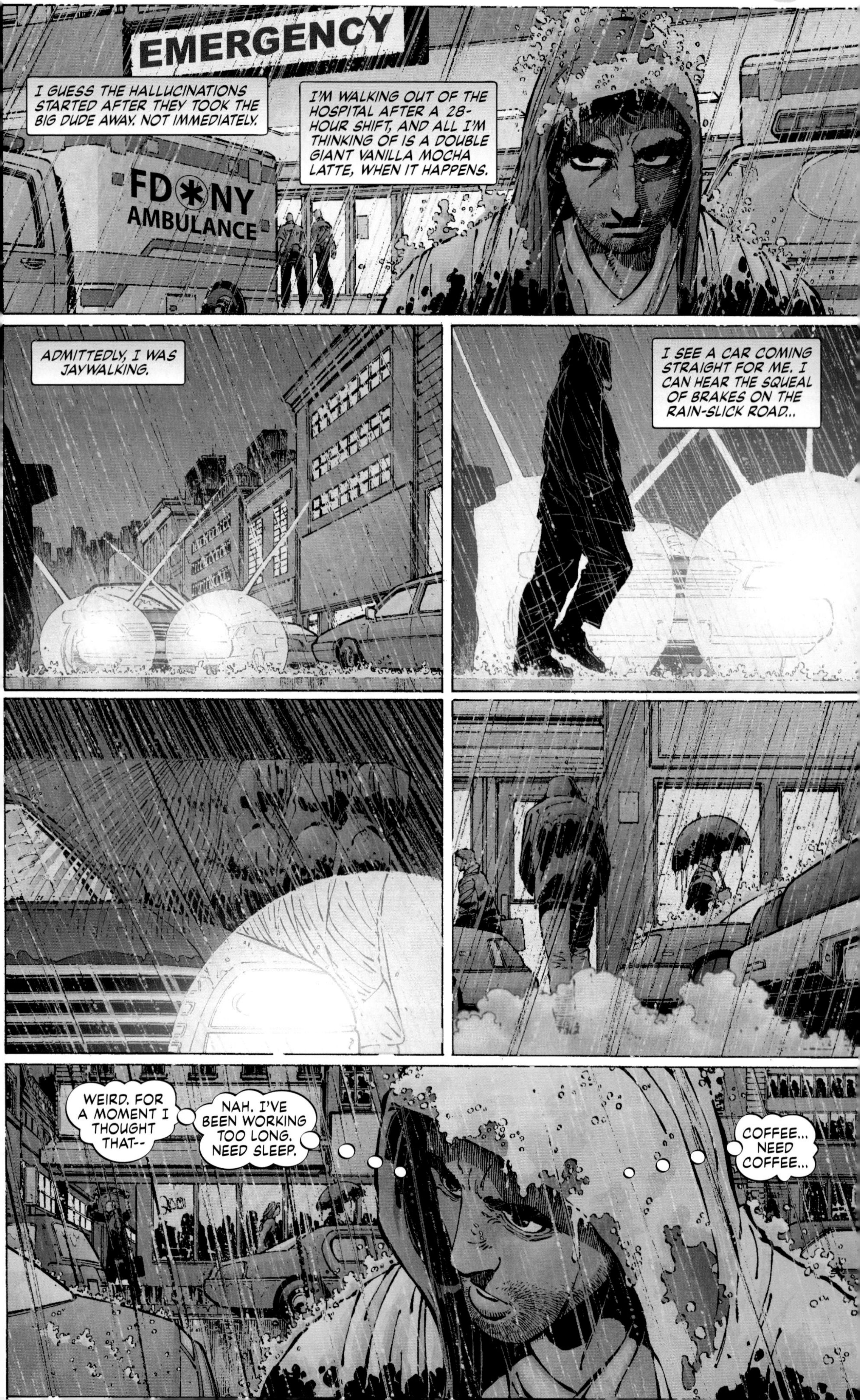
EMERGENCY
I GUESS THE HALLUCINATIONS STARTED AFTER THEY TOOK THE BIG DUDE AWAY. NOT IMMEDIATELY.
I'M WALKING OUT OF THE HOSPITAL AFTER A 28-HOUR SHIFT, AND ALL I'M THINKING OF IS A DOUBLE GIANT VANILLA MOCHA LATTE, WHEN IT HAPPENS.
FD✱NY AMBULANCE
ADMITTEDLY, I WAS JAYWALKING.
I SEE A CAR COMING STRAIGHT FOR ME. I CAN HEAR THE SQUEAL OF BRAKES ON THE RAIN-SLICK ROAD...
WEIRD. FOR A MOMENT I THOUGHT THAT--
NAH. I'VE BEEN WORKING TOO LONG. NEED SLEEP.
COFFEE... NEED COFFEE...

DOUBLE GIANT VANILLA MOCHA LATTE?

THAT'S ME. THAT'S MINE.

MARK CURRY. I'M A MED STUDENT, WORKING DOWN AT THE HOSPITAL...

I'M A PARTY ORGANIZER. AND I'M PUTTING ON THIS *HUGE* PARTY FOR THE VOROZHEIKAN EMBASSY. IT'S LIKE THIS MASSIVE RUSH JOB. I'VE NOT SLEPT FOR 26 HOURS, ORGANIZING THE CATERERS, CONFIRMING GUESTS...

28 HOURS OVER HERE.

WOW.

SO HOW MANY OF THESE BIG PARTIES HAVE YOU PUT ON?

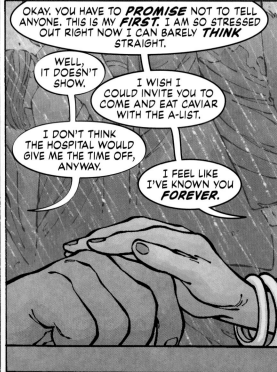

OKAY. YOU HAVE TO *PROMISE* NOT TO TELL ANYONE. THIS IS MY *FIRST.* I AM SO STRESSED OUT RIGHT NOW I CAN BARELY *THINK* STRAIGHT.

WELL, IT DOESN'T SHOW.

I WISH I COULD INVITE YOU TO COME AND EAT CAVIAR WITH THE A-LIST.

I DON'T THINK THE HOSPITAL WOULD GIVE ME THE TIME OFF, ANYWAY.

I FEEL LIKE I'VE KNOWN YOU *FOREVER.*

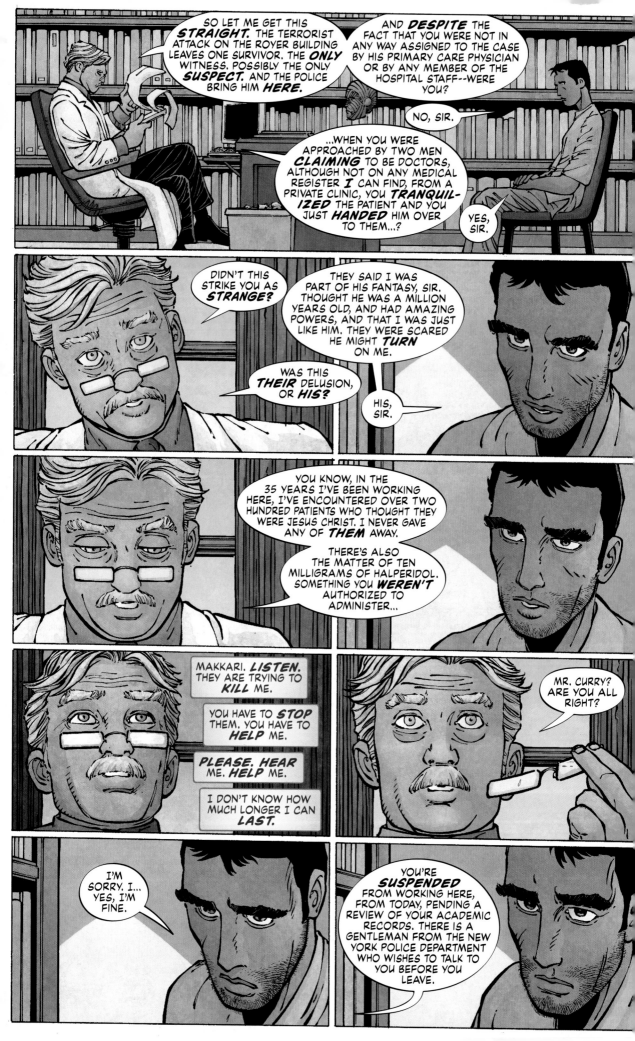

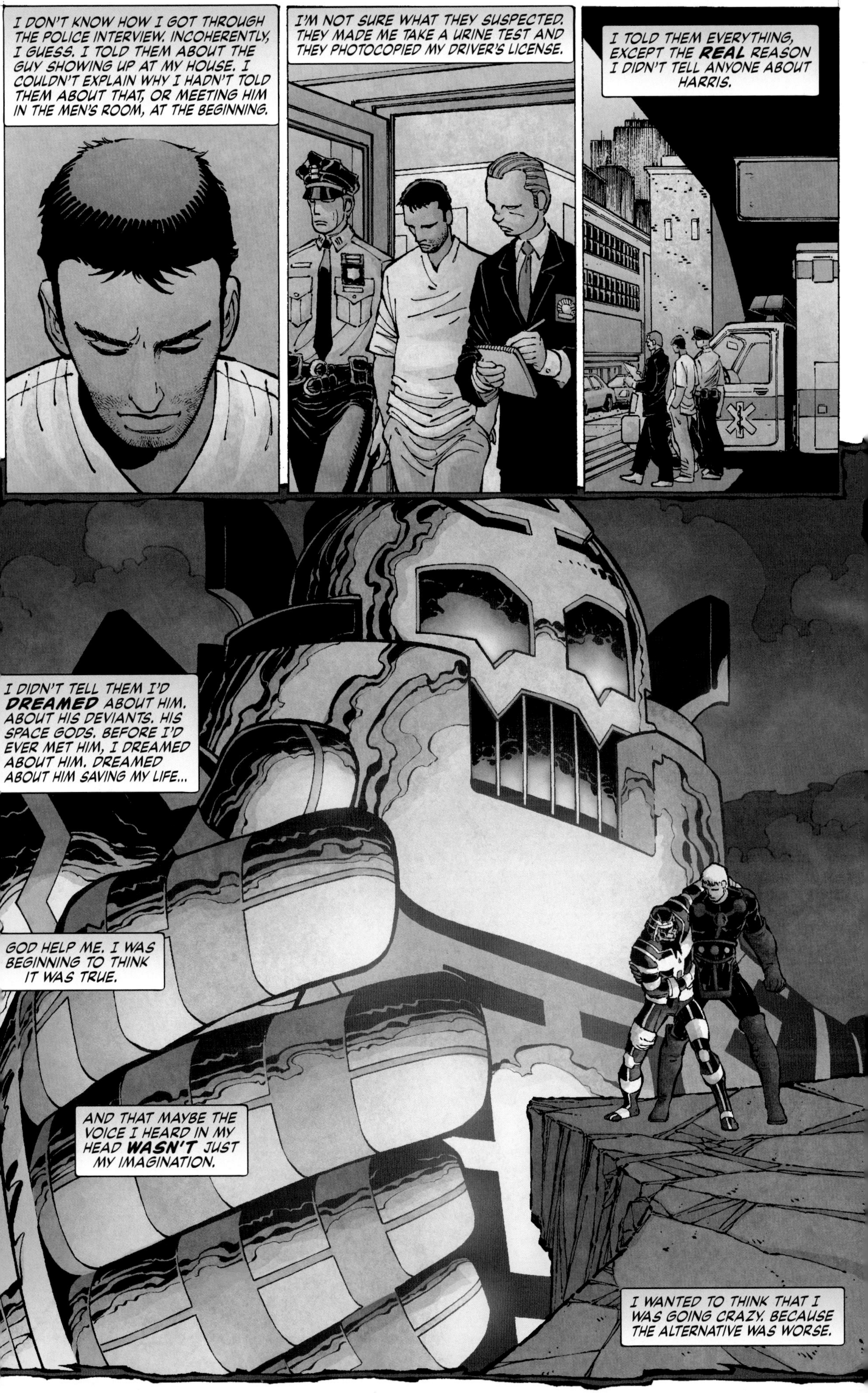
I DON'T KNOW HOW I GOT THROUGH THE POLICE INTERVIEW. INCOHERENTLY, I GUESS. I TOLD THEM ABOUT THE GUY SHOWING UP AT MY HOUSE. I COULDN'T EXPLAIN WHY I HADN'T TOLD THEM ABOUT THAT, OR MEETING HIM IN THE MEN'S ROOM, AT THE BEGINNING.
I'M NOT SURE WHAT THEY SUSPECTED. THEY MADE ME TAKE A URINE TEST AND THEY PHOTOCOPIED MY DRIVER'S LICENSE.
I TOLD THEM EVERYTHING, EXCEPT THE REAL REASON I DIDN'T TELL ANYONE ABOUT HARRIS.
I DIDN'T TELL THEM I'D DREAMED ABOUT HIM. ABOUT HIS DEVIANTS. HIS SPACE GODS. BEFORE I'D EVER MET HIM, I DREAMED ABOUT HIM. DREAMED ABOUT HIM SAVING MY LIFE...
GOD HELP ME. I WAS BEGINNING TO THINK IT WAS TRUE.
AND THAT MAYBE THE VOICE I HEARD IN MY HEAD WASN'T JUST MY IMAGINATION.
I WANTED TO THINK THAT I WAS GOING CRAZY. BECAUSE THE ALTERNATIVE WAS WORSE.

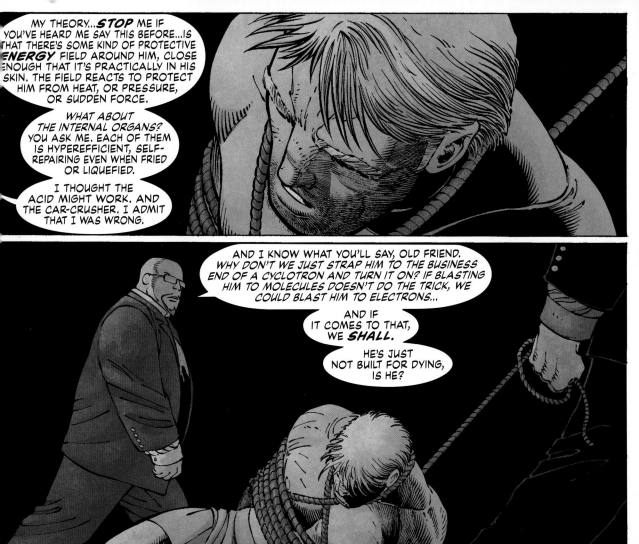

MY THEORY...*STOP* ME IF YOU'VE HEARD ME SAY THIS BEFORE...IS THAT THERE'S SOME KIND OF PROTECTIVE *ENERGY* FIELD AROUND HIM, CLOSE ENOUGH THAT IT'S PRACTICALLY IN HIS SKIN. THE FIELD REACTS TO PROTECT HIM FROM HEAT, OR PRESSURE, OR SUDDEN FORCE.

WHAT ABOUT THE INTERNAL ORGANS? YOU ASK ME. EACH OF THEM IS HYPEREFFICIENT, SELF-REPAIRING EVEN WHEN FRIED OR LIQUEFIED.

I THOUGHT THE ACID MIGHT WORK. AND THE CAR-CRUSHER. I ADMIT THAT I WAS WRONG.

AND I KNOW WHAT YOU'LL SAY, OLD FRIEND. WHY DON'T WE JUST STRAP HIM TO THE BUSINESS END OF A CYCLOTRON AND TURN IT ON? IF BLASTING HIM TO MOLECULES DOESN'T DO THE TRICK, WE COULD BLAST HIM TO ELECTRONS...

AND IF IT COMES TO THAT, WE *SHALL.*

HE'S JUST NOT BUILT FOR DYING, IS HE?

YOU KNOW, MY GUESS IS THAT THIS SMELTER WON'T DO ANYTHING AT ALL.

BUT LET'S FIND OUT.

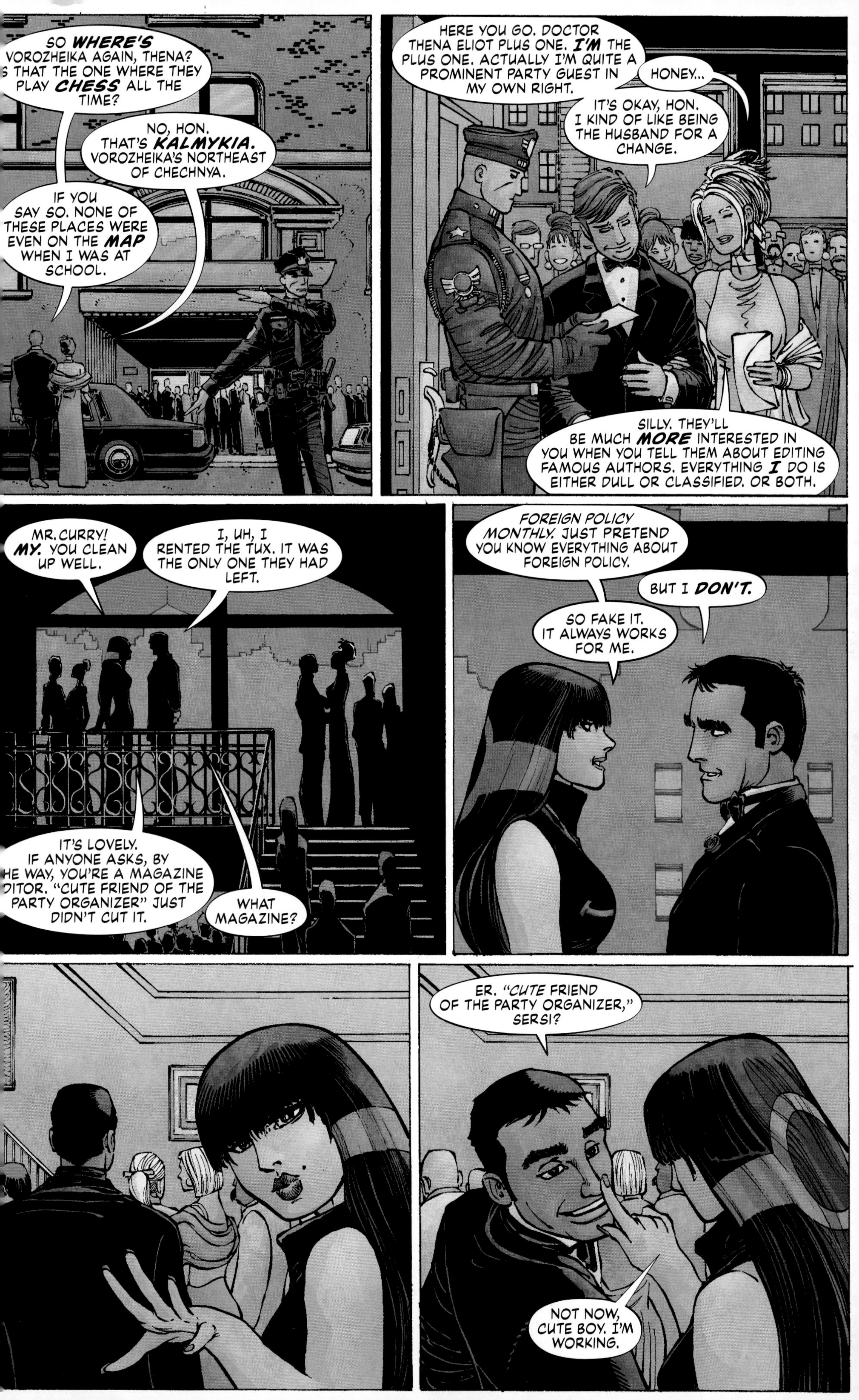
SO WHERE'S VOROZHEIKA AGAIN, THENA? S THAT THE ONE WHERE THEY PLAY CHESS ALL THE TIME?
NO, HON. THAT'S KALMYKIA. VOROZHEIKA'S NORTHEAST OF CHECHNYA.
IF YOU SAY SO. NONE OF THESE PLACES WERE EVEN ON THE MAP WHEN I WAS AT SCHOOL.
HERE YOU GO. DOCTOR THENA ELIOT PLUS ONE. I'M THE PLUS ONE. ACTUALLY I'M QUITE A PROMINENT PARTY GUEST IN MY OWN RIGHT.
HONEY...
IT'S OKAY, HON. I KIND OF LIKE BEING THE HUSBAND FOR A CHANGE.
SILLY. THEY'LL BE MUCH MORE INTERESTED IN YOU WHEN YOU TELL THEM ABOUT EDITING FAMOUS AUTHORS. EVERYTHING I DO IS EITHER DULL OR CLASSIFIED. OR BOTH.
MR. CURRY! MY. YOU CLEAN UP WELL.
I, UH, I RENTED THE TUX. IT WAS THE ONLY ONE THEY HAD LEFT.
IT'S LOVELY. IF ANYONE ASKS, BY HE WAY, YOU'RE A MAGAZINE DITOR. "CUTE FRIEND OF THE PARTY ORGANIZER" JUST DIDN'T CUT IT.
WHAT MAGAZINE?
FOREIGN POLICY MONTHLY. JUST PRETEND YOU KNOW EVERYTHING ABOUT FOREIGN POLICY.
BUT I DON'T.
SO FAKE IT. IT ALWAYS WORKS FOR ME.
ER. "CUTE FRIEND OF THE PARTY ORGANIZER," SERSI?
NOT NOW, CUTE BOY. I'M WORKING.

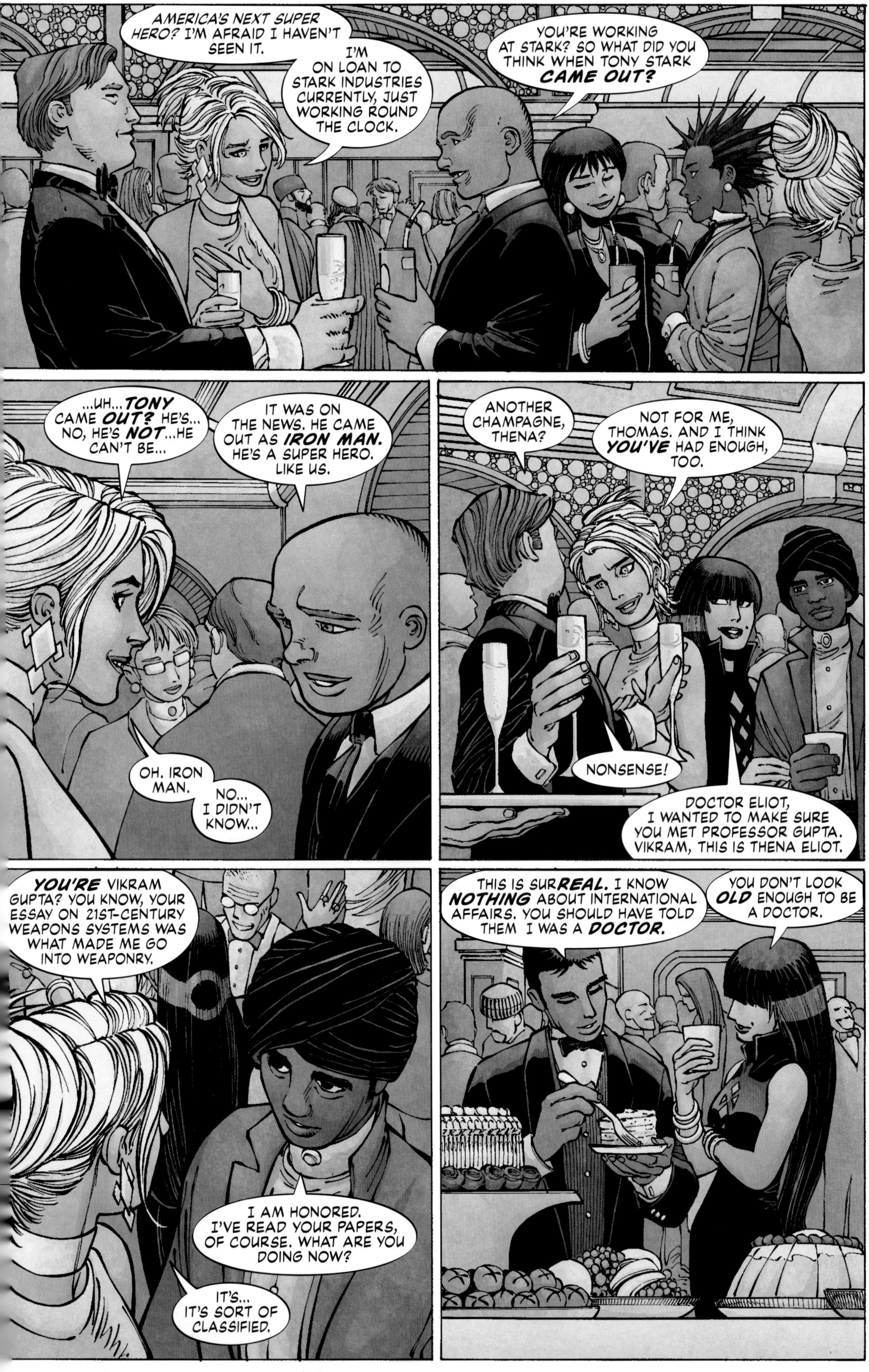
AMERICA'S NEXT SUPER HERO? I'M AFRAID I HAVEN'T SEEN IT.
I'M ON LOAN TO STARK INDUSTRIES CURRENTLY, JUST WORKING ROUND THE CLOCK.
YOU'RE WORKING AT STARK? SO WHAT DID YOU THINK WHEN TONY STARK **CAME OUT?**
...UH...**TONY** CAME **OUT?** HE'S... NO, HE'S **NOT**...HE CAN'T BE...
IT WAS ON THE NEWS. HE CAME OUT AS **IRON MAN.** HE'S A SUPER HERO. LIKE US.
OH. IRON MAN.
NO... I DIDN'T KNOW...
ANOTHER CHAMPAGNE, THENA?
NOT FOR ME, THOMAS. AND I THINK **YOU'VE** HAD ENOUGH, TOO.
NONSENSE!
DOCTOR ELIOT, I WANTED TO MAKE SURE YOU MET PROFESSOR GUPTA. VIKRAM, THIS IS THENA ELIOT.
YOU'RE VIKRAM GUPTA? YOU KNOW, YOUR ESSAY ON 21ST-CENTURY WEAPONS SYSTEMS WAS WHAT MADE ME GO INTO WEAPONRY.
I AM HONORED. I'VE READ YOUR PAPERS, OF COURSE. WHAT ARE YOU DOING NOW?
IT'S... IT'S SORT OF CLASSIFIED.
THIS IS SUR**REAL.** I KNOW **NOTHING** ABOUT INTERNATIONAL AFFAIRS. YOU SHOULD HAVE TOLD THEM I WAS A **DOCTOR.**
YOU DON'T LOOK **OLD** ENOUGH TO BE A DOCTOR.

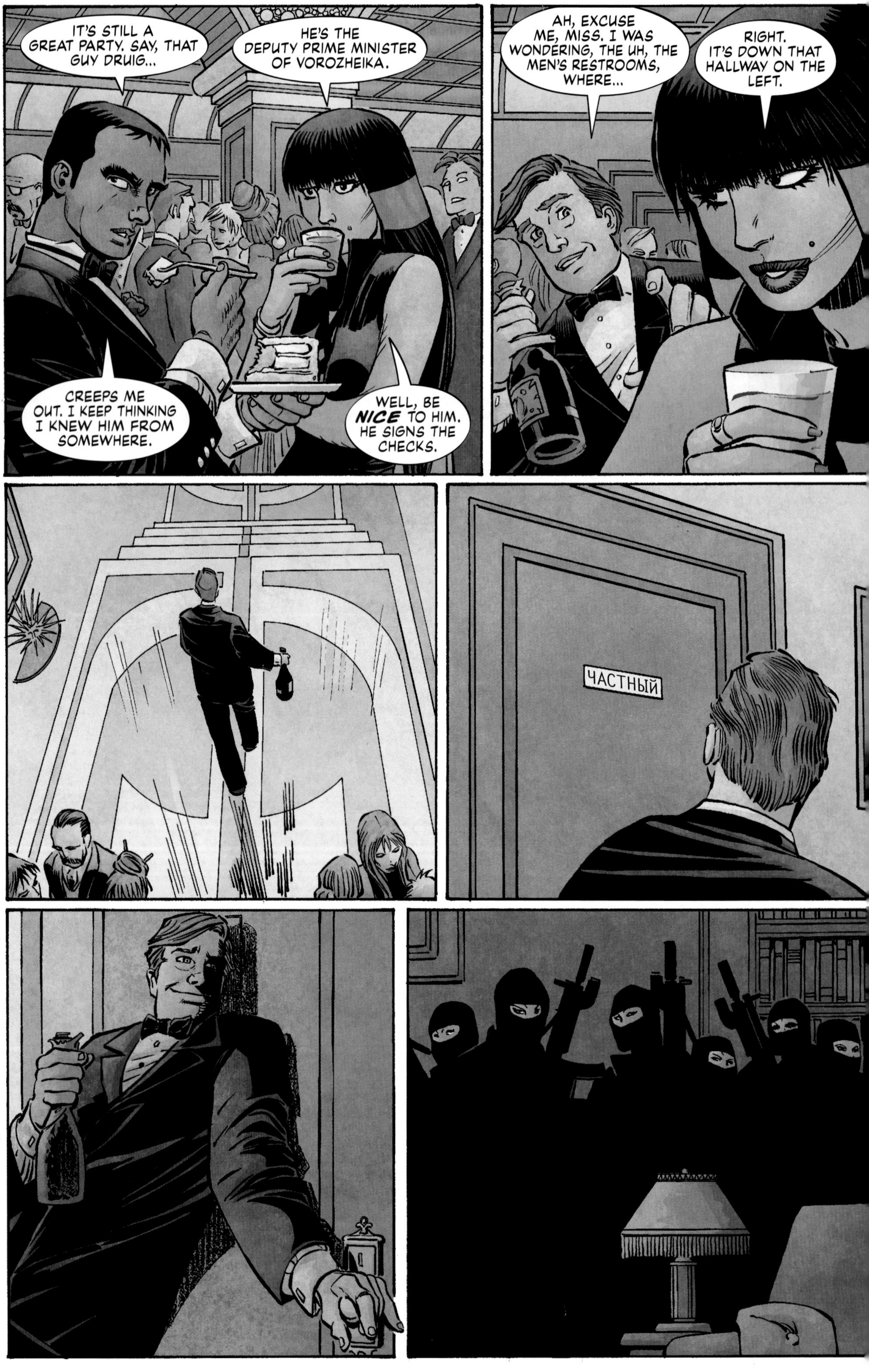
IT'S STILL A GREAT PARTY. SAY, THAT GUY DRUIG...
HE'S THE DEPUTY PRIME MINISTER OF VOROZHEIKA.
CREEPS ME OUT. I KEEP THINKING I KNEW HIM FROM SOMEWHERE.
WELL, BE NICE TO HIM. HE SIGNS THE CHECKS.
AH, EXCUSE ME, MISS. I WAS WONDERING, THE UH, THE MEN'S RESTROOMS, WHERE...
RIGHT. IT'S DOWN THAT HALLWAY ON THE LEFT.
ЧАСТНЫЙ

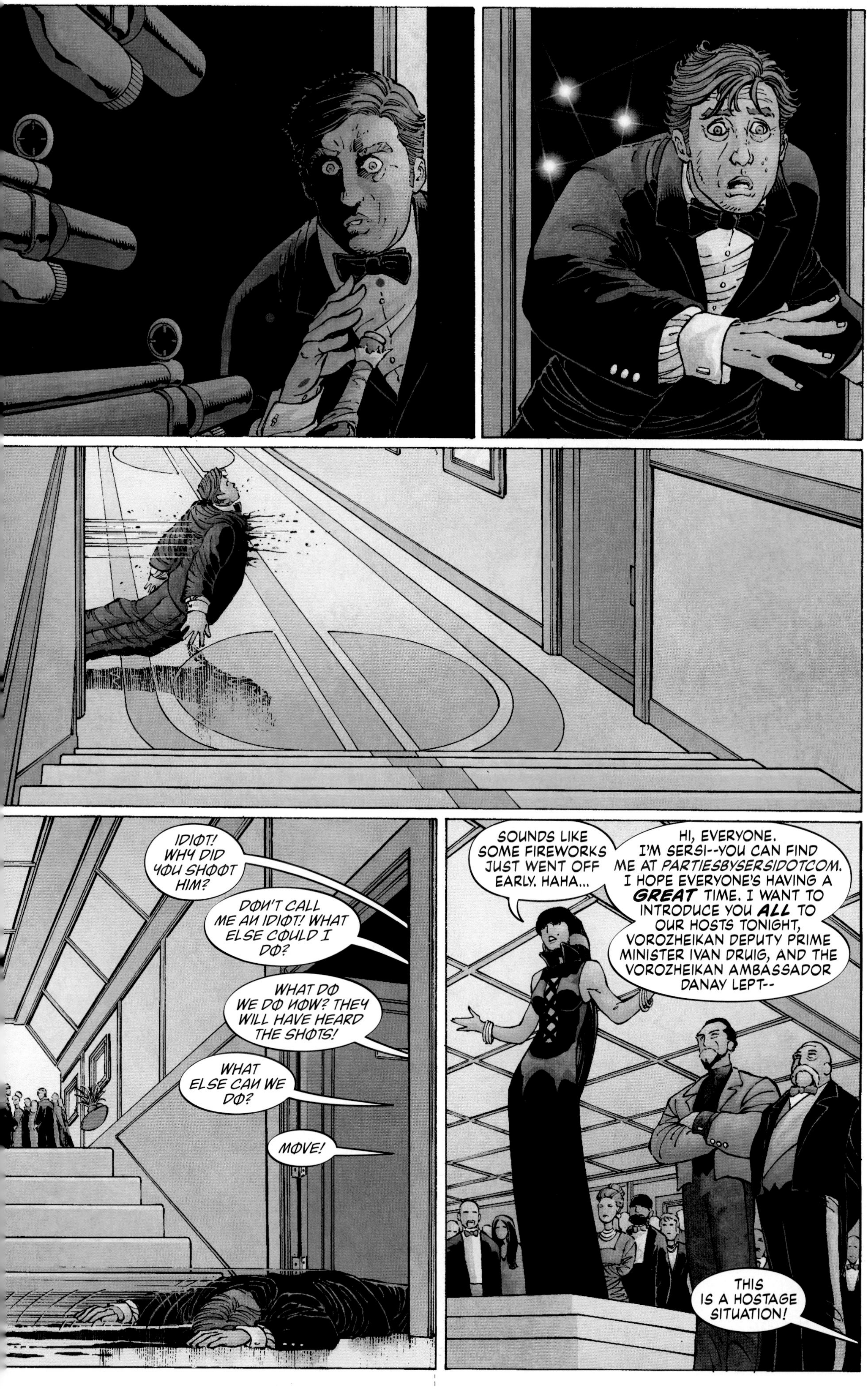
IDIOT! WHY DID YOU SHOOT HIM?
DON'T CALL ME AN IDIOT! WHAT ELSE COULD I DO?
WHAT DO WE DO NOW? THEY WILL HAVE HEARD THE SHOTS!
WHAT ELSE CAN WE DO?
MOVE!
SOUNDS LIKE SOME FIREWORKS JUST WENT OFF EARLY. HAHA...
HI, EVERYONE. I'M SERSI--YOU CAN FIND ME AT PARTIESBYSERSIDOTCOM. I HOPE EVERYONE'S HAVING A GREAT TIME. I WANT TO INTRODUCE YOU ALL TO OUR HOSTS TONIGHT, VOROZHEIKAN DEPUTY PRIME MINISTER IVAN DRUIG, AND THE VOROZHEIKAN AMBASSADOR DANAY LEPT--
THIS IS A HOSTAGE SITUATION!

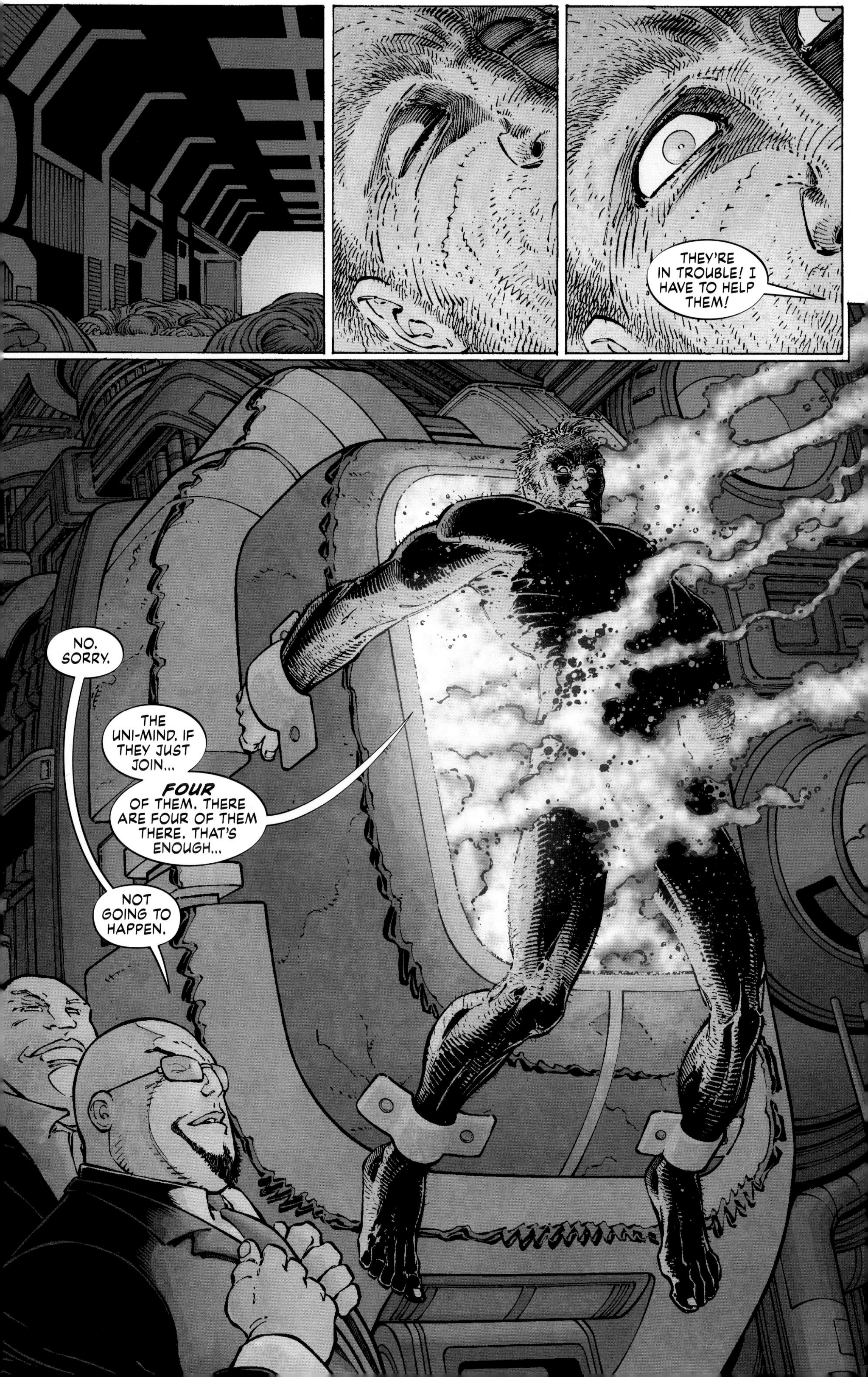
THEY'RE IN TROUBLE! I HAVE TO HELP THEM!
NO. SORRY.
THE UNI-MIND. IF THEY JUST JOIN...
FOUR OF THEM. THERE ARE FOUR OF THEM THERE. THAT'S ENOUGH...
NOT GOING TO HAPPEN.

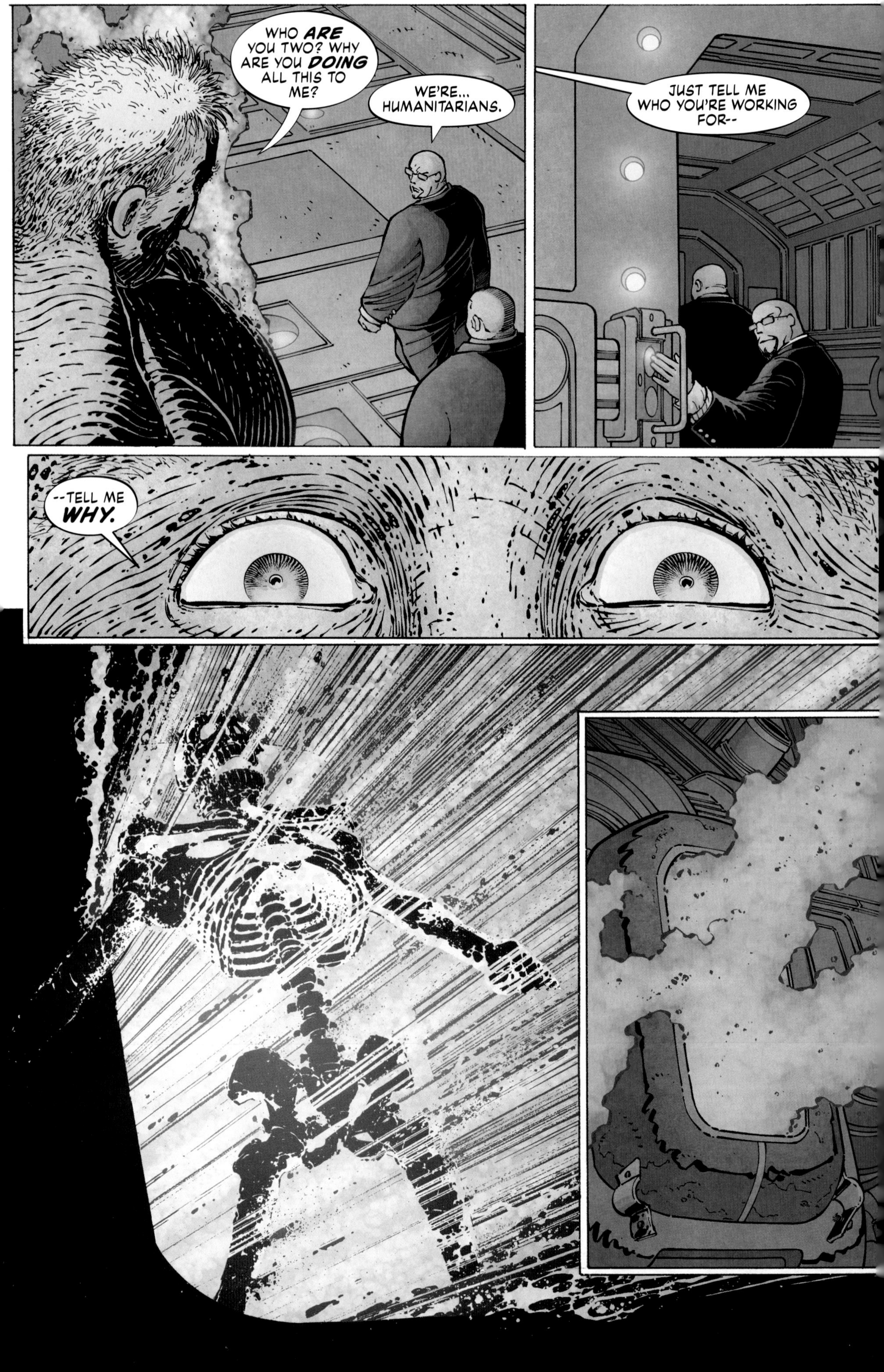
WHO ARE YOU TWO? WHY ARE YOU DOING ALL THIS TO ME?
WE'RE... HUMANITARIANS.
JUST TELL ME WHO YOU'RE WORKING FOR--
--TELL ME WHY.

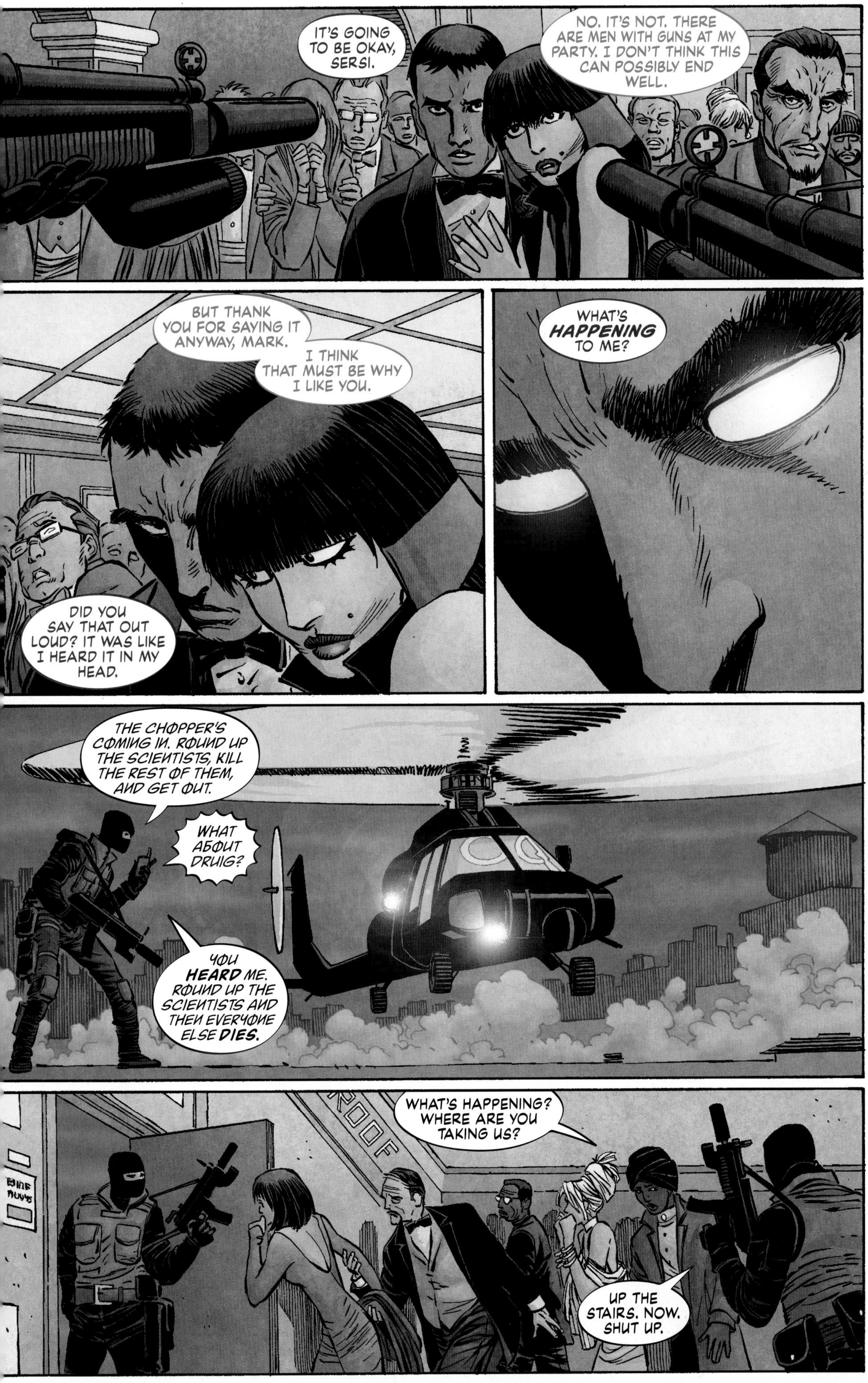
IT'S GOING TO BE OKAY, SERSI.
NO. IT'S NOT. THERE ARE MEN WITH GUNS AT MY PARTY. I DON'T THINK THIS CAN POSSIBLY END WELL.
BUT THANK YOU FOR SAYING IT ANYWAY, MARK.
I THINK THAT MUST BE WHY I LIKE YOU.
DID YOU SAY THAT OUT LOUD? IT WAS LIKE I HEARD IT IN MY HEAD.
WHAT'S HAPPENING TO ME?
THE CHOPPER'S COMING IN. ROUND UP THE SCIENTISTS, KILL THE REST OF THEM, AND GET OUT.
WHAT ABOUT DRUIG?
YOU HEARD ME. ROUND UP THE SCIENTISTS AND THEN EVERYONE ELSE DIES.
ROOF
WHAT'S HAPPENING? WHERE ARE YOU TAKING US?
UP THE STAIRS. NOW. SHUT UP.

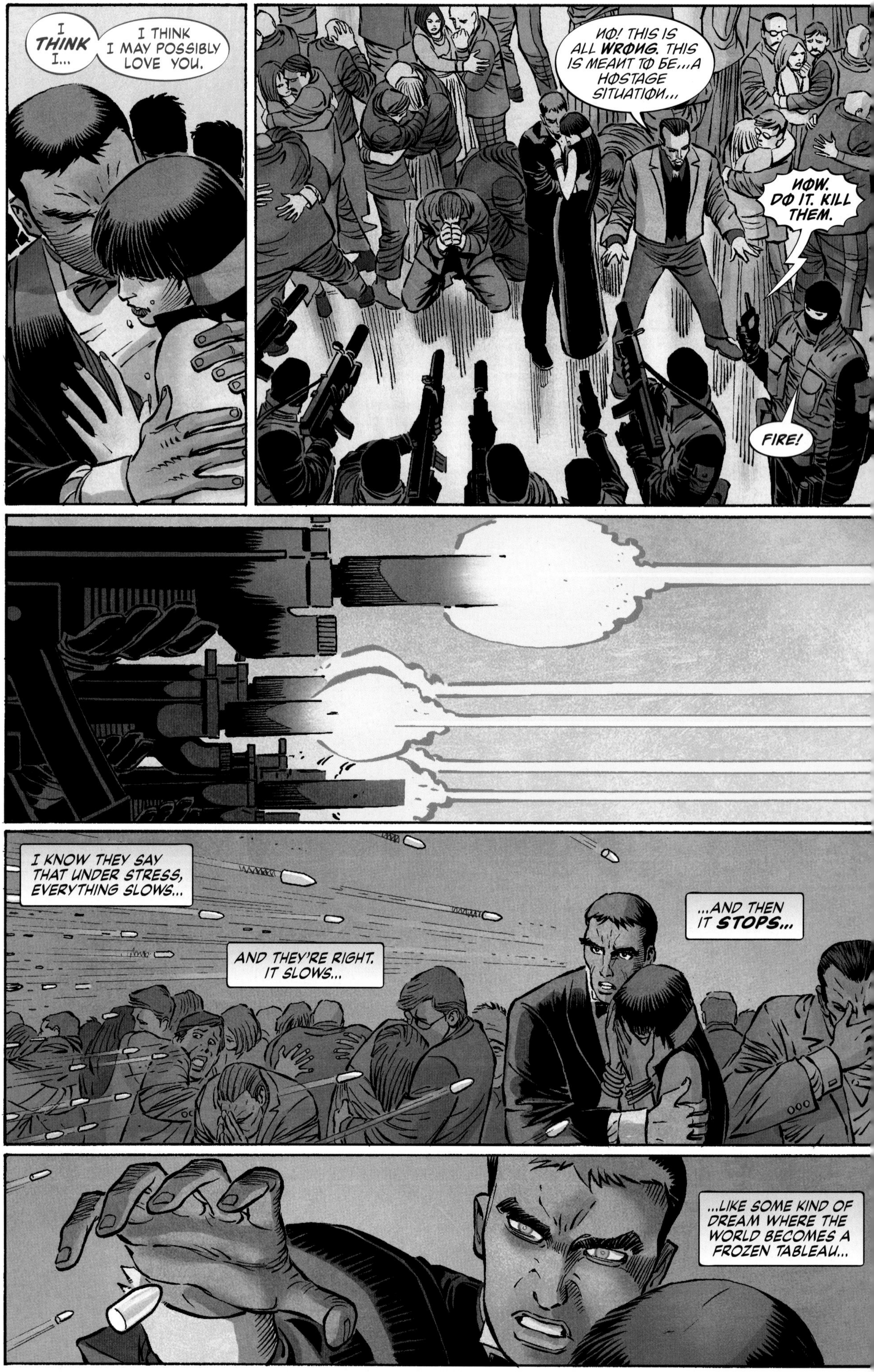
I THINK I...
I THINK I MAY POSSIBLY LOVE YOU.
NO! THIS IS ALL WRONG. THIS IS MEANT TO BE...A HOSTAGE SITUATION...
NOW. DO IT. KILL THEM.
FIRE!
I KNOW THEY SAY THAT UNDER STRESS, EVERYTHING SLOWS...
AND THEY'RE RIGHT. IT SLOWS...
...AND THEN IT STOPS...
...LIKE SOME KIND OF DREAM WHERE THE WORLD BECOMES A FROZEN TABLEAU...

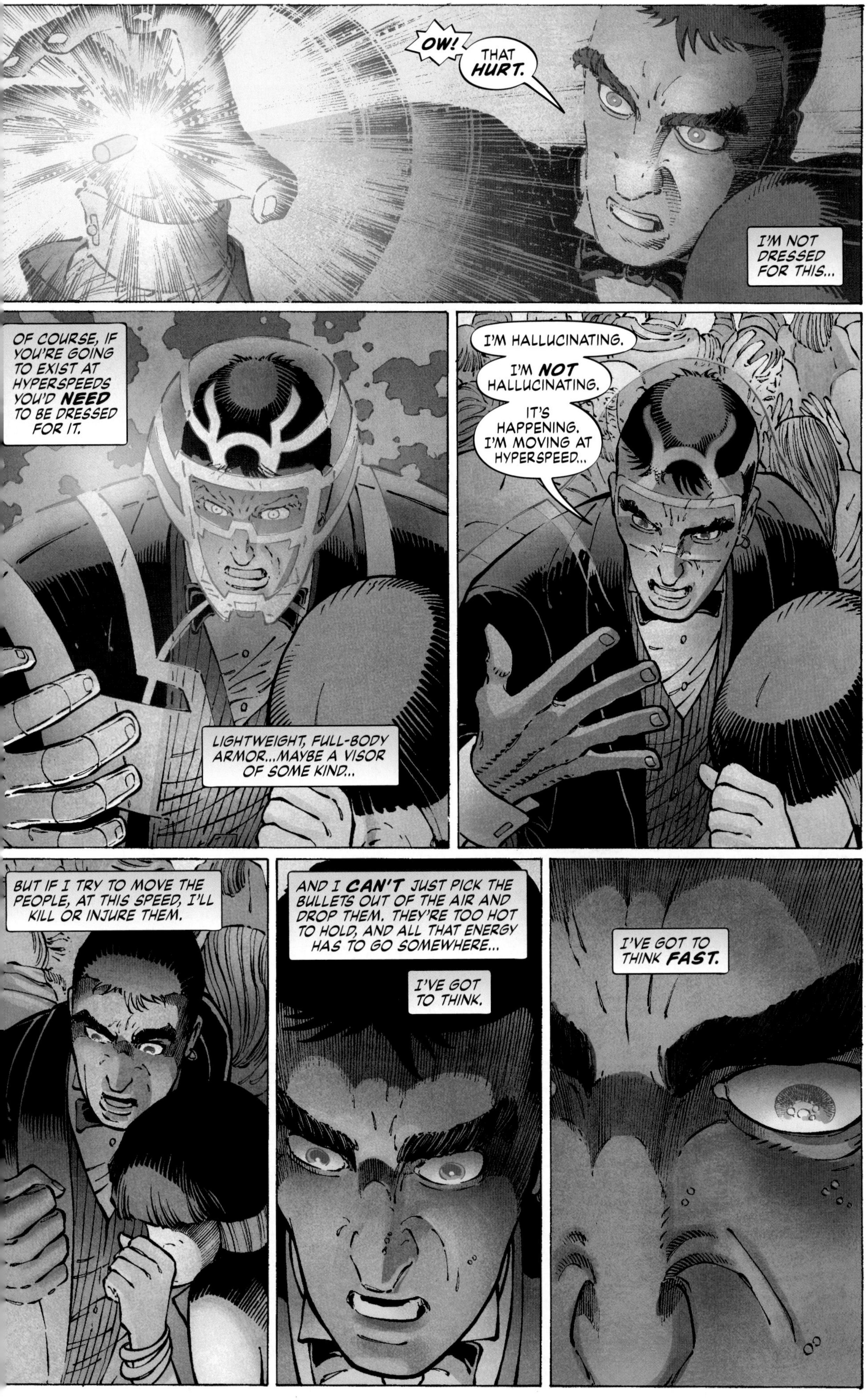
OW!
THAT HURT.
I'M NOT DRESSED FOR THIS...
OF COURSE, IF YOU'RE GOING TO EXIST AT HYPERSPEEDS YOU'D NEED TO BE DRESSED FOR IT.
LIGHTWEIGHT, FULL-BODY ARMOR...MAYBE A VISOR OF SOME KIND...
I'M HALLUCINATING.
I'M NOT HALLUCINATING.
IT'S HAPPENING. I'M MOVING AT HYPERSPEED...
BUT IF I TRY TO MOVE THE PEOPLE, AT THIS SPEED, I'LL KILL OR INJURE THEM.
AND I CAN'T JUST PICK THE BULLETS OUT OF THE AIR AND DROP THEM. THEY'RE TOO HOT TO HOLD, AND ALL THAT ENERGY HAS TO GO SOMEWHERE...
I'VE GOT TO THINK.
I'VE GOT TO THINK FAST.

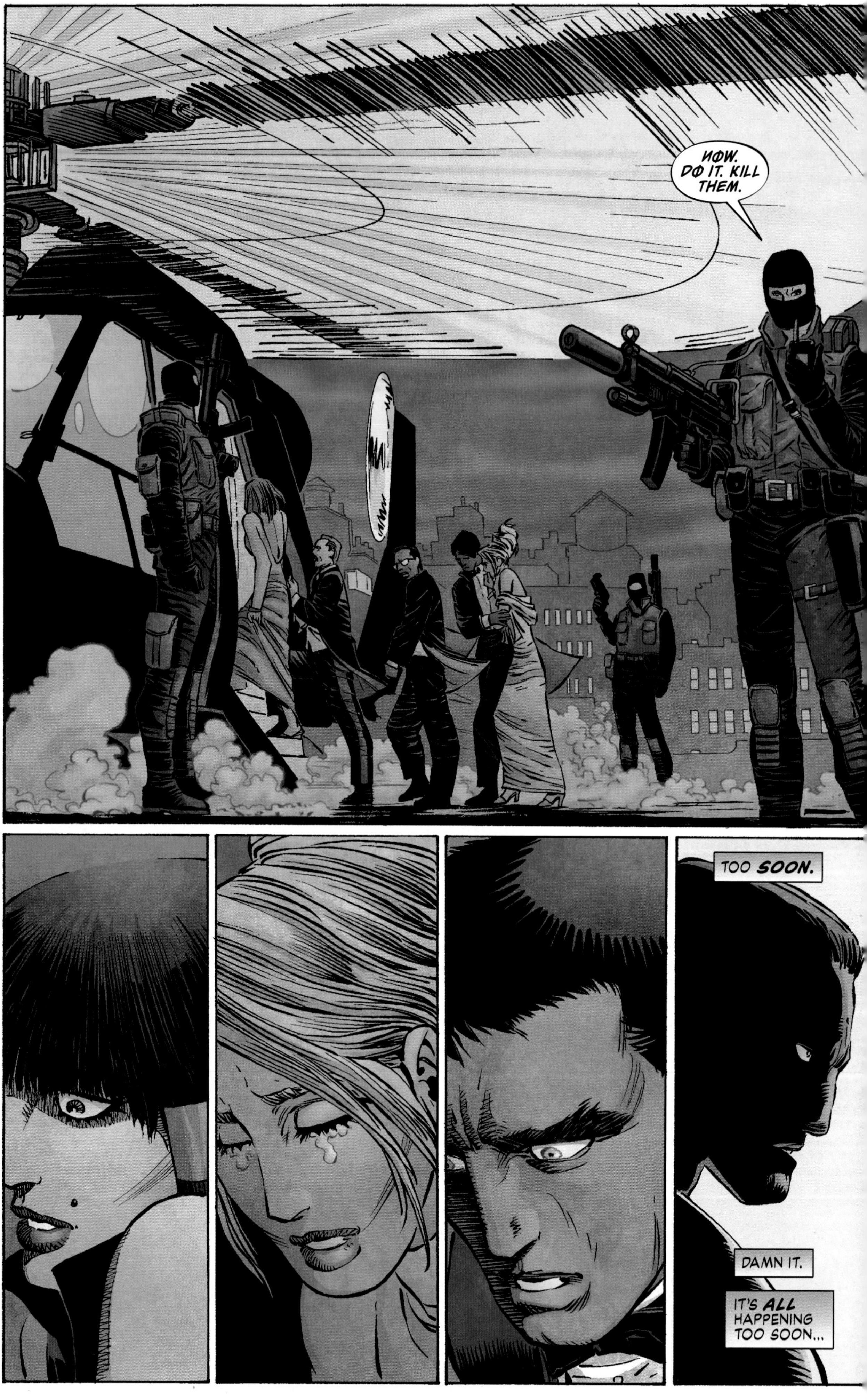
NOW. DO IT. KILL THEM.
TOO SOON.
DAMN IT.
IT'S ALL HAPPENING TOO SOON...

CHAPTER THREE: HOSTAGE SITUATION

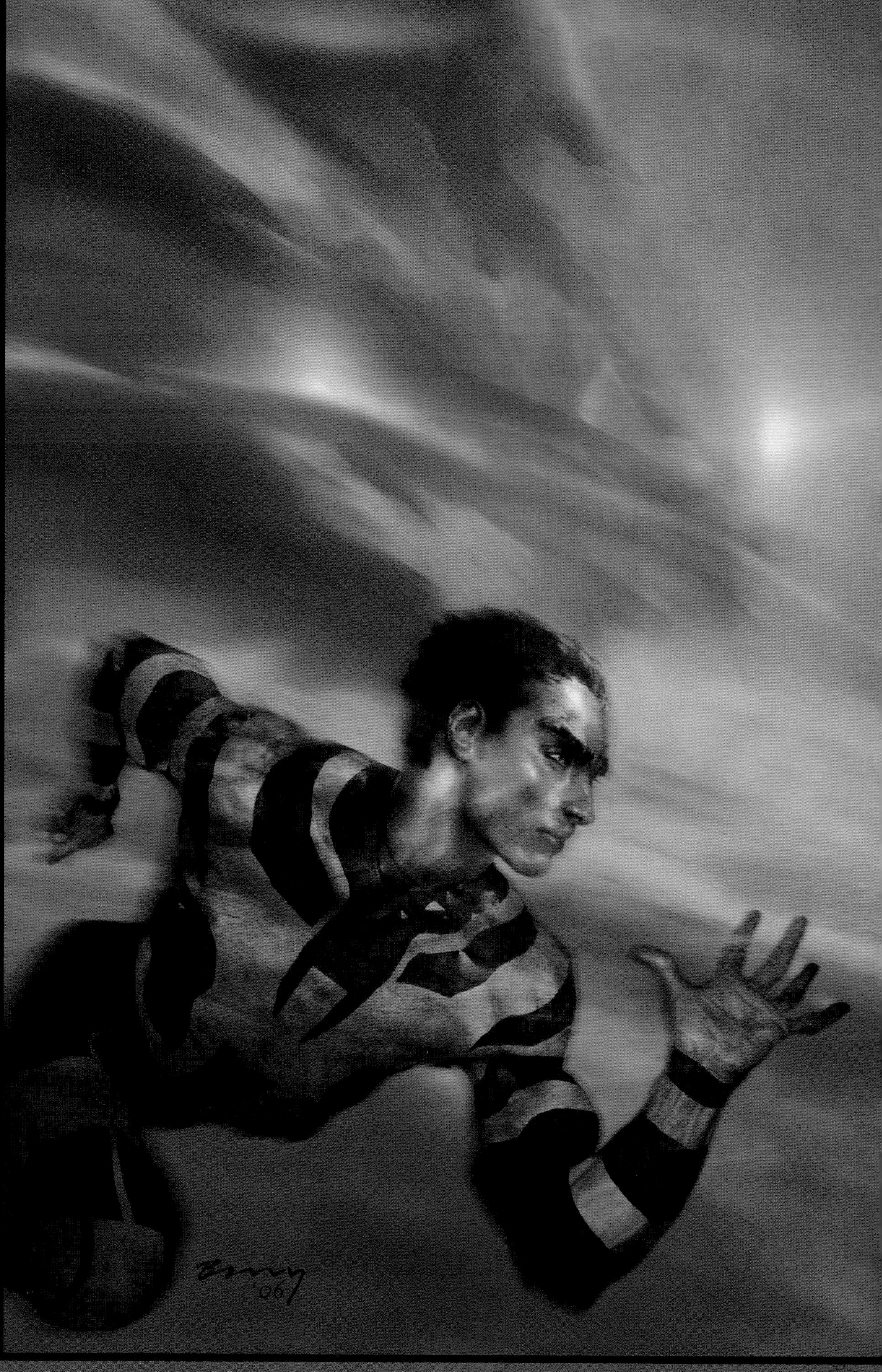

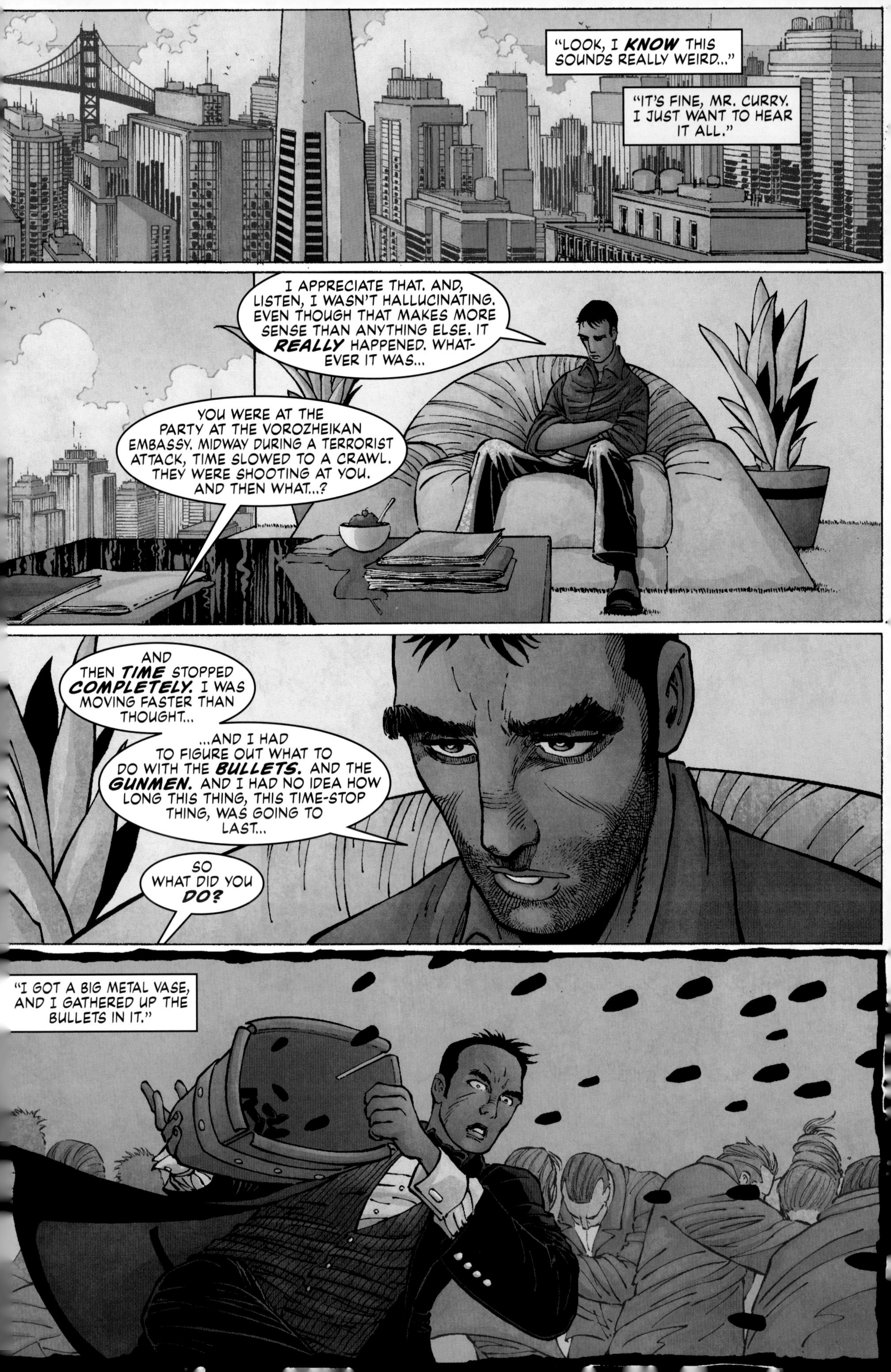
"LOOK, I KNOW THIS SOUNDS REALLY WEIRD..."
"IT'S FINE, MR. CURRY. I JUST WANT TO HEAR IT ALL."
I APPRECIATE THAT. AND, LISTEN, I WASN'T HALLUCINATING. EVEN THOUGH THAT MAKES MORE SENSE THAN ANYTHING ELSE. IT REALLY HAPPENED. WHAT-EVER IT WAS...
YOU WERE AT THE PARTY AT THE VOROZHEIKAN EMBASSY. MIDWAY DURING A TERRORIST ATTACK, TIME SLOWED TO A CRAWL. THEY WERE SHOOTING AT YOU. AND THEN WHAT...?
AND THEN TIME STOPPED COMPLETELY. I WAS MOVING FASTER THAN THOUGHT...
...AND I HAD TO FIGURE OUT WHAT TO DO WITH THE BULLETS. AND THE GUNMEN. AND I HAD NO IDEA HOW LONG THIS THING, THIS TIME-STOP THING, WAS GOING TO LAST...
SO WHAT DID YOU DO?
"I GOT A BIG METAL VASE, AND I GATHERED UP THE BULLETS IN IT."

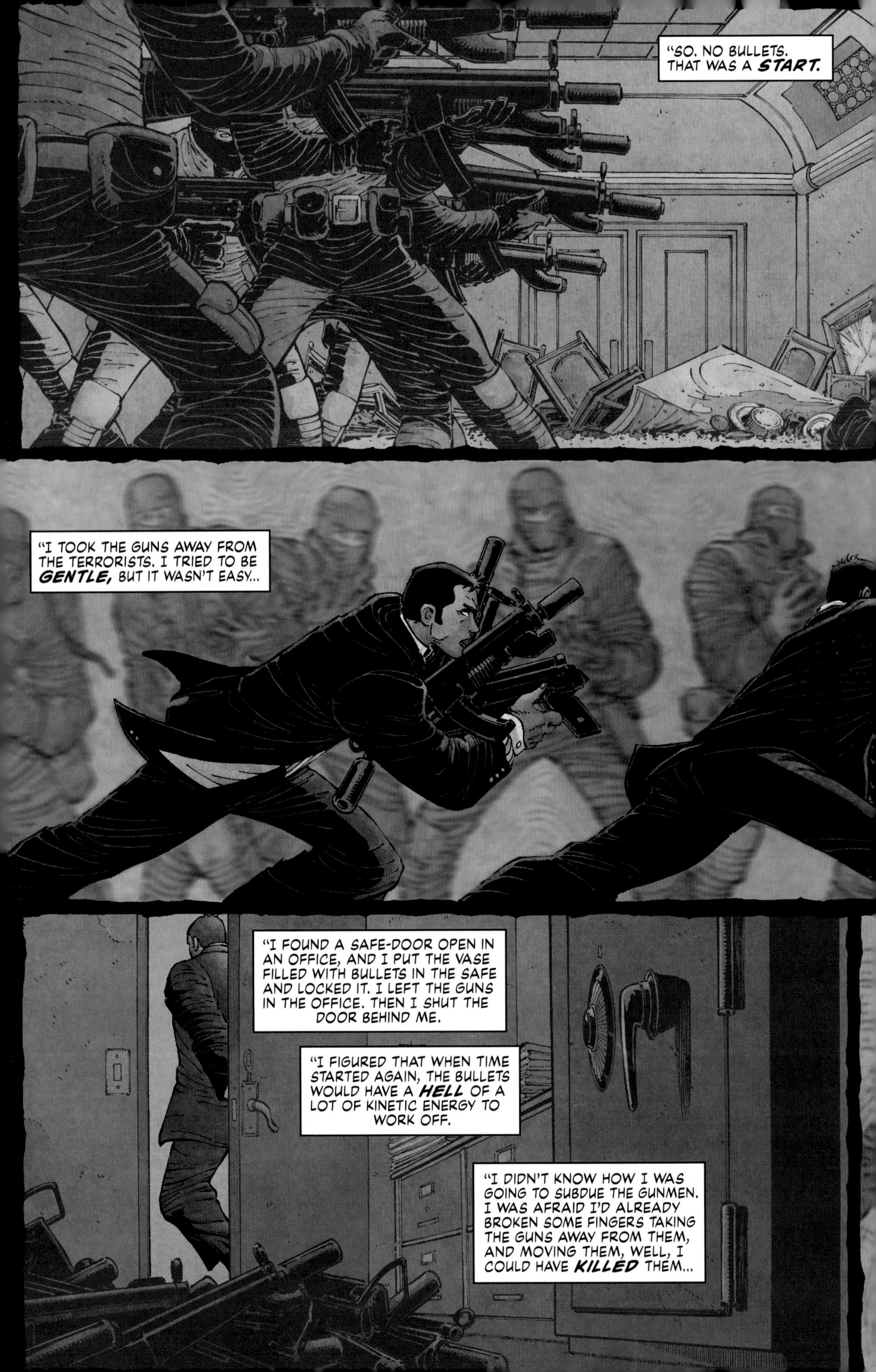
"SO. NO BULLETS. THAT WAS A START.
"I TOOK THE GUNS AWAY FROM THE TERRORISTS. I TRIED TO BE GENTLE, BUT IT WASN'T EASY...
"I FOUND A SAFE-DOOR OPEN IN AN OFFICE, AND I PUT THE VASE FILLED WITH BULLETS IN THE SAFE AND LOCKED IT. I LEFT THE GUNS IN THE OFFICE. THEN I SHUT THE DOOR BEHIND ME.
"I FIGURED THAT WHEN TIME STARTED AGAIN, THE BULLETS WOULD HAVE A HELL OF A LOT OF KINETIC ENERGY TO WORK OFF.
"I DIDN'T KNOW HOW I WAS GOING TO SUBDUE THE GUNMEN. I WAS AFRAID I'D ALREADY BROKEN SOME FINGERS TAKING THE GUNS AWAY FROM THEM, AND MOVING THEM, WELL, I COULD HAVE KILLED THEM...

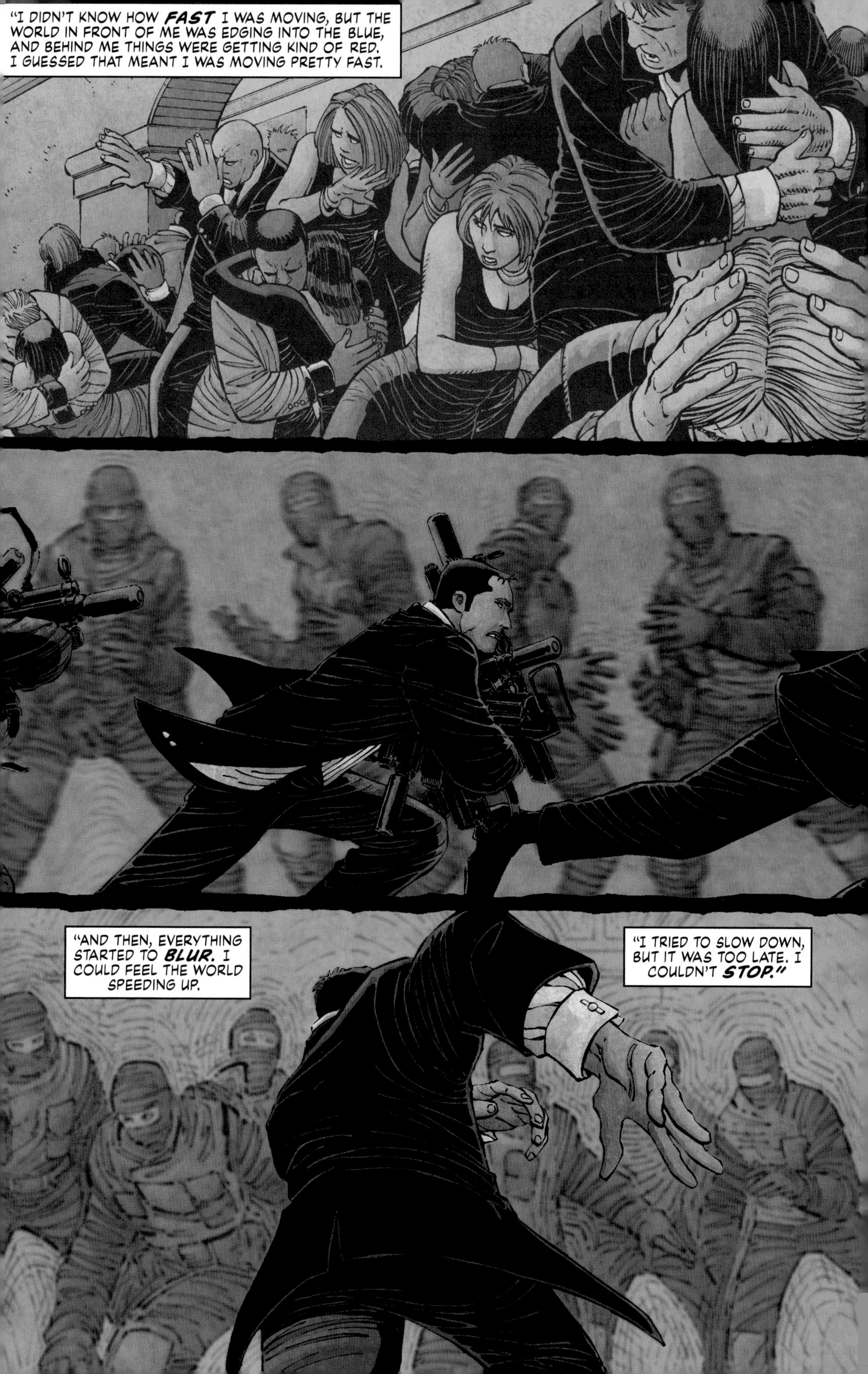
"I DIDN'T KNOW HOW **FAST** I WAS MOVING, BUT THE WORLD IN FRONT OF ME WAS EDGING INTO THE BLUE, AND BEHIND ME THINGS WERE GETTING KIND OF RED. I GUESSED THAT MEANT I WAS MOVING PRETTY FAST.
"AND THEN, EVERYTHING STARTED TO **BLUR.** I COULD FEEL THE WORLD SPEEDING UP.
"I TRIED TO SLOW DOWN, BUT IT WAS TOO LATE. I COULDN'T **STOP."**

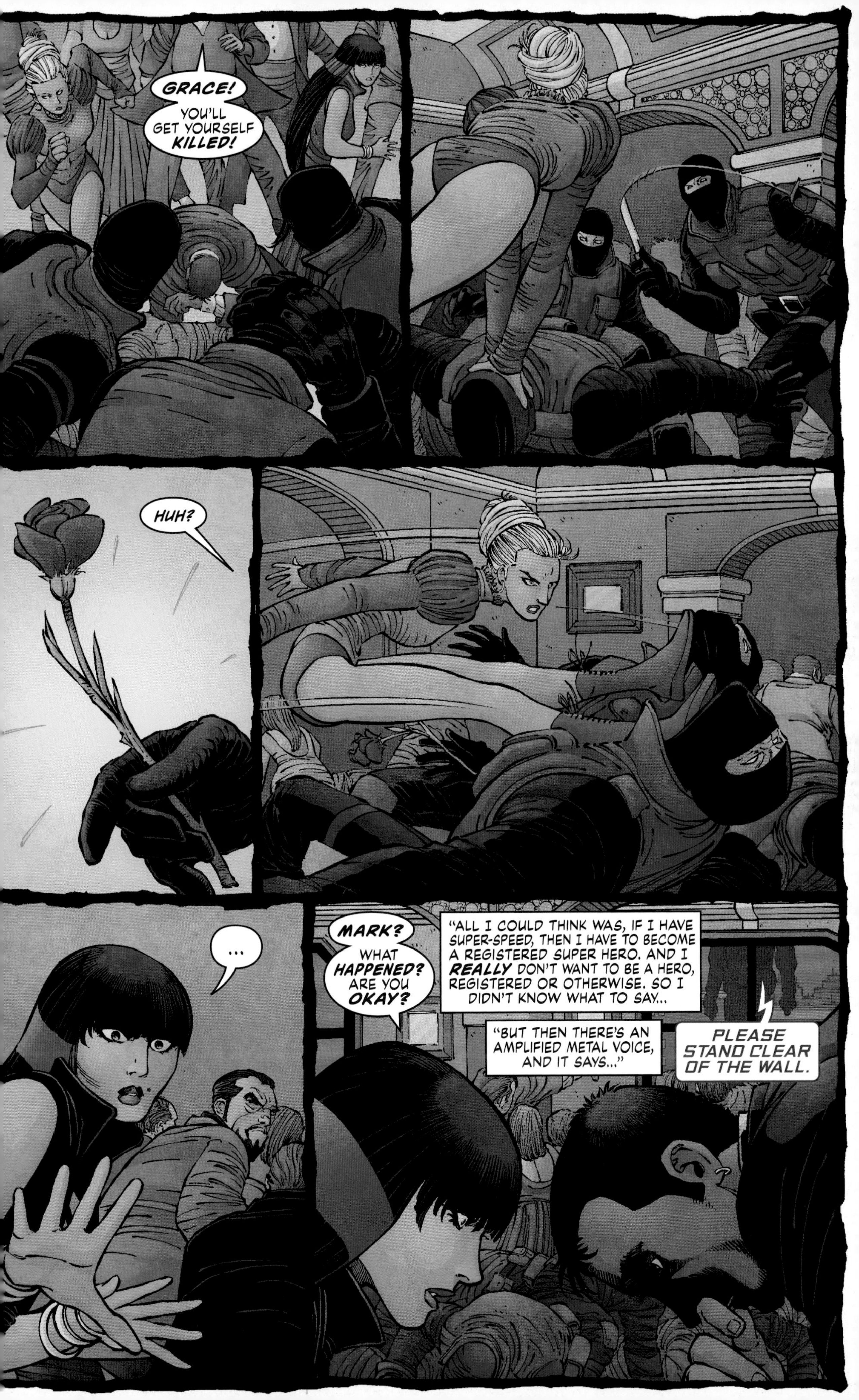
GRACE! YOU'LL GET YOURSELF KILLED!
HUH?
...
MARK? WHAT HAPPENED? ARE YOU OKAY?
"ALL I COULD THINK WAS, IF I HAVE SUPER-SPEED, THEN I HAVE TO BECOME A REGISTERED SUPER HERO. AND I REALLY DON'T WANT TO BE A HERO, REGISTERED OR OTHERWISE. SO I DIDN'T KNOW WHAT TO SAY...
"BUT THEN THERE'S AN AMPLIFIED METAL VOICE, AND IT SAYS..."
PLEASE STAND CLEAR OF THE WALL.

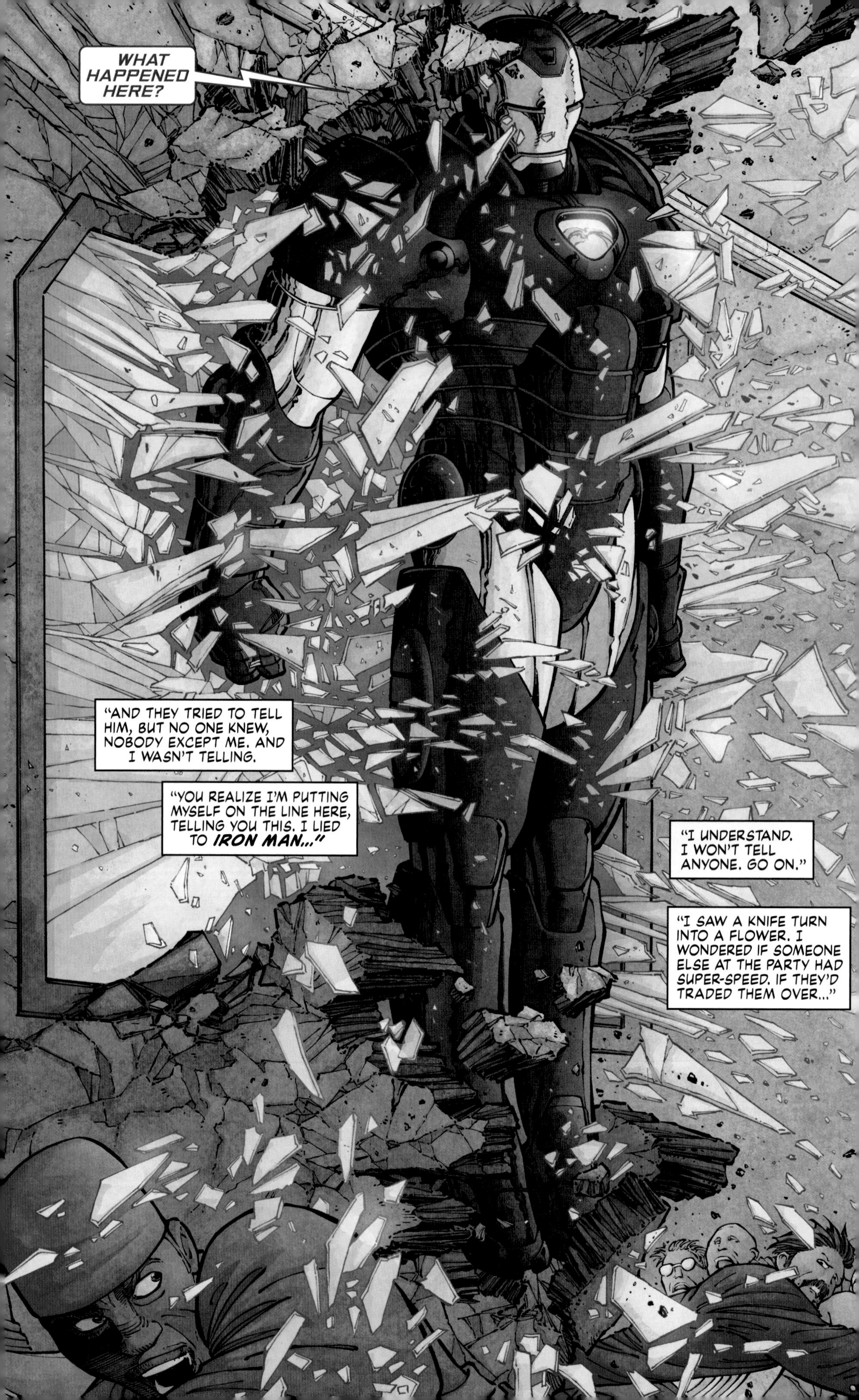
WHAT HAPPENED HERE?
"AND THEY TRIED TO TELL HIM, BUT NO ONE KNEW, NOBODY EXCEPT ME. AND I WASN'T TELLING.
"YOU REALIZE I'M PUTTING MYSELF ON THE LINE HERE, TELLING YOU THIS. I LIED TO IRON MAN..."
"I UNDERSTAND. I WON'T TELL ANYONE. GO ON."
"I SAW A KNIFE TURN INTO A FLOWER. I WONDERED IF SOMEONE ELSE AT THE PARTY HAD SUPER-SPEED. IF THEY'D TRADED THEM OVER..."

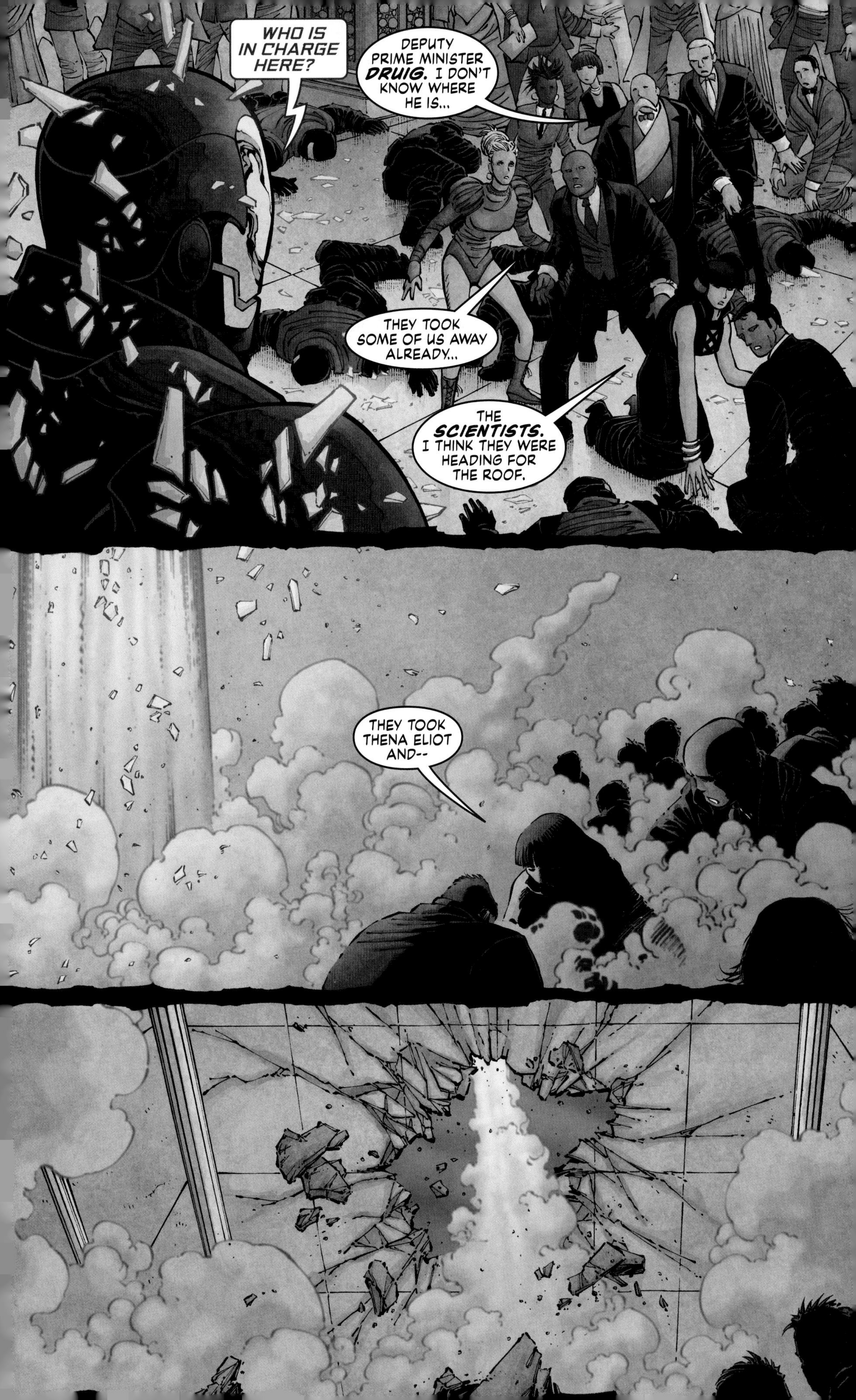
WHO IS IN CHARGE HERE?
DEPUTY PRIME MINISTER DRUIG. I DON'T KNOW WHERE HE IS...
THEY TOOK SOME OF US AWAY ALREADY...
THE SCIENTISTS. I THINK THEY WERE HEADING FOR THE ROOF.
THEY TOOK THENA ELIOT AND--

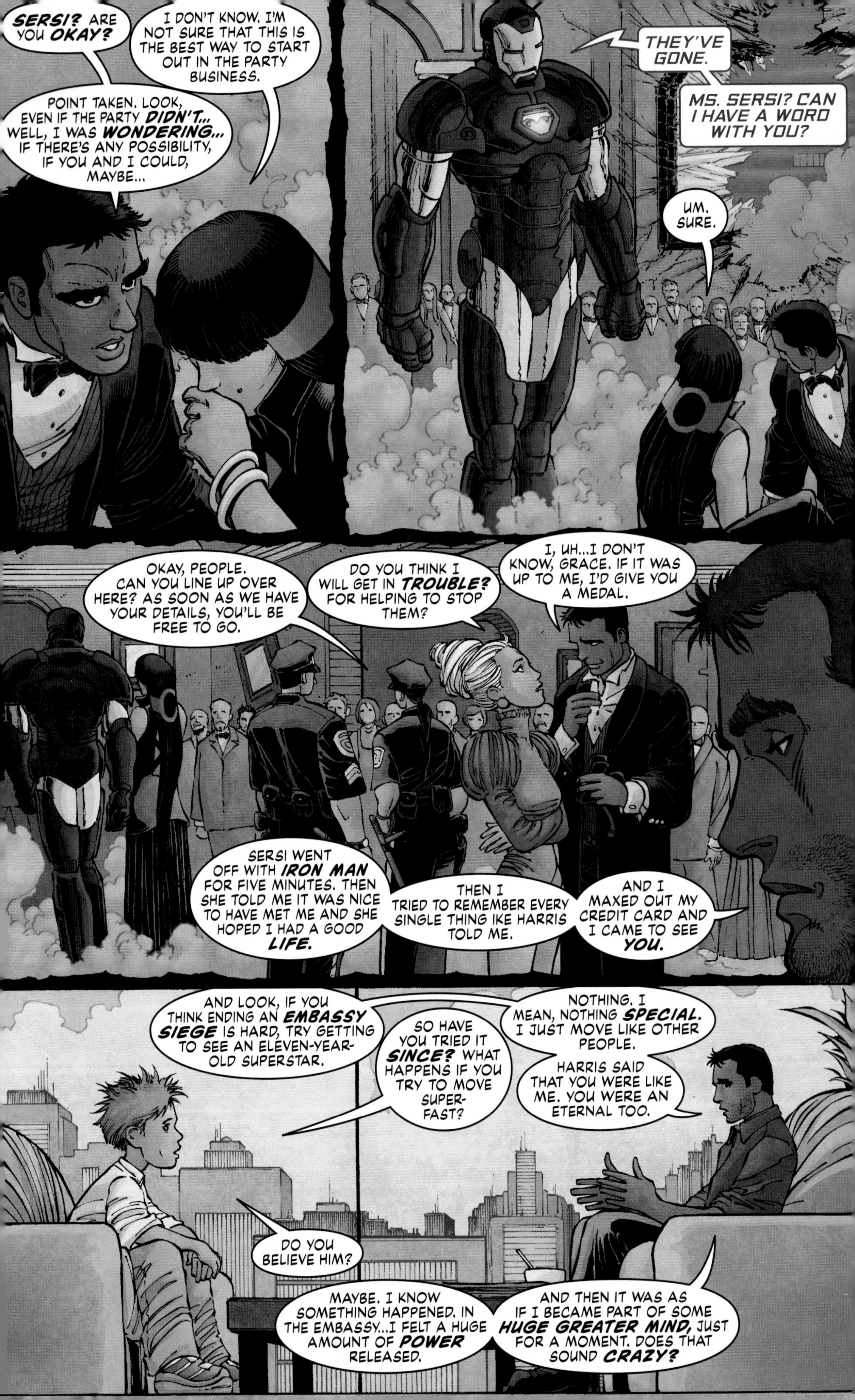
SERSI? ARE YOU OKAY?
I DON'T KNOW. I'M NOT SURE THAT THIS IS THE BEST WAY TO START OUT IN THE PARTY BUSINESS.
POINT TAKEN. LOOK, EVEN IF THE PARTY DIDN'T... WELL, I WAS WONDERING... IF THERE'S ANY POSSIBILITY, IF YOU AND I COULD, MAYBE...
THEY'VE GONE.
MS. SERSI? CAN I HAVE A WORD WITH YOU?
UM. SURE.
OKAY, PEOPLE. CAN YOU LINE UP OVER HERE? AS SOON AS WE HAVE YOUR DETAILS, YOU'LL BE FREE TO GO.
DO YOU THINK I WILL GET IN TROUBLE? FOR HELPING TO STOP THEM?
I, UH...I DON'T KNOW, GRACE. IF IT WAS UP TO ME, I'D GIVE YOU A MEDAL.
SERSI WENT OFF WITH IRON MAN FOR FIVE MINUTES. THEN SHE TOLD ME IT WAS NICE TO HAVE MET ME AND SHE HOPED I HAD A GOOD LIFE.
THEN I TRIED TO REMEMBER EVERY SINGLE THING IKE HARRIS TOLD ME.
AND I MAXED OUT MY CREDIT CARD AND I CAME TO SEE YOU.
AND LOOK, IF YOU THINK ENDING AN EMBASSY SIEGE IS HARD, TRY GETTING TO SEE AN ELEVEN-YEAR-OLD SUPERSTAR.
SO HAVE YOU TRIED IT SINCE? WHAT HAPPENS IF YOU TRY TO MOVE SUPER-FAST?
NOTHING. I MEAN, NOTHING SPECIAL. I JUST MOVE LIKE OTHER PEOPLE.
HARRIS SAID THAT YOU WERE LIKE ME. YOU WERE AN ETERNAL TOO.
DO YOU BELIEVE HIM?
MAYBE. I KNOW SOMETHING HAPPENED. IN THE EMBASSY...I FELT A HUGE AMOUNT OF POWER RELEASED.
AND THEN IT WAS AS IF I BECAME PART OF SOME HUGE GREATER MIND, JUST FOR A MOMENT. DOES THAT SOUND CRAZY?

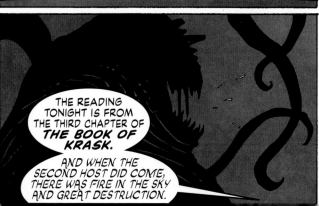

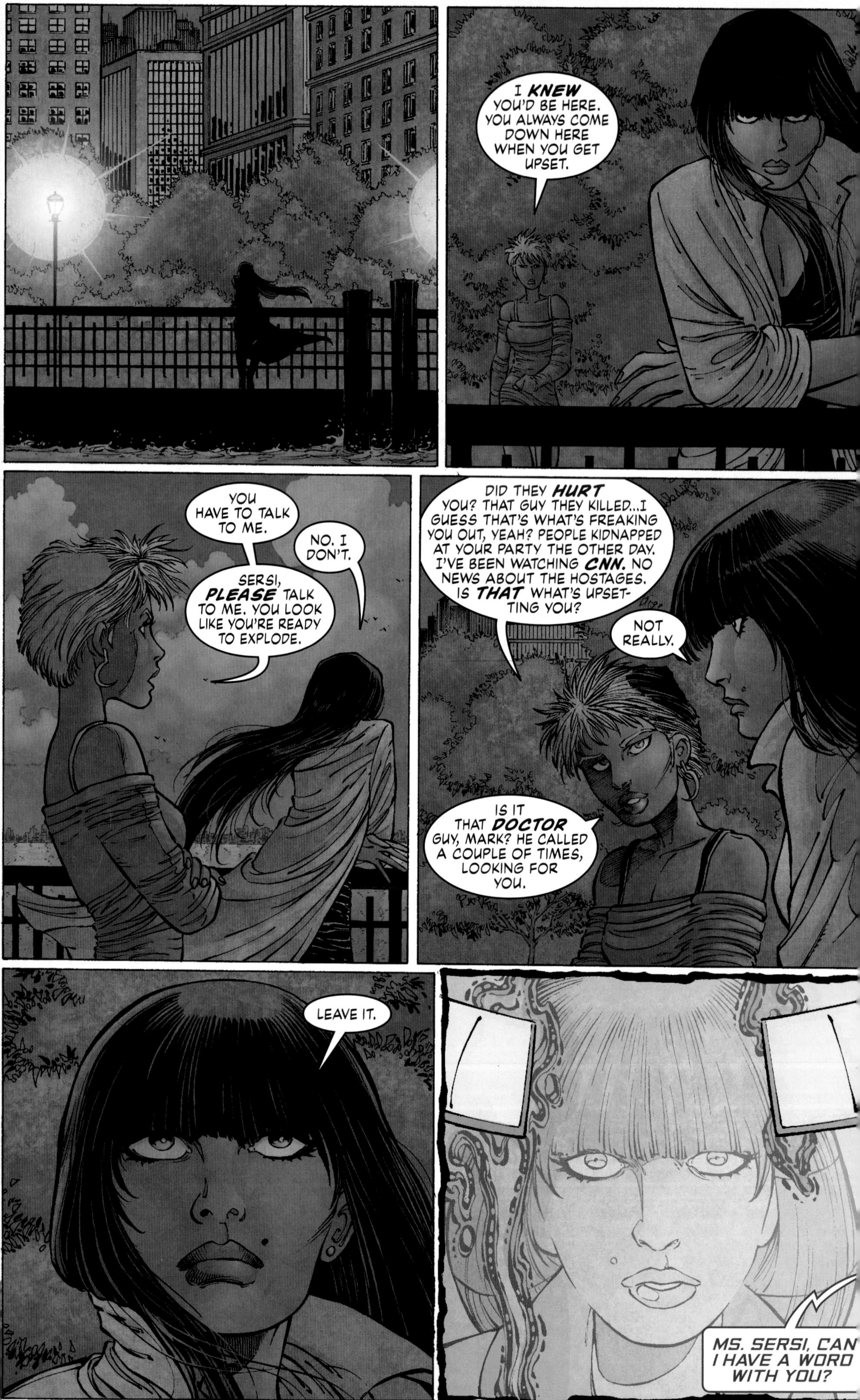
I KNEW YOU'D BE HERE. YOU ALWAYS COME DOWN HERE WHEN YOU GET UPSET.
YOU HAVE TO TALK TO ME.
NO. I DON'T.
SERSI, PLEASE TALK TO ME. YOU LOOK LIKE YOU'RE READY TO EXPLODE.
DID THEY HURT YOU? THAT GUY THEY KILLED...I GUESS THAT'S WHAT'S FREAKING YOU OUT, YEAH? PEOPLE KIDNAPPED AT YOUR PARTY THE OTHER DAY. I'VE BEEN WATCHING CNN. NO NEWS ABOUT THE HOSTAGES. IS THAT WHAT'S UPSETTING YOU?
NOT REALLY.
IS IT THAT DOCTOR GUY, MARK? HE CALLED A COUPLE OF TIMES, LOOKING FOR YOU.
LEAVE IT.
MS. SERSI, CAN I HAVE A WORD WITH YOU?

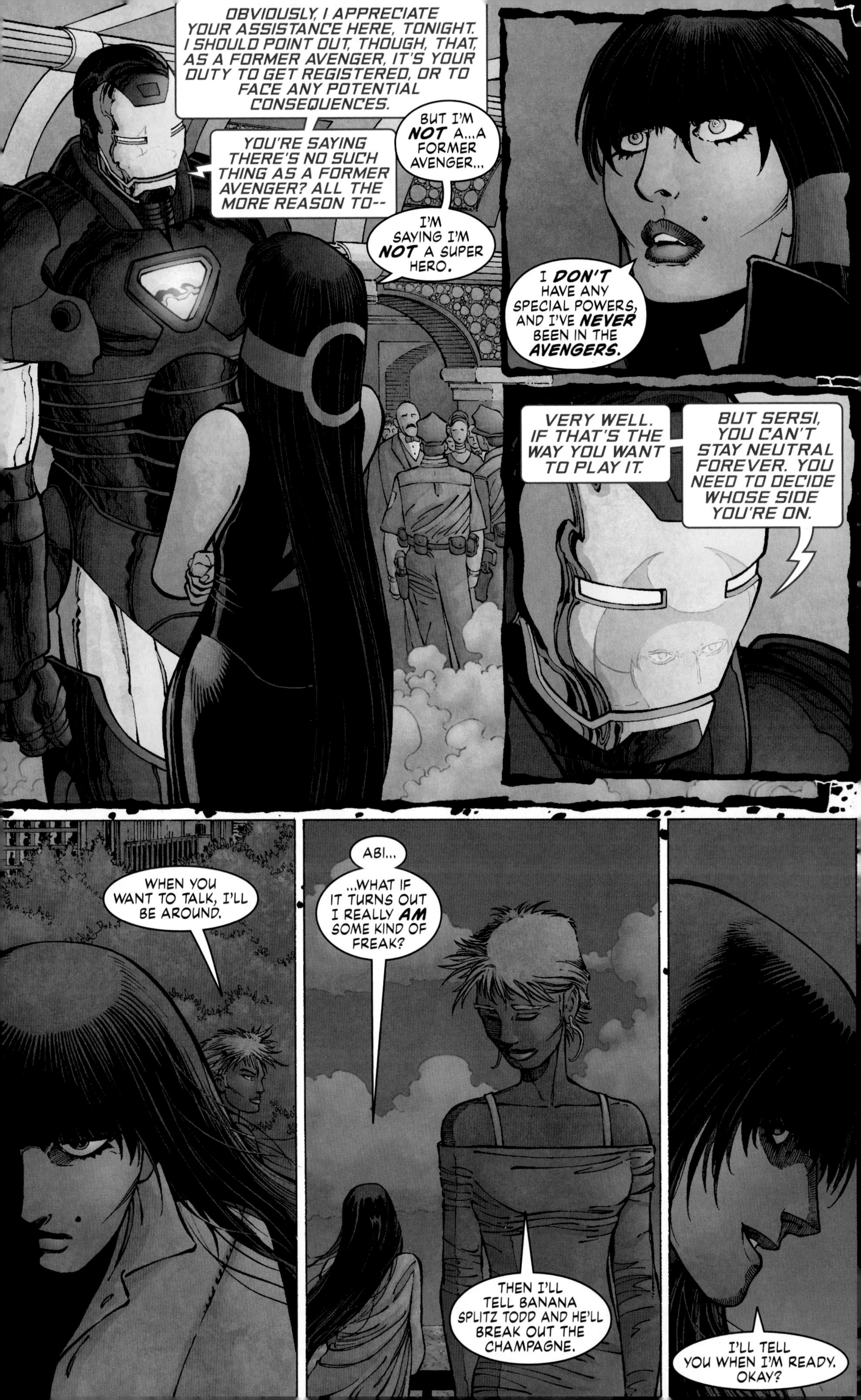
OBVIOUSLY, I APPRECIATE YOUR ASSISTANCE HERE, TONIGHT. I SHOULD POINT OUT, THOUGH, THAT, AS A FORMER AVENGER, IT'S YOUR DUTY TO GET REGISTERED, OR TO FACE ANY POTENTIAL CONSEQUENCES.
BUT I'M NOT A...A FORMER AVENGER...
YOU'RE SAYING THERE'S NO SUCH THING AS A FORMER AVENGER? ALL THE MORE REASON TO--
I'M SAYING I'M NOT A SUPER HERO.
I DON'T HAVE ANY SPECIAL POWERS, AND I'VE NEVER BEEN IN THE AVENGERS.
VERY WELL. IF THAT'S THE WAY YOU WANT TO PLAY IT.
BUT SERSI, YOU CAN'T STAY NEUTRAL FOREVER. YOU NEED TO DECIDE WHOSE SIDE YOU'RE ON.
WHEN YOU WANT TO TALK, I'LL BE AROUND.
ABI...
...WHAT IF IT TURNS OUT I REALLY AM SOME KIND OF FREAK?
THEN I'LL TELL BANANA SPLITZ TODD AND HE'LL BREAK OUT THE CHAMPAGNE.
I'LL TELL YOU WHEN I'M READY. OKAY?

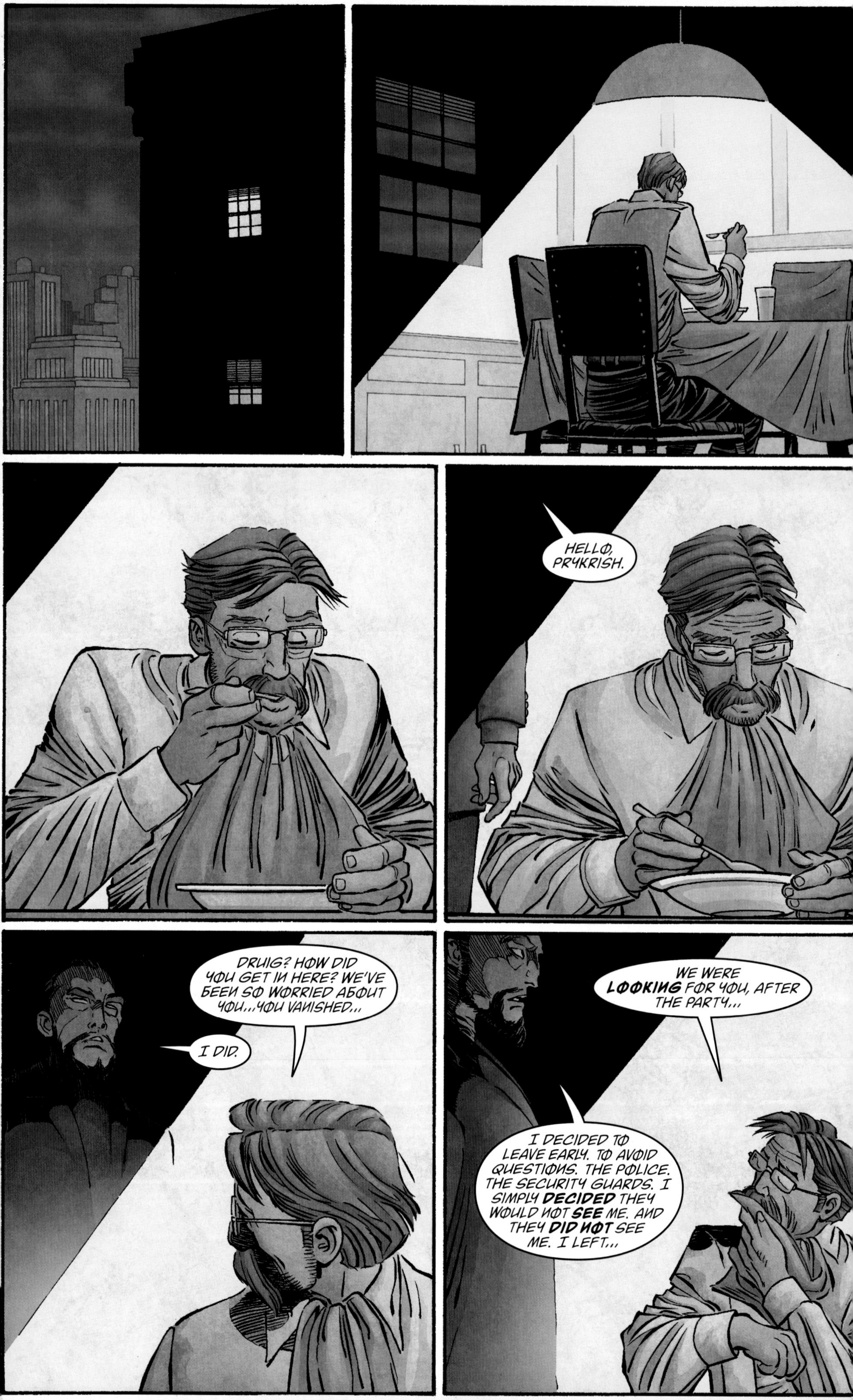
HELLO, PRYKRISH.
DRUIG? HOW DID YOU GET IN HERE? WE'VE BEEN SO WORRIED ABOUT YOU... YOU VANISHED...
I DID.
WE WERE LOOKING FOR YOU, AFTER THE PARTY...
I DECIDED TO LEAVE EARLY. TO AVOID QUESTIONS. THE POLICE. THE SECURITY GUARDS. I SIMPLY DECIDED THEY WOULD NOT SEE ME. AND THEY DID NOT SEE ME. I LEFT...

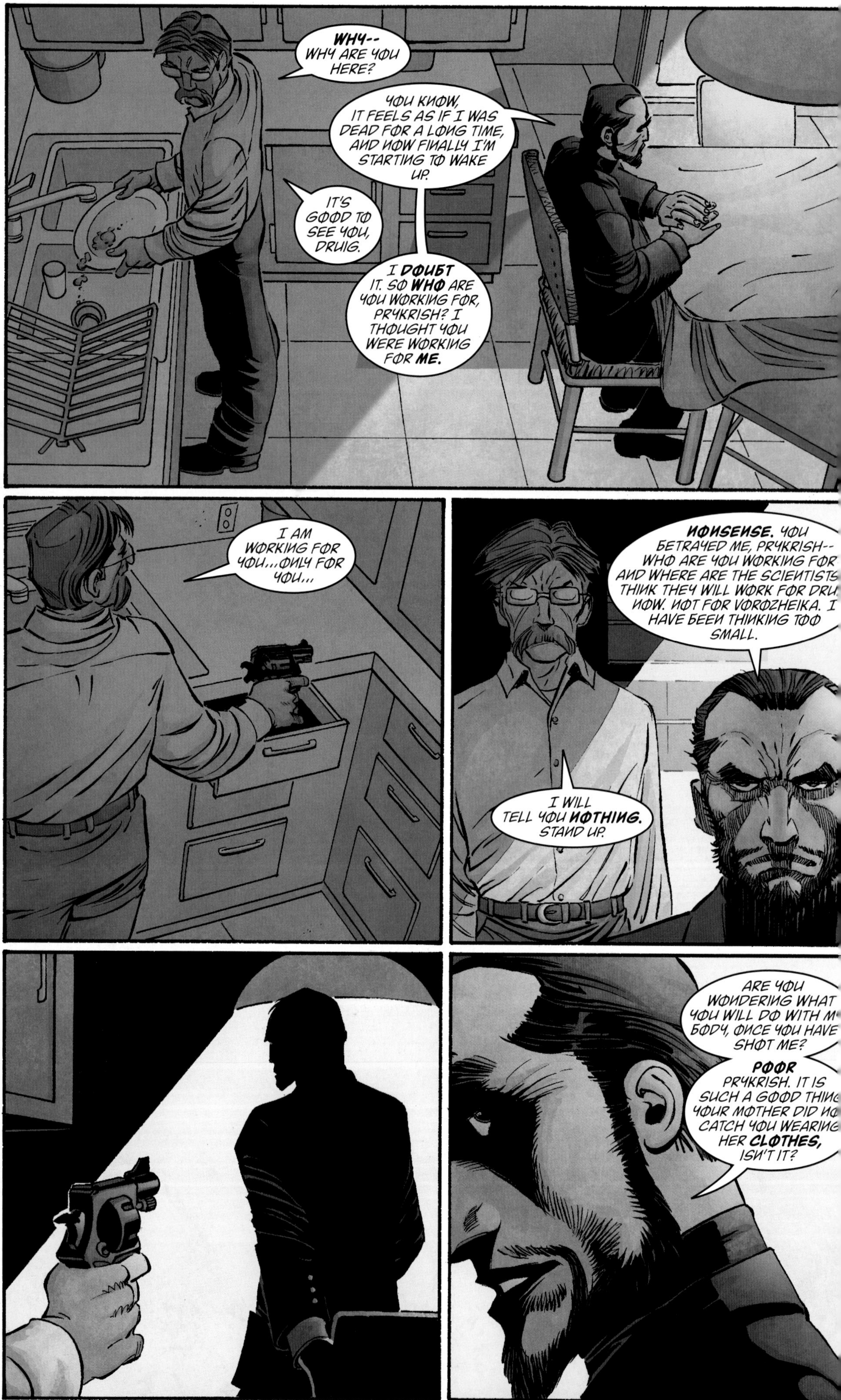
WHY-- WHY ARE YOU HERE?
YOU KNOW, IT FEELS AS IF I WAS DEAD FOR A LONG TIME, AND NOW FINALLY I'M STARTING TO WAKE UP.
IT'S GOOD TO SEE YOU, DRUIG.
I DOUBT IT. SO WHO ARE YOU WORKING FOR, PRYKRISH? I THOUGHT YOU WERE WORKING FOR ME.
I AM WORKING FOR YOU...ONLY FOR YOU...
NONSENSE. YOU BETRAYED ME, PRYKRISH-- WHO ARE YOU WORKING FOR AND WHERE ARE THE SCIENTISTS THINK THEY WILL WORK FOR DRU NOW. NOT FOR VOROZHEIKA. I HAVE BEEN THINKING TOO SMALL.
I WILL TELL YOU NOTHING. STAND UP.
ARE YOU WONDERING WHAT YOU WILL DO WITH M BODY, ONCE YOU HAVE SHOT ME?
POOR PRYKRISH. IT IS SUCH A GOOD THING YOUR MOTHER DID NO CATCH YOU WEARING HER CLOTHES, ISN'T IT?

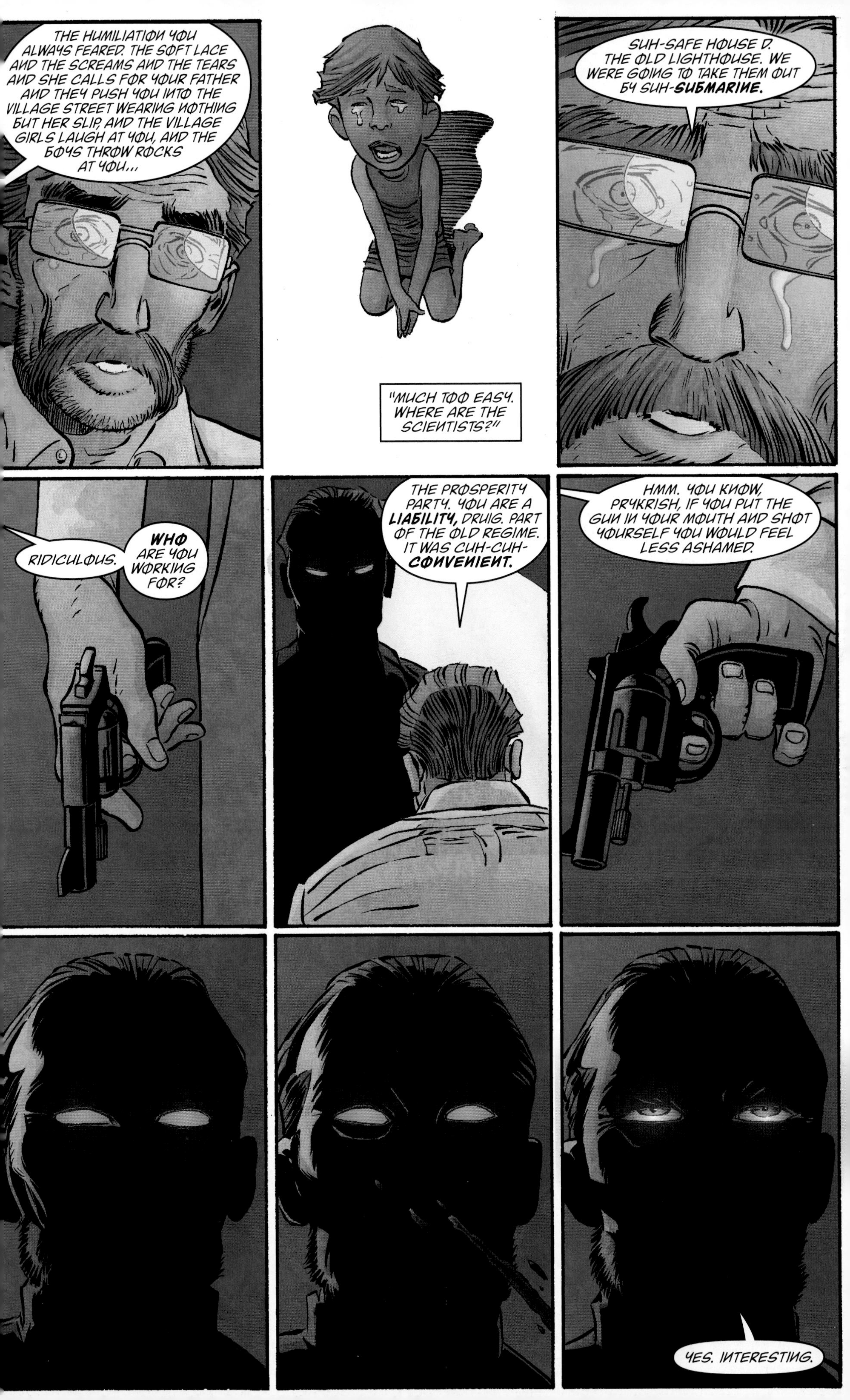
THE HUMILIATION YOU ALWAYS FEARED. THE SOFT LACE AND THE SCREAMS AND THE TEARS AND SHE CALLS FOR YOUR FATHER AND THEY PUSH YOU INTO THE VILLAGE STREET WEARING NOTHING BUT HER SLIP, AND THE VILLAGE GIRLS LAUGH AT YOU, AND THE BOYS THROW ROCKS AT YOU...
"MUCH TOO EASY. WHERE ARE THE SCIENTISTS?"
SUH-SAFE HOUSE D. THE OLD LIGHTHOUSE. WE WERE GOING TO TAKE THEM OUT BY SUH-SUBMARINE.
RIDICULOUS.
WHO ARE YOU WORKING FOR?
THE PROSPERITY PARTY. YOU ARE A LIABILITY, DRUIG. PART OF THE OLD REGIME. IT WAS CUH-CUH-CONVENIENT.
HMM. YOU KNOW, PRYKRISH, IF YOU PUT THE GUN IN YOUR MOUTH AND SHOT YOURSELF YOU WOULD FEEL LESS ASHAMED.
YES. INTERESTING.

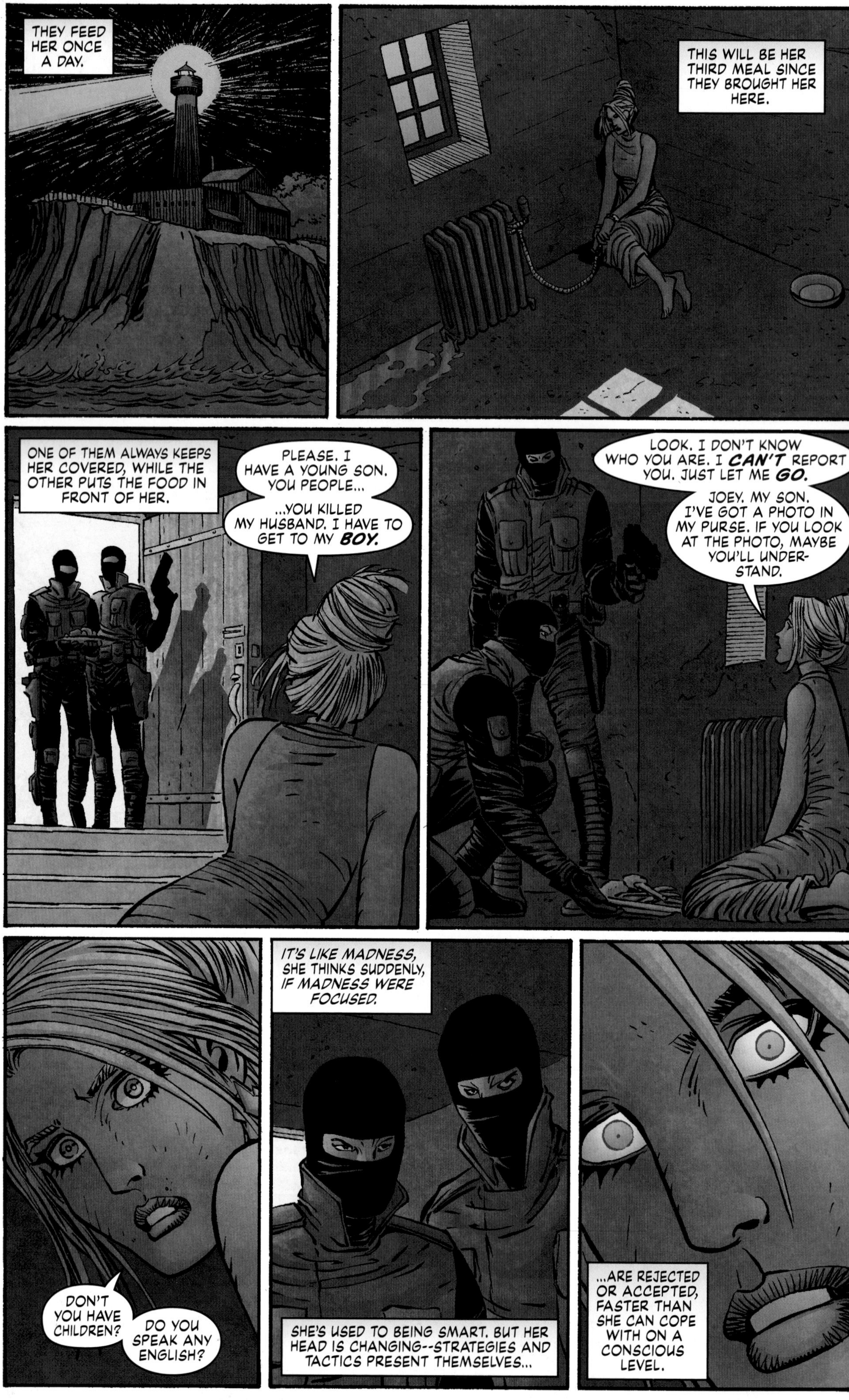
THEY FEED HER ONCE A DAY.
THIS WILL BE HER THIRD MEAL SINCE THEY BROUGHT HER HERE.
ONE OF THEM ALWAYS KEEPS HER COVERED, WHILE THE OTHER PUTS THE FOOD IN FRONT OF HER.
PLEASE. I HAVE A YOUNG SON. YOU PEOPLE...
...YOU KILLED MY HUSBAND. I HAVE TO GET TO MY **BOY.**
LOOK. I DON'T KNOW WHO YOU ARE. I ***CAN'T*** REPORT YOU. JUST LET ME ***GO.***
JOEY. MY SON. I'VE GOT A PHOTO IN MY PURSE. IF YOU LOOK AT THE PHOTO, MAYBE YOU'LL UNDER-STAND.
DON'T YOU HAVE CHILDREN?
DO YOU SPEAK ANY ENGLISH?
IT'S LIKE MADNESS, SHE THINKS SUDDENLY, IF MADNESS WERE FOCUSED.
SHE'S USED TO BEING SMART. BUT HER HEAD IS CHANGING--STRATEGIES AND TACTICS PRESENT THEMSELVES...
...ARE REJECTED OR ACCEPTED, FASTER THAN SHE CAN COPE WITH ON A CONSCIOUS LEVEL.

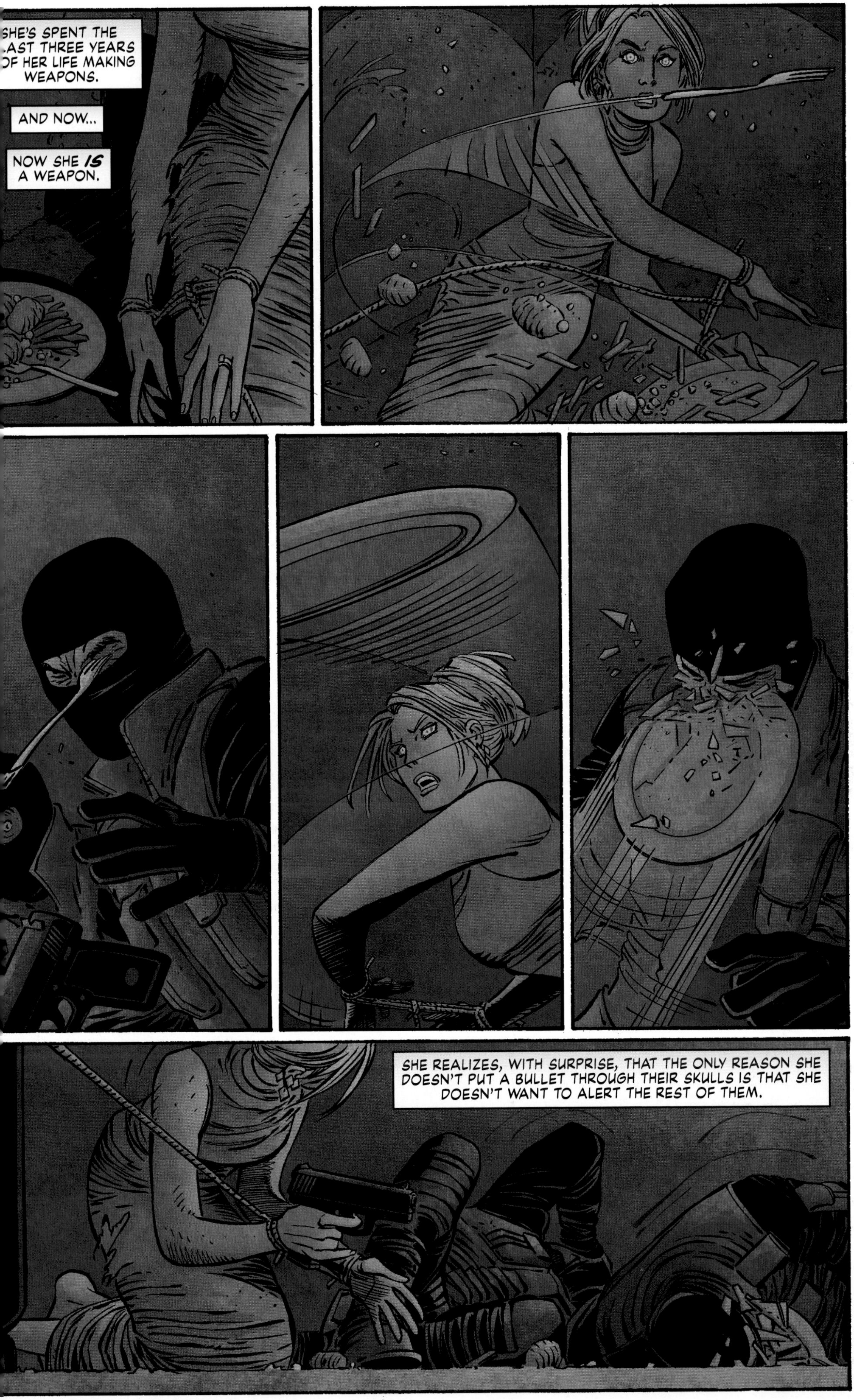
SHE'S SPENT THE LAST THREE YEARS OF HER LIFE MAKING WEAPONS.
AND NOW...
NOW SHE IS A WEAPON.
SHE REALIZES, WITH SURPRISE, THAT THE ONLY REASON SHE DOESN'T PUT A BULLET THROUGH THEIR SKULLS IS THAT SHE DOESN'T WANT TO ALERT THE REST OF THEM.

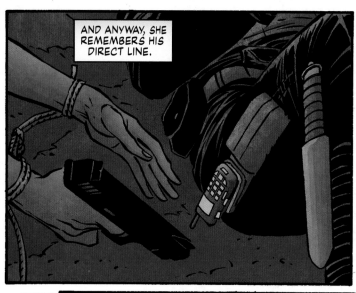

AND ANYWAY, SHE REMEMBERS HIS DIRECT LINE.

AVENGERS HEADQUARTERS, STARK TOWER...

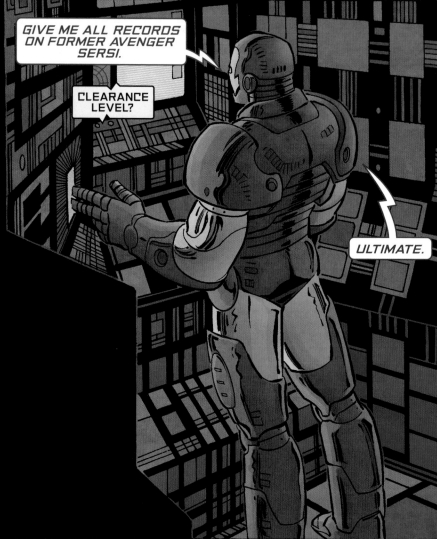

GIVE ME ALL RECORDS ON FORMER AVENGER SERSI.

CLEARANCE LEVEL?

ULTIMATE.

NO RECORDS FOUND.

HUH?

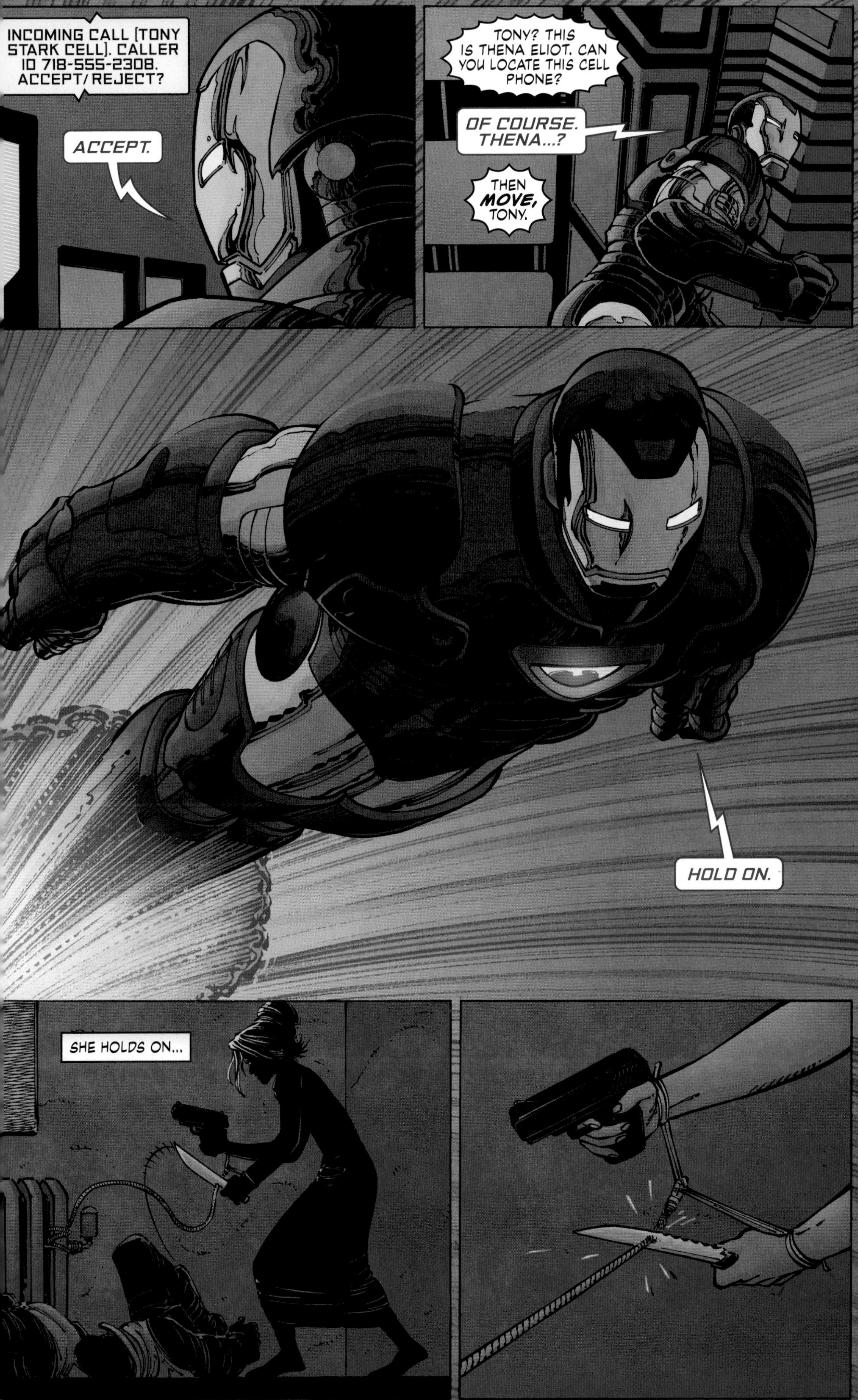
INCOMING CALL [TONY STARK CELL]. CALLER ID 718-555-2308. ACCEPT/ REJECT?
ACCEPT.
TONY? THIS IS THENA ELIOT. CAN YOU LOCATE THIS CELL PHONE?
OF COURSE. THENA...?
THEN MOVE, TONY.
HOLD ON.
SHE HOLDS ON...

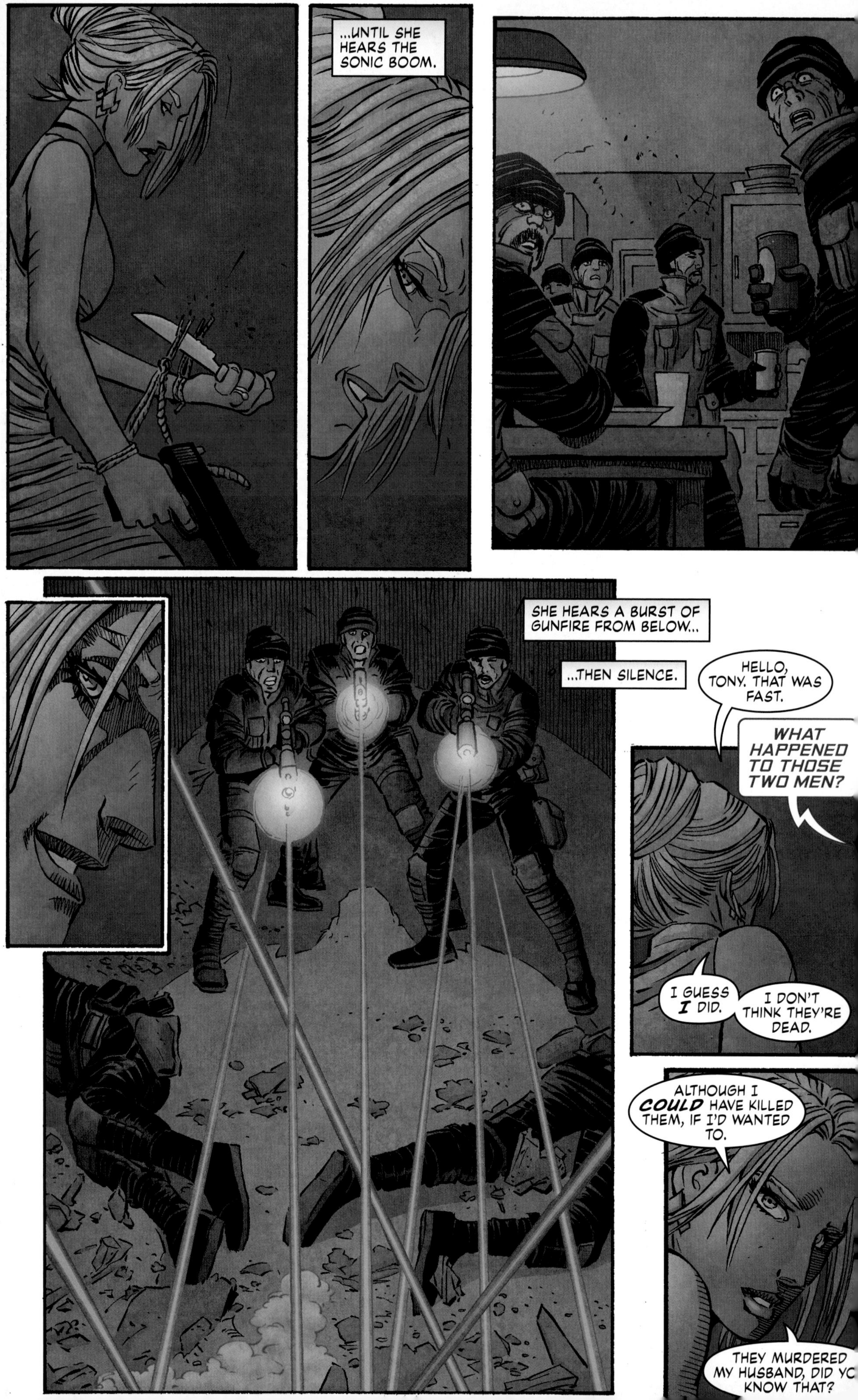

...UNTIL SHE HEARS THE SONIC BOOM.
SHE HEARS A BURST OF GUNFIRE FROM BELOW...
...THEN SILENCE.
HELLO, TONY. THAT WAS FAST.
WHAT HAPPENED TO THOSE TWO MEN?
I GUESS I DID.
I DON'T THINK THEY'RE DEAD.
ALTHOUGH I COULD HAVE KILLED THEM, IF I'D WANTED TO.
THEY MURDERED MY HUSBAND, DID YO KNOW THAT?

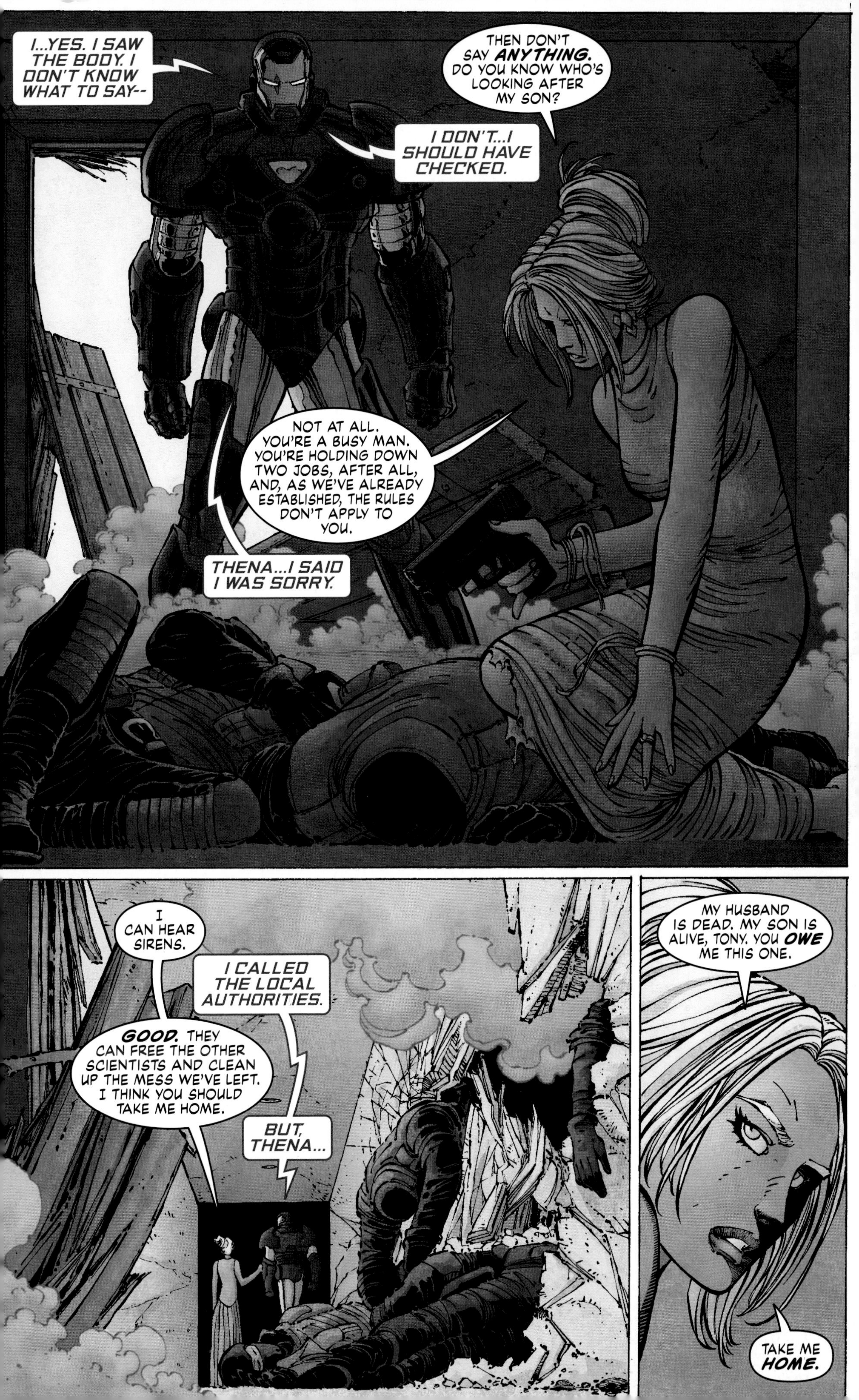
I...YES. I SAW THE BODY. I DON'T KNOW WHAT TO SAY--
THEN DON'T SAY ANYTHING. DO YOU KNOW WHO'S LOOKING AFTER MY SON?
I DON'T...I SHOULD HAVE CHECKED.
NOT AT ALL. YOU'RE A BUSY MAN. YOU'RE HOLDING DOWN TWO JOBS, AFTER ALL, AND, AS WE'VE ALREADY ESTABLISHED, THE RULES DON'T APPLY TO YOU.
THENA...I SAID I WAS SORRY.
I CAN HEAR SIRENS.
I CALLED THE LOCAL AUTHORITIES.
GOOD. THEY CAN FREE THE OTHER SCIENTISTS AND CLEAN UP THE MESS WE'VE LEFT. I THINK YOU SHOULD TAKE ME HOME.
BUT, THENA...
MY HUSBAND IS DEAD. MY SON IS ALIVE, TONY. YOU OWE ME THIS ONE.
TAKE ME HOME.

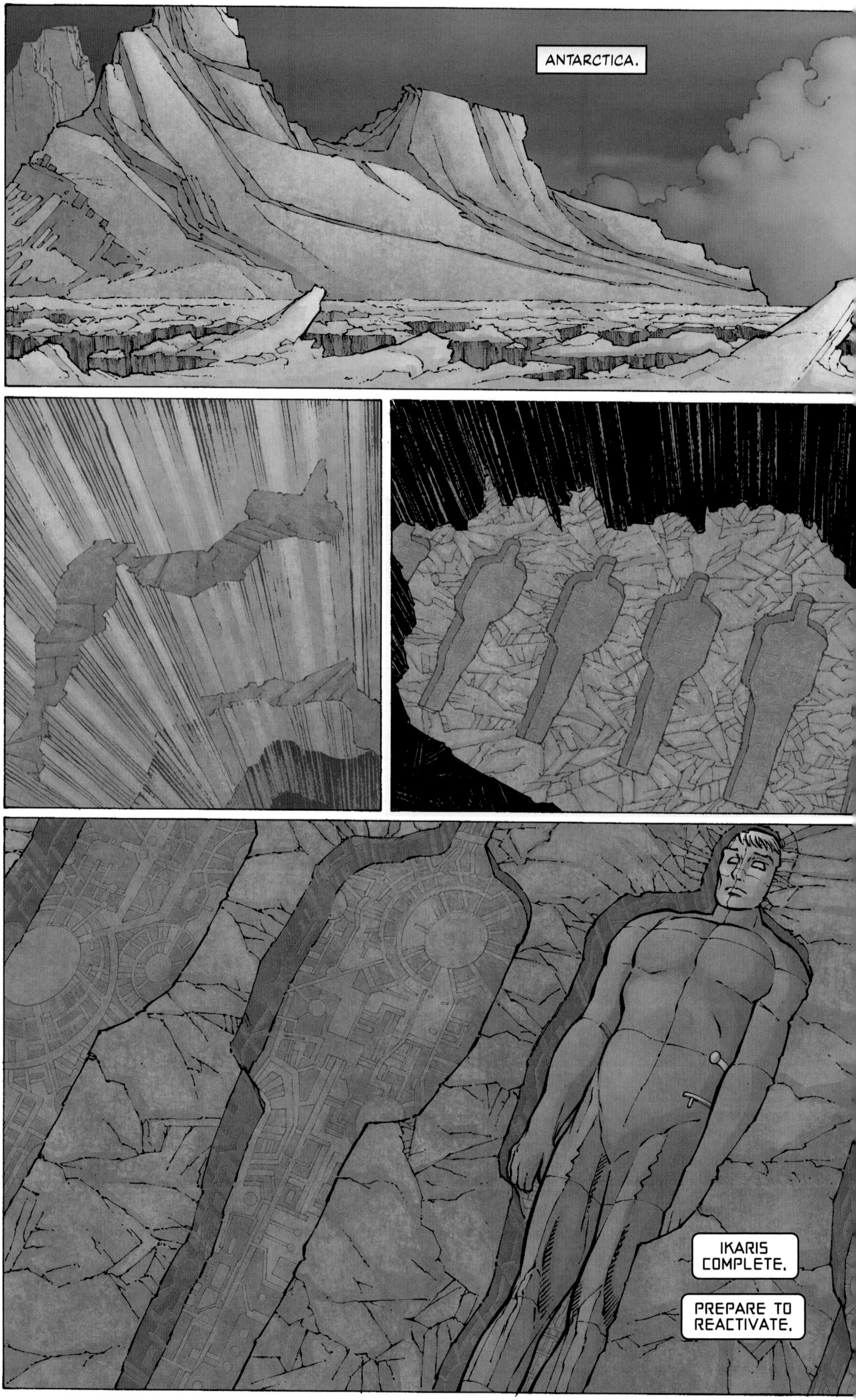
ANTARCTICA.
IKARIS COMPLETE.
PREPARE TO REACTIVATE.

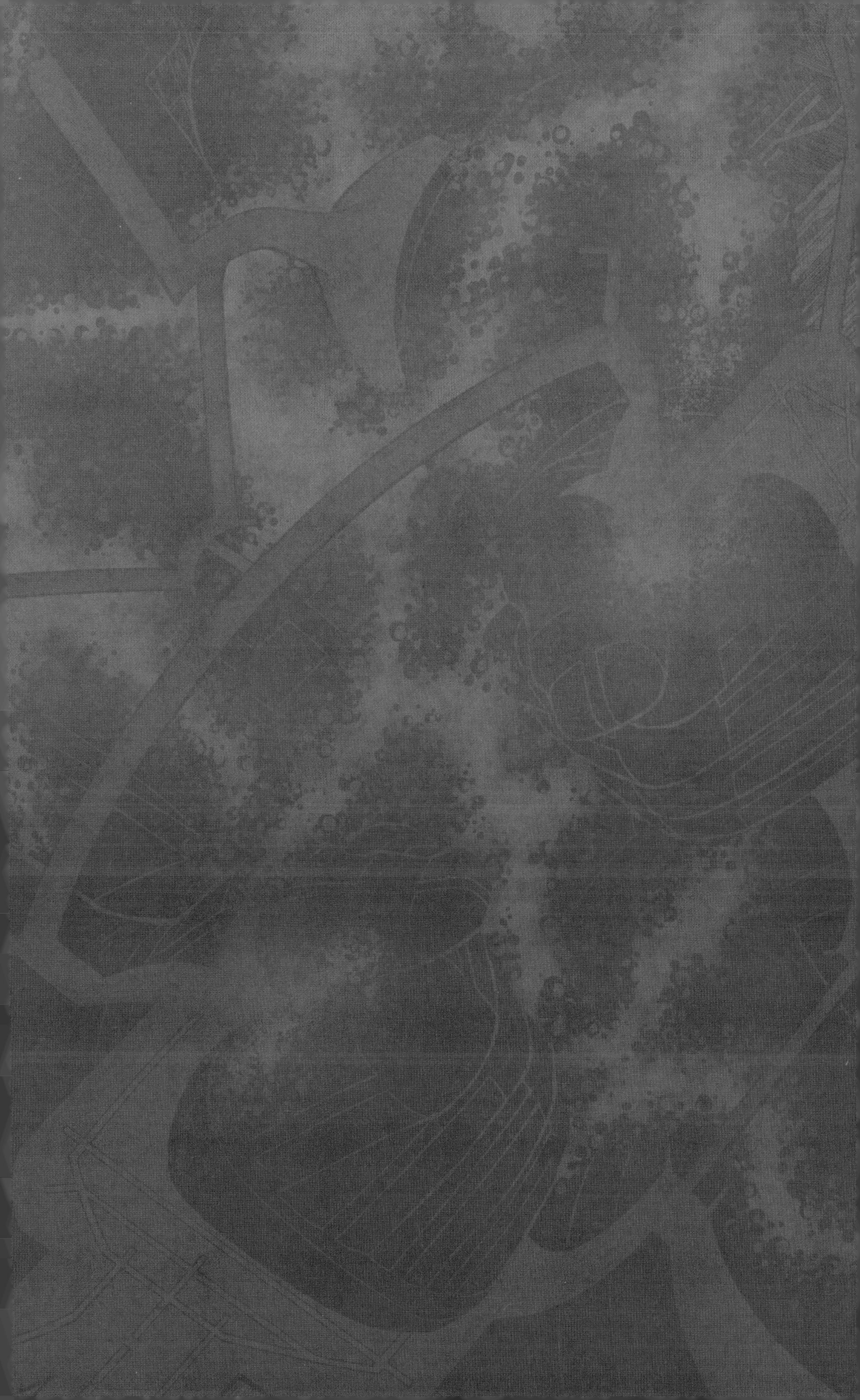

CHAPTER FOUR: FROM GENESIS TO REVELATIONS

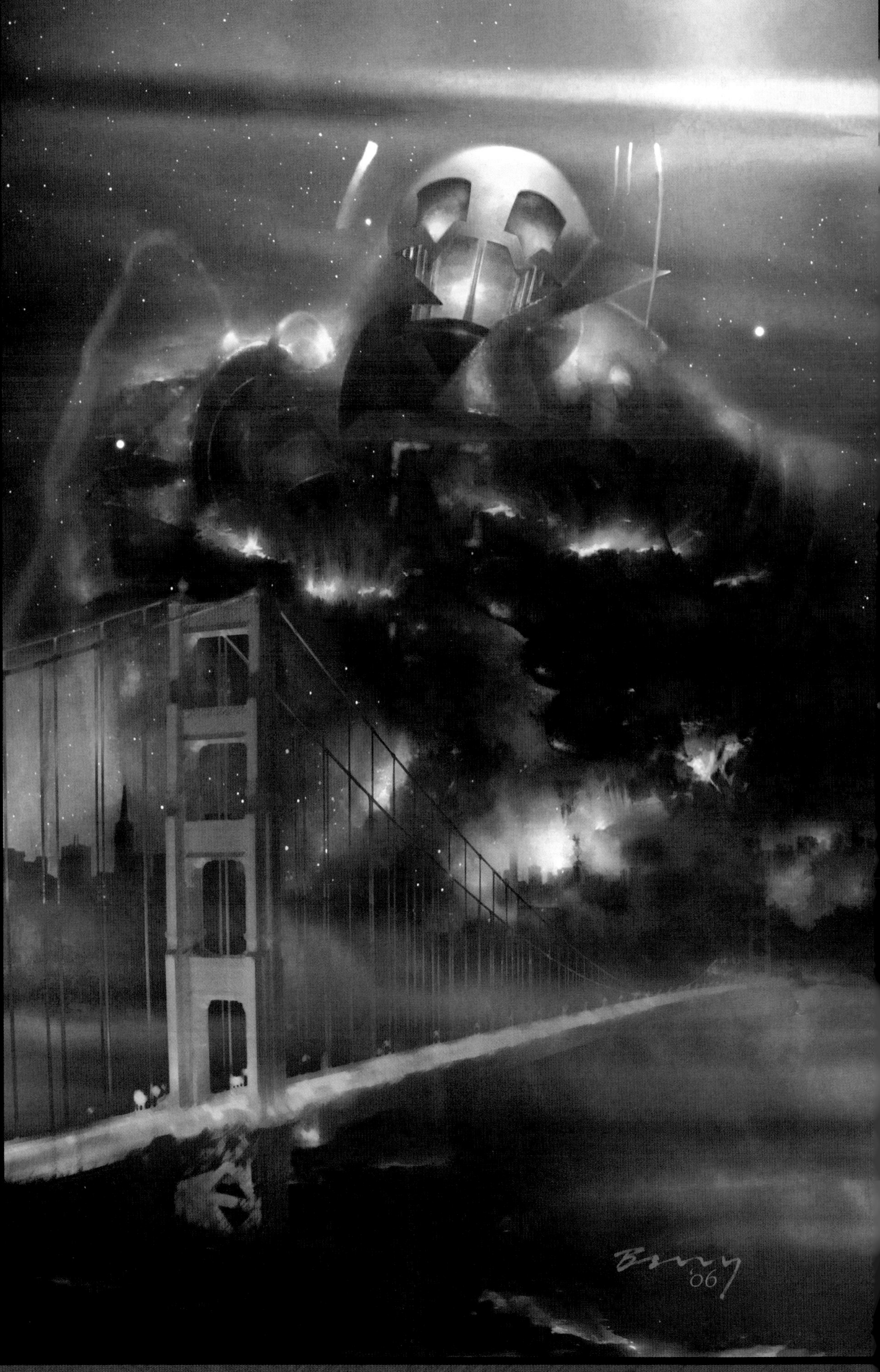

ANTARCTICA.

...TO AWAKE, PLEASE GET UP AND GO THROUGH THE DOORS.

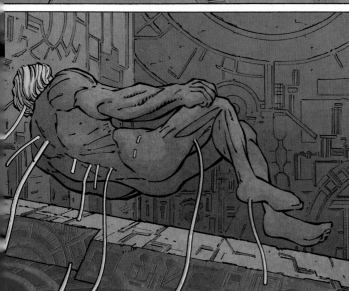

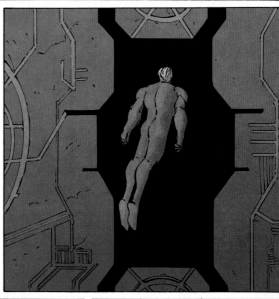

ETERNAL, IKARIS, IDENTIFIED.

ETERNAL IKARIS, REACTIVATION COMPLETE.

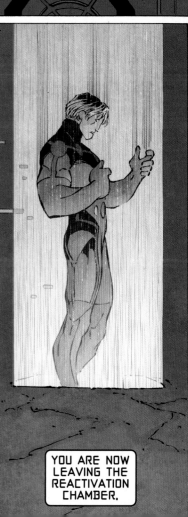

YOU ARE NOW LEAVING THE REACTIVATION CHAMBER.

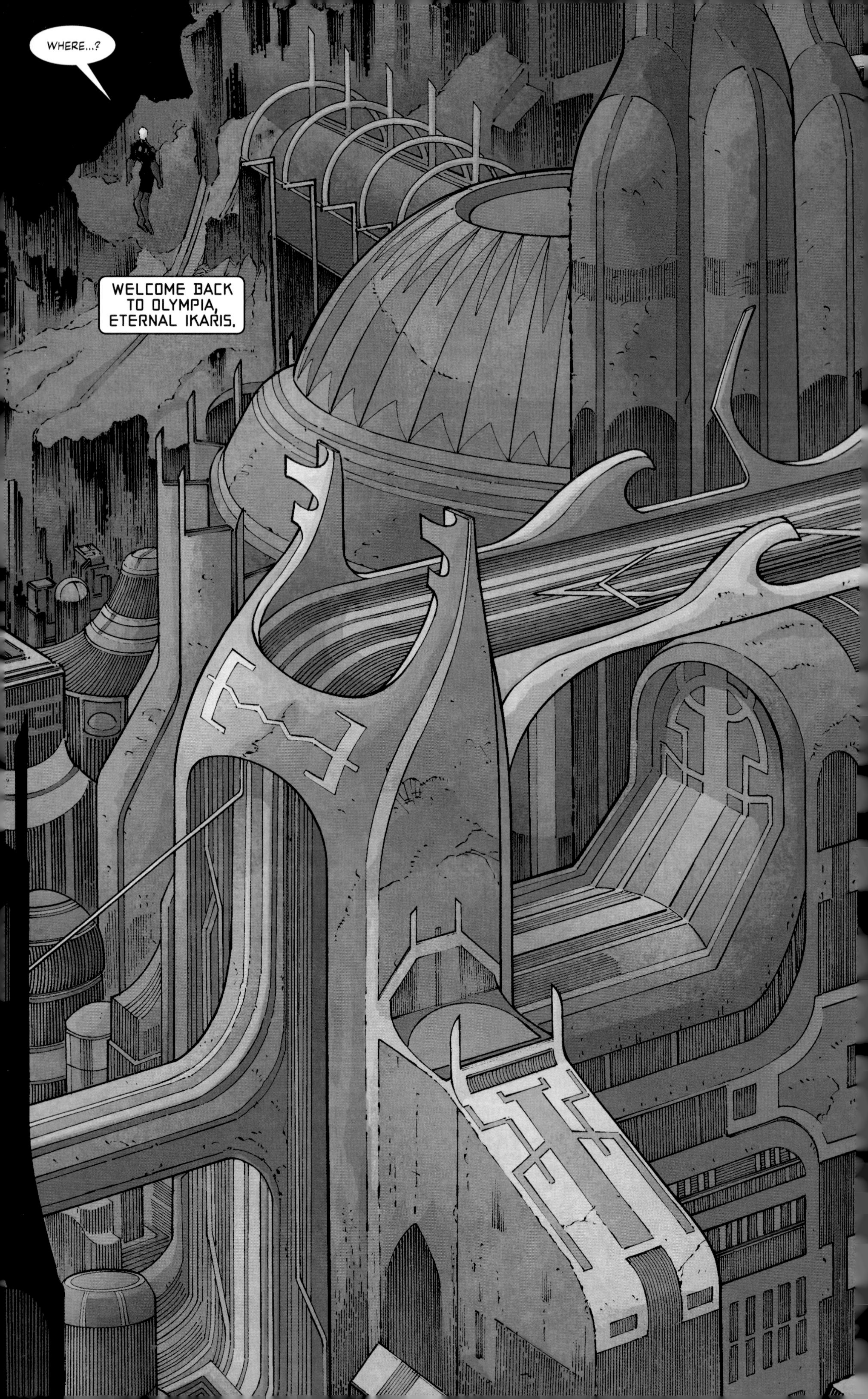
WHERE...?
WELCOME BACK TO OLYMPIA, ETERNAL IKARIS.

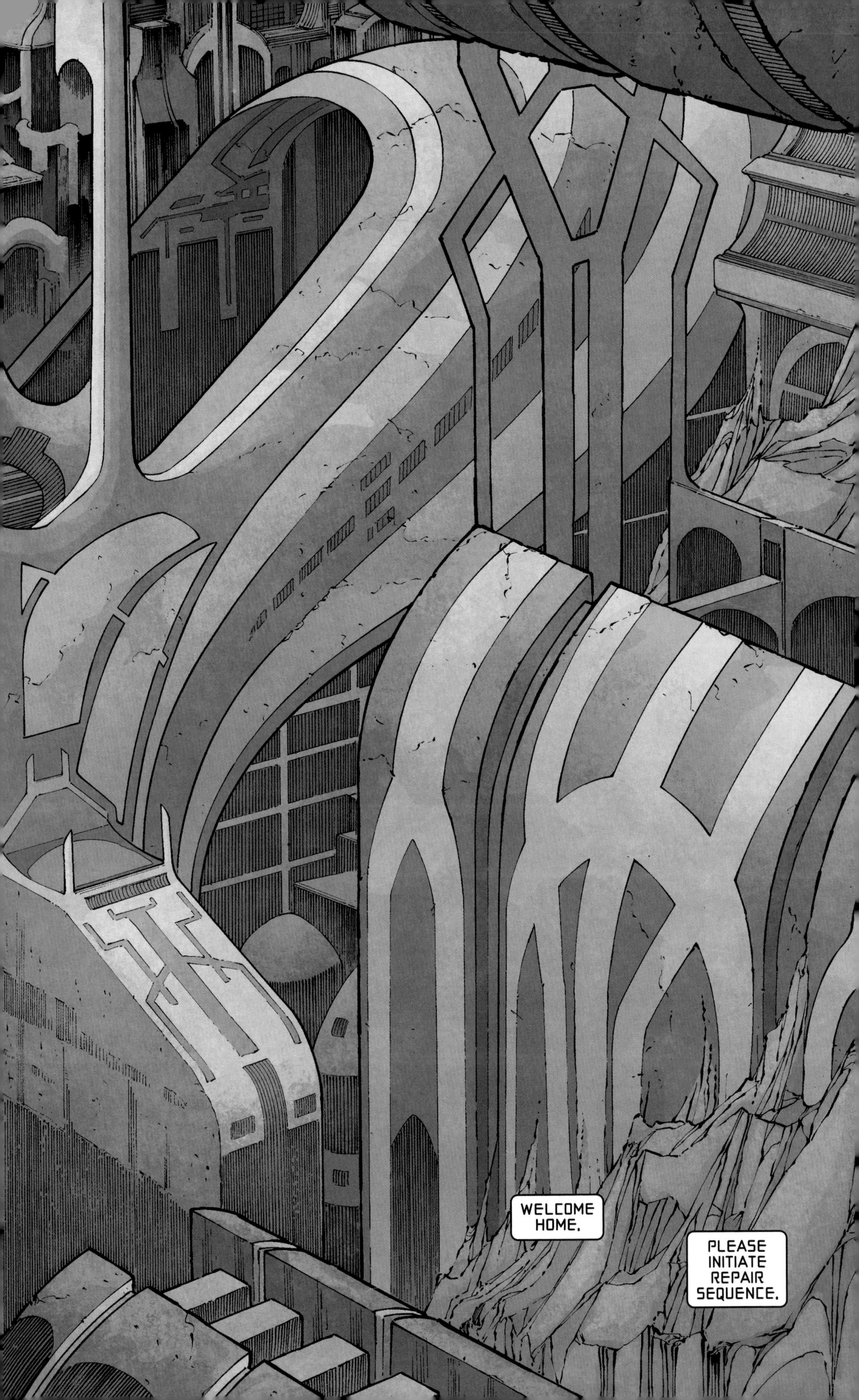
WELCOME HOME.
PLEASE INITIATE REPAIR SEQUENCE.

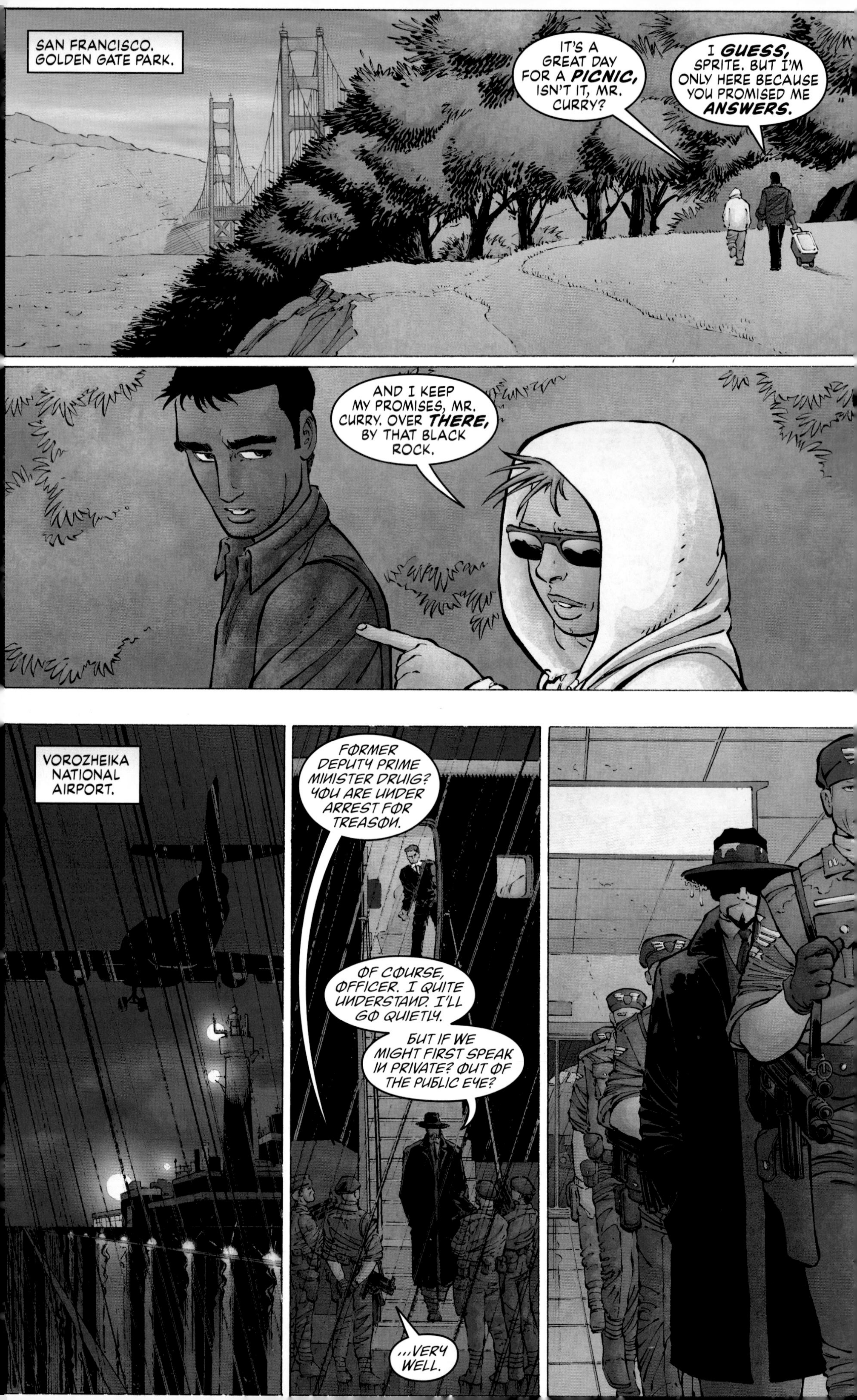
SAN FRANCISCO. GOLDEN GATE PARK.
IT'S A GREAT DAY FOR A PICNIC, ISN'T IT, MR. CURRY?
I GUESS, SPRITE. BUT I'M ONLY HERE BECAUSE YOU PROMISED ME ANSWERS.
AND I KEEP MY PROMISES, MR. CURRY. OVER THERE, BY THAT BLACK ROCK.
VOROZHEIKA NATIONAL AIRPORT.
FORMER DEPUTY PRIME MINISTER DRUIG? YOU ARE UNDER ARREST FOR TREASON.
OF COURSE, OFFICER. I QUITE UNDERSTAND. I'LL GO QUIETLY.
BUT IF WE MIGHT FIRST SPEAK IN PRIVATE? OUT OF THE PUBLIC EYE?
...VERY WELL.

NOW. SAY WHAT YOU HAVE TO SAY. AND MAKE IT QUICK.

ЧАСТНЫЙ

THERE, GENTLEMEN.

AS LONG AS YOU WORK FOR ME, I PROMISE YOU WILL NEVER SEE THOSE THINGS AGAIN. NOW...

THE PROSPERITY PARTY HEADQUARTERS, I THINK.

I HAVE A COUNTRY TO TAKE OVER.

I LOVE PICNICS. WICKED.

AND MR. CURRY, YOU MUSTN'T GET UPSET ABOUT SERSI BREAKING YOUR HEART. IT'S NOT THE FIRST TIME.

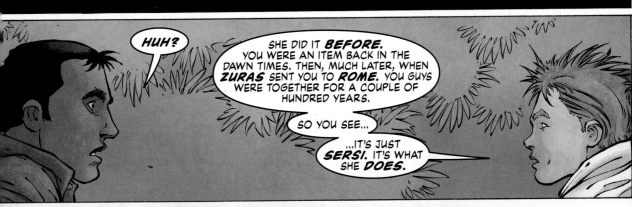

HUH?

SHE DID IT BEFORE. YOU WERE AN ITEM BACK IN THE DAWN TIMES. THEN, MUCH LATER, WHEN ZURAS SENT YOU TO ROME. YOU GUYS WERE TOGETHER FOR A COUPLE OF HUNDRED YEARS.

SO YOU SEE...

...IT'S JUST SERSI. IT'S WHAT SHE DOES.

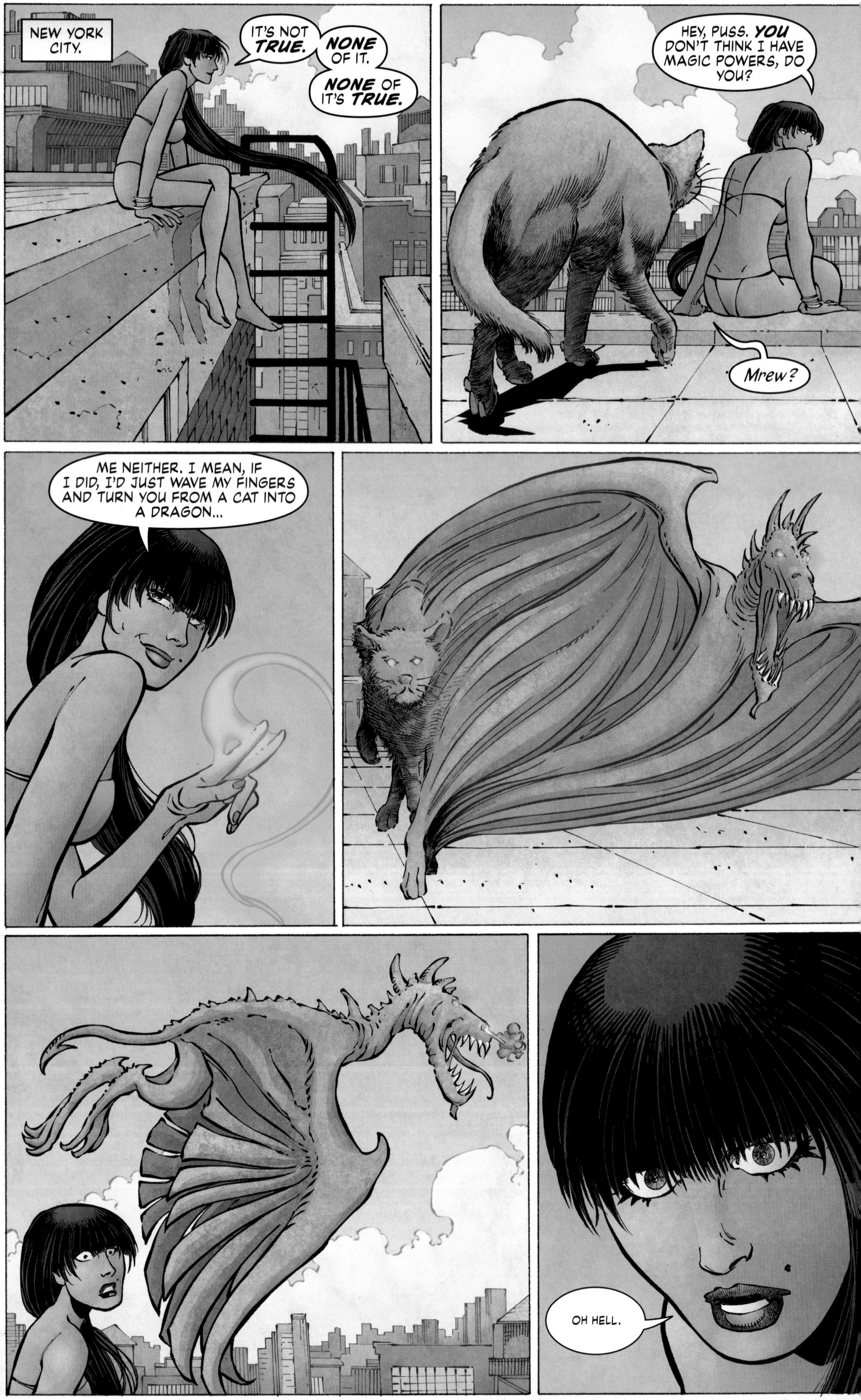
NEW YORK CITY.
IT'S NOT TRUE.
NONE OF IT.
NONE OF IT'S TRUE.
HEY, PUSS. YOU DON'T THINK I HAVE MAGIC POWERS, DO YOU?
Mrew?
ME NEITHER. I MEAN, IF I DID, I'D JUST WAVE MY FINGERS AND TURN YOU FROM A CAT INTO A DRAGON...
OH HELL.

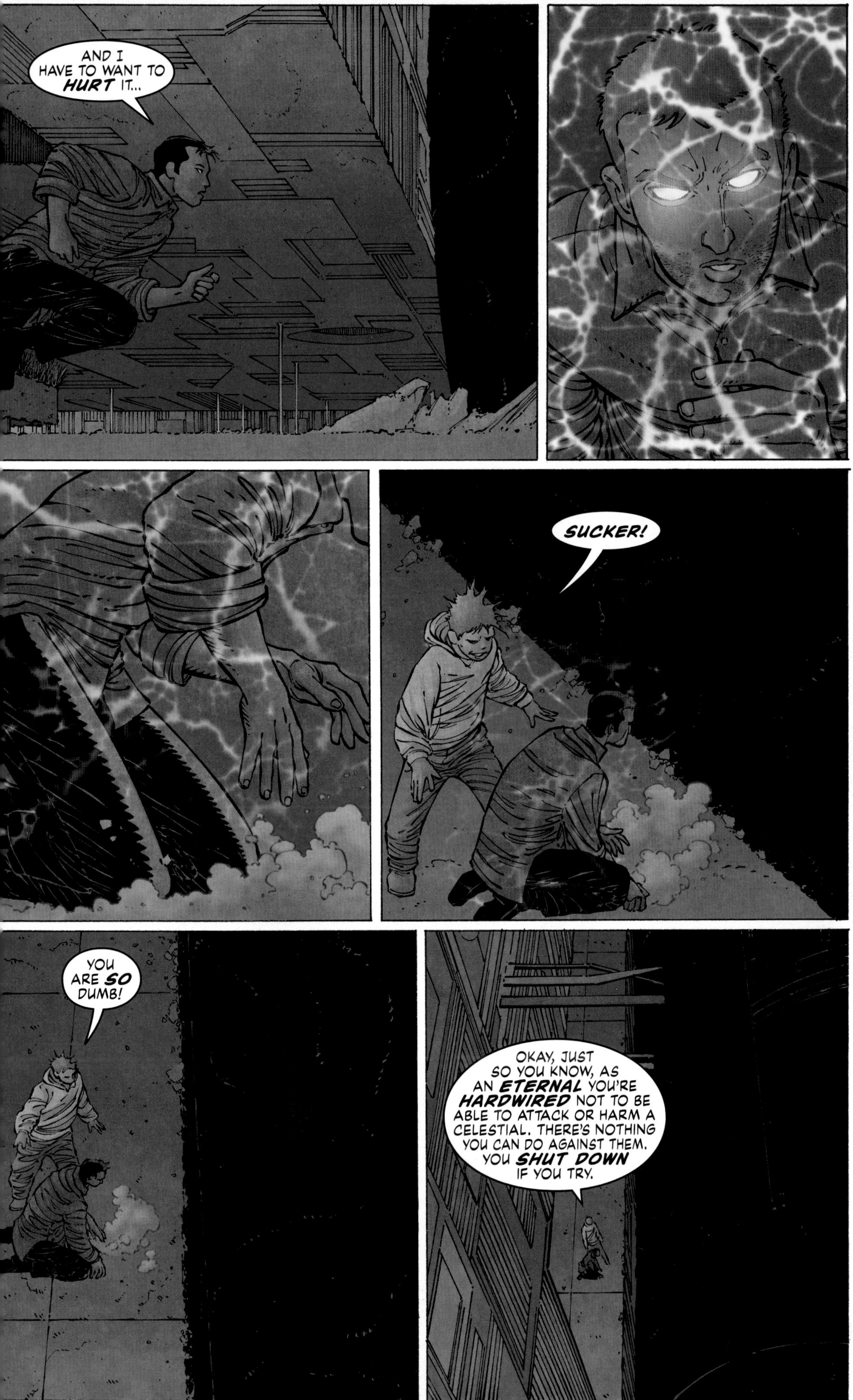
AND I HAVE TO WANT TO *HURT* IT...
SUCKER!
YOU ARE *SO* DUMB!
OKAY, JUST SO YOU KNOW, AS AN *ETERNAL* YOU'RE *HARDWIRED* NOT TO BE ABLE TO ATTACK OR HARM A CELESTIAL. THERE'S NOTHING YOU CAN DO AGAINST THEM. YOU *SHUT DOWN* IF YOU TRY.

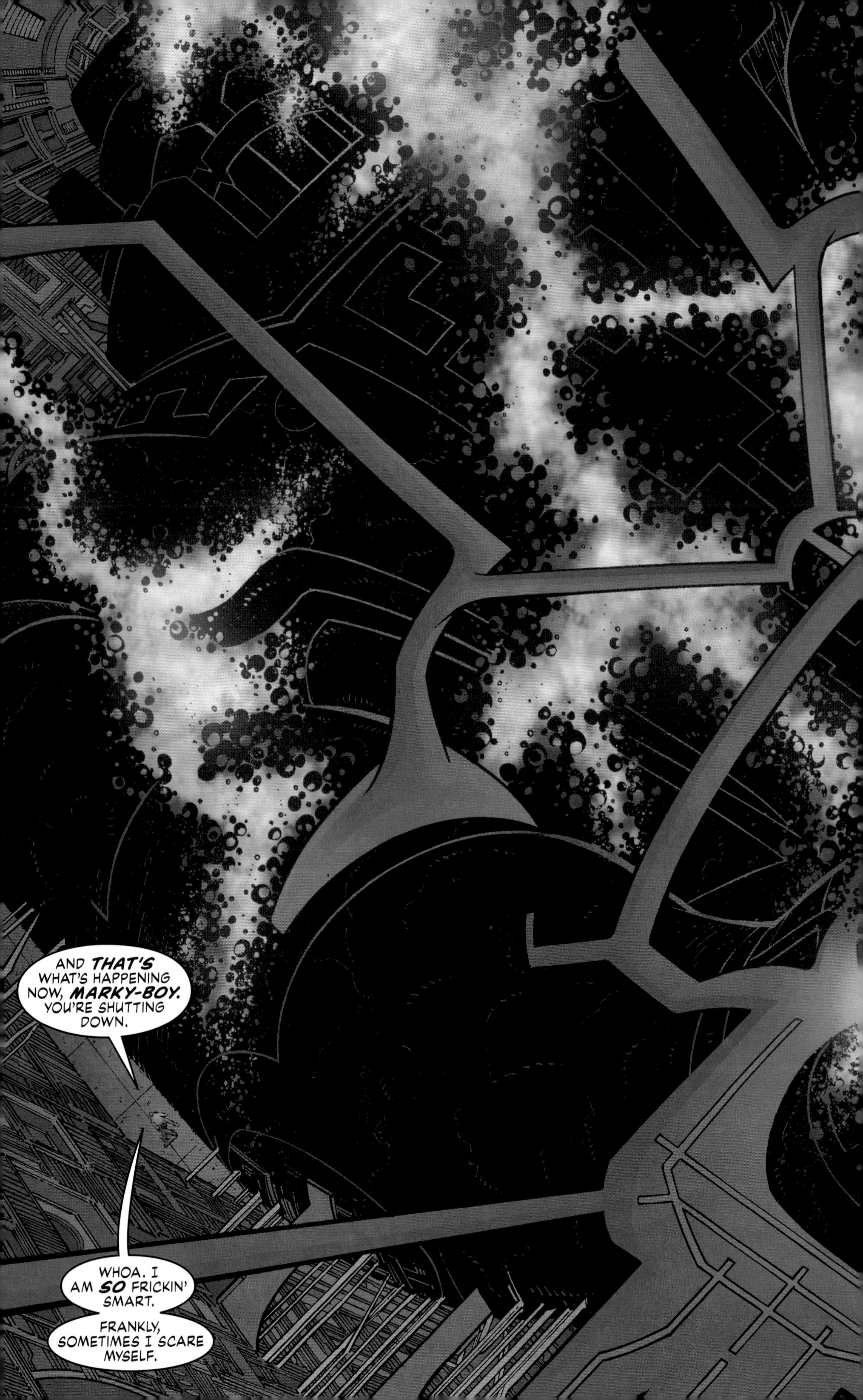
AND **THAT'S** WHAT'S HAPPENING NOW, **MARKY-BOY.** YOU'RE SHUTTING DOWN.
WHOA. I AM **SO** FRICKIN' SMART.
FRANKLY, SOMETIMES I SCARE MYSELF.

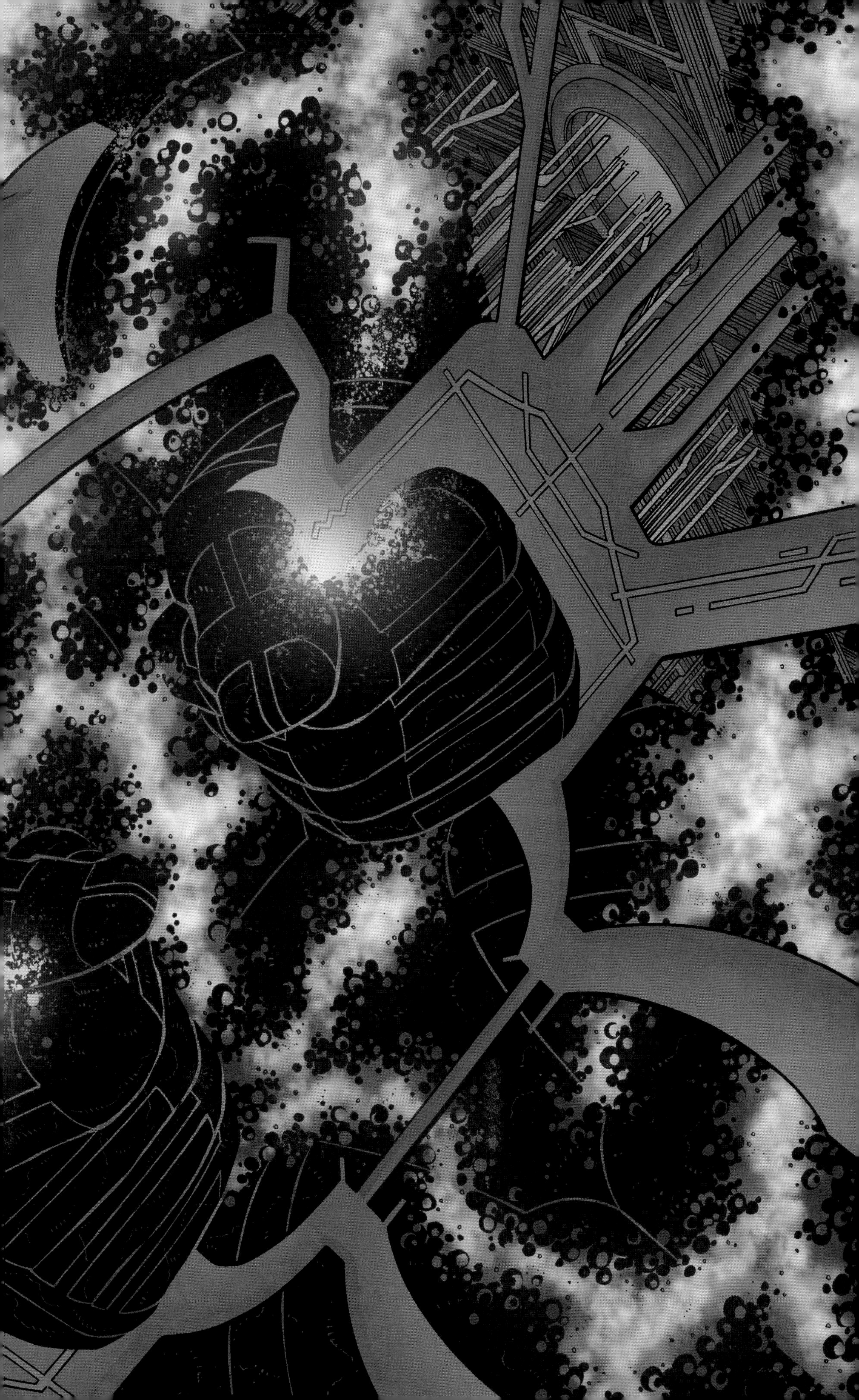

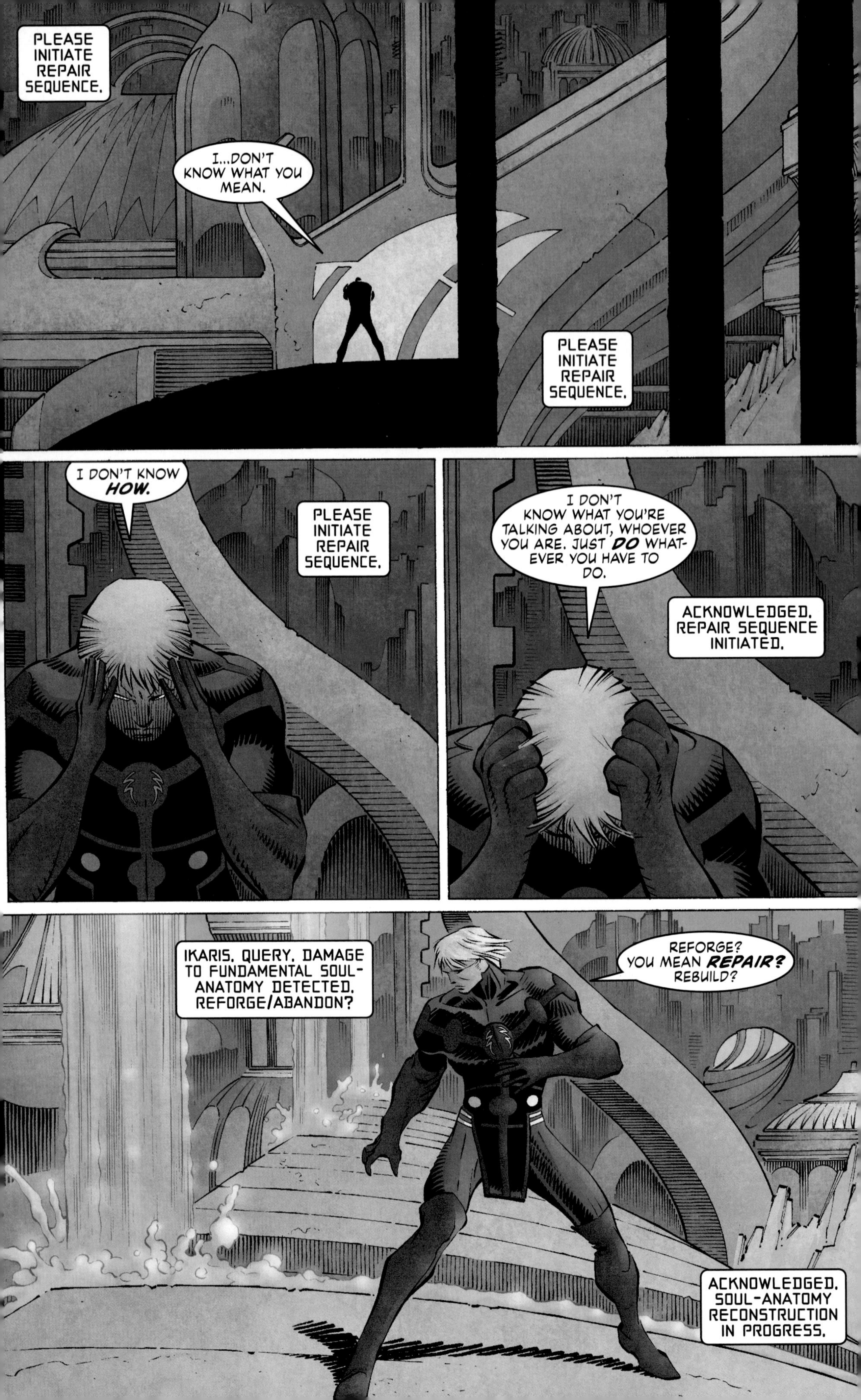

PLEASE INITIATE REPAIR SEQUENCE.
I...DON'T KNOW WHAT YOU MEAN.
PLEASE INITIATE REPAIR SEQUENCE.
I DON'T KNOW *HOW.*
PLEASE INITIATE REPAIR SEQUENCE.
I DON'T KNOW WHAT YOU'RE TALKING ABOUT, WHOEVER YOU ARE. JUST *DO* WHATEVER YOU HAVE TO DO.
ACKNOWLEDGED. REPAIR SEQUENCE INITIATED.
IKARIS. QUERY. DAMAGE TO FUNDAMENTAL SOUL-ANATOMY DETECTED. REFORGE/ABANDON?
REFORGE? YOU MEAN *REPAIR?* REBUILD?
ACKNOWLEDGED. SOUL-ANATOMY RECONSTRUCTION IN PROGRESS.

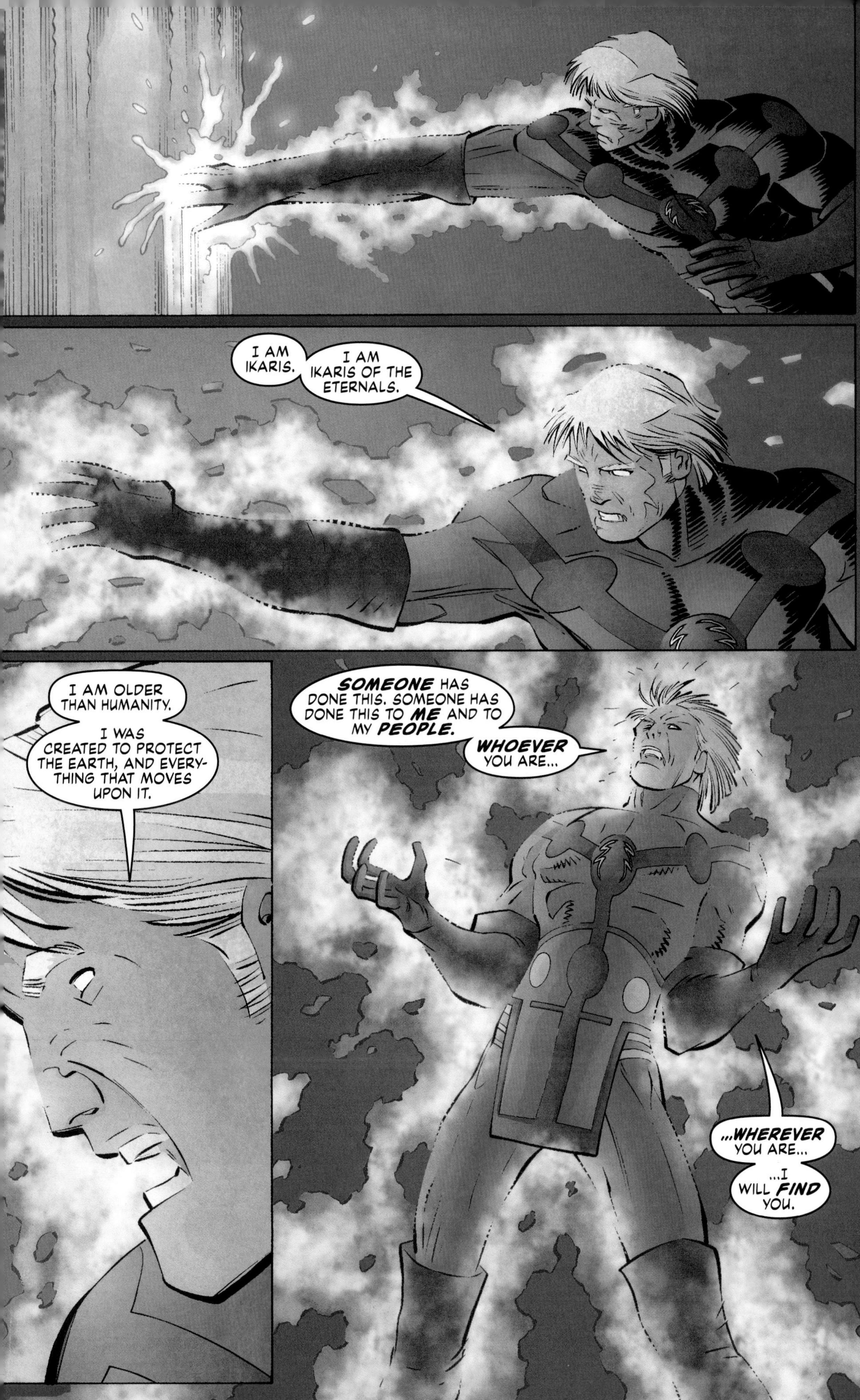
I AM IKARIS.
I AM IKARIS OF THE ETERNALS.
I AM OLDER THAN HUMANITY.
I WAS CREATED TO PROTECT THE EARTH, AND EVERYTHING THAT MOVES UPON IT.
SOMEONE HAS DONE THIS. SOMEONE HAS DONE THIS TO ME AND TO MY PEOPLE.
WHOEVER YOU ARE...
...WHEREVER YOU ARE...
...I WILL FIND YOU.

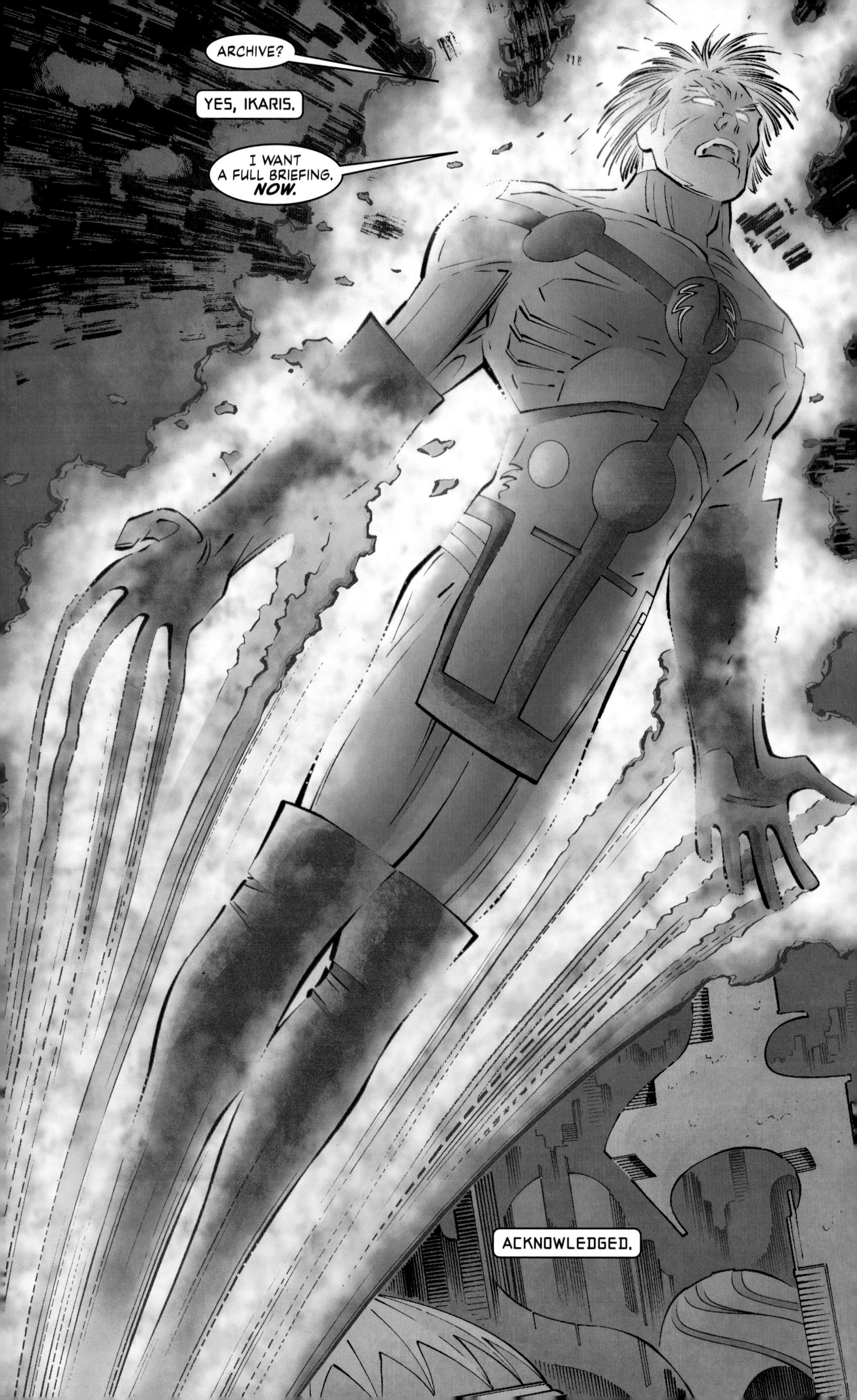
ARCHIVE?
YES, IKARIS.
I WANT A FULL BRIEFING. NOW.
ACKNOWLEDGED.

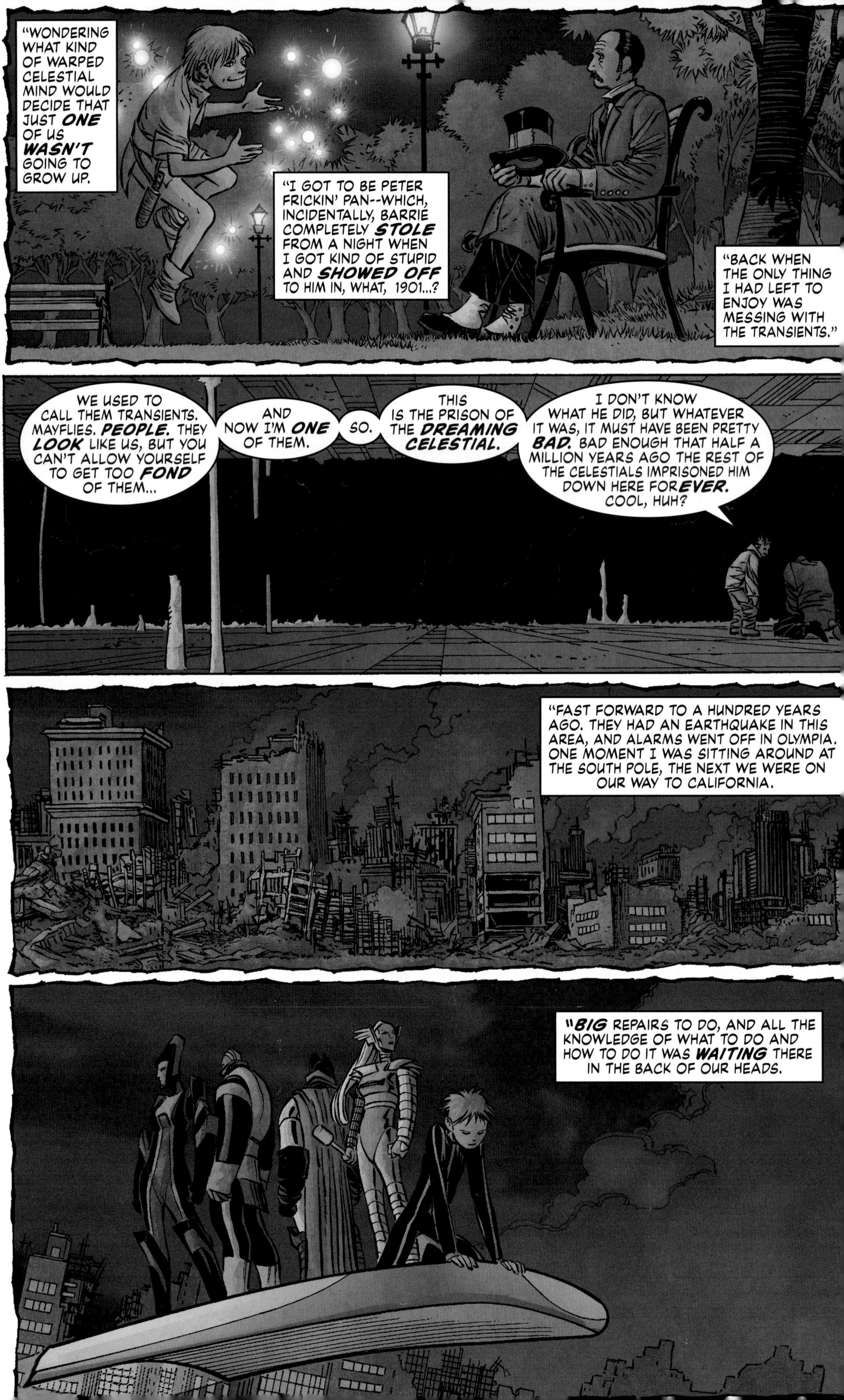
"WONDERING WHAT KIND OF WARPED CELESTIAL MIND WOULD DECIDE THAT JUST ONE OF US WASN'T GOING TO GROW UP.
"I GOT TO BE PETER FRICKIN' PAN--WHICH, INCIDENTALLY, BARRIE COMPLETELY STOLE FROM A NIGHT WHEN I GOT KIND OF STUPID AND SHOWED OFF TO HIM IN, WHAT, 1901...?
"BACK WHEN THE ONLY THING I HAD LEFT TO ENJOY WAS MESSING WITH THE TRANSIENTS."
WE USED TO CALL THEM TRANSIENTS. MAYFLIES. PEOPLE. THEY LOOK LIKE US, BUT YOU CAN'T ALLOW YOURSELF TO GET TOO FOND OF THEM...
AND NOW I'M ONE OF THEM.
SO.
THIS IS THE PRISON OF THE DREAMING CELESTIAL.
I DON'T KNOW WHAT HE DID, BUT WHATEVER IT WAS, IT MUST HAVE BEEN PRETTY BAD. BAD ENOUGH THAT HALF A MILLION YEARS AGO THE REST OF THE CELESTIALS IMPRISONED HIM DOWN HERE FOREVER. COOL, HUH?
"FAST FORWARD TO A HUNDRED YEARS AGO. THEY HAD AN EARTHQUAKE IN THIS AREA, AND ALARMS WENT OFF IN OLYMPIA. ONE MOMENT I WAS SITTING AROUND AT THE SOUTH POLE, THE NEXT WE WERE ON OUR WAY TO CALIFORNIA.
"BIG REPAIRS TO DO, AND ALL THE KNOWLEDGE OF WHAT TO DO AND HOW TO DO IT WAS WAITING THERE IN THE BACK OF OUR HEADS.

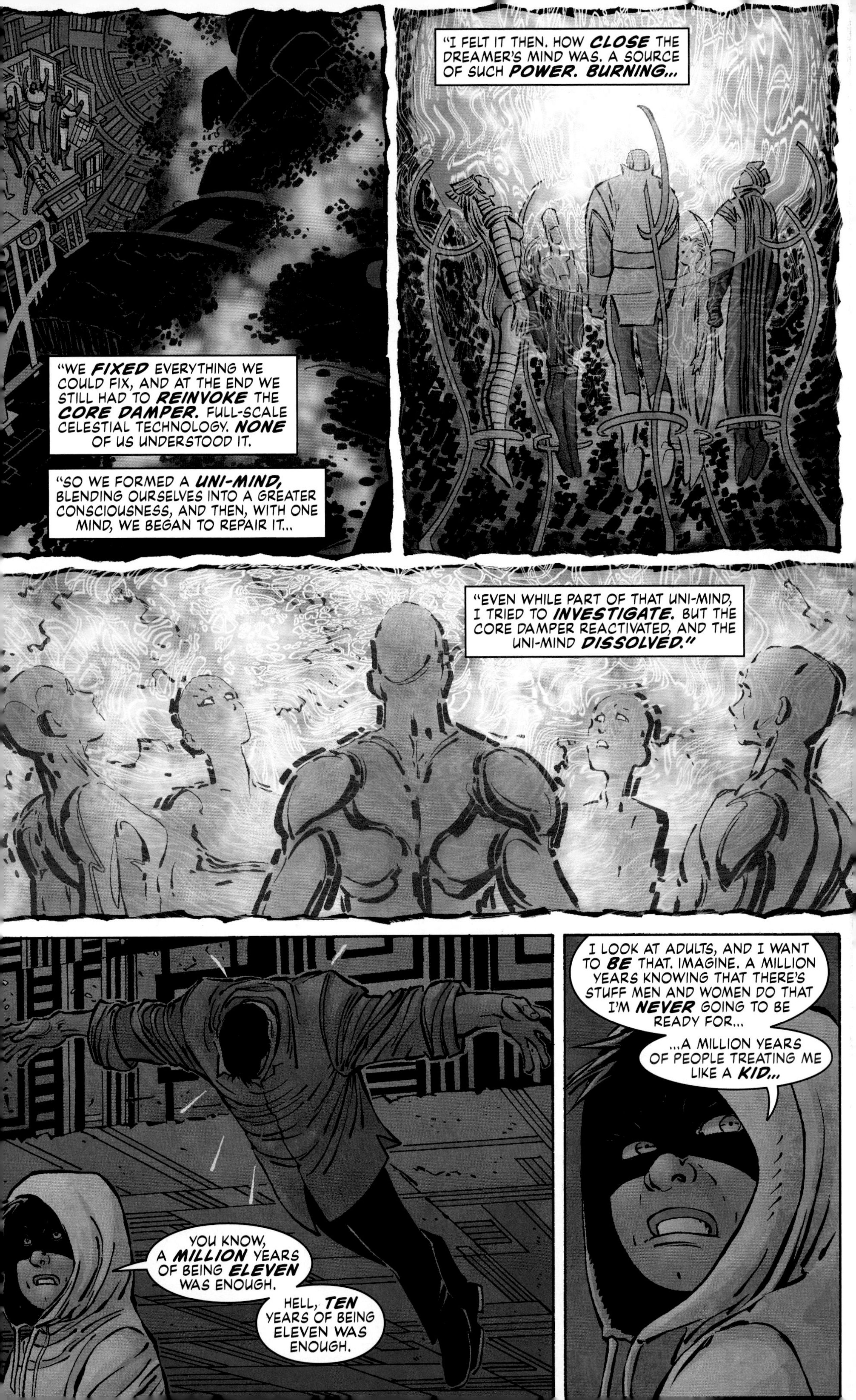

"WE FIXED EVERYTHING WE COULD FIX, AND AT THE END WE STILL HAD TO REINVOKE THE CORE DAMPER. FULL-SCALE CELESTIAL TECHNOLOGY. NONE OF US UNDERSTOOD IT.
"SO WE FORMED A UNI-MIND, BLENDING OURSELVES INTO A GREATER CONSCIOUSNESS, AND THEN, WITH ONE MIND, WE BEGAN TO REPAIR IT...
"I FELT IT THEN. HOW CLOSE THE DREAMER'S MIND WAS. A SOURCE OF SUCH POWER. BURNING...
"EVEN WHILE PART OF THAT UNI-MIND, I TRIED TO INVESTIGATE. BUT THE CORE DAMPER REACTIVATED, AND THE UNI-MIND DISSOLVED."
YOU KNOW, A MILLION YEARS OF BEING ELEVEN WAS ENOUGH.
HELL, TEN YEARS OF BEING ELEVEN WAS ENOUGH.
I LOOK AT ADULTS, AND I WANT TO BE THAT. IMAGINE. A MILLION YEARS KNOWING THAT THERE'S STUFF MEN AND WOMEN DO THAT I'M NEVER GOING TO BE READY FOR...
...A MILLION YEARS OF PEOPLE TREATING ME LIKE A KID...

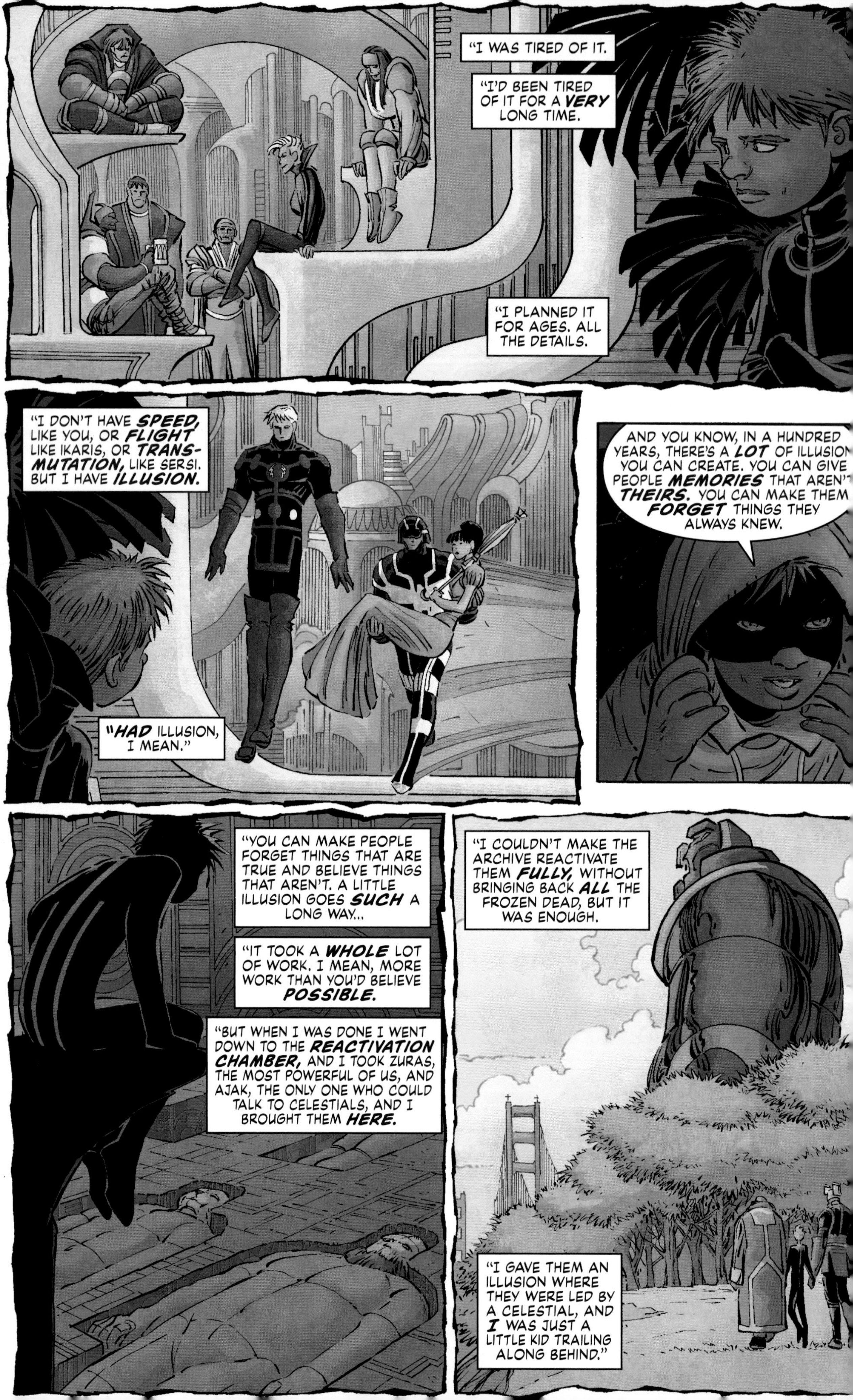
"I WAS TIRED OF IT.
"I'D BEEN TIRED OF IT FOR A VERY LONG TIME.
"I PLANNED IT FOR AGES. ALL THE DETAILS.
"I DON'T HAVE SPEED, LIKE YOU, OR FLIGHT LIKE IKARIS, OR TRANS-MUTATION, LIKE SERSI. BUT I HAVE ILLUSION.
"HAD ILLUSION, I MEAN."
AND YOU KNOW, IN A HUNDRED YEARS, THERE'S A LOT OF ILLUSION YOU CAN CREATE. YOU CAN GIVE PEOPLE MEMORIES THAT AREN'T THEIRS. YOU CAN MAKE THEM FORGET THINGS THEY ALWAYS KNEW.
"YOU CAN MAKE PEOPLE FORGET THINGS THAT ARE TRUE AND BELIEVE THINGS THAT AREN'T. A LITTLE ILLUSION GOES SUCH A LONG WAY...
"IT TOOK A WHOLE LOT OF WORK. I MEAN, MORE WORK THAN YOU'D BELIEVE POSSIBLE.
"BUT WHEN I WAS DONE I WENT DOWN TO THE REACTIVATION CHAMBER, AND I TOOK ZURAS, THE MOST POWERFUL OF US, AND AJAK, THE ONLY ONE WHO COULD TALK TO CELESTIALS, AND I BROUGHT THEM HERE.
"I COULDN'T MAKE THE ARCHIVE REACTIVATE THEM FULLY, WITHOUT BRINGING BACK ALL THE FROZEN DEAD, BUT IT WAS ENOUGH.
"I GAVE THEM AN ILLUSION WHERE THEY WERE LED BY A CELESTIAL, AND I WAS JUST A LITTLE KID TRAILING ALONG BEHIND."

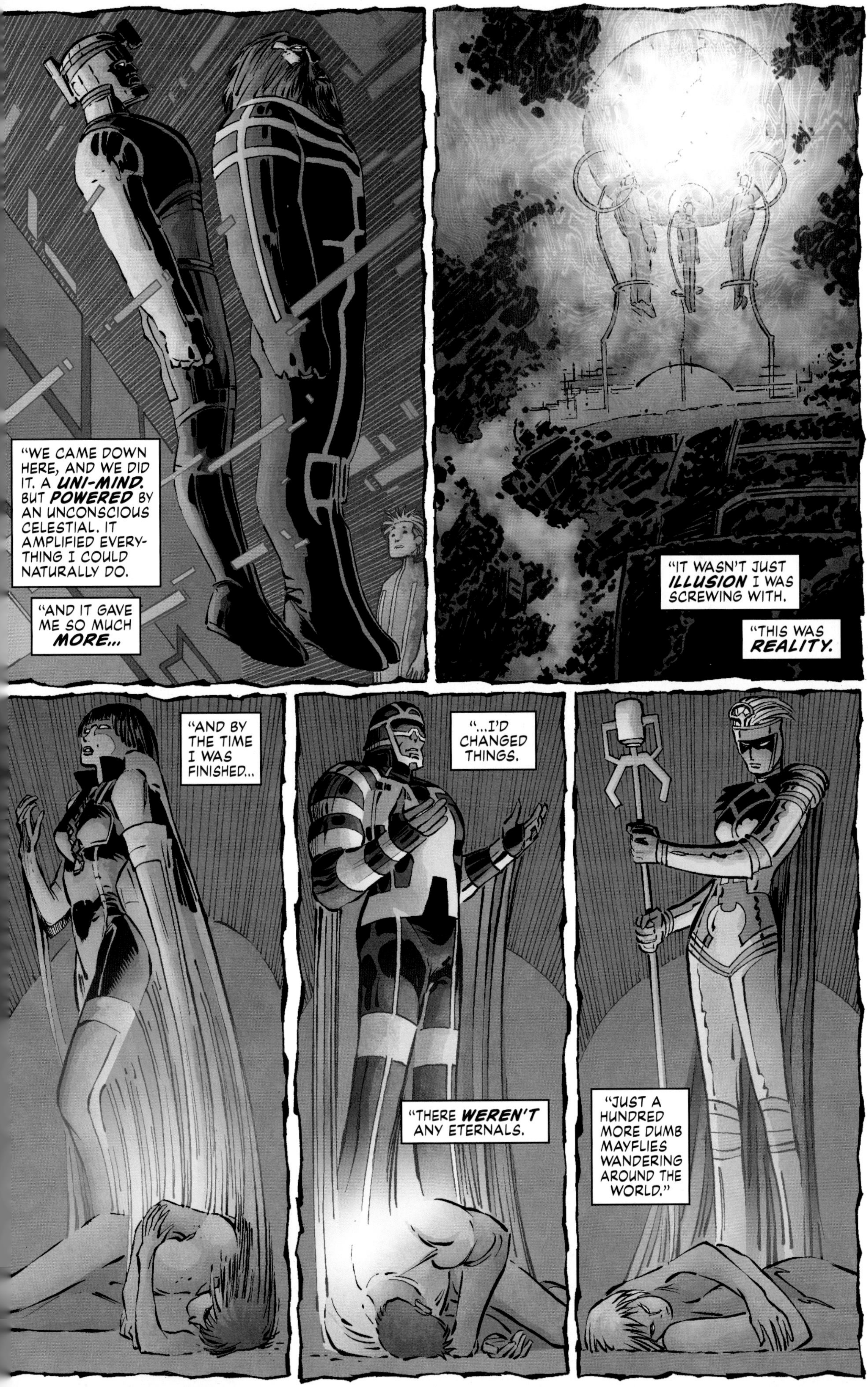
"WE CAME DOWN HERE, AND WE DID IT. A UNI-MIND. BUT POWERED BY AN UNCONSCIOUS CELESTIAL. IT AMPLIFIED EVERYTHING I COULD NATURALLY DO.
"AND IT GAVE ME SO MUCH MORE...
"IT WASN'T JUST ILLUSION I WAS SCREWING WITH.
"THIS WAS REALITY.
"AND BY THE TIME I WAS FINISHED...
"...I'D CHANGED THINGS.
"THERE WEREN'T ANY ETERNALS.
"JUST A HUNDRED MORE DUMB MAYFLIES WANDERING AROUND THE WORLD."

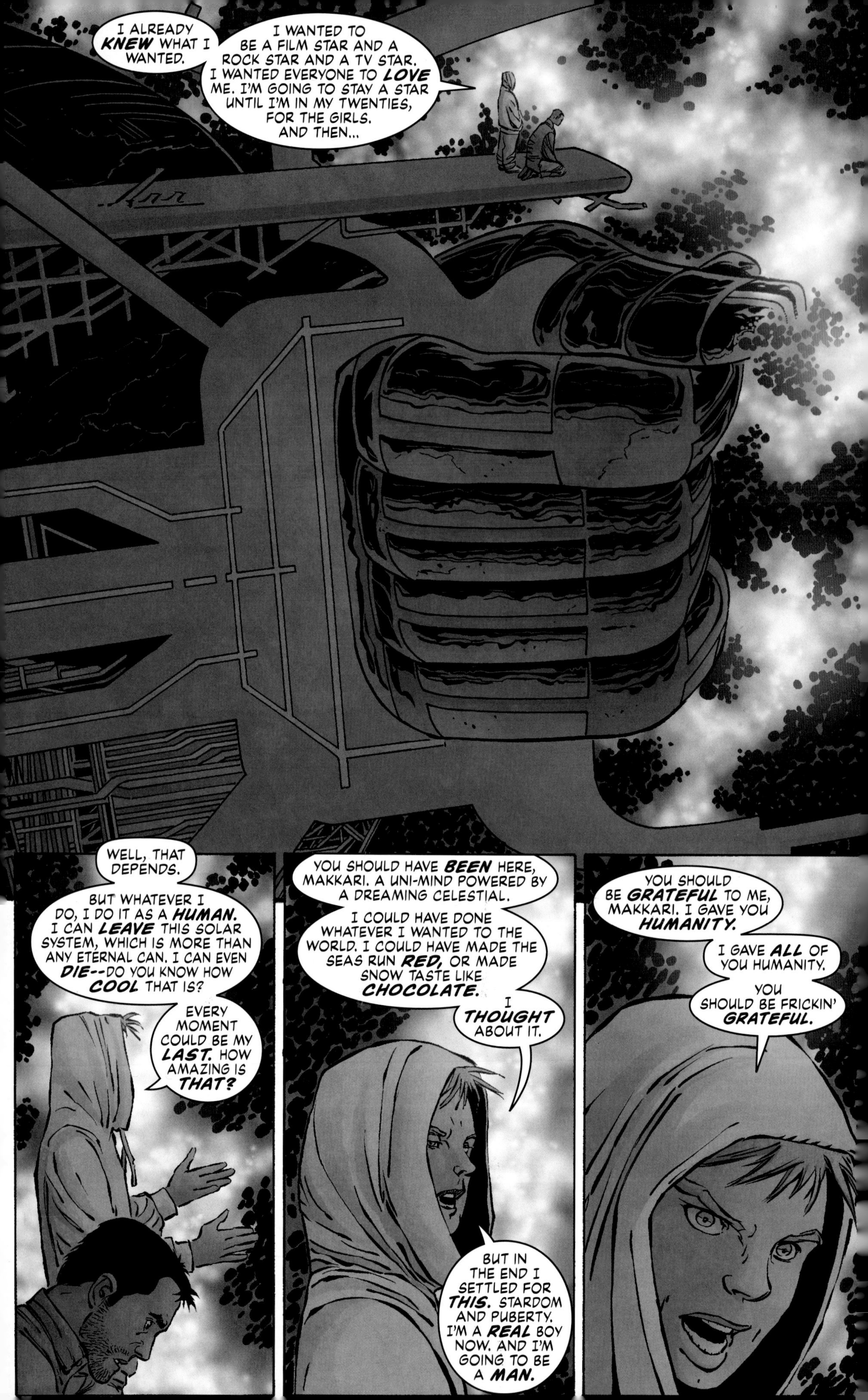
I ALREADY KNEW WHAT I WANTED.
I WANTED TO BE A FILM STAR AND A ROCK STAR AND A TV STAR. I WANTED EVERYONE TO LOVE ME. I'M GOING TO STAY A STAR UNTIL I'M IN MY TWENTIES, FOR THE GIRLS. AND THEN...
WELL, THAT DEPENDS.
BUT WHATEVER I DO, I DO IT AS A HUMAN. I CAN LEAVE THIS SOLAR SYSTEM, WHICH IS MORE THAN ANY ETERNAL CAN. I CAN EVEN DIE--DO YOU KNOW HOW COOL THAT IS?
EVERY MOMENT COULD BE MY LAST. HOW AMAZING IS THAT?
YOU SHOULD HAVE BEEN HERE, MAKKARI. A UNI-MIND POWERED BY A DREAMING CELESTIAL.
I COULD HAVE DONE WHATEVER I WANTED TO THE WORLD. I COULD HAVE MADE THE SEAS RUN RED, OR MADE SNOW TASTE LIKE CHOCOLATE.
I THOUGHT ABOUT IT.
BUT IN THE END I SETTLED FOR THIS. STARDOM AND PUBERTY. I'M A REAL BOY NOW. AND I'M GOING TO BE A MAN.
YOU SHOULD BE GRATEFUL TO ME, MAKKARI. I GAVE YOU HUMANITY.
I GAVE ALL OF YOU HUMANITY.
YOU SHOULD BE FRICKIN' GRATEFUL.

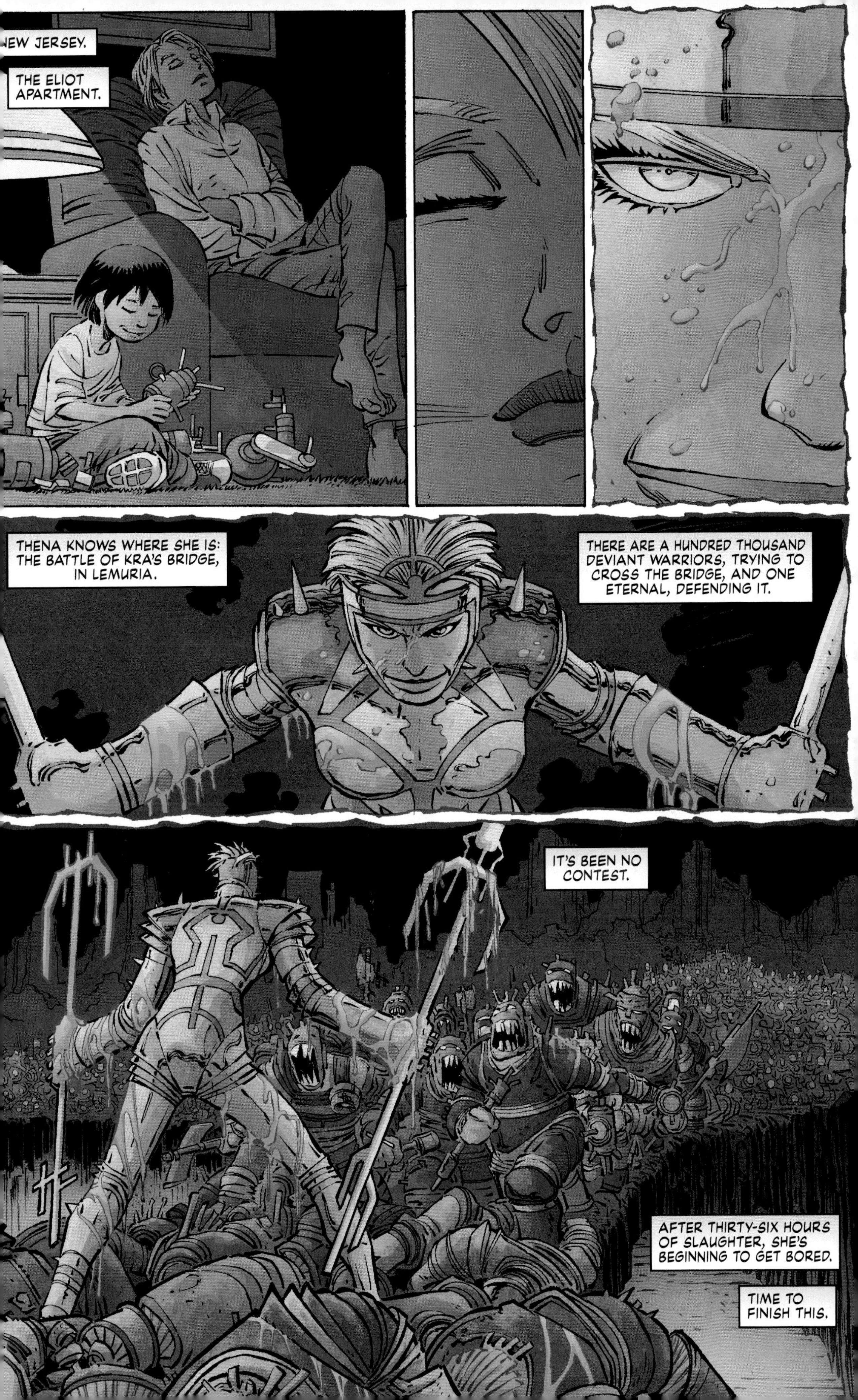
NEW JERSEY.
THE ELIOT APARTMENT.
THENA KNOWS WHERE SHE IS: THE BATTLE OF KRA'S BRIDGE, IN LEMURIA.
THERE ARE A HUNDRED THOUSAND DEVIANT WARRIORS, TRYING TO CROSS THE BRIDGE, AND ONE ETERNAL, DEFENDING IT.
IT'S BEEN NO CONTEST.
AFTER THIRTY-SIX HOURS OF SLAUGHTER, SHE'S BEGINNING TO GET BORED.
TIME TO FINISH THIS.

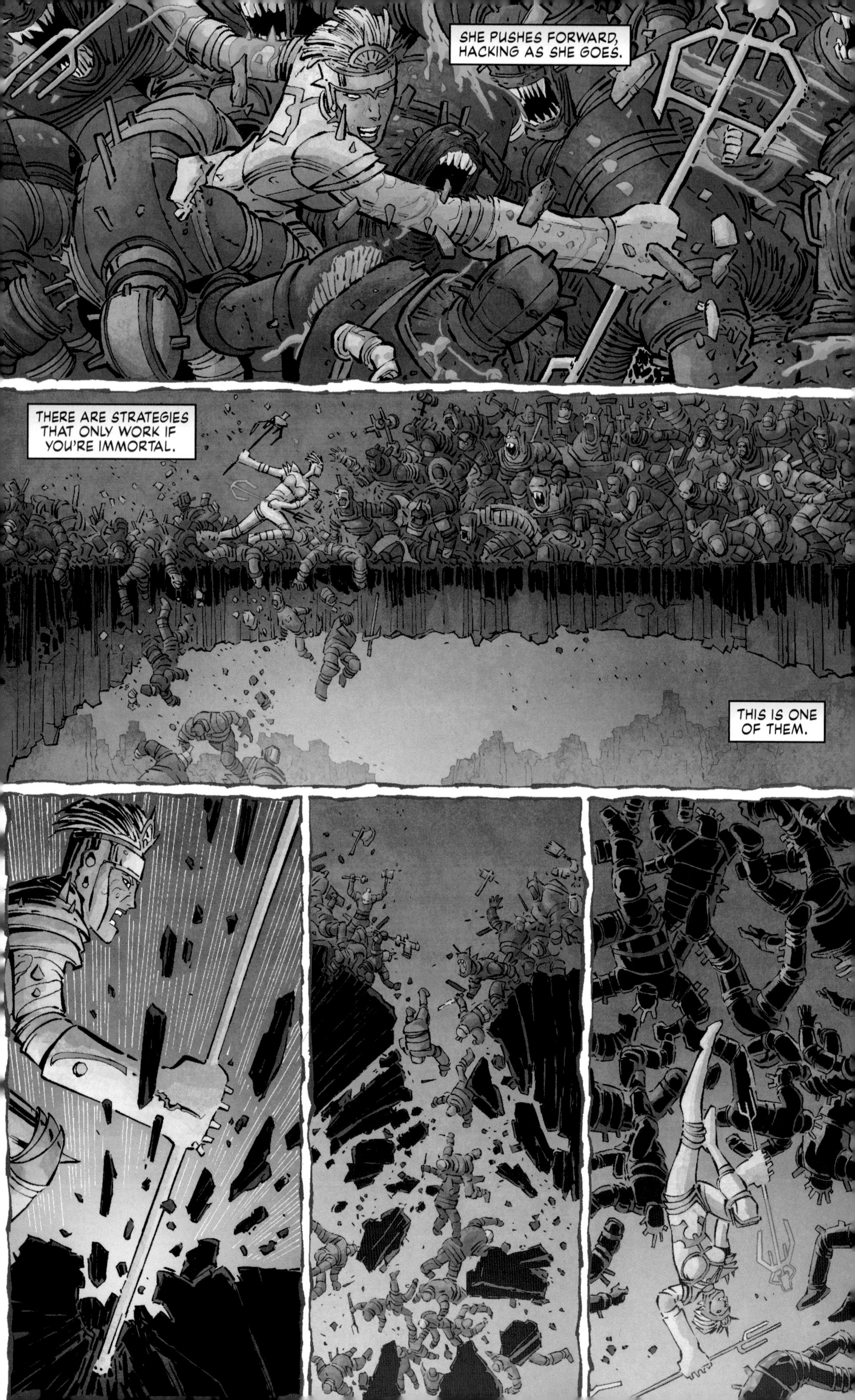
SHE PUSHES FORWARD, HACKING AS SHE GOES.
THERE ARE STRATEGIES THAT ONLY WORK IF YOU'RE IMMORTAL.
THIS IS ONE OF THEM.

MOMMA?

JOEY? MOMMA HAD A **BAD DREAM...** THAT'S ALL.

IT'S OKAY. I'M **SORRY,** HON. EVERYTHING'S OKAY.

MOMMA?

AND AS SHE LOOKS AT HER HANDS, SHE UNDERSTANDS.

SHE KNOWS **WHAT** SHE IS.

IT'S **STILL** MOMMA, JOEY. COME TO MOMMA.

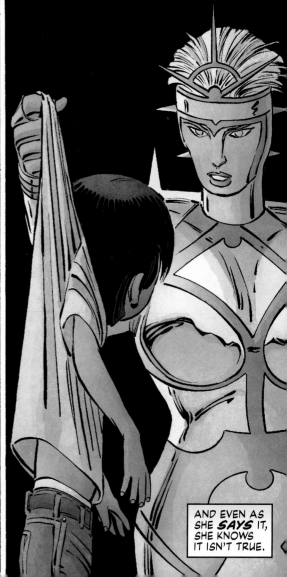

AND EVEN AS SHE **SAYS** IT, SHE KNOWS IT ISN'T TRUE.

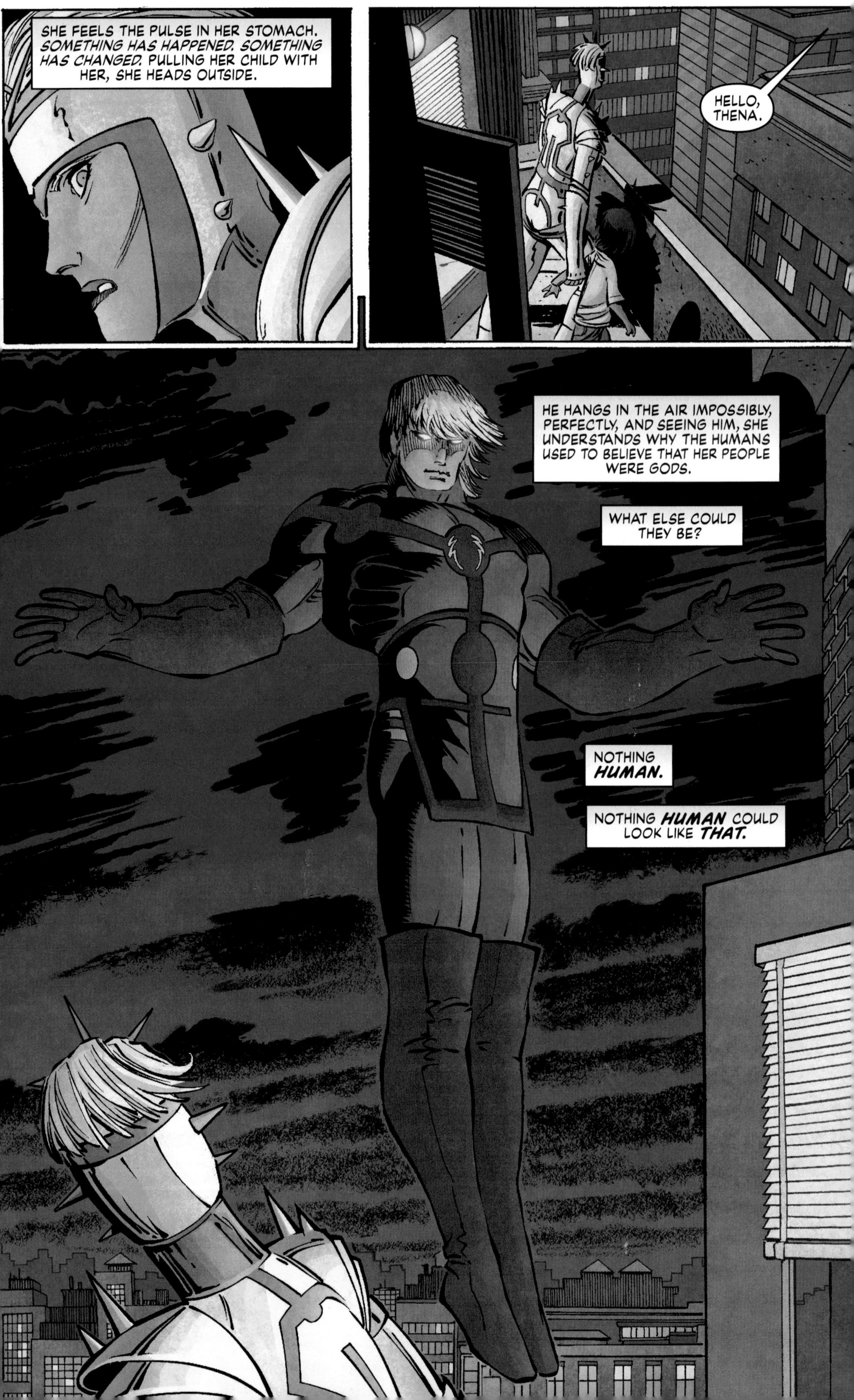
SHE FEELS THE PULSE IN HER STOMACH. *SOMETHING HAS HAPPENED. SOMETHING HAS CHANGED.* PULLING HER CHILD WITH HER, SHE HEADS OUTSIDE.
HELLO, THENA.
HE HANGS IN THE AIR IMPOSSIBLY, PERFECTLY, AND SEEING HIM, SHE UNDERSTANDS WHY THE HUMANS USED TO BELIEVE THAT HER PEOPLE WERE GODS.
WHAT ELSE COULD THEY BE?
NOTHING ***HUMAN.***
NOTHING ***HUMAN*** COULD LOOK LIKE ***THAT.***

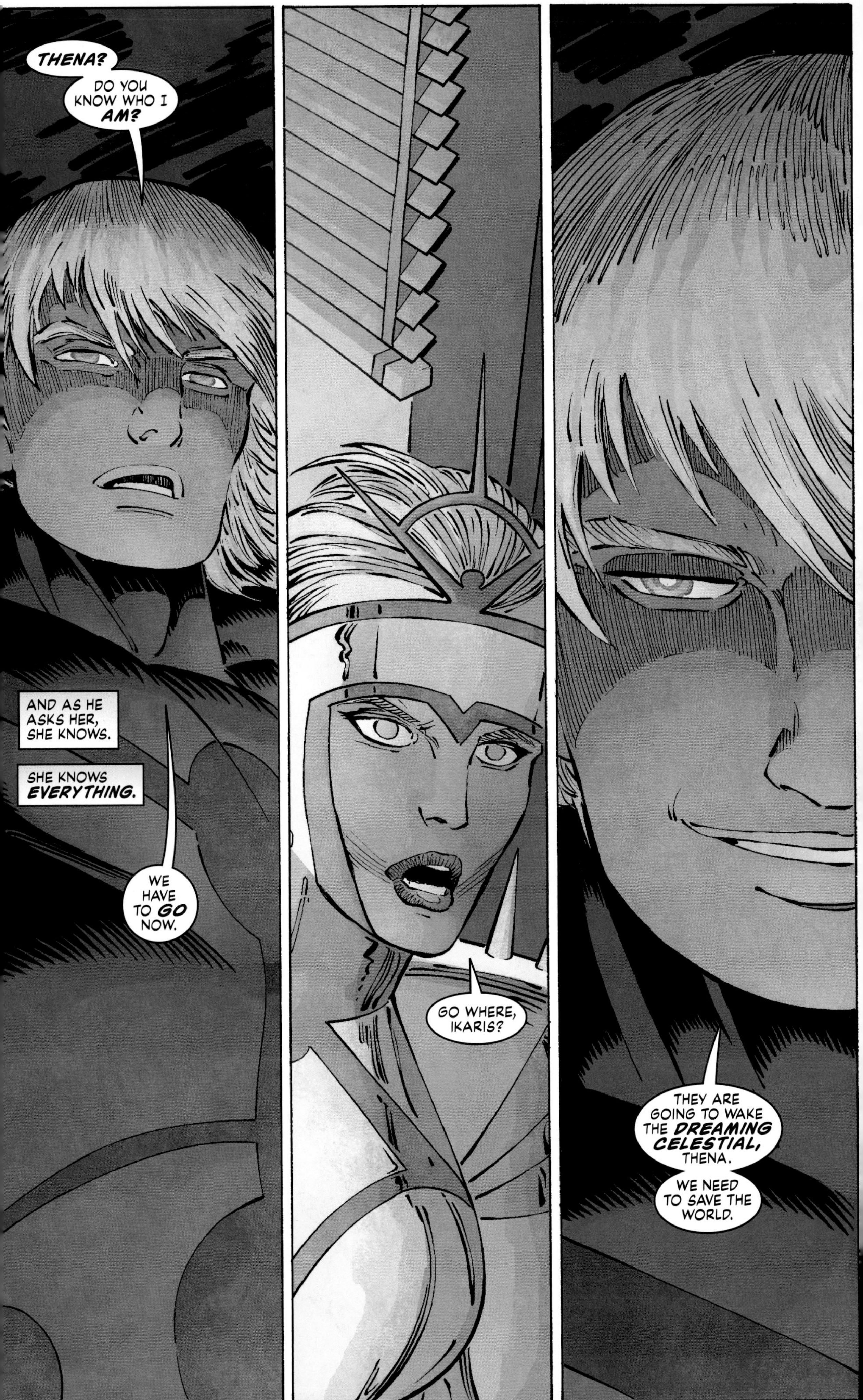
THENA?
DO YOU KNOW WHO I AM?
AND AS HE ASKS HER, SHE KNOWS.
SHE KNOWS EVERYTHING.
WE HAVE TO GO NOW.
GO WHERE, IKARIS?
THEY ARE GOING TO WAKE THE DREAMING CELESTIAL, THENA.
WE NEED TO SAVE THE WORLD.

CHAPTER FIVE: RIGHT TO LIFE

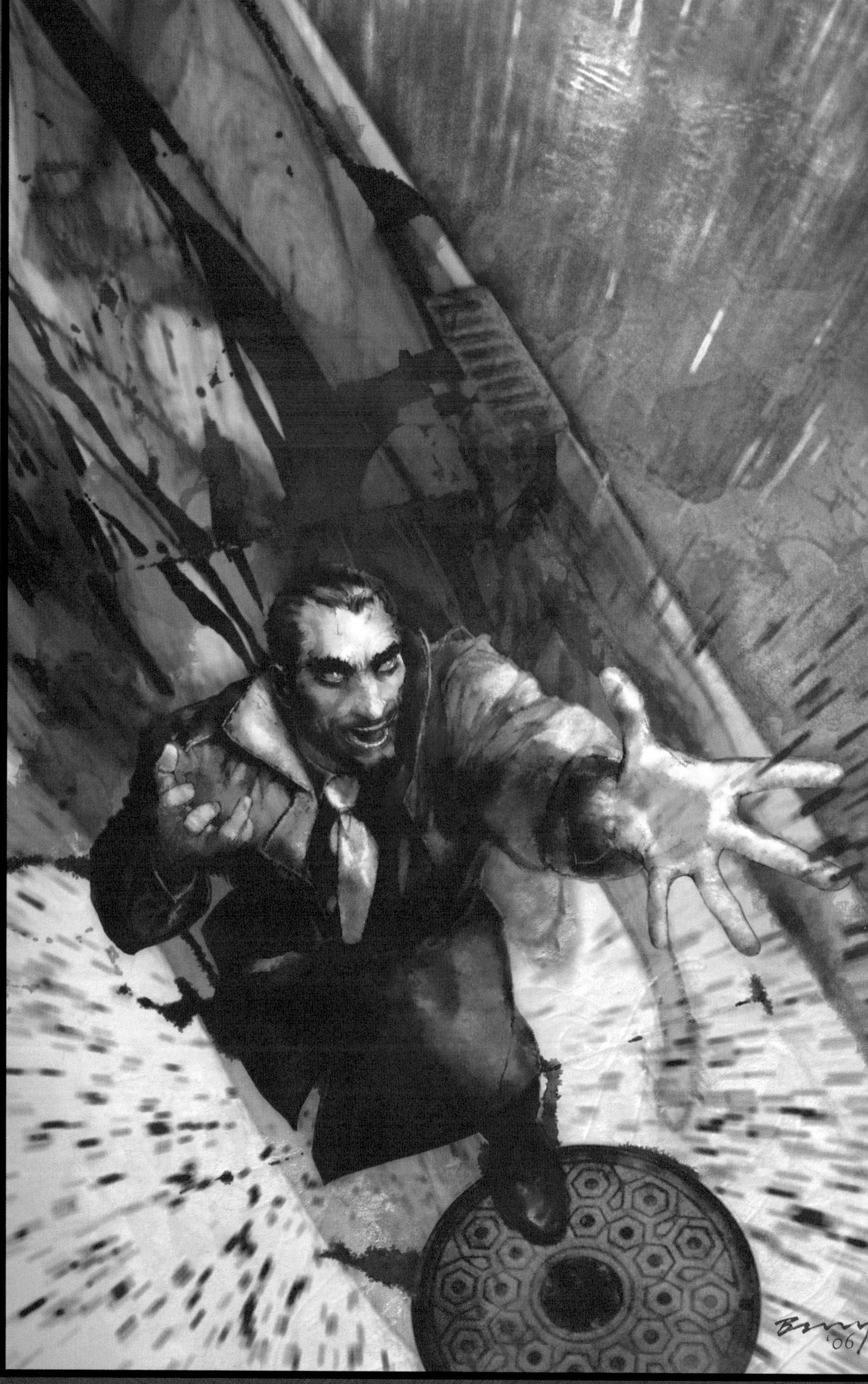

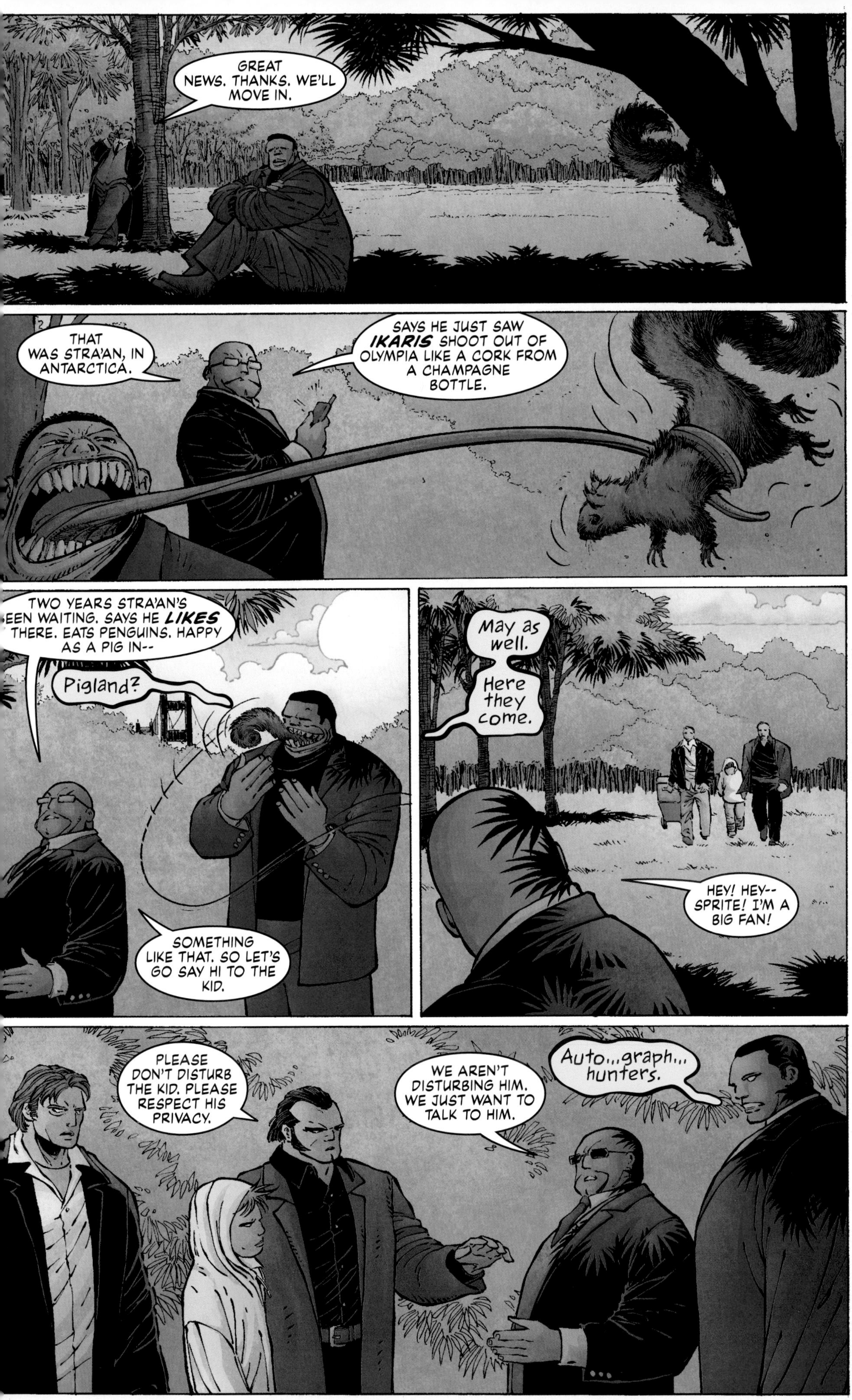
GREAT NEWS. THANKS. WE'LL MOVE IN.
THAT WAS STRA'AN, IN ANTARCTICA.
SAYS HE JUST SAW IKARIS SHOOT OUT OF OLYMPIA LIKE A CORK FROM A CHAMPAGNE BOTTLE.
TWO YEARS STRA'AN'S BEEN WAITING. SAYS HE LIKES THERE. EATS PENGUINS. HAPPY AS A PIG IN--
Pigland?
SOMETHING LIKE THAT. SO LET'S GO SAY HI TO THE KID.
May as well.
Here they come.
HEY! HEY-- SPRITE! I'M A BIG FAN!
PLEASE DON'T DISTURB THE KID. PLEASE RESPECT HIS PRIVACY.
WE AREN'T DISTURBING HIM. WE JUST WANT TO TALK TO HIM.
Auto...graph... hunters.

UHHH...THE HOSPITAL?

GOOD CALL.

GO FAR AND GO FAST...

"...AND DO NOT LOOK BACK."

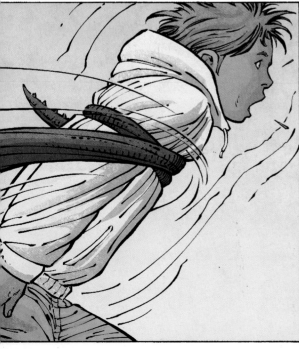

Tag. You're it.

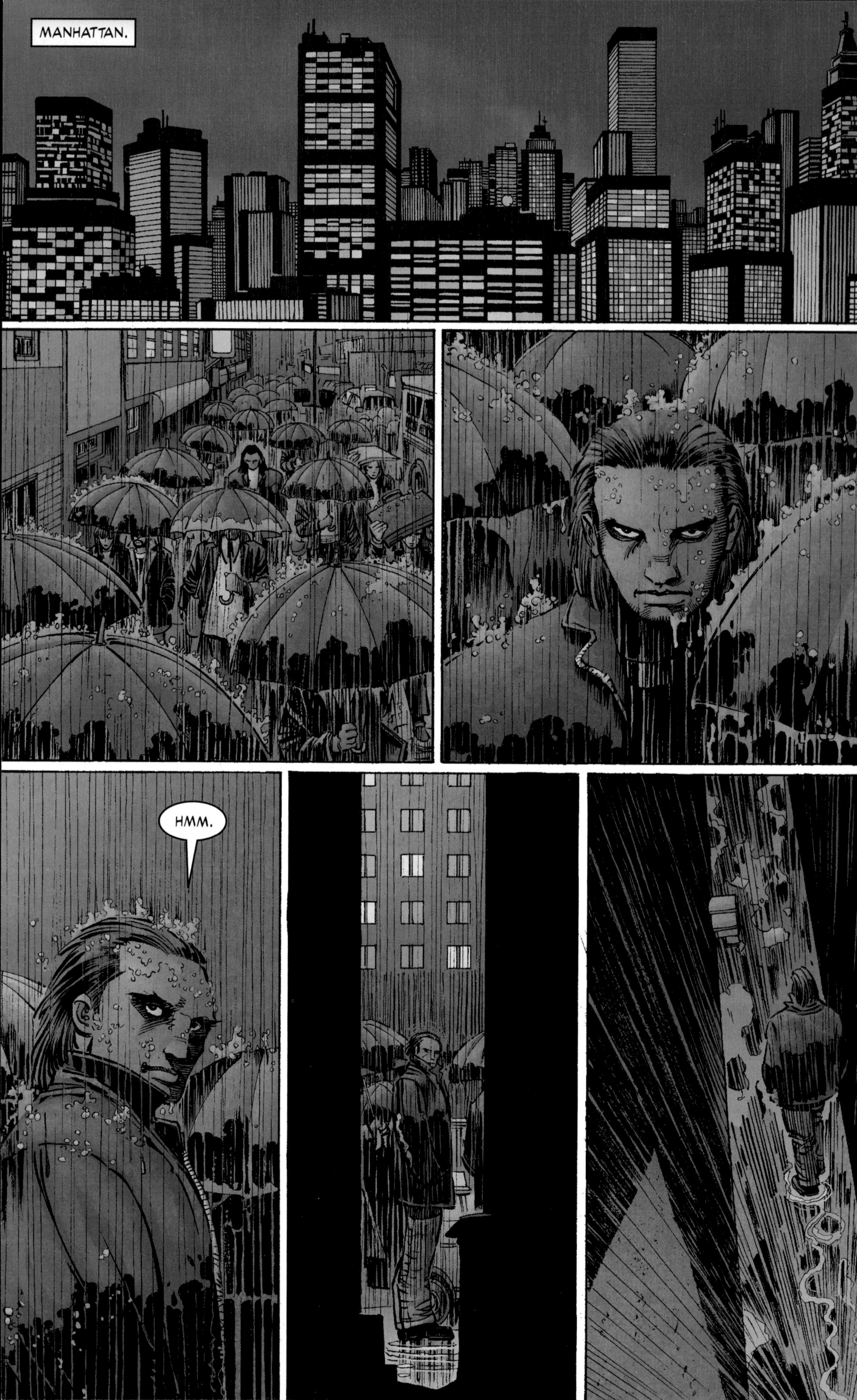
MANHATTAN.
HMM.

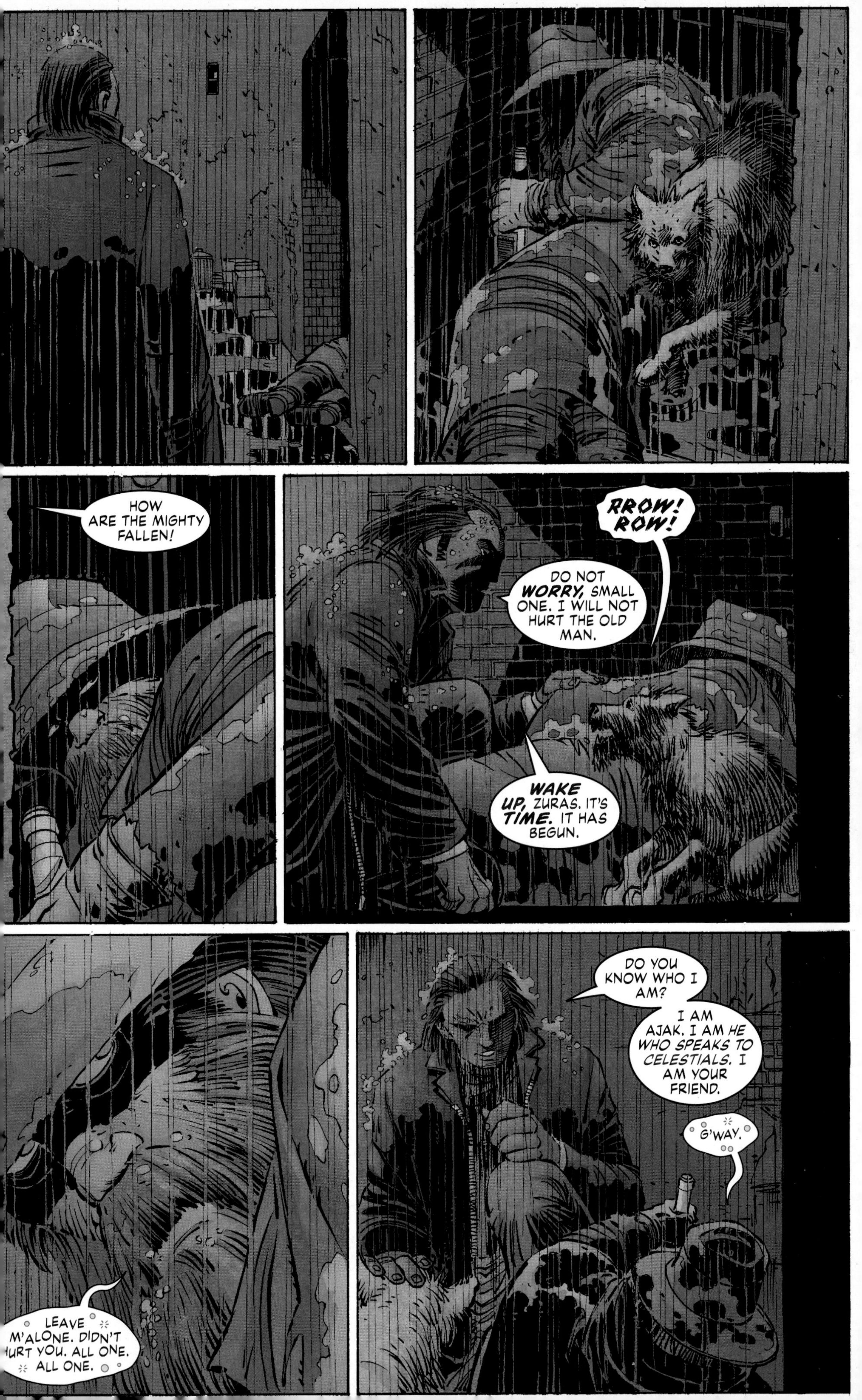
HOW ARE THE MIGHTY FALLEN!
RROW! ROW!
DO NOT WORRY, SMALL ONE. I WILL NOT HURT THE OLD MAN.
WAKE UP, ZURAS. IT'S TIME. IT HAS BEGUN.
LEAVE M'ALONE. DIDN'T HURT YOU. ALL ONE. ALL ONE.
DO YOU KNOW WHO I AM?
I AM AJAK. I AM HE WHO SPEAKS TO CELESTIALS. I AM YOUR FRIEND.
G'WAY.

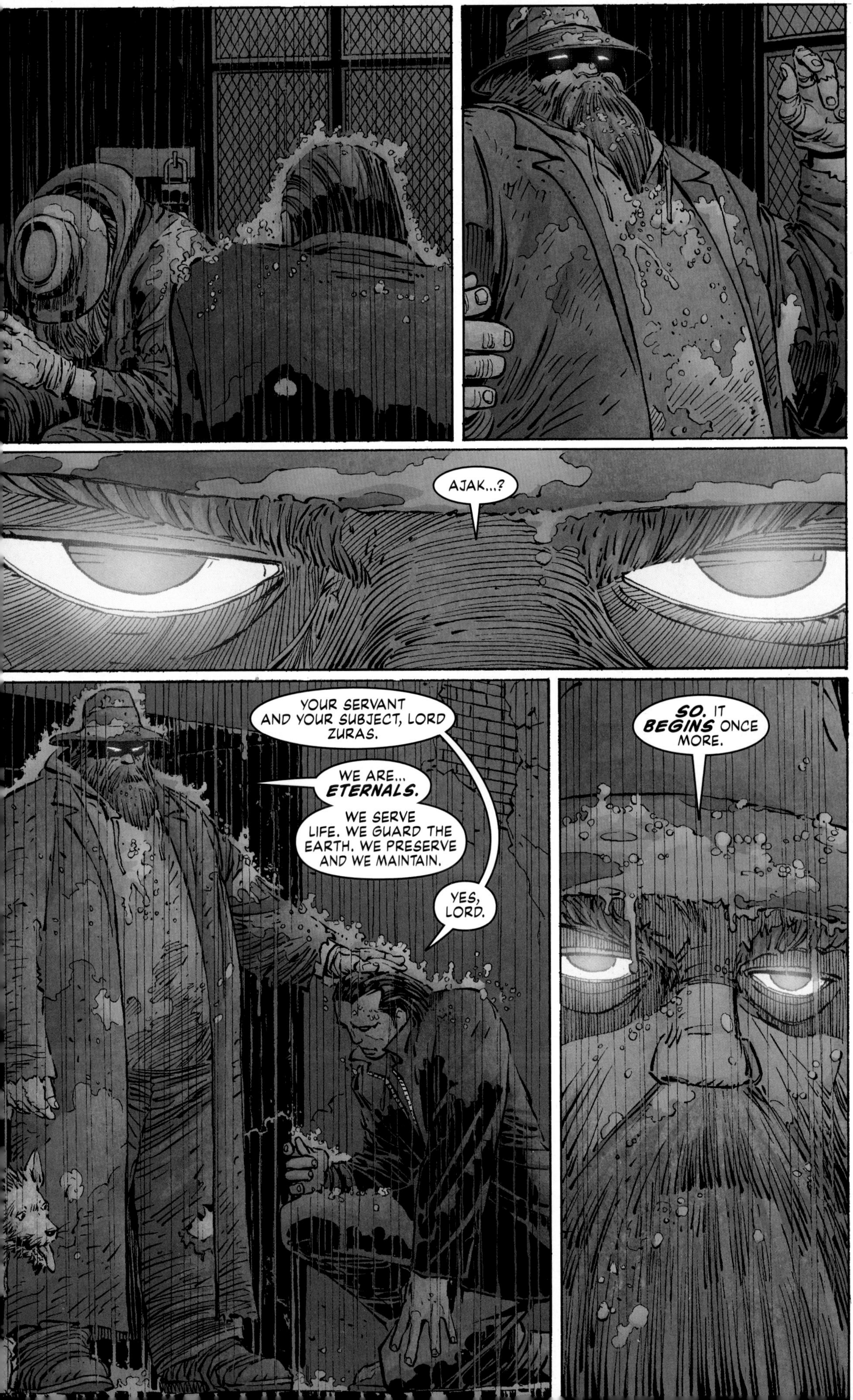
AJAK...?
YOUR SERVANT AND YOUR SUBJECT, LORD ZURAS.
WE ARE... ETERNALS.
WE SERVE LIFE. WE GUARD THE EARTH. WE PRESERVE AND WE MAINTAIN.
YES, LORD.
SO. IT BEGINS ONCE MORE.

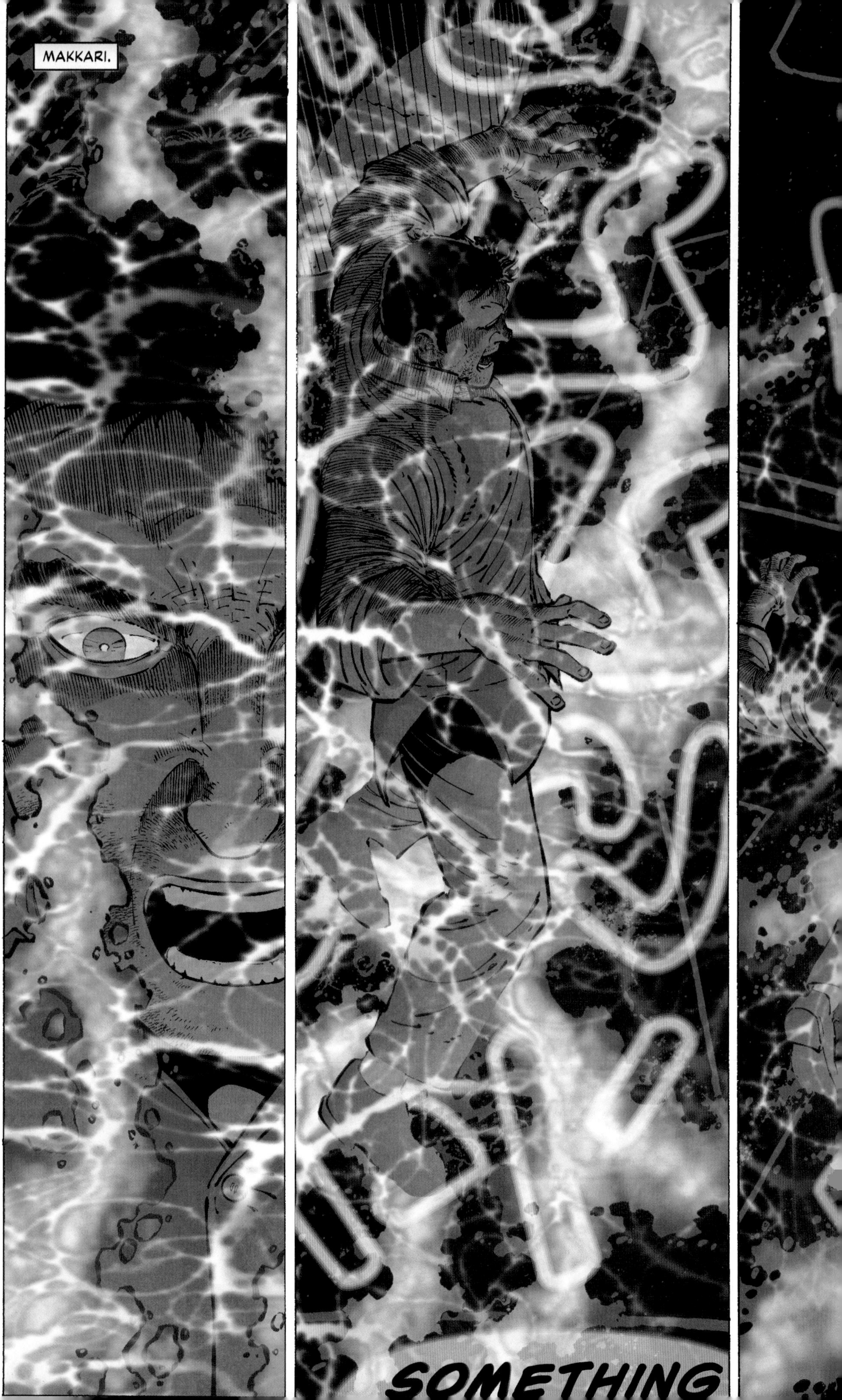
MAKKARI.
SOMETHING

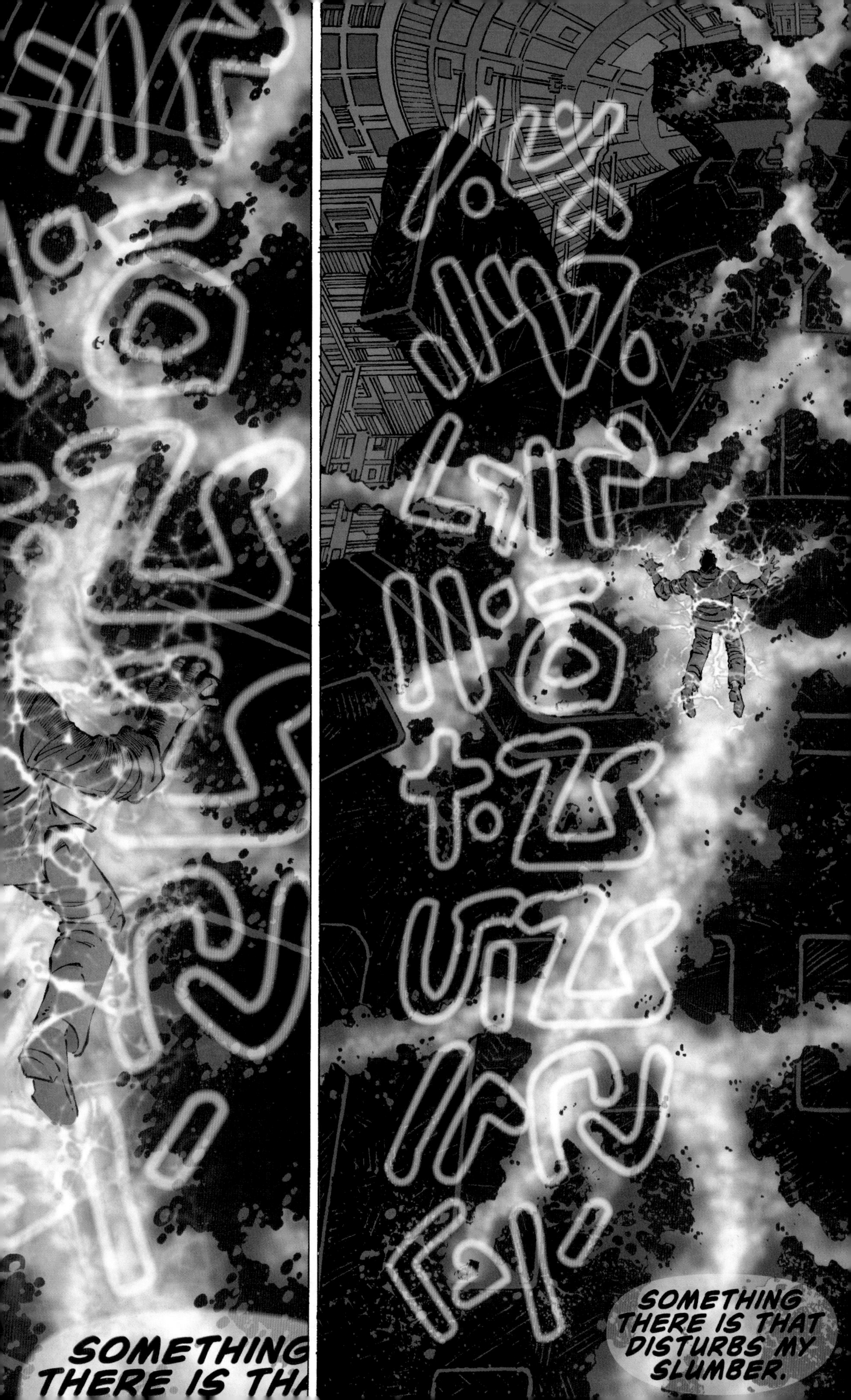
SOMETHING THERE IS THA
SOMETHING THERE IS THAT DISTURBS MY SLUMBER.

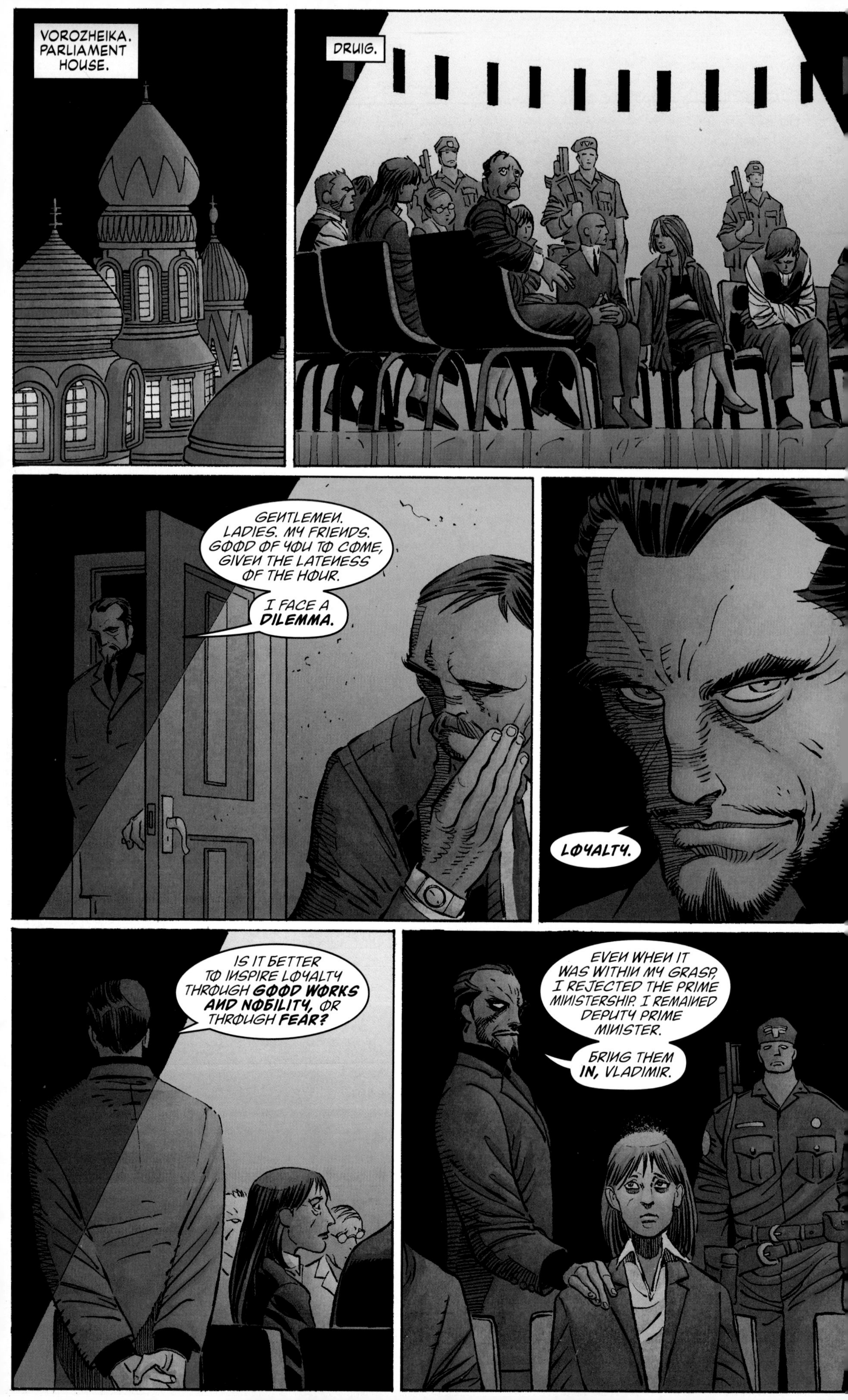
VOROZHEIKA. PARLIAMENT HOUSE.
DRUIG.
GENTLEMEN. LADIES. MY FRIENDS. GOOD OF YOU TO COME, GIVEN THE LATENESS OF THE HOUR.
I FACE A DILEMMA.
LOYALTY.
IS IT BETTER TO INSPIRE LOYALTY THROUGH GOOD WORKS AND NOBILITY, OR THROUGH FEAR?
EVEN WHEN IT WAS WITHIN MY GRASP, I REJECTED THE PRIME MINISTERSHIP. I REMAINED DEPUTY PRIME MINISTER.
BRING THEM IN, VLADIMIR.

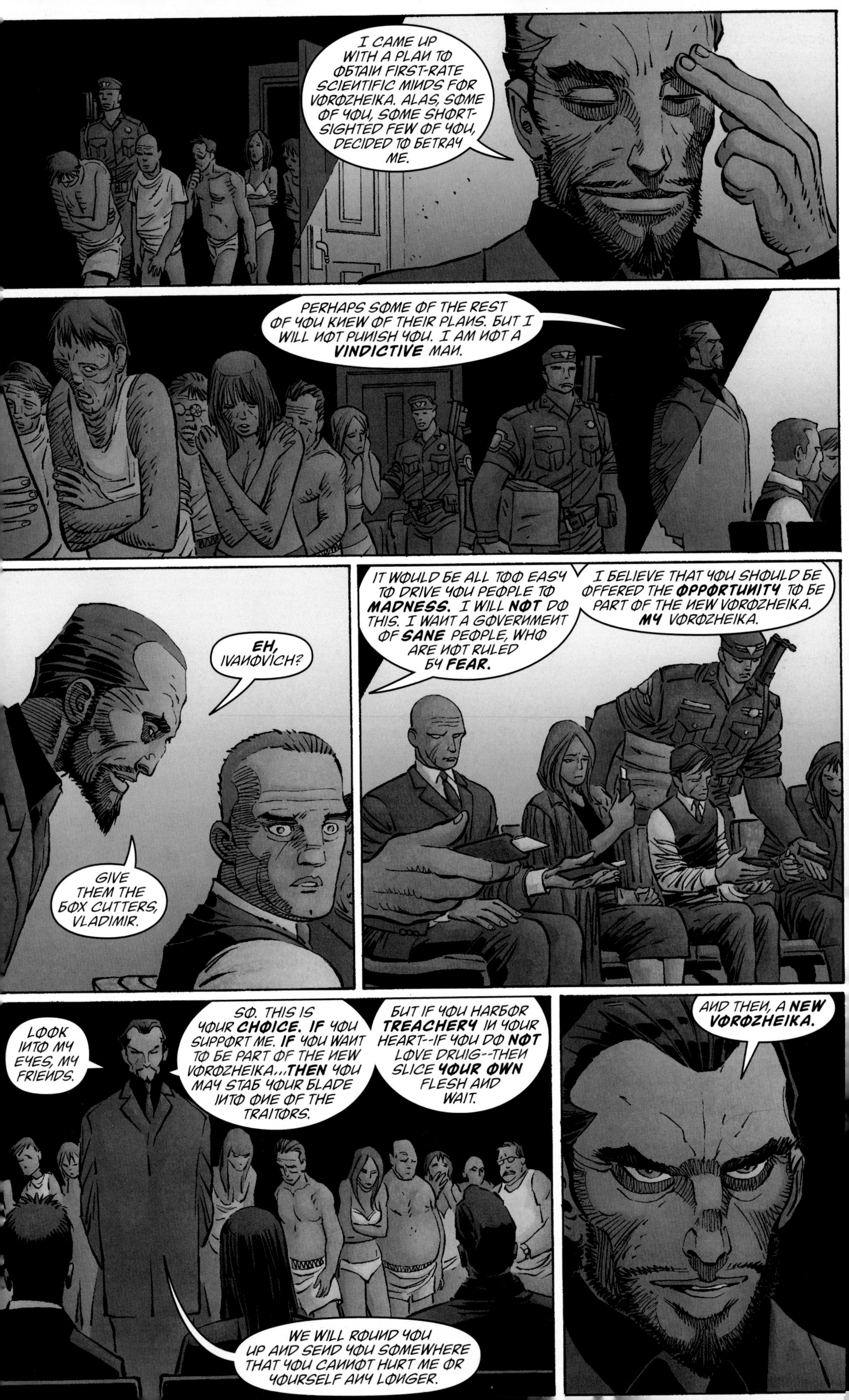
I CAME UP WITH A PLAN TO OBTAIN FIRST-RATE SCIENTIFIC MINDS FOR VOROZHEIKA. ALAS, SOME OF YOU, SOME SHORT-SIGHTED FEW OF YOU, DECIDED TO BETRAY ME.
PERHAPS SOME OF THE REST OF YOU KNEW OF THEIR PLANS. BUT I WILL NOT PUNISH YOU. I AM NOT A **VINDICTIVE** MAN.
EH, IVANOVICH?
GIVE THEM THE BOX CUTTERS, VLADIMIR.
IT WOULD BE ALL TOO EASY TO DRIVE YOU PEOPLE TO **MADNESS.** I WILL **NOT** DO THIS. I WANT A GOVERNMENT OF **SANE** PEOPLE, WHO ARE NOT RULED BY **FEAR.**
I BELIEVE THAT YOU SHOULD BE OFFERED THE **OPPORTUNITY** TO BE PART OF THE NEW VOROZHEIKA. **MY** VOROZHEIKA.
LOOK INTO MY EYES, MY FRIENDS.
SO. THIS IS YOUR **CHOICE. IF** YOU SUPPORT ME. **IF** YOU WANT TO BE PART OF THE NEW VOROZHEIKA... **THEN** YOU MAY STAB YOUR BLADE INTO ONE OF THE TRAITORS.
BUT IF YOU HARBOR **TREACHERY** IN YOUR HEART--IF YOU DO **NOT** LOVE DRUIG--THEN SLICE **YOUR OWN** FLESH AND WAIT.
WE WILL ROUND YOU UP AND SEND YOU SOMEWHERE THAT YOU CANNOT HURT ME OR YOURSELF ANY LONGER.
AND THEN, A **NEW VOROZHEIKA.**

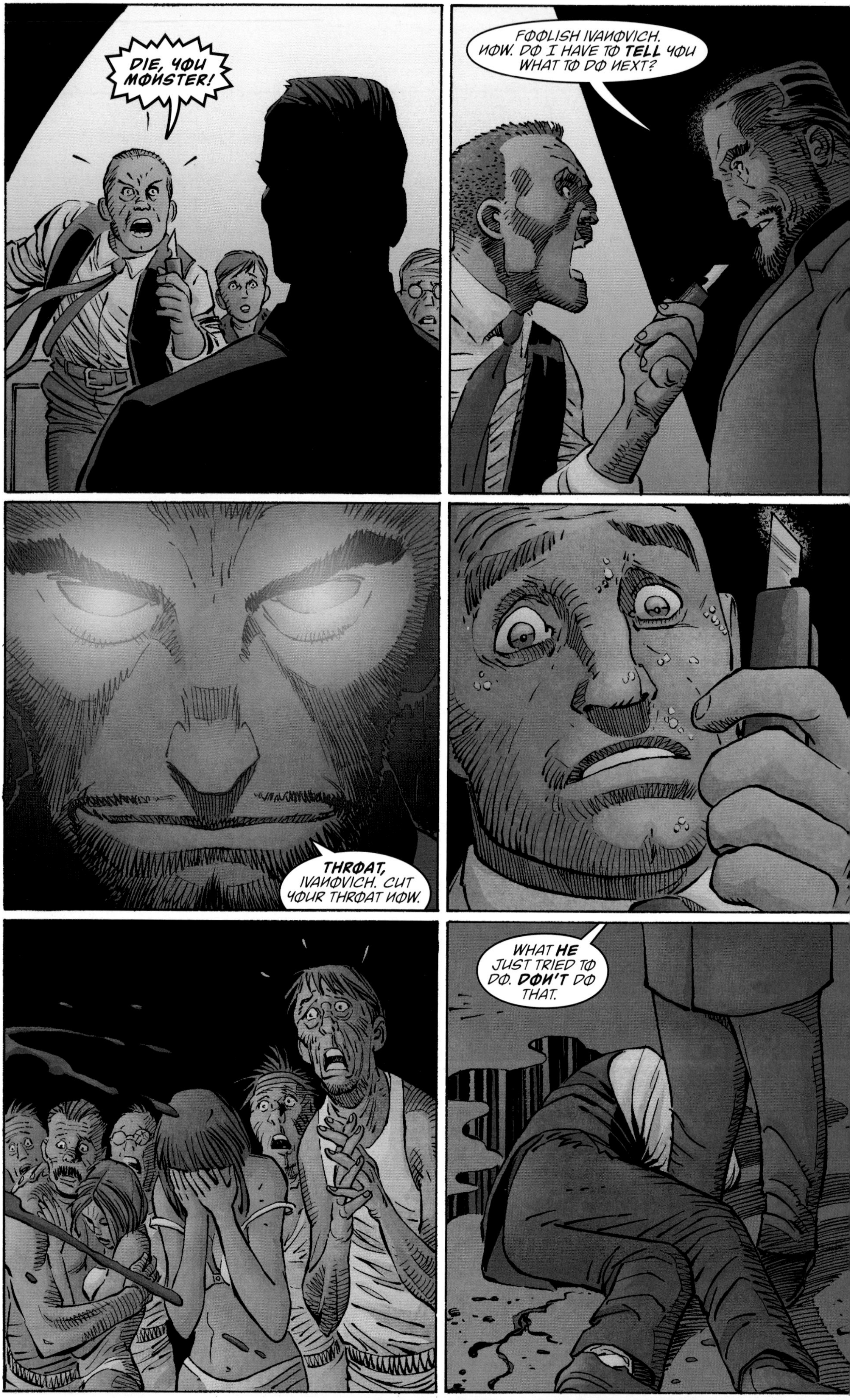
DIE, YOU MONSTER!
FOOLISH IVANOVICH. NOW. DO I HAVE TO TELL YOU WHAT TO DO NEXT?
THROAT, IVANOVICH. CUT YOUR THROAT NOW.
WHAT HE JUST TRIED TO DO. DON'T DO THAT.

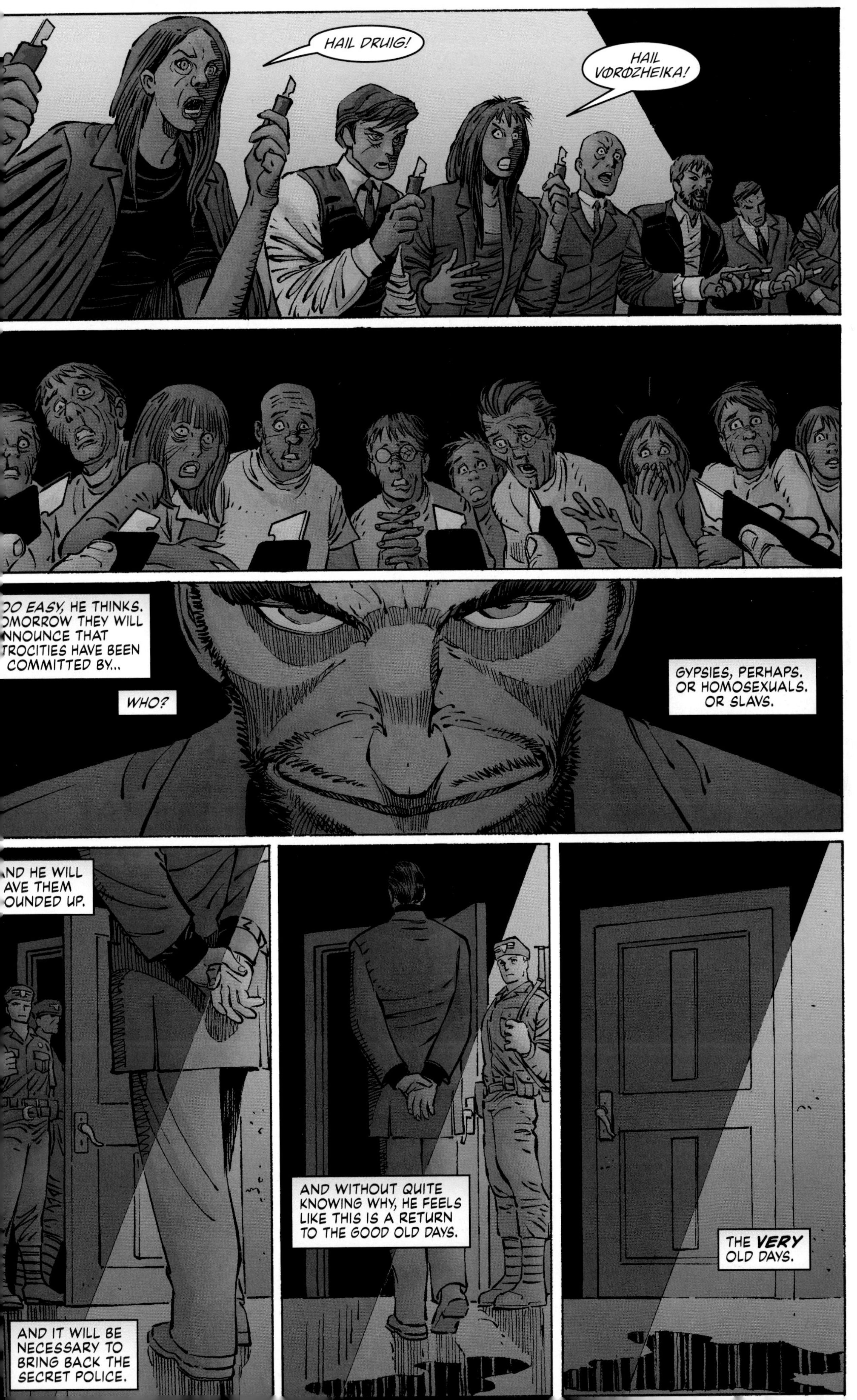
HAIL DRUIG!
HAIL VØRØZHEIKA!
OO EASY, HE THINKS. OMORROW THEY WILL NNOUNCE THAT TROCITIES HAVE BEEN COMMITTED BY...
WHO?
GYPSIES, PERHAPS. OR HOMOSEXUALS. OR SLAVS.
ND HE WILL AVE THEM OUNDED UP.
AND IT WILL BE NECESSARY TO BRING BACK THE SECRET POLICE.
AND WITHOUT QUITE KNOWING WHY, HE FEELS LIKE THIS IS A RETURN TO THE GOOD OLD DAYS.
THE VERY OLD DAYS.

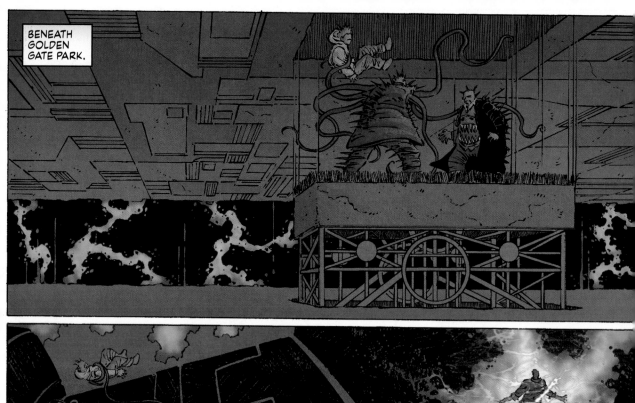

BENEATH GOLDEN GATE PARK.

WHAT *HO*, MR. CURRY! SUCH FUN TO SEE YOU AGAIN SO SOON. REMEMBER *US*?

I'M AFRAID THAT LAST TIME WE SPOKE WE TOLD YOU A FEW LITTLE WHITE LIES, FOR THE GREATER GOOD. I TRUST THAT YOU CAN FIND IT IN YOUR HEART TO *FORGIVE* US.

I AM *MORJAK*. MY FRIEND OVER THERE IS *GELT*. WE ARE TWO OF THE *CHANGING PEOPLE*. THAT'S WHAT WE CALL OURSELVES, ANYWAY.

YOU ETERNALS HAVE YOUR OWN NAMES FOR US.

Deviants. Mongrels. Subhumans. Scum.

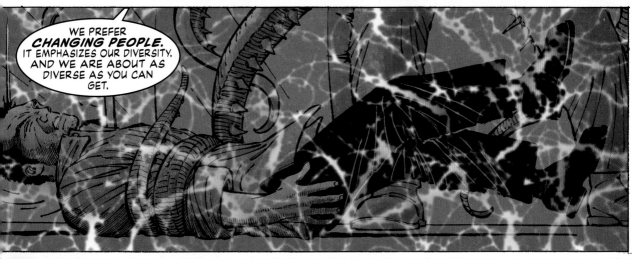

WE PREFER *CHANGING PEOPLE.* IT EMPHASIZES OUR DIVERSITY. AND WE ARE ABOUT AS DIVERSE AS YOU CAN GET.

LET *GO* OF ME!

GELT, PUT SOMETHING IN THE LITTLE ONE'S MOUTH. OR CHEW OFF ITS TONGUE.

NO!

Then you...be quiet...

YOU ETERNALS HAVE *LONG LIVES,* BUT *SHORT MEMORIES.* THE CHANGING PEOPLE HAVE SHORT LIVES, BUT WE DO NOT FORGET.

DON'T EXPECT US TO *KILL* YOU, EITHER. IT WAS HARD ENOUGH KILLING IKARIS. *HE* WON'T BE GRATEFUL. YOU'LL SEE. ANYWAY, ONE FULL ETERNAL IS ENOUGH.

IT WAS A *CRIME AGAINST LIFE.* THAT WAS WHAT THE CELESTIALS TOLD AJAK. AND THAT WAS TRUE IN ITS WAY.

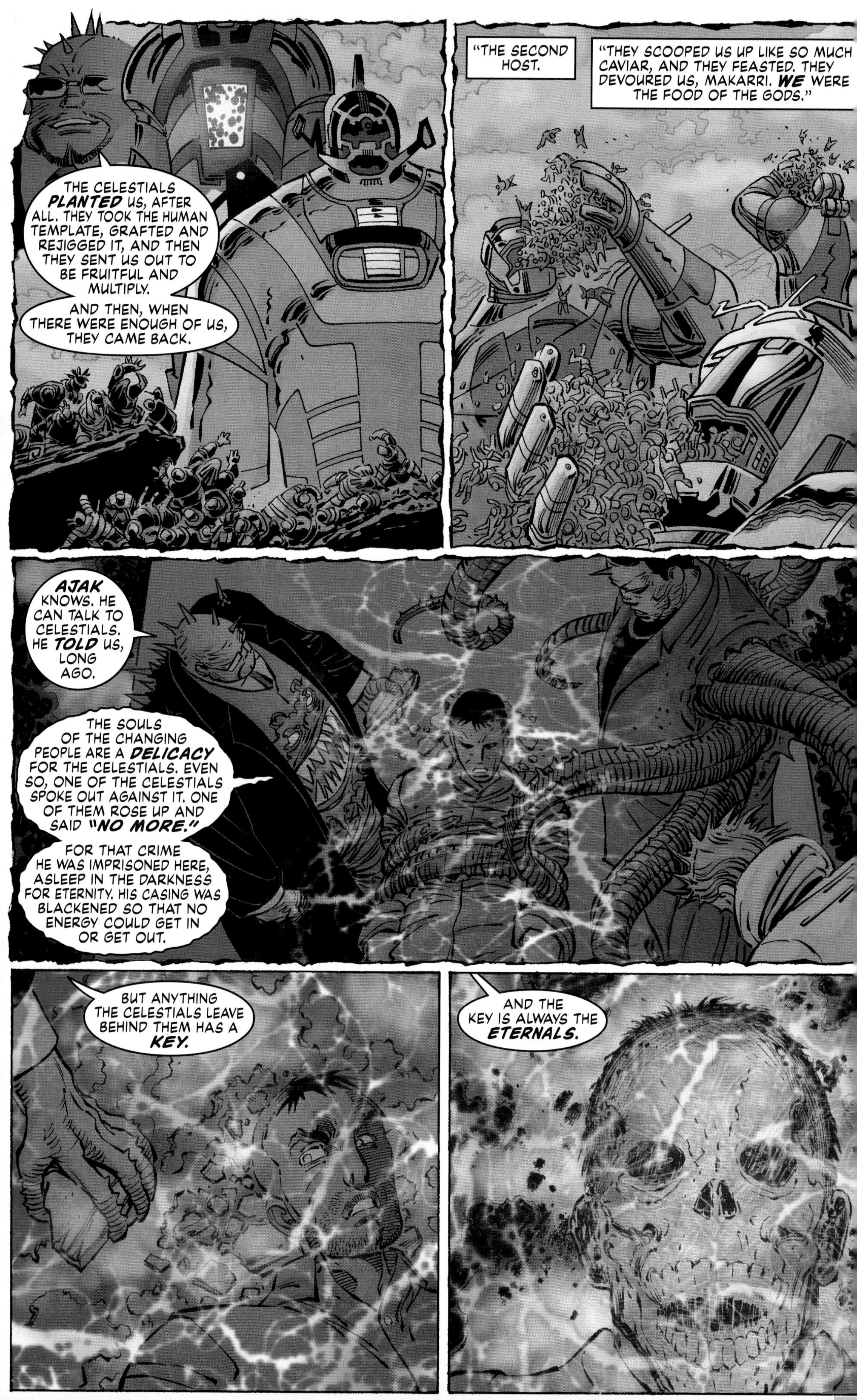
THE CELESTIALS PLANTED US, AFTER ALL. THEY TOOK THE HUMAN TEMPLATE, GRAFTED AND REJIGGED IT, AND THEN THEY SENT US OUT TO BE FRUITFUL AND MULTIPLY.
AND THEN, WHEN THERE WERE ENOUGH OF US, THEY CAME BACK.
"THE SECOND HOST.
"THEY SCOOPED US UP LIKE SO MUCH CAVIAR, AND THEY FEASTED. THEY DEVOURED US, MAKARRI. WE WERE THE FOOD OF THE GODS."
AJAK KNOWS. HE CAN TALK TO CELESTIALS. HE TOLD US, LONG AGO.
THE SOULS OF THE CHANGING PEOPLE ARE A DELICACY FOR THE CELESTIALS. EVEN SO, ONE OF THE CELESTIALS SPOKE OUT AGAINST IT. ONE OF THEM ROSE UP AND SAID "NO MORE."
FOR THAT CRIME HE WAS IMPRISONED HERE, ASLEEP IN THE DARKNESS FOR ETERNITY. HIS CASING WAS BLACKENED SO THAT NO ENERGY COULD GET IN OR GET OUT.
BUT ANYTHING THE CELESTIALS LEAVE BEHIND THEM HAS A KEY.
AND THE KEY IS ALWAYS THE ETERNALS.

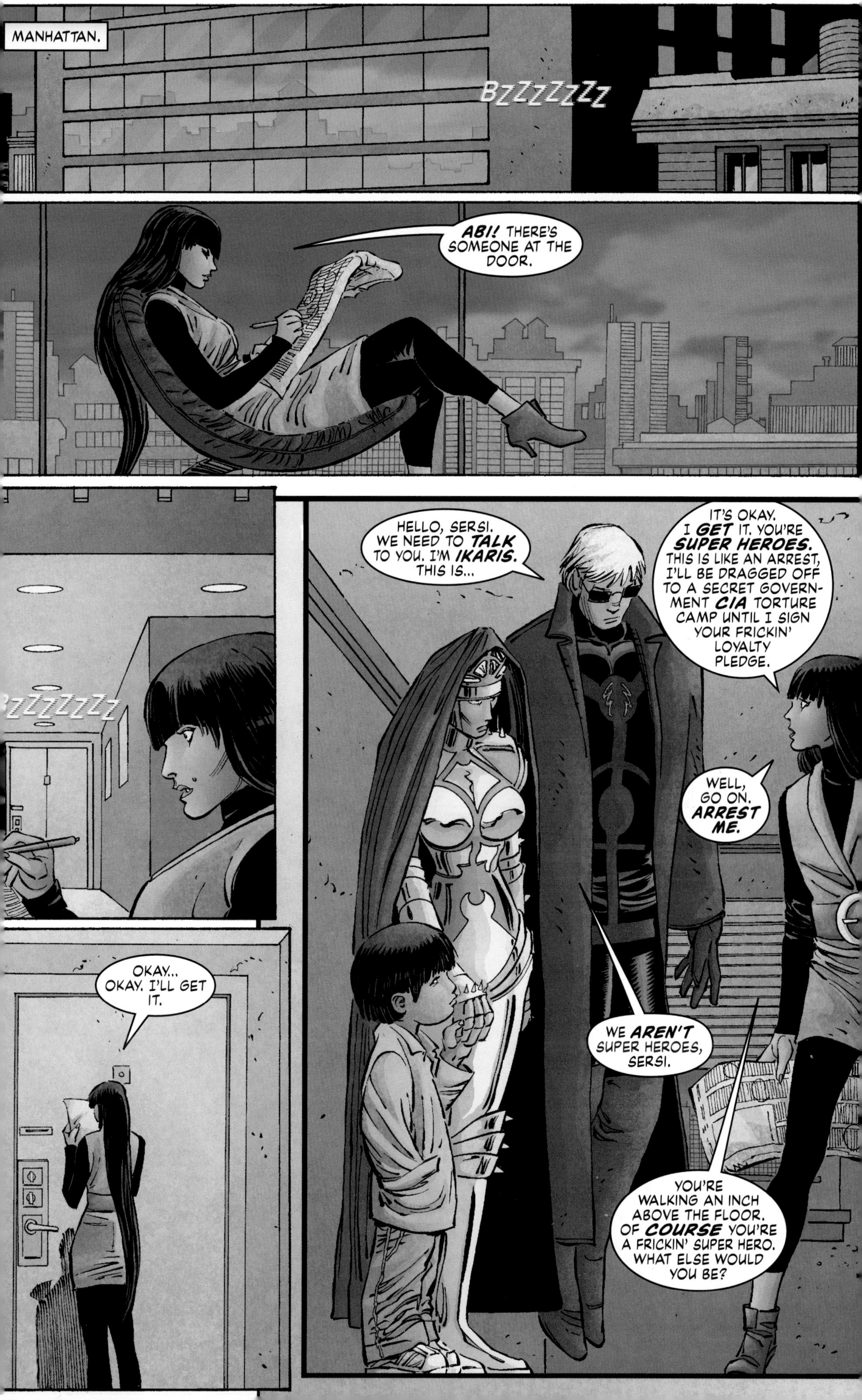
MANHATTAN.
BZZZZZZZ
ABI! THERE'S SOMEONE AT THE DOOR.
BZZZZZZZZ
OKAY... OKAY. I'LL GET IT.
HELLO, SERSI. WE NEED TO TALK TO YOU. I'M IKARIS. THIS IS...
IT'S OKAY. I GET IT. YOU'RE SUPER HEROES. THIS IS LIKE AN ARREST, I'LL BE DRAGGED OFF TO A SECRET GOVERNMENT CIA TORTURE CAMP UNTIL I SIGN YOUR FRICKIN' LOYALTY PLEDGE.
WELL, GO ON. ARREST ME.
WE AREN'T SUPER HEROES, SERSI.
YOU'RE WALKING AN INCH ABOVE THE FLOOR. OF COURSE YOU'RE A FRICKIN' SUPER HERO. WHAT ELSE WOULD YOU BE?

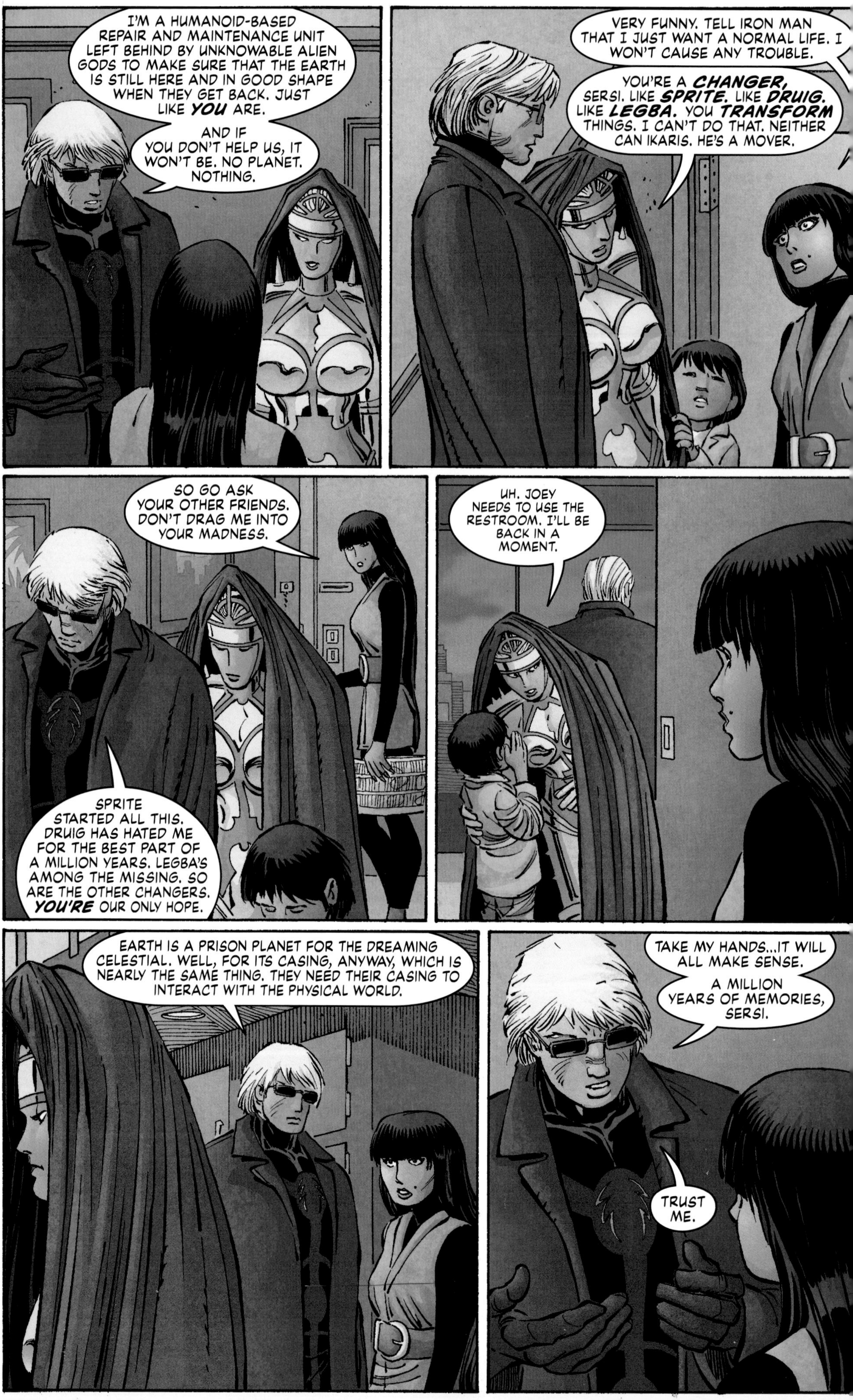
I'M A HUMANOID-BASED REPAIR AND MAINTENANCE UNIT LEFT BEHIND BY UNKNOWABLE ALIEN GODS TO MAKE SURE THAT THE EARTH IS STILL HERE AND IN GOOD SHAPE WHEN THEY GET BACK. JUST LIKE *YOU* ARE.
AND IF YOU DON'T HELP US, IT WON'T BE. NO PLANET. NOTHING.
VERY FUNNY. TELL IRON MAN THAT I JUST WANT A NORMAL LIFE. I WON'T CAUSE ANY TROUBLE.
YOU'RE A *CHANGER,* SERSI. LIKE *SPRITE.* LIKE *DRUIG.* LIKE *LEGBA.* YOU *TRANSFORM* THINGS. I CAN'T DO THAT. NEITHER CAN IKARIS. HE'S A MOVER.
SO GO ASK YOUR OTHER FRIENDS. DON'T DRAG ME INTO YOUR MADNESS.
SPRITE STARTED ALL THIS. DRUIG HAS HATED ME FOR THE BEST PART OF A MILLION YEARS. LEGBA'S AMONG THE MISSING. SO ARE THE OTHER CHANGERS. *YOU'RE* OUR ONLY HOPE.
UH. JOEY NEEDS TO USE THE RESTROOM. I'LL BE BACK IN A MOMENT.
EARTH IS A PRISON PLANET FOR THE DREAMING CELESTIAL. WELL, FOR ITS CASING, ANYWAY, WHICH IS NEARLY THE SAME THING. THEY NEED THEIR CASING TO INTERACT WITH THE PHYSICAL WORLD.
TAKE MY HANDS...IT WILL ALL MAKE SENSE.
A MILLION YEARS OF MEMORIES, SERSI.
TRUST ME.

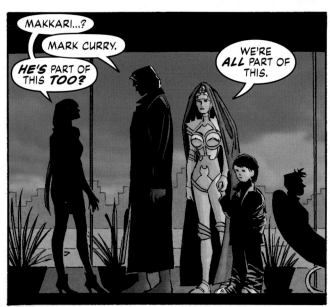

MAKKARI...?

MARK CURRY.

HE'S PART OF THIS *TOO?*

WE'RE *ALL* PART OF THIS.

LET ME INTO YOUR *MIND*, SERSI. I CAN MAKE YOU WHOLE AGAIN.

OVER MY DEAD FRICKIN' BODY WHAT ABOUT THE *KID* WHAT'S THE DEAL WITH *HIM?*

THIS IS JOEY. HE'S MY SON. I'M *NOT* LEAVING HIM BEHIND.

HOLD ON. YOU'RE DOCTOR ELIOT? YOU WERE AT MY PARTY.

YES, HON. THAT'S WHERE JOEY'S DADDY WAS K-I-L-L-E-D.

DADDY WAS WHAT?

AND IKARIS TURNED YOU INTO *THAT?*

I WAS THIS ALL ALONG.

IF I...IF I GO ALONG WITH THIS...WHAT WOULD *I* TURN INTO?

YOU'RE JUST THE SAME. BETTER *HAIR*, MAYBE.

IF I HELP YOU, WILL YOU MAKE IT SO THAT ABI KNOWS WHO I *AM* AGAIN?

YOU COULD DO THAT YOURSELF.

I AM *SO* GOING TO REGRET THIS.

DO IT.

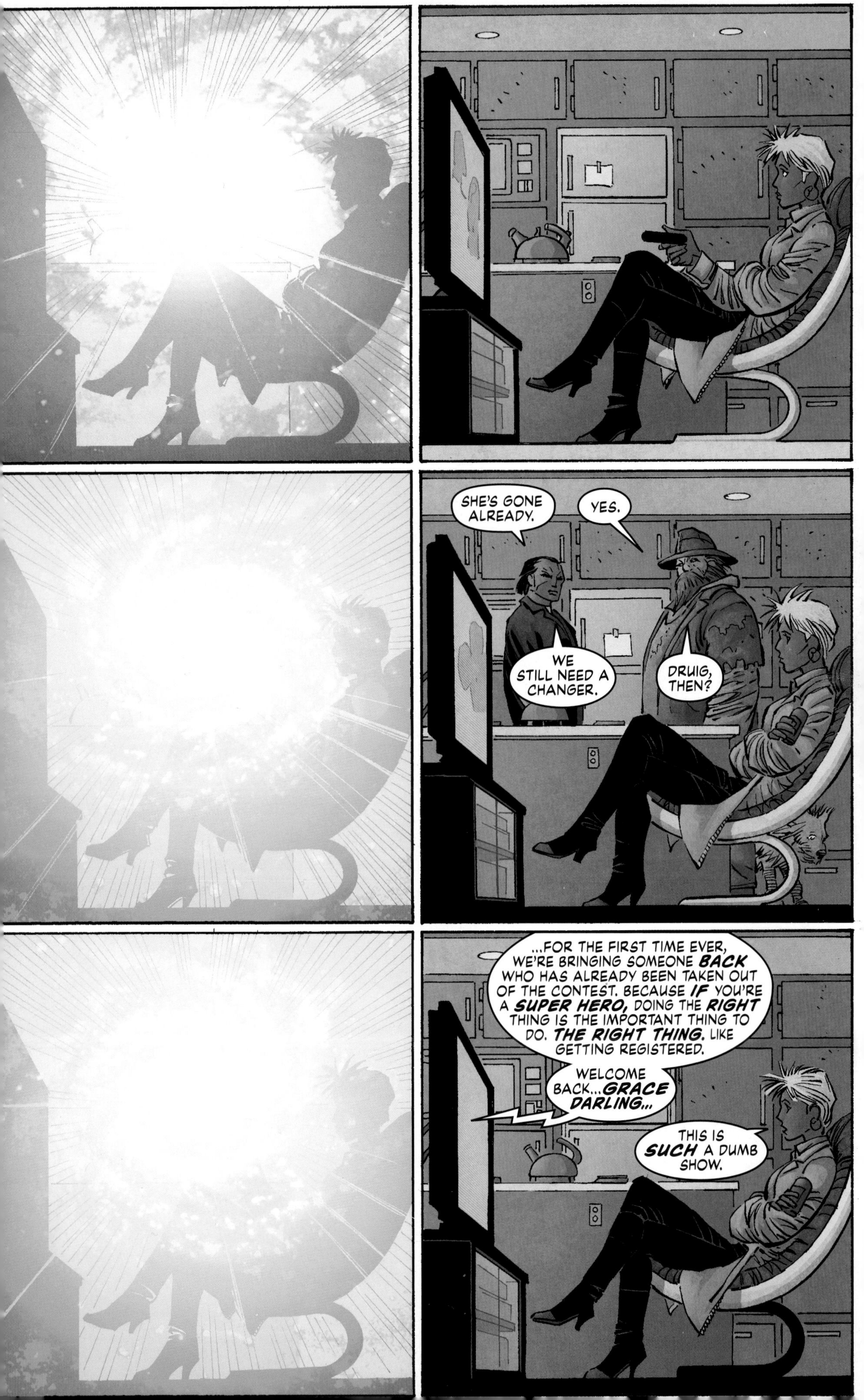
SHE'S GONE ALREADY.
YES.
WE STILL NEED A CHANGER.
DRUIG, THEN?
...FOR THE FIRST TIME EVER, WE'RE BRINGING SOMEONE BACK WHO HAS ALREADY BEEN TAKEN OUT OF THE CONTEST. BECAUSE IF YOU'RE A SUPER HERO, DOING THE RIGHT THING IS THE IMPORTANT THING TO DO. THE RIGHT THING. LIKE GETTING REGISTERED.
WELCOME BACK...GRACE DARLING...
THIS IS SUCH A DUMB SHOW.

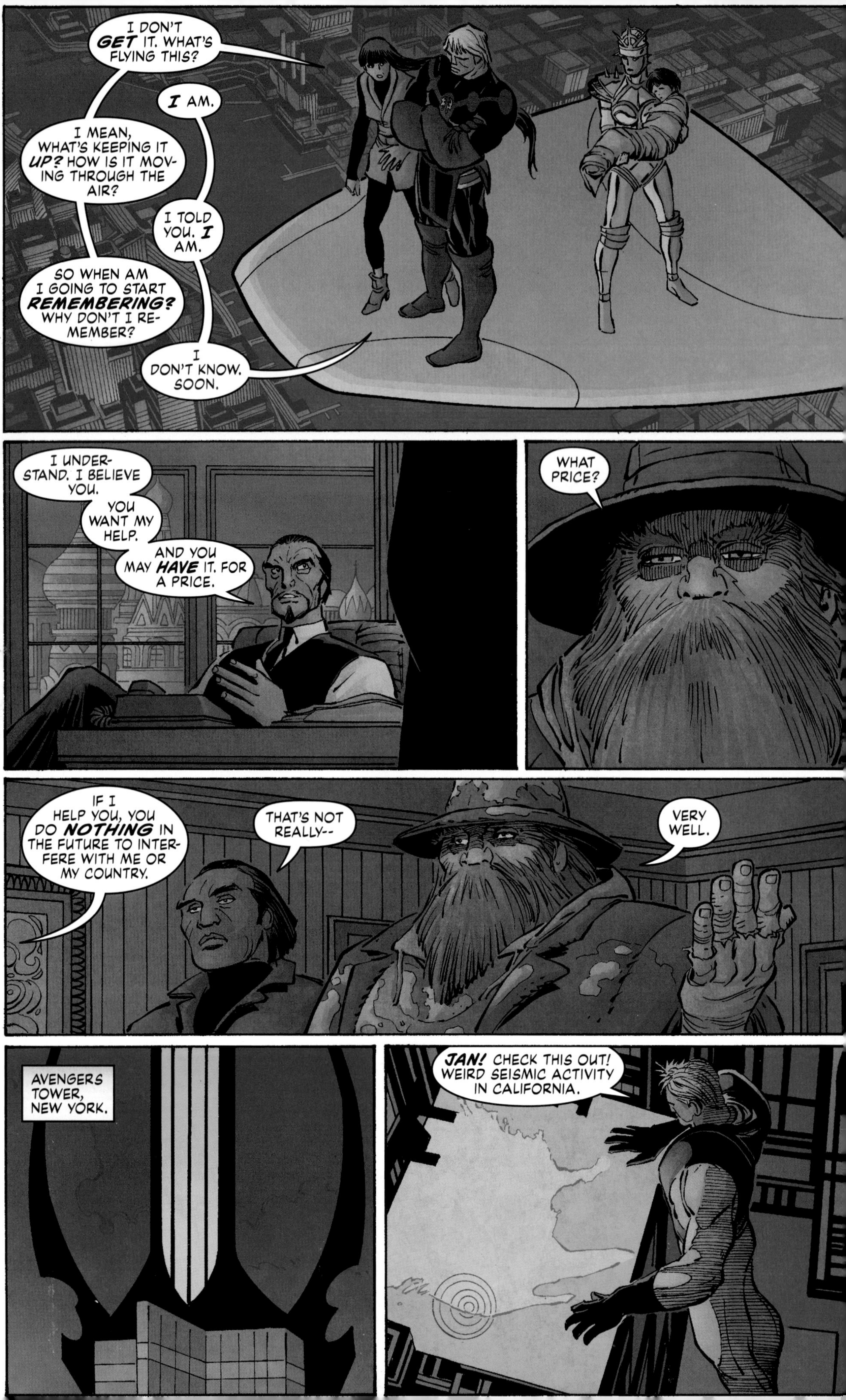
I DON'T GET IT. WHAT'S FLYING THIS?
I AM.
I MEAN, WHAT'S KEEPING IT UP? HOW IS IT MOVING THROUGH THE AIR?
I TOLD YOU. I AM.
SO WHEN AM I GOING TO START REMEMBERING? WHY DON'T I REMEMBER?
I DON'T KNOW. SOON.
I UNDERSTAND. I BELIEVE YOU.
YOU WANT MY HELP.
AND YOU MAY HAVE IT. FOR A PRICE.
WHAT PRICE?
IF I HELP YOU, YOU DO NOTHING IN THE FUTURE TO INTERFERE WITH ME OR MY COUNTRY.
THAT'S NOT REALLY--
VERY WELL.
AVENGERS TOWER, NEW YORK.
JAN! CHECK THIS OUT! WEIRD SEISMIC ACTIVITY IN CALIFORNIA.

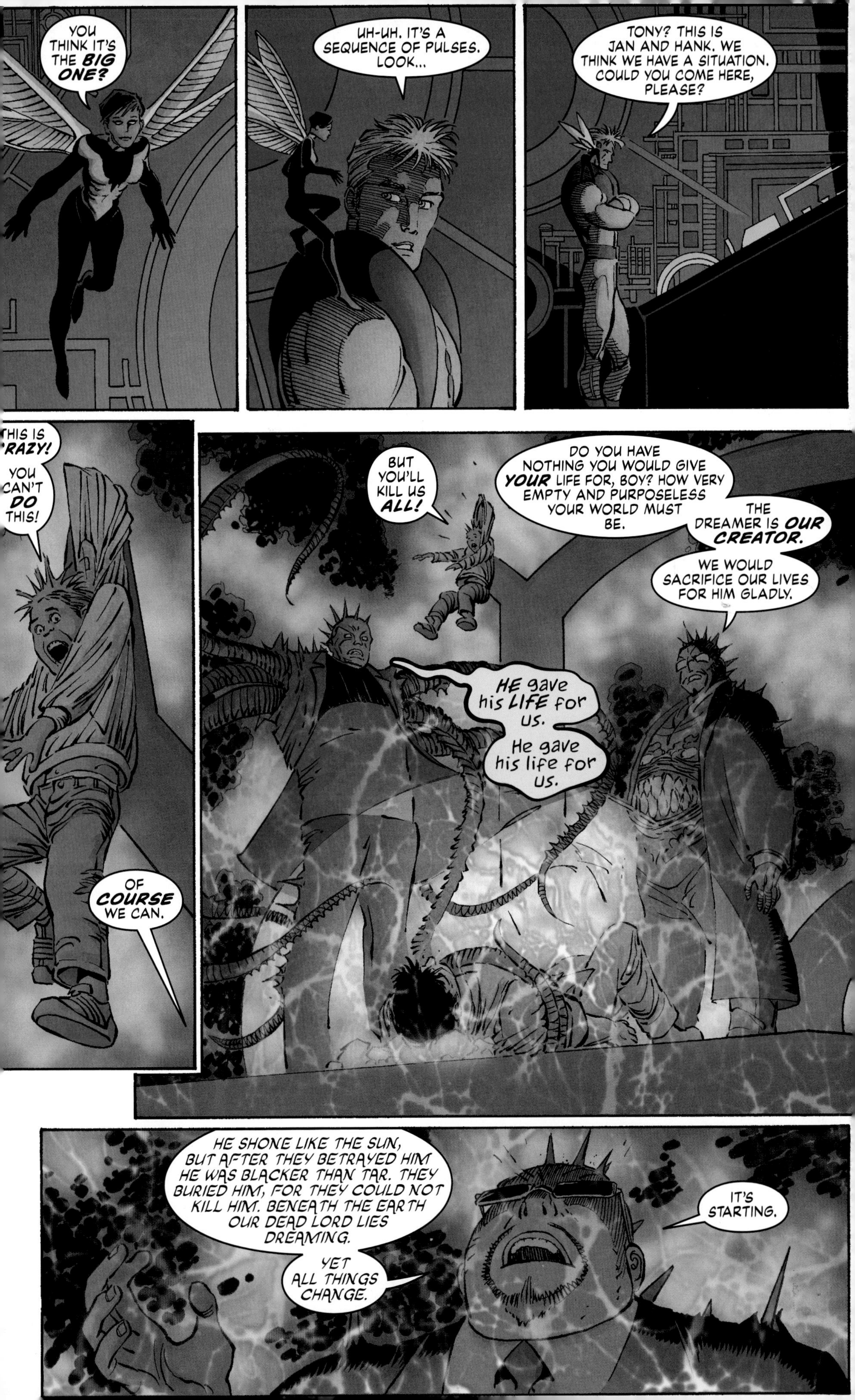

YOU THINK IT'S THE **BIG ONE?**
UH-UH. IT'S A SEQUENCE OF PULSES. LOOK...
TONY? THIS IS JAN AND HANK. WE THINK WE HAVE A SITUATION. COULD YOU COME HERE, PLEASE?
THIS IS *RAZY!*
YOU CAN'T **DO** THIS!
OF **COURSE** WE CAN.
BUT YOU'LL KILL US **ALL!**
DO YOU HAVE NOTHING YOU WOULD GIVE **YOUR** LIFE FOR, BOY? HOW VERY EMPTY AND PURPOSELESS YOUR WORLD MUST BE.
THE DREAMER IS **OUR CREATOR.**
WE WOULD SACRIFICE OUR LIVES FOR HIM GLADLY.
HE gave his **LIFE** for us.
He gave his life for us.
HE SHONE LIKE THE SUN, BUT AFTER THEY BETRAYED HIM HE WAS BLACKER THAN TAR. THEY BURIED HIM, FOR THEY COULD NOT KILL HIM. BENEATH THE EARTH OUR DEAD LORD LIES DREAMING.
YET ALL THINGS CHANGE.
IT'S STARTING.

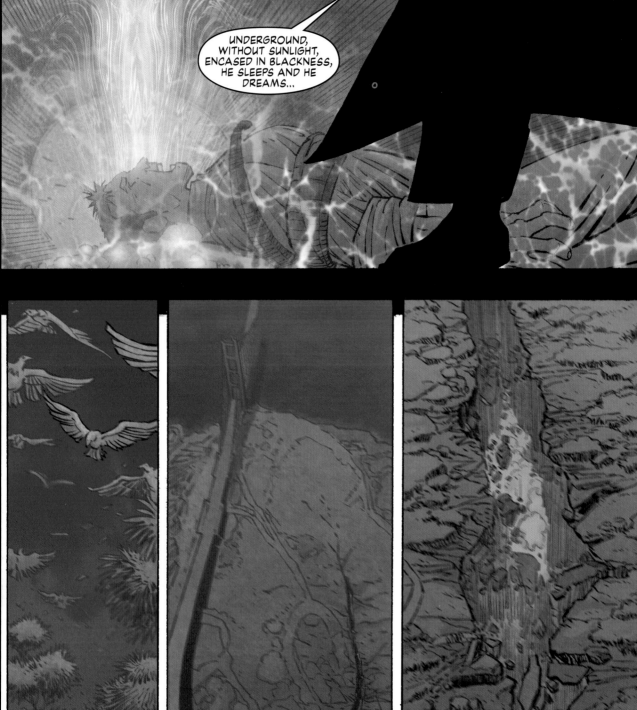

UNDERGROUND, WITHOUT SUNLIGHT, ENCASED IN BLACKNESS, HE SLEEPS AND HE DREAMS...

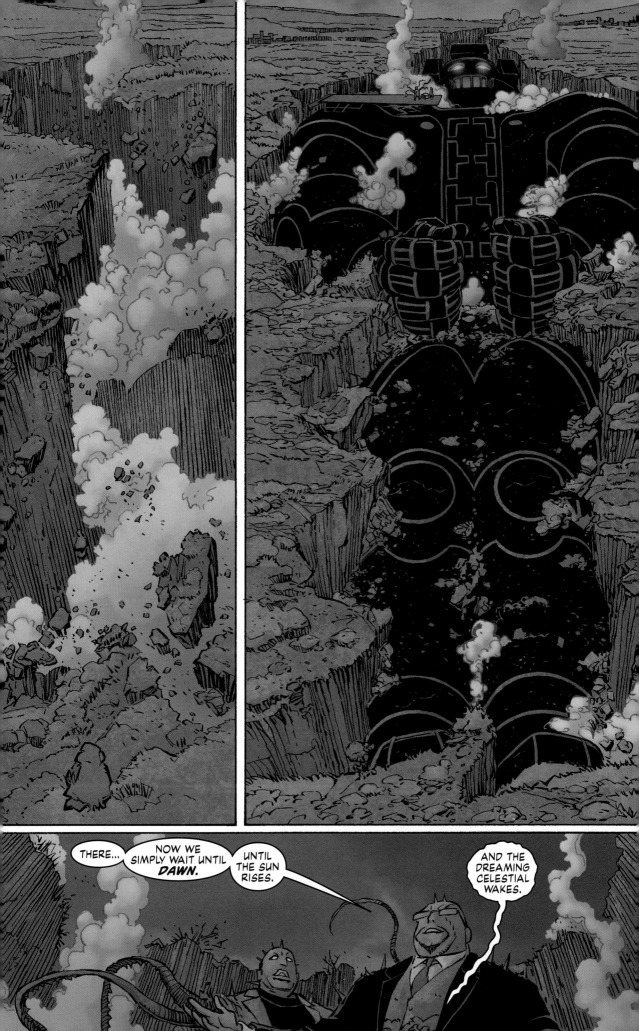

THERE... NOW WE SIMPLY WAIT UNTIL **DAWN**. UNTIL THE SUN RISES.

AND THE DREAMING CELESTIAL WAKES.

CHAPTER SIX: MODIFIED RAPTURE

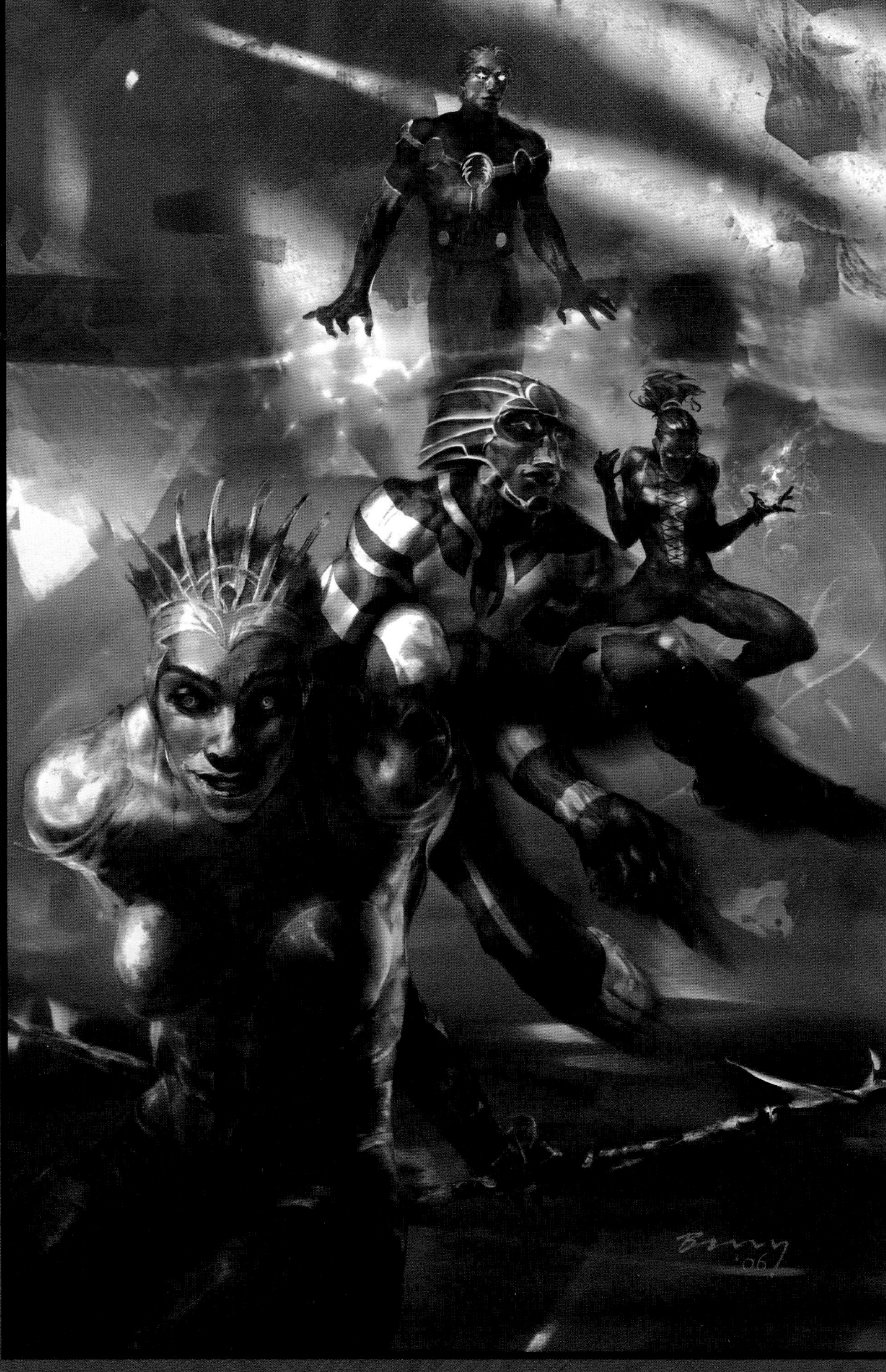

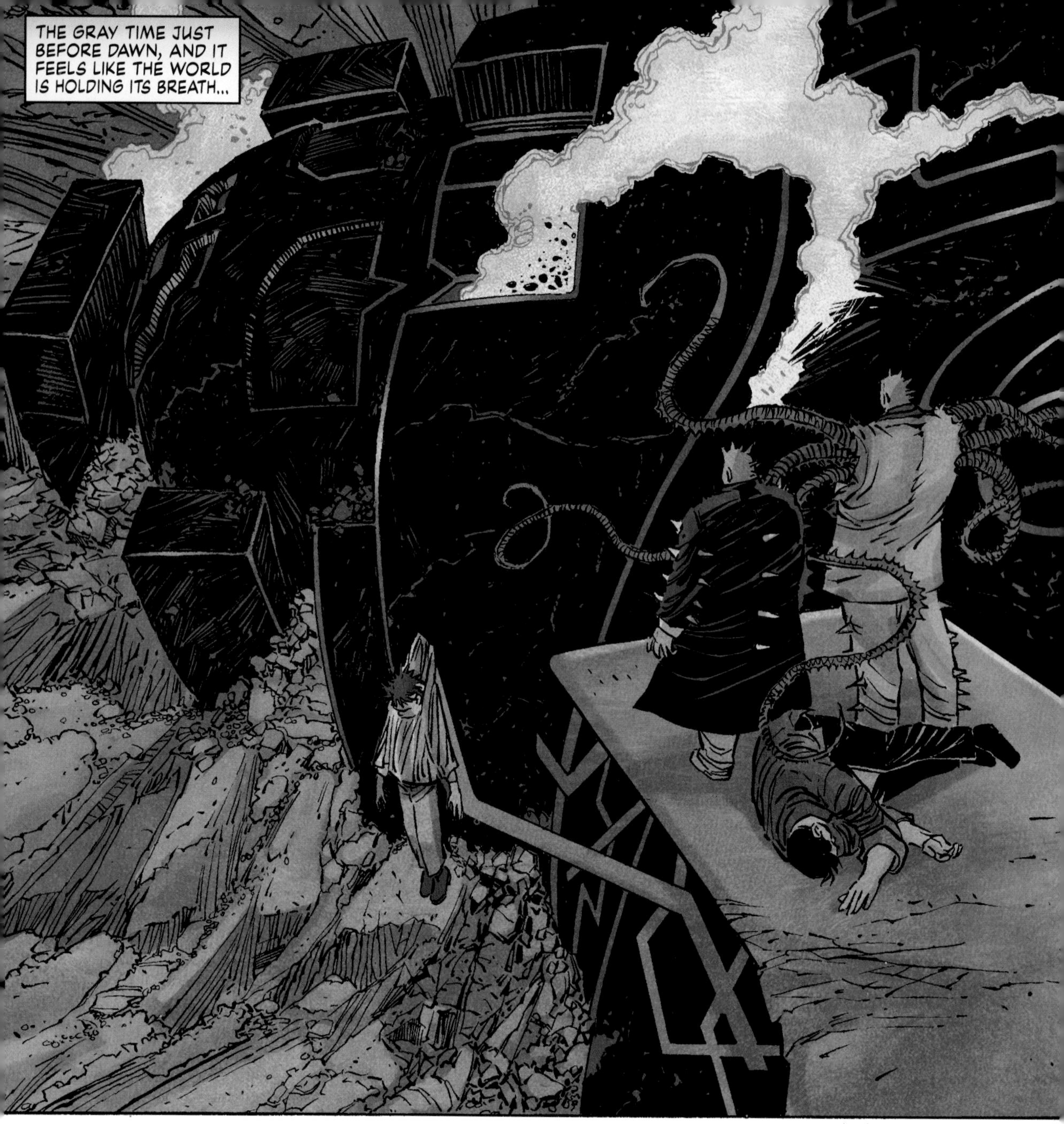
THE GRAY TIME JUST BEFORE DAWN, AND IT FEELS LIKE THE WORLD IS HOLDING ITS BREATH...

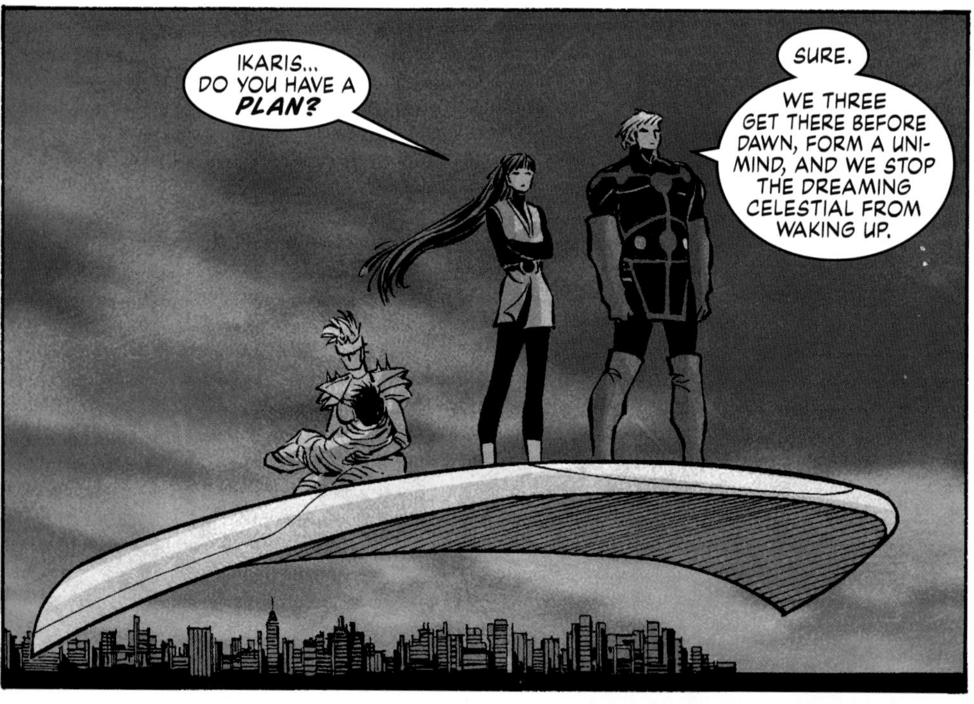
IKARIS... DO YOU HAVE A **PLAN?**
SURE.
WE THREE GET THERE BEFORE DAWN, FORM A UNI-MIND, AND WE STOP THE DREAMING CELESTIAL FROM WAKING UP.

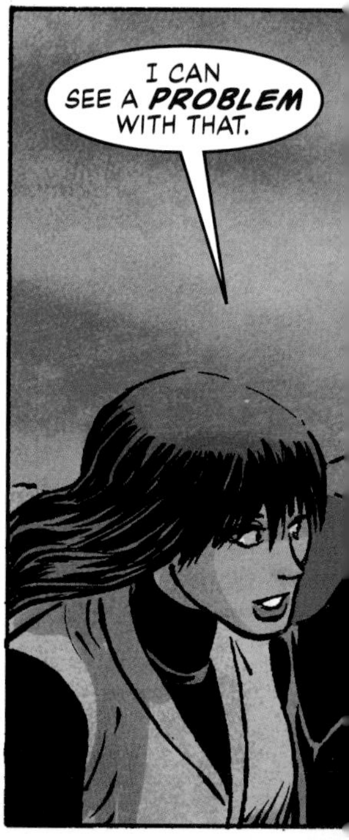
I CAN SEE A **PROBLEM** WITH THAT.

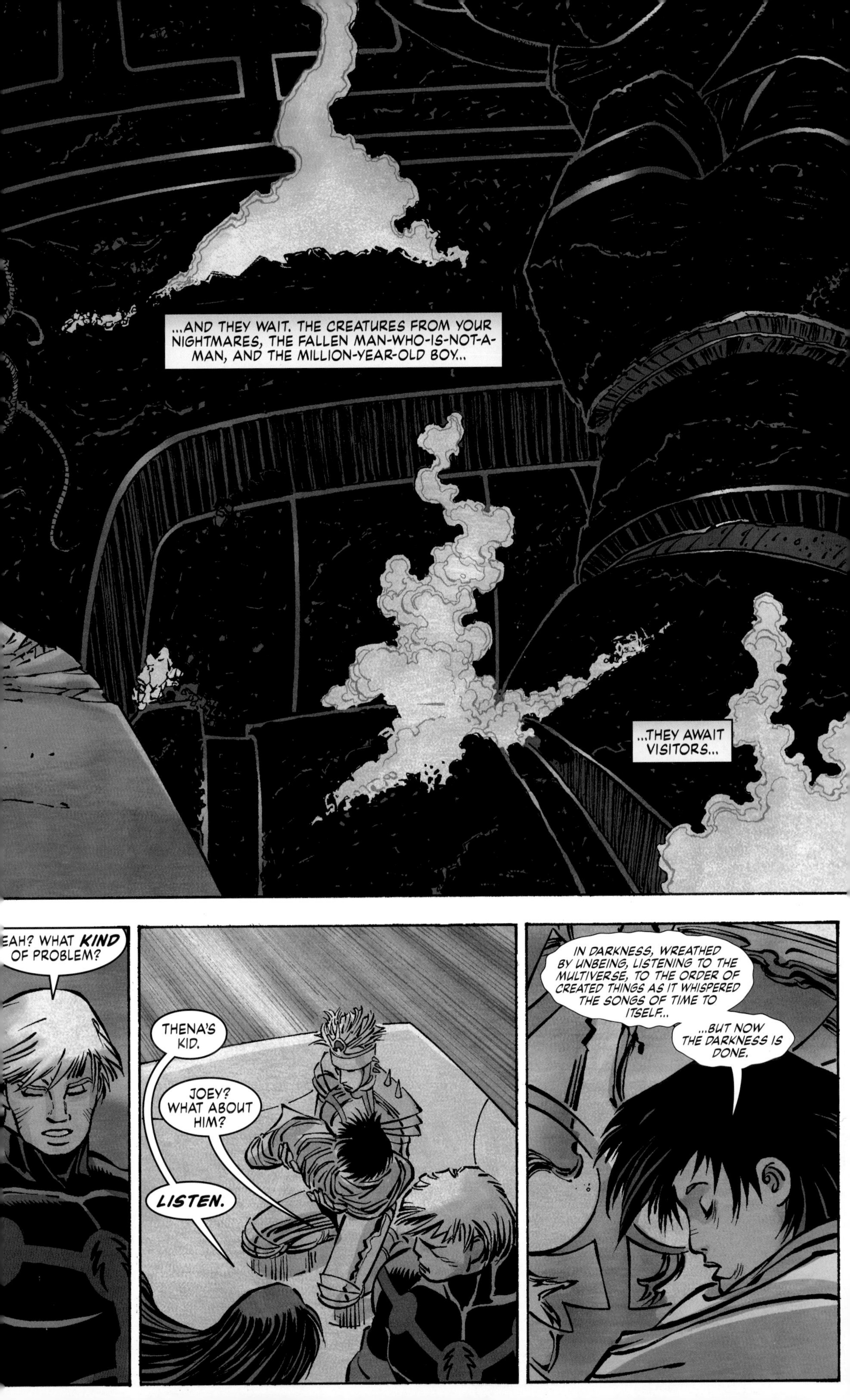
...AND THEY WAIT. THE CREATURES FROM YOUR NIGHTMARES, THE FALLEN MAN-WHO-IS-NOT-A-MAN, AND THE MILLION-YEAR-OLD BOY...
...THEY AWAIT VISITORS...
EAH? WHAT KIND OF PROBLEM?
THENA'S KID.
JOEY? WHAT ABOUT HIM?
LISTEN.
IN DARKNESS, WREATHED BY UNBEING, LISTENING TO THE MULTIVERSE, TO THE ORDER OF CREATED THINGS AS IT WHISPERED THE SONGS OF TIME TO ITSELF...
...BUT NOW THE DARKNESS IS DONE.

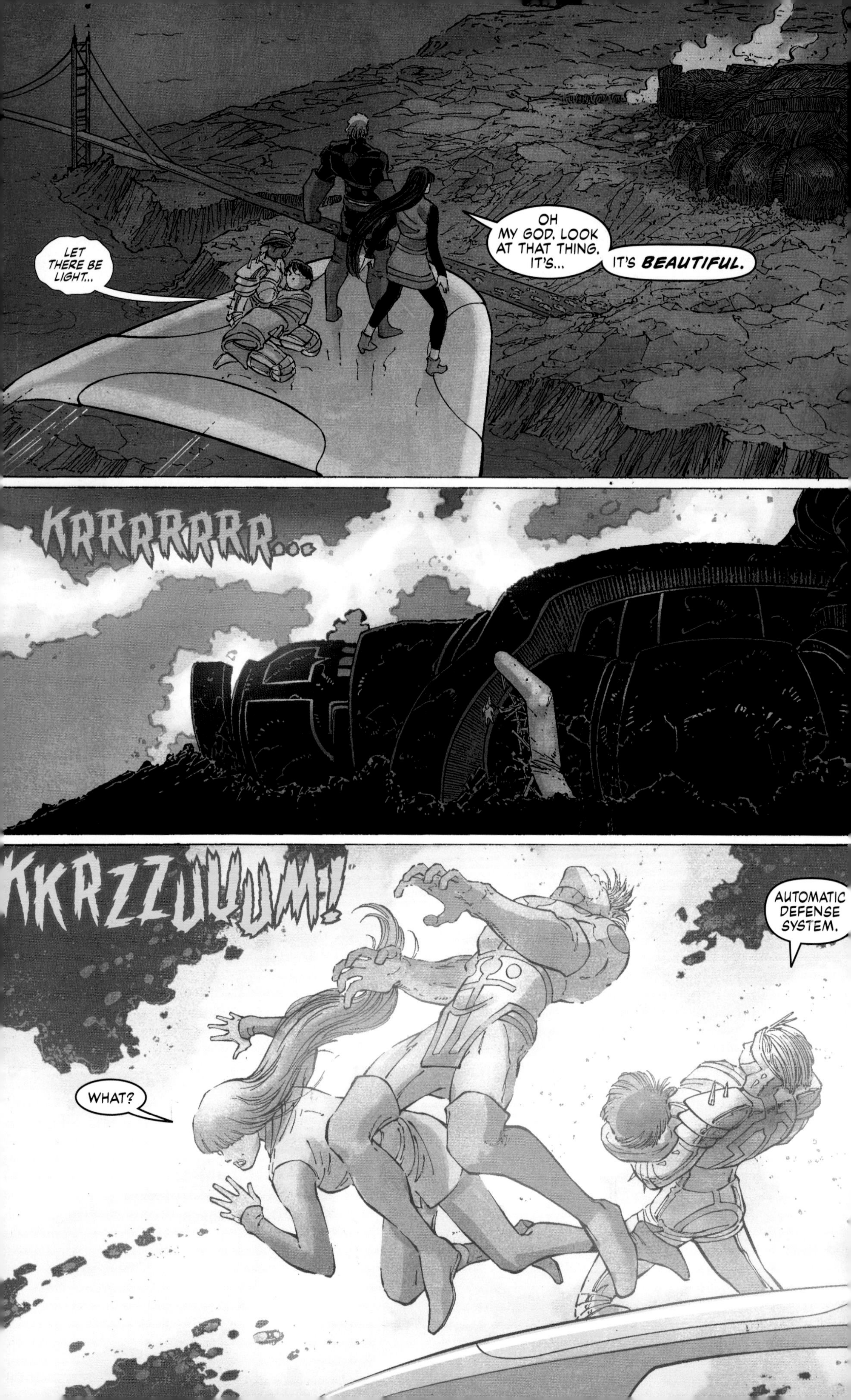
OH MY GOD. LOOK AT THAT THING. IT'S...
IT'S **BEAUTIFUL.**
LET THERE BE LIGHT...
KRRRRRRR...
KKRZZUUM!
AUTOMATIC DEFENSE SYSTEM.
WHAT?

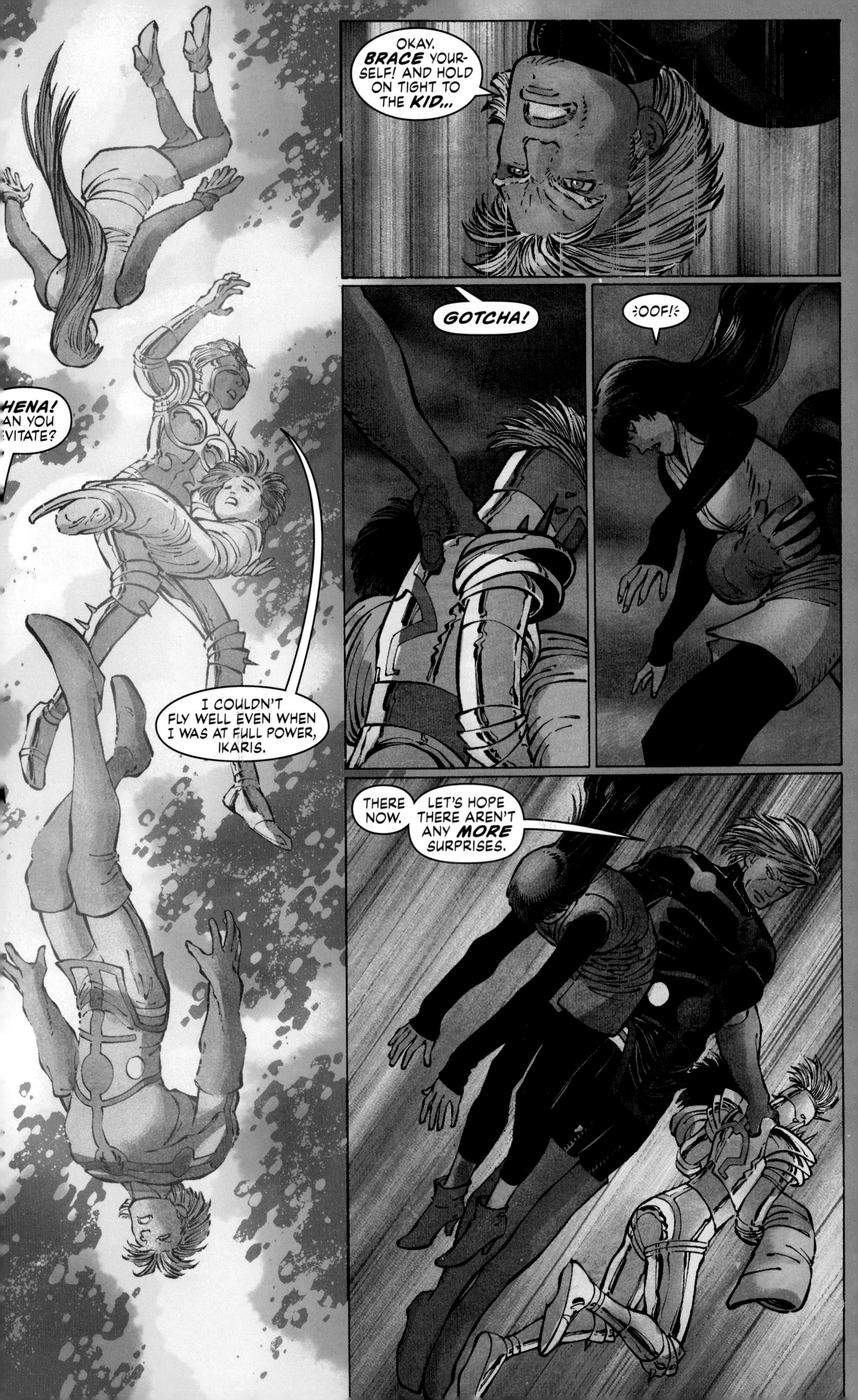

HENA! AN YOU EVITATE?
I COULDN'T FLY WELL EVEN WHEN I WAS AT FULL POWER, IKARIS.
OKAY. BRACE YOURSELF! AND HOLD ON TIGHT TO THE KID...
GOTCHA!
OOF!
THERE NOW.
LET'S HOPE THERE AREN'T ANY MORE SURPRISES.

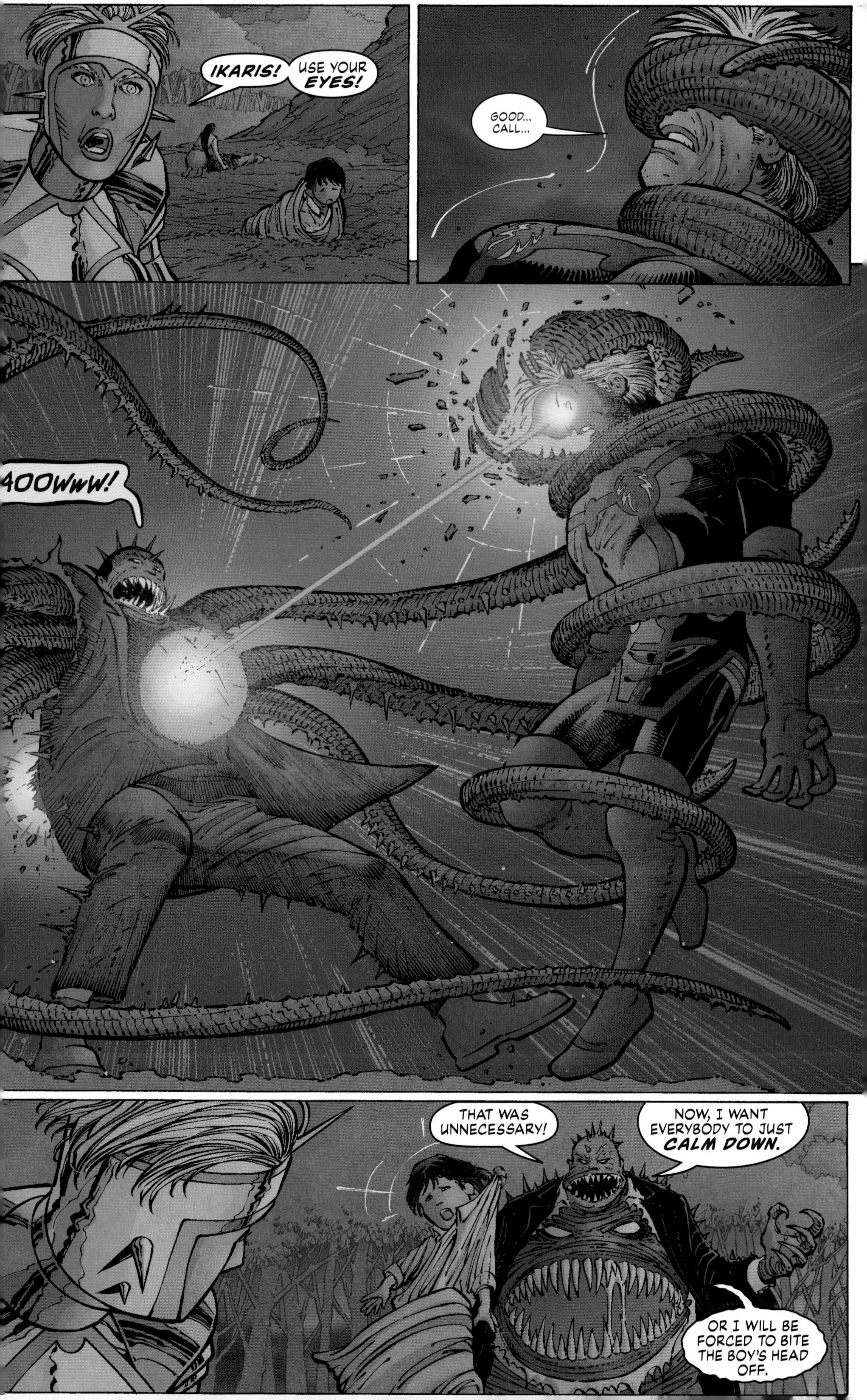
IKARIS!
USE YOUR EYES!
GOOD... CALL...
AOOWWW!
THAT WAS UNNECESSARY!
NOW, I WANT EVERYBODY TO JUST CALM DOWN.
OR I WILL BE FORCED TO BITE THE BOY'S HEAD OFF.

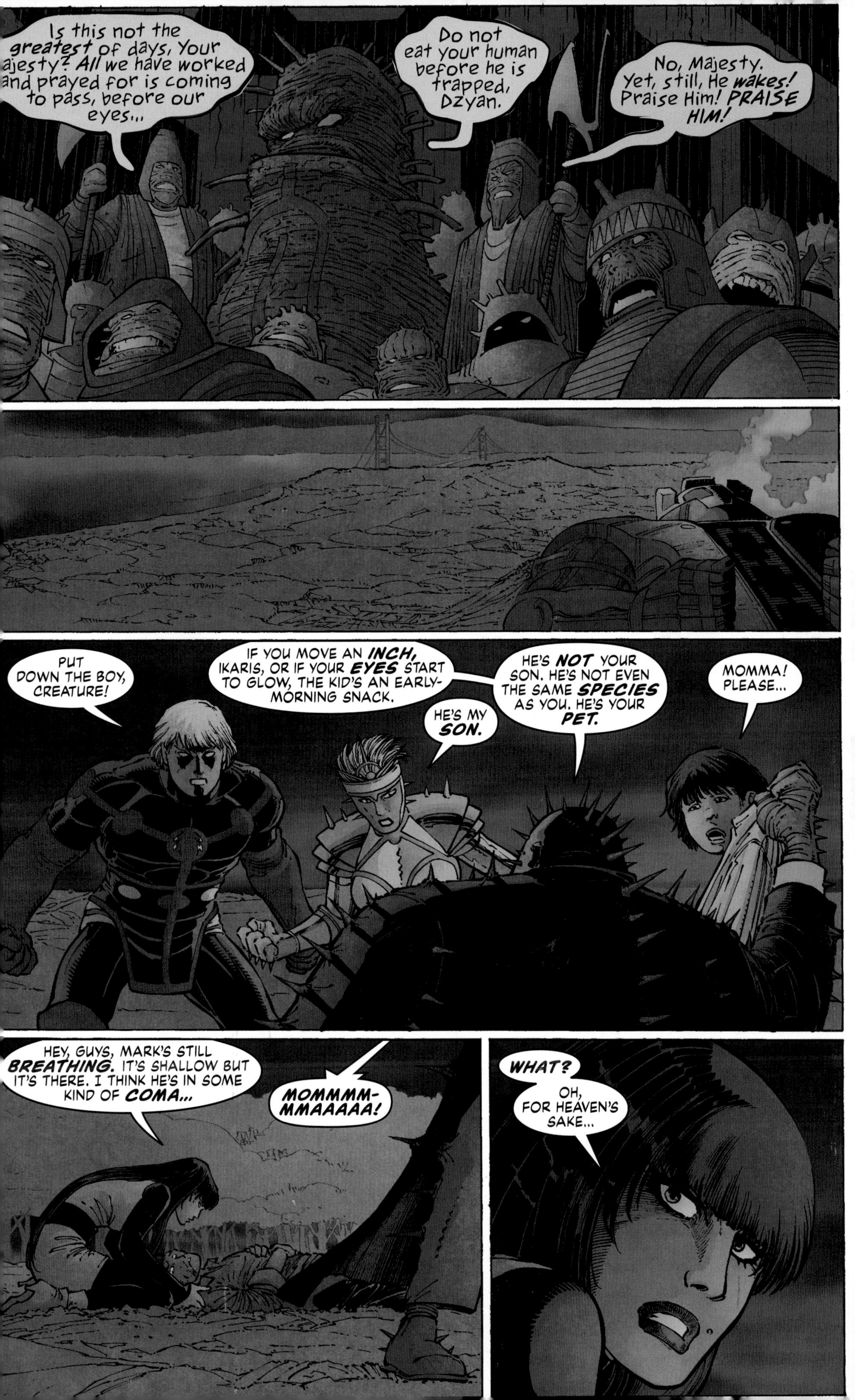

Is this not the greatest of days, Your Majesty? All we have worked and prayed for is coming to pass, before our eyes...
Do not eat your human before he is trapped, Dzyan.
No, Majesty. Yet, still, He wakes! Praise Him! PRAISE HIM!
PUT DOWN THE BOY, CREATURE!
IF YOU MOVE AN INCH, IKARIS, OR IF YOUR EYES START TO GLOW, THE KID'S AN EARLY-MORNING SNACK.
HE'S MY SON.
HE'S NOT YOUR SON. HE'S NOT EVEN THE SAME SPECIES AS YOU. HE'S YOUR PET.
MOMMA! PLEASE...
HEY, GUYS, MARK'S STILL BREATHING. IT'S SHALLOW BUT IT'S THERE. I THINK HE'S IN SOME KIND OF COMA...
MOMMMM-MMAAAAAA!
WHAT?
OH, FOR HEAVEN'S SAKE...

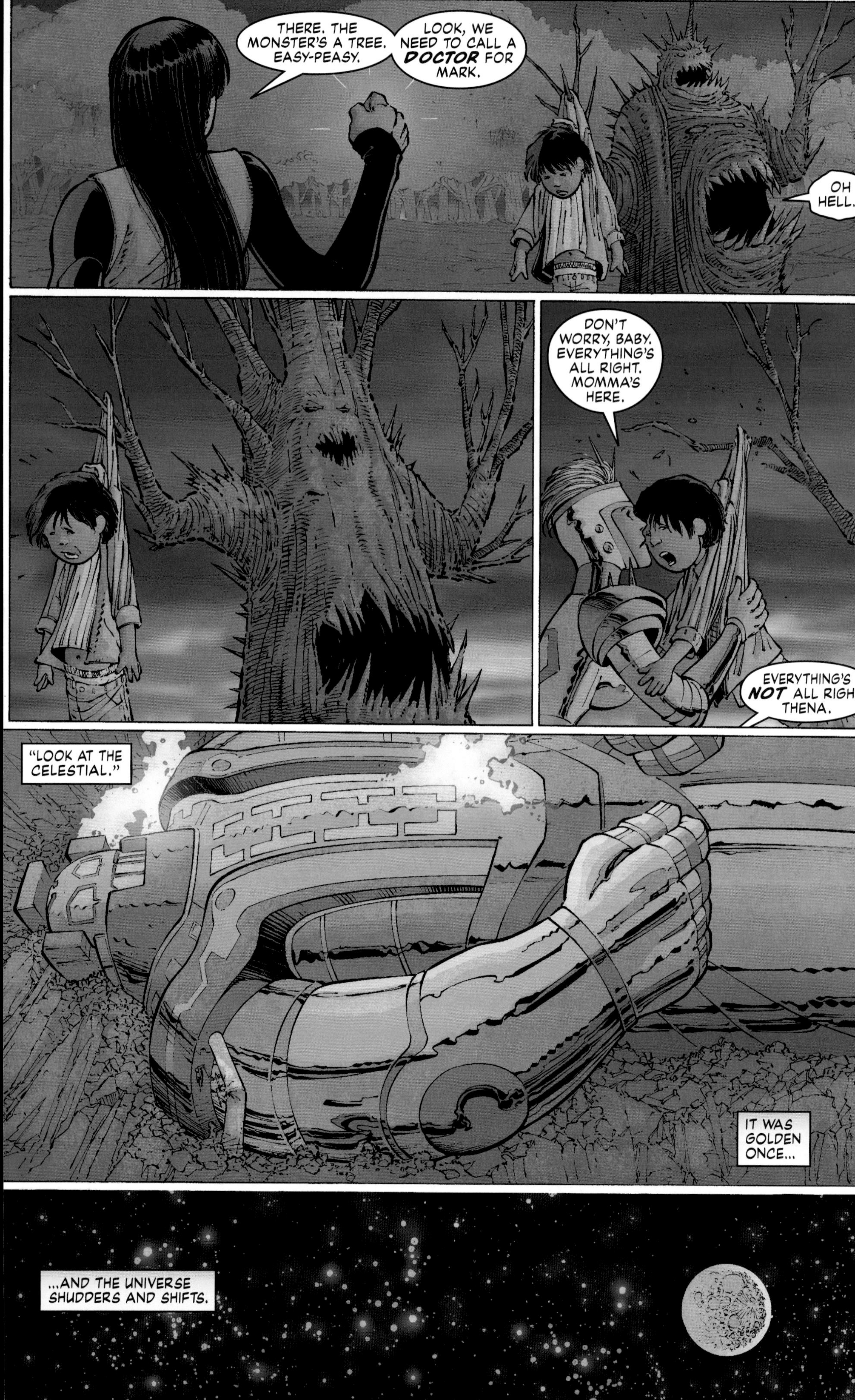
THERE. THE MONSTER'S A TREE. EASY-PEASY.
LOOK, WE NEED TO CALL A **DOCTOR** FOR MARK.
OH HELL.
DON'T WORRY, BABY. EVERYTHING'S ALL RIGHT. MOMMA'S HERE.
EVERYTHING'S **NOT** ALL RIGH THENA.
"LOOK AT THE CELESTIAL."
IT WAS GOLDEN ONCE...
...AND THE UNIVERSE SHUDDERS AND SHIFTS.

IN THE BLUE CITY, ON EARTH'S MOON, THE WATCHER FEELS THE TWIST AND TEAR IN THE COSMIC FLUX...

AND, IF FOR ONLY A MOMENT, HE CANNOT WATCH.

HALFWAY ACROSS THE MILKY WAY, GALACTUS PAUSES, A METHANE GIANT TEEMING WITH AMMONIACAL LIFE STILL HALF-CONSUMED.

HAS BEEN HALF A MILLION YEARS.

HE HAD THOUGHT THE MATTER DEALT WITH AND OVER.

BUT THE UNIVERSE ECHOES IN A WAY HE THOUGHT HE WOULD NEVER FEEL AGAIN...

...AND GALACTUS REMEMBERS WHAT IT IS TO BE AFRAID.

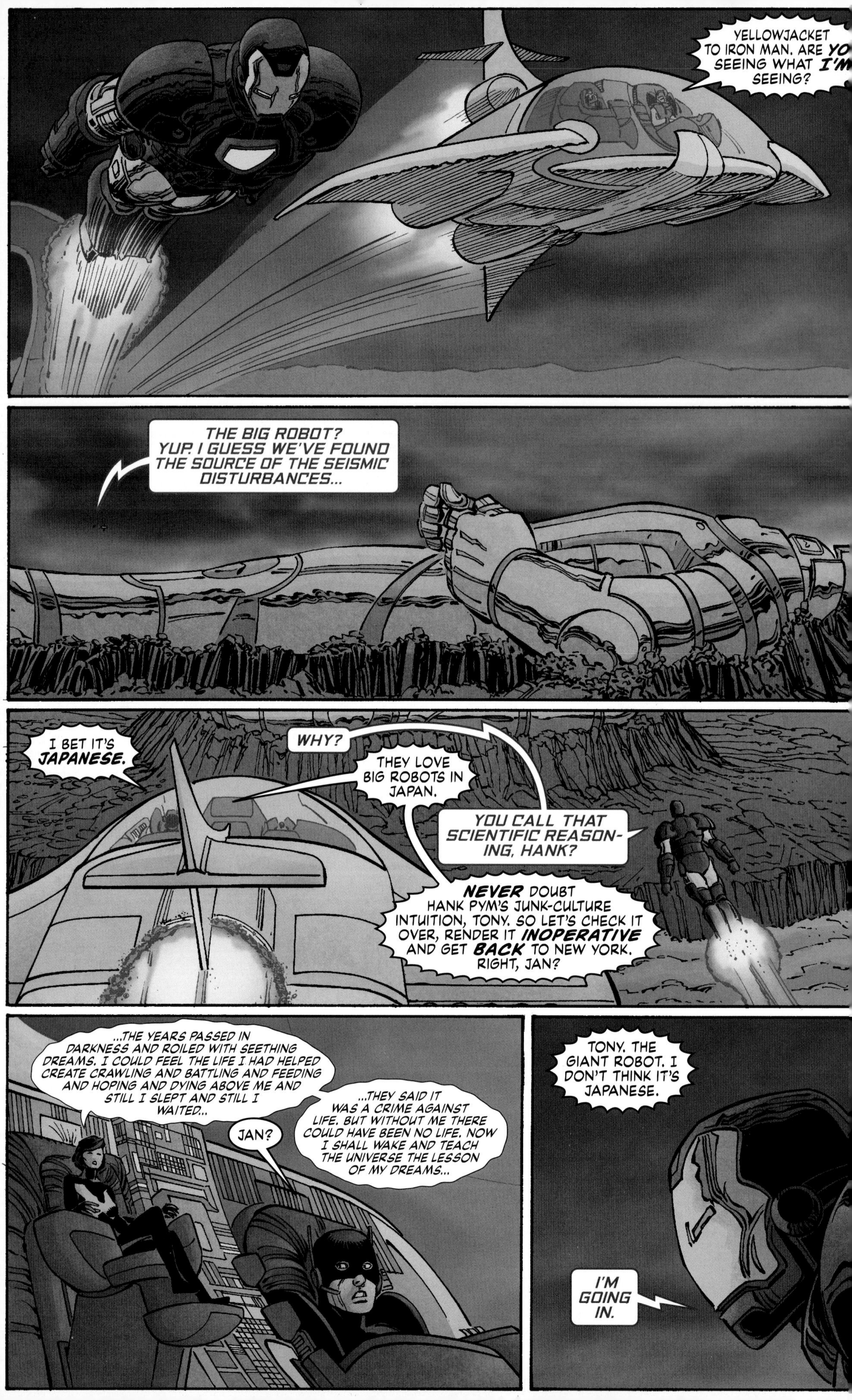
YELLOWJACKET TO IRON MAN. ARE YO[U] SEEING WHAT I'M SEEING?
THE BIG ROBOT? YUP. I GUESS WE'VE FOUND THE SOURCE OF THE SEISMIC DISTURBANCES...
I BET IT'S JAPANESE.
WHY?
THEY LOVE BIG ROBOTS IN JAPAN.
YOU CALL THAT SCIENTIFIC REASONING, HANK?
NEVER DOUBT HANK PYM'S JUNK-CULTURE INTUITION, TONY. SO LET'S CHECK IT OVER, RENDER IT INOPERATIVE AND GET BACK TO NEW YORK. RIGHT, JAN?
...THE YEARS PASSED IN DARKNESS AND ROILED WITH SEETHING DREAMS. I COULD FEEL THE LIFE I HAD HELPED CREATE CRAWLING AND BATTLING AND FEEDING AND HOPING AND DYING ABOVE ME AND STILL I SLEPT AND STILL I WAITED...
...THEY SAID IT WAS A CRIME AGAINST LIFE. BUT WITHOUT ME THERE COULD HAVE BEEN NO LIFE. NOW I SHALL WAKE AND TEACH THE UNIVERSE THE LESSON OF MY DREAMS...
JAN?
TONY. THE GIANT ROBOT. I DON'T THINK IT'S JAPANESE.
I'M GOING IN.

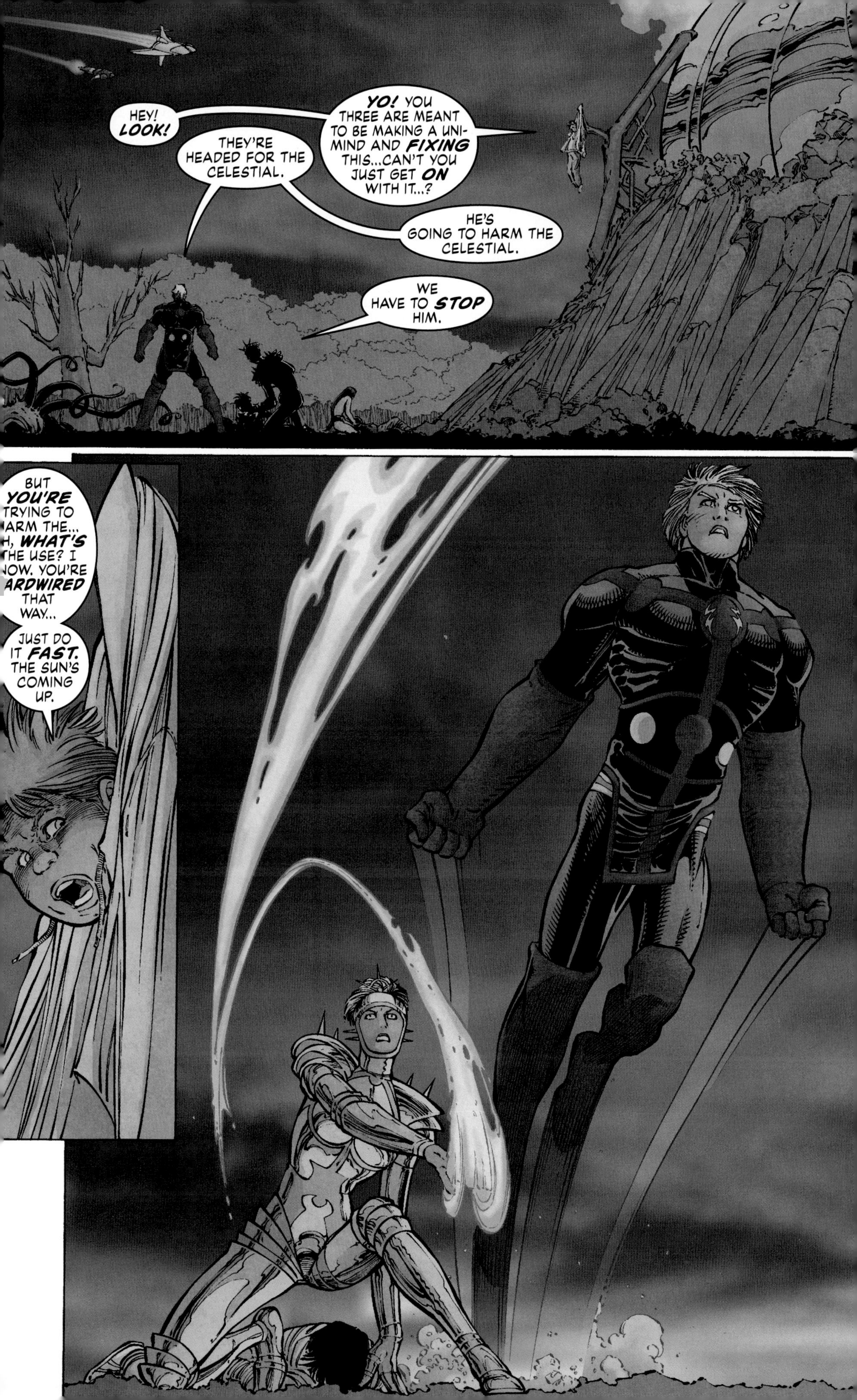

HEY! **LOOK!**
YO! YOU THREE ARE MEANT TO BE MAKING A UNI-MIND AND **FIXING** THIS...CAN'T YOU JUST GET **ON** WITH IT...?
THEY'RE HEADED FOR THE CELESTIAL.
HE'S GOING TO HARM THE CELESTIAL.
WE HAVE TO **STOP** HIM.
BUT **YOU'RE** TRYING TO ARM THE... H, **WHAT'S** THE USE? I NOW. YOU'RE **ARDWIRED** THAT WAY...
JUST DO IT **FAST.** THE SUN'S COMING UP.

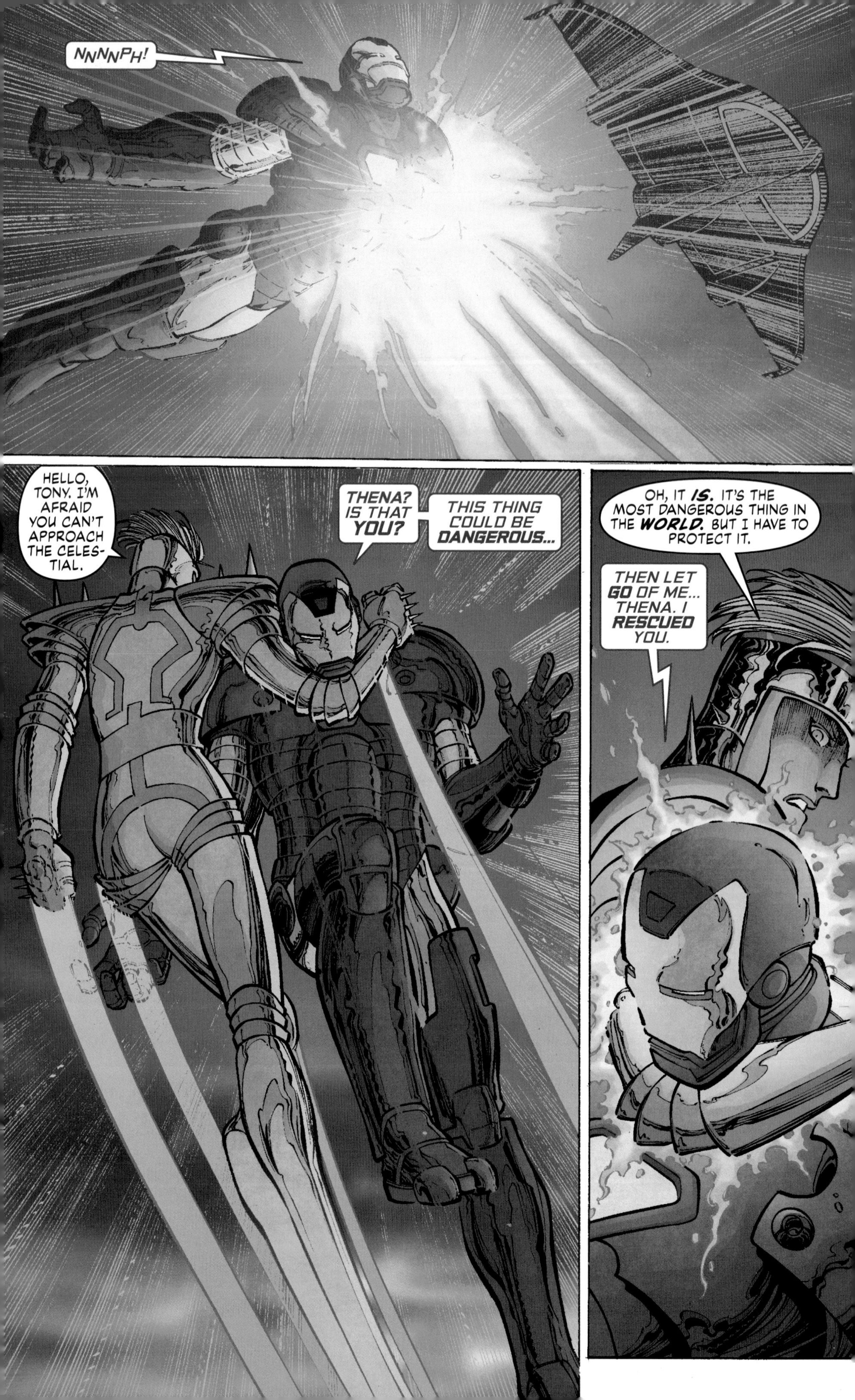
NNNNPH!
HELLO, TONY. I'M AFRAID YOU CAN'T APPROACH THE CELESTIAL.
THENA? IS THAT YOU?
THIS THING COULD BE DANGEROUS...
OH, IT IS. IT'S THE MOST DANGEROUS THING IN THE WORLD. BUT I HAVE TO PROTECT IT.
THEN LET GO OF ME... THENA. I RESCUED YOU.

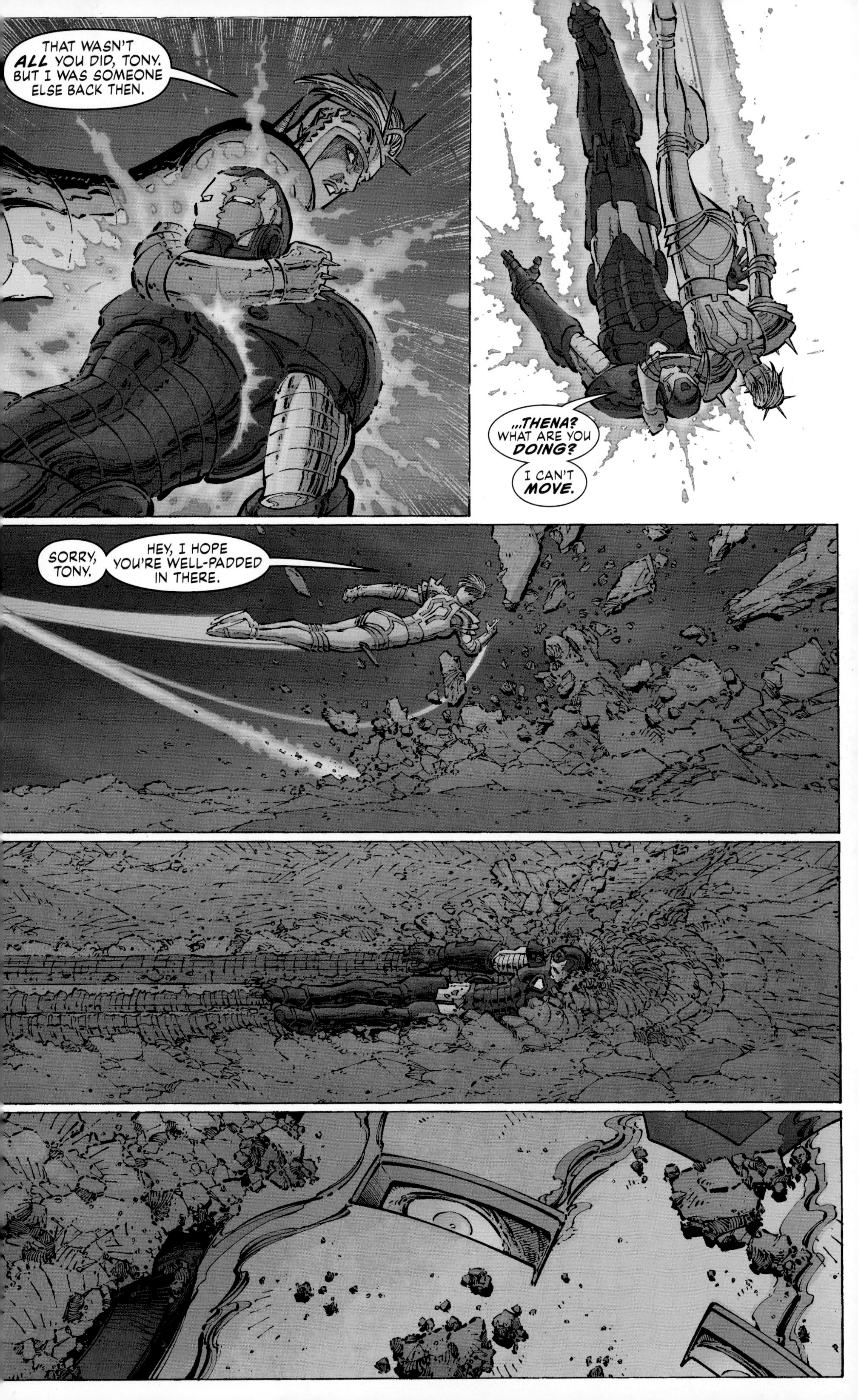
THAT WASN'T ALL YOU DID, TONY. BUT I WAS SOMEONE ELSE BACK THEN.
...THENA? WHAT ARE YOU DOING?
I CAN'T MOVE.
SORRY, TONY.
HEY, I HOPE YOU'RE WELL-PADDED IN THERE.

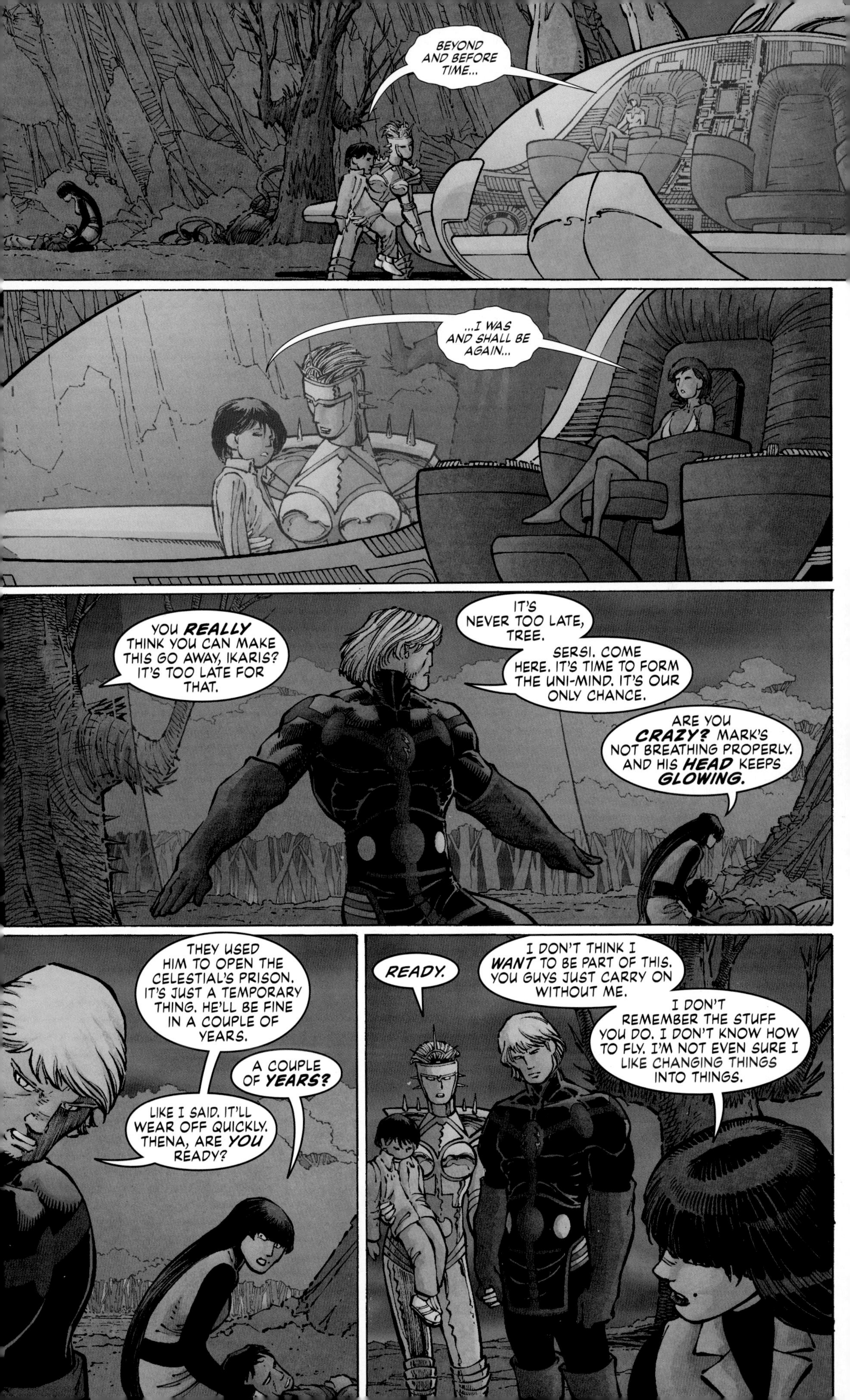
BEYOND AND BEFORE TIME...
...I WAS AND SHALL BE AGAIN...
YOU REALLY THINK YOU CAN MAKE THIS GO AWAY, IKARIS? IT'S TOO LATE FOR THAT.
IT'S NEVER TOO LATE, TREE.
SERSI. COME HERE. IT'S TIME TO FORM THE UNI-MIND. IT'S OUR ONLY CHANCE.
ARE YOU CRAZY? MARK'S NOT BREATHING PROPERLY. AND HIS HEAD KEEPS GLOWING.
THEY USED HIM TO OPEN THE CELESTIAL'S PRISON. IT'S JUST A TEMPORARY THING. HE'LL BE FINE IN A COUPLE OF YEARS.
A COUPLE OF YEARS?
LIKE I SAID. IT'LL WEAR OFF QUICKLY. THENA, ARE YOU READY?
READY.
I DON'T THINK I WANT TO BE PART OF THIS. YOU GUYS JUST CARRY ON WITHOUT ME.
I DON'T REMEMBER THE STUFF YOU DO. I DON'T KNOW HOW TO FLY. I'M NOT EVEN SURE I LIKE CHANGING THINGS INTO THINGS.

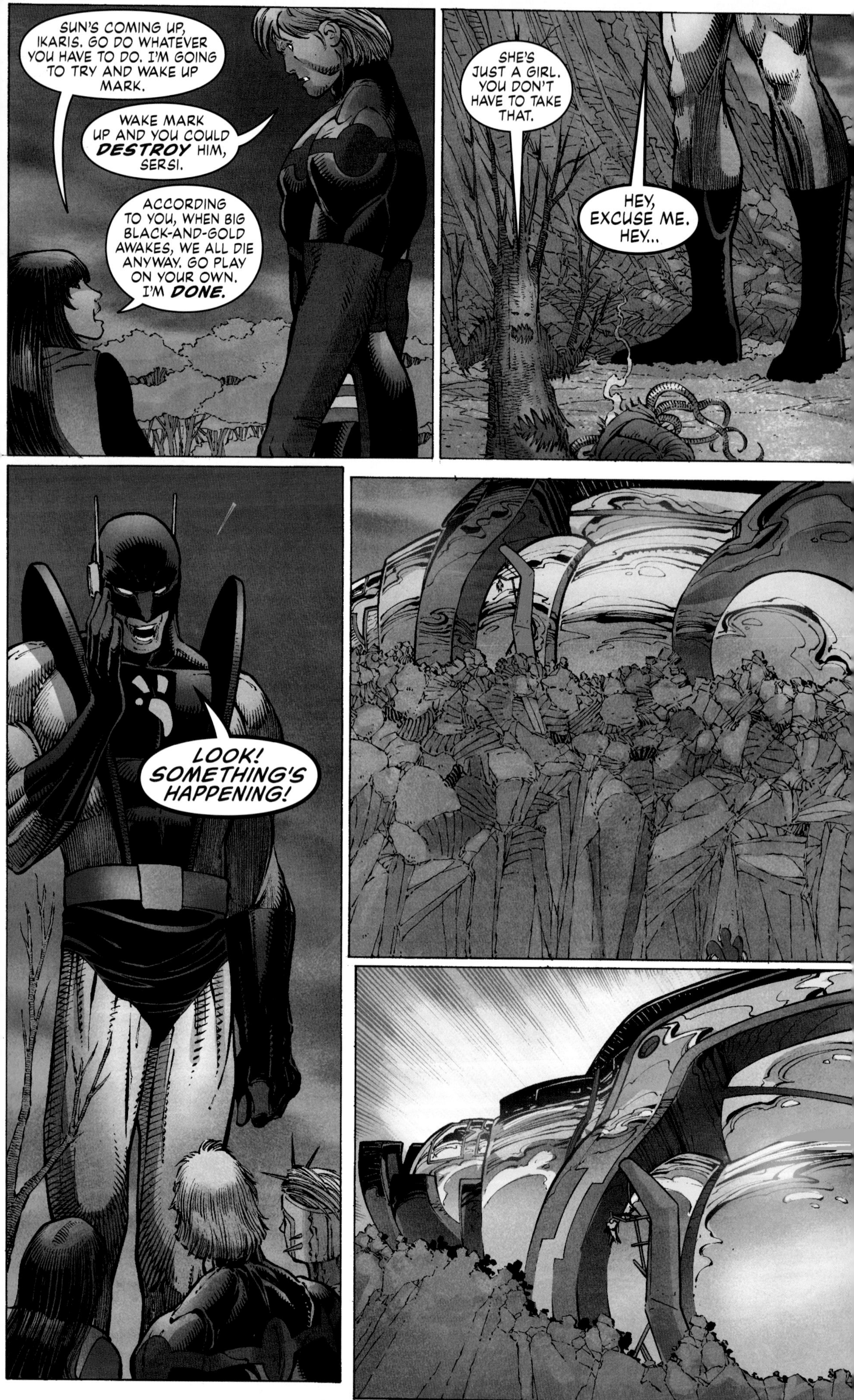
SUN'S COMING UP, IKARIS. GO DO WHATEVER YOU HAVE TO DO. I'M GOING TO TRY AND WAKE UP MARK.
WAKE MARK UP AND YOU COULD DESTROY HIM, SERSI.
ACCORDING TO YOU, WHEN BIG BLACK-AND-GOLD AWAKES, WE ALL DIE ANYWAY. GO PLAY ON YOUR OWN. I'M DONE.
SHE'S JUST A GIRL. YOU DON'T HAVE TO TAKE THAT.
HEY, EXCUSE ME. HEY...
LOOK! SOMETHING'S HAPPENING!

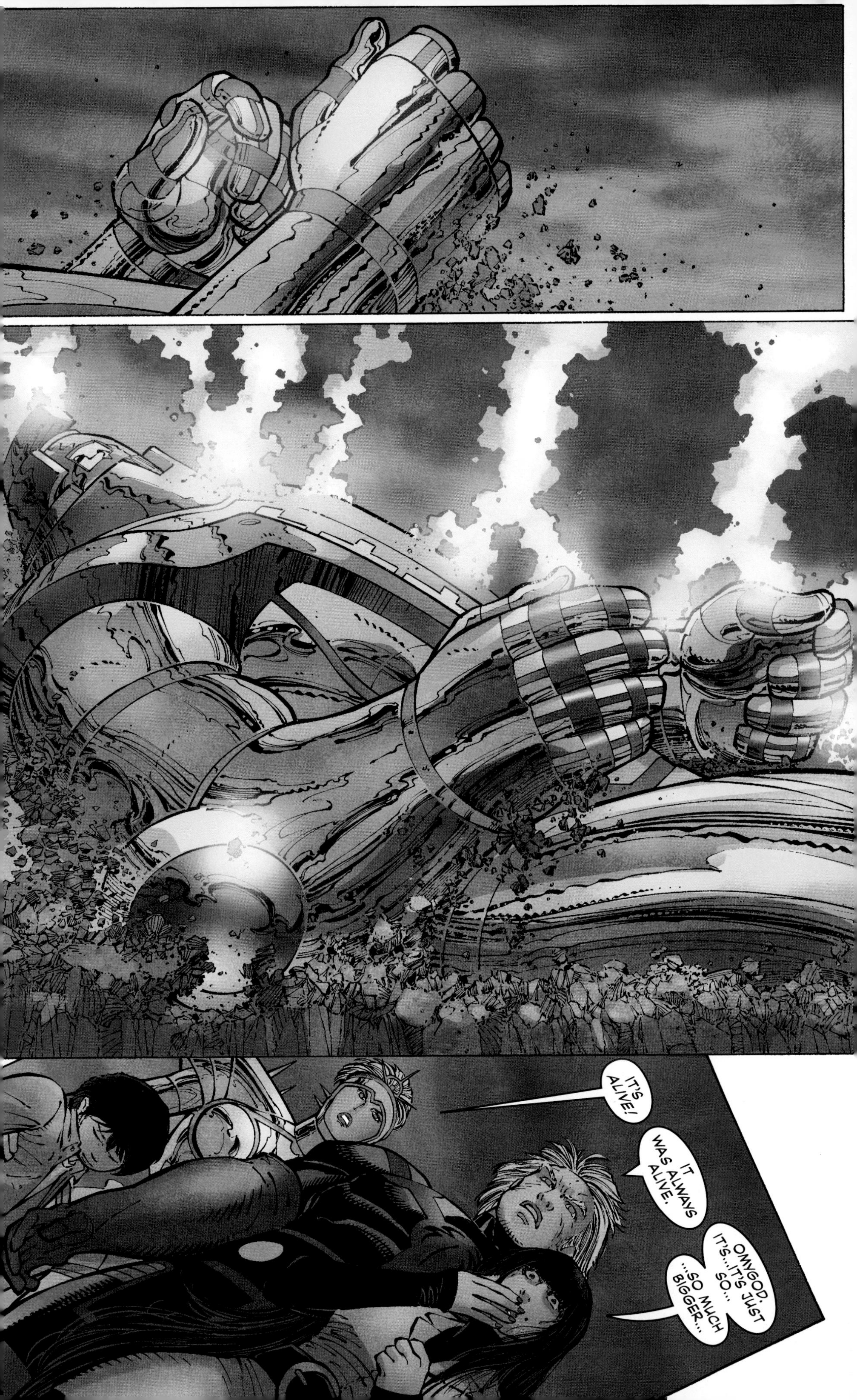
IT'S ALIVE!
IT WAS ALWAYS ALIVE.
OMYGOD. IT'S...IT'S JUST SO... ...SO MUCH BIGGER...

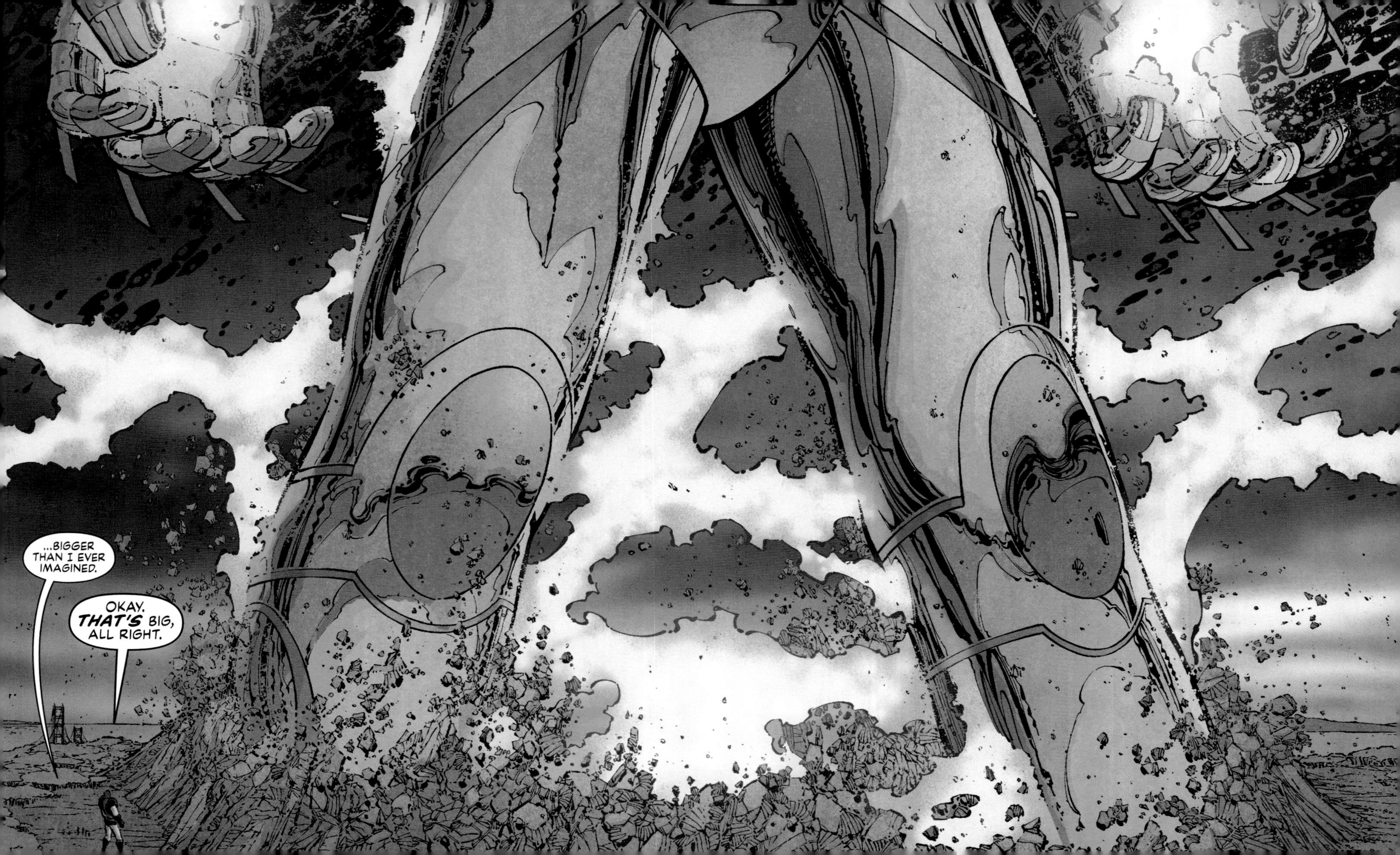
...BIGGER THAN I EVER IMAGINED.
OKAY. THAT'S BIG, ALL RIGHT.

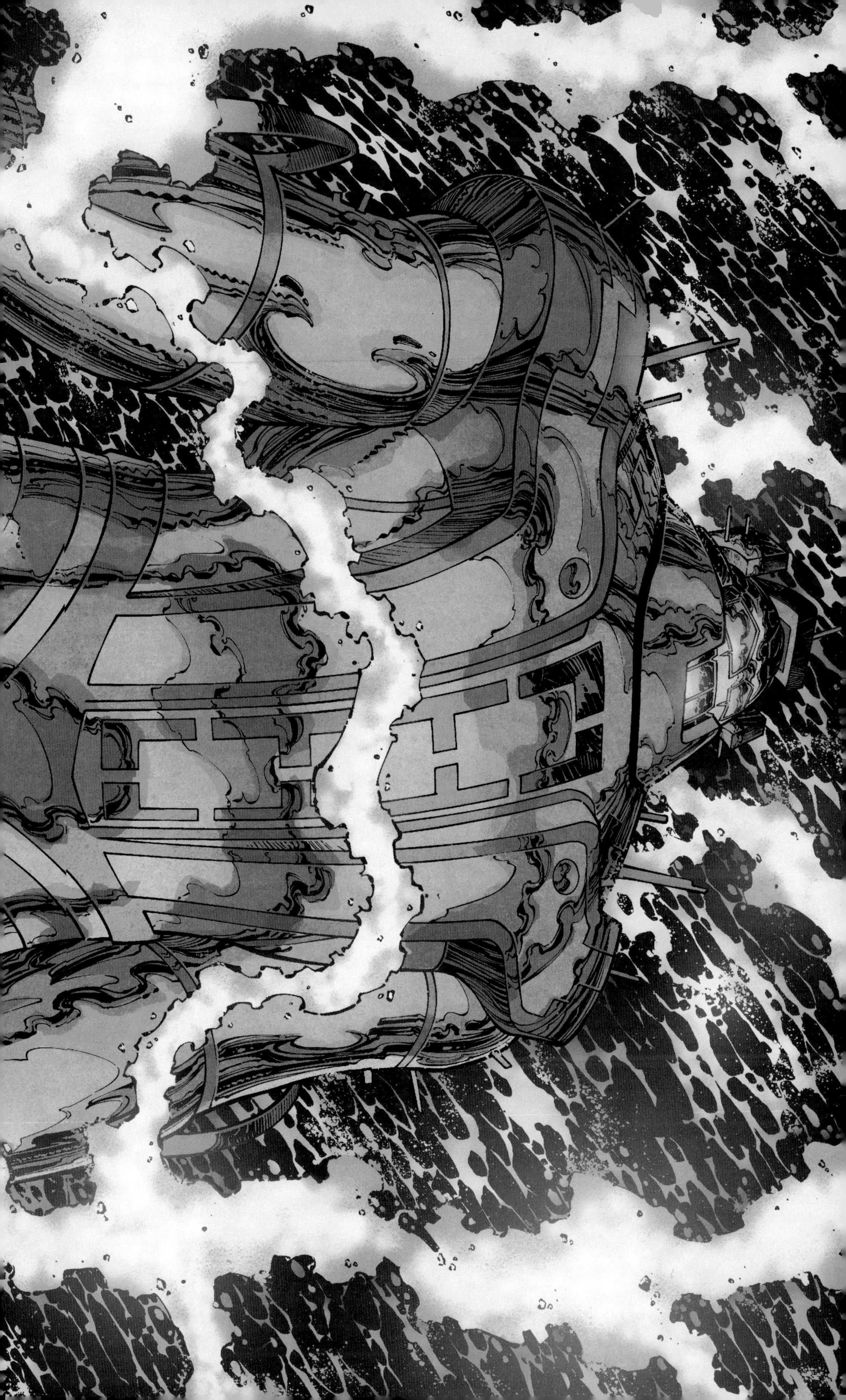

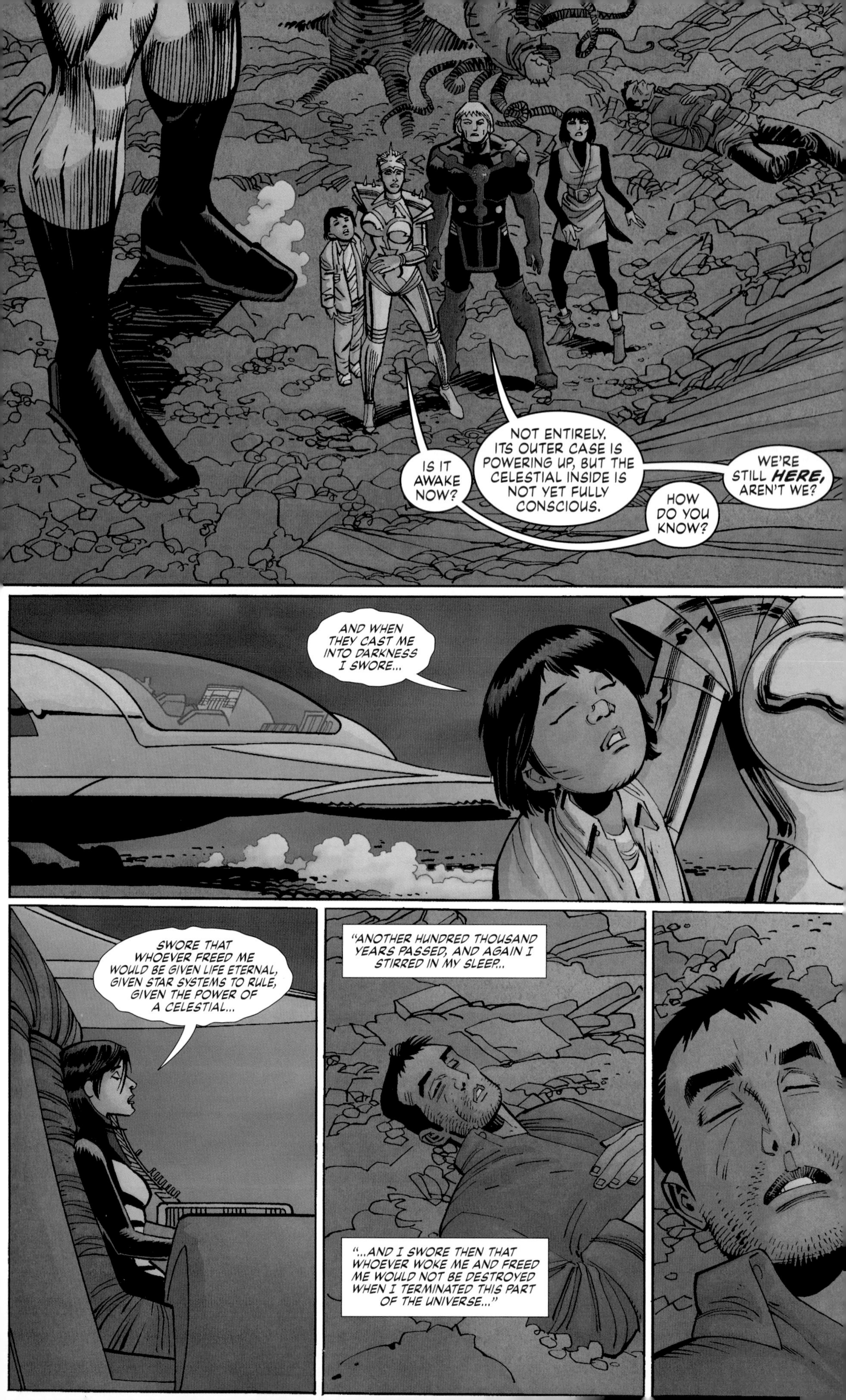
IS IT AWAKE NOW?
NOT ENTIRELY. ITS OUTER CASE IS POWERING UP, BUT THE CELESTIAL INSIDE IS NOT YET FULLY CONSCIOUS.
HOW DO YOU KNOW?
WE'RE STILL **HERE,** AREN'T WE?
AND WHEN THEY CAST ME INTO DARKNESS I SWORE...
SWORE THAT WHOEVER FREED ME WOULD BE GIVEN LIFE ETERNAL, GIVEN STAR SYSTEMS TO RULE, GIVEN THE POWER OF A CELESTIAL...
"ANOTHER HUNDRED THOUSAND YEARS PASSED, AND AGAIN I STIRRED IN MY SLEEP...
"...AND I SWORE THEN THAT WHOEVER WOKE ME AND FREED ME WOULD NOT BE DESTROYED WHEN I TERMINATED THIS PART OF THE UNIVERSE..."

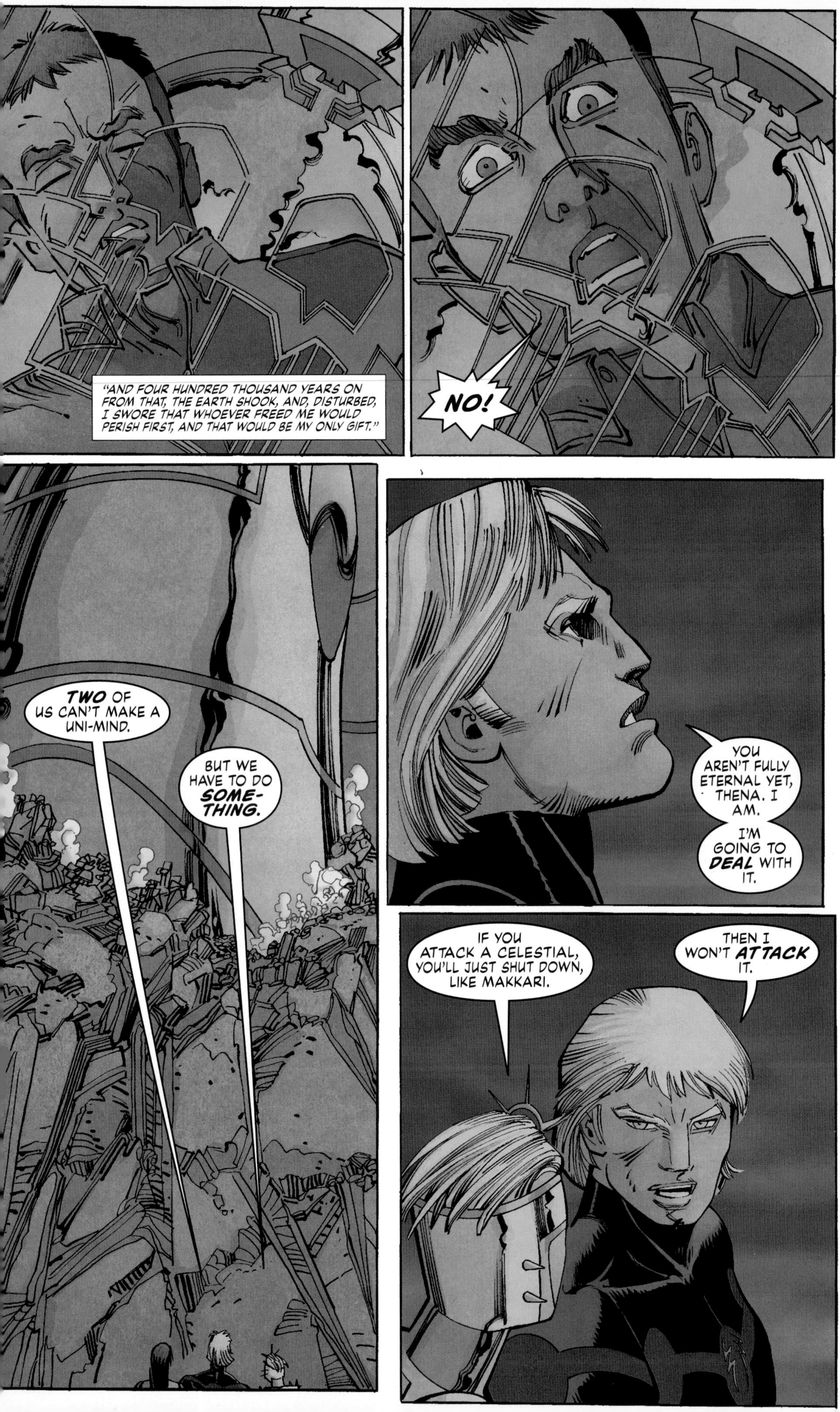
"AND FOUR HUNDRED THOUSAND YEARS ON FROM THAT, THE EARTH SHOOK, AND, DISTURBED, I SWORE THAT WHOEVER FREED ME WOULD PERISH FIRST, AND THAT WOULD BE MY ONLY GIFT."
NO!
TWO OF US CAN'T MAKE A UNI-MIND.
BUT WE HAVE TO DO SOME-THING.
YOU AREN'T FULLY ETERNAL YET, THENA. I AM.
I'M GOING TO DEAL WITH IT.
IF YOU ATTACK A CELESTIAL, YOU'LL JUST SHUT DOWN, LIKE MAKKARI.
THEN I WON'T ATTACK IT.

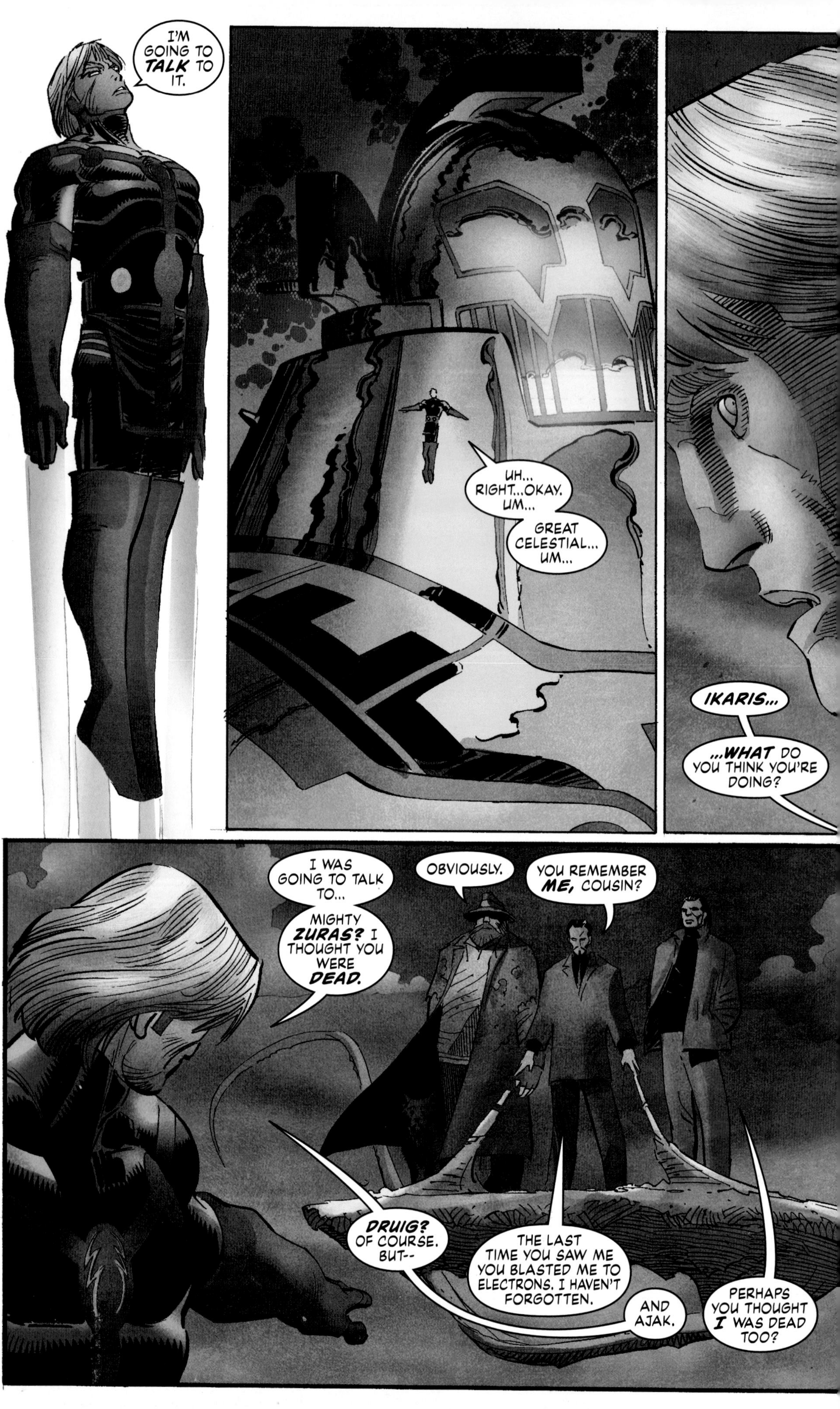

I'M GOING TO TALK TO IT.
UH... RIGHT...OKAY. UM...
GREAT CELESTIAL... UM...
IKARIS...
...WHAT DO YOU THINK YOU'RE DOING?
I WAS GOING TO TALK TO...
OBVIOUSLY.
MIGHTY ZURAS? I THOUGHT YOU WERE DEAD.
YOU REMEMBER ME, COUSIN?
DRUIG? OF COURSE. BUT--
THE LAST TIME YOU SAW ME YOU BLASTED ME TO ELECTRONS. I HAVEN'T FORGOTTEN.
AND AJAK.
PERHAPS YOU THOUGHT I WAS DEAD TOO?

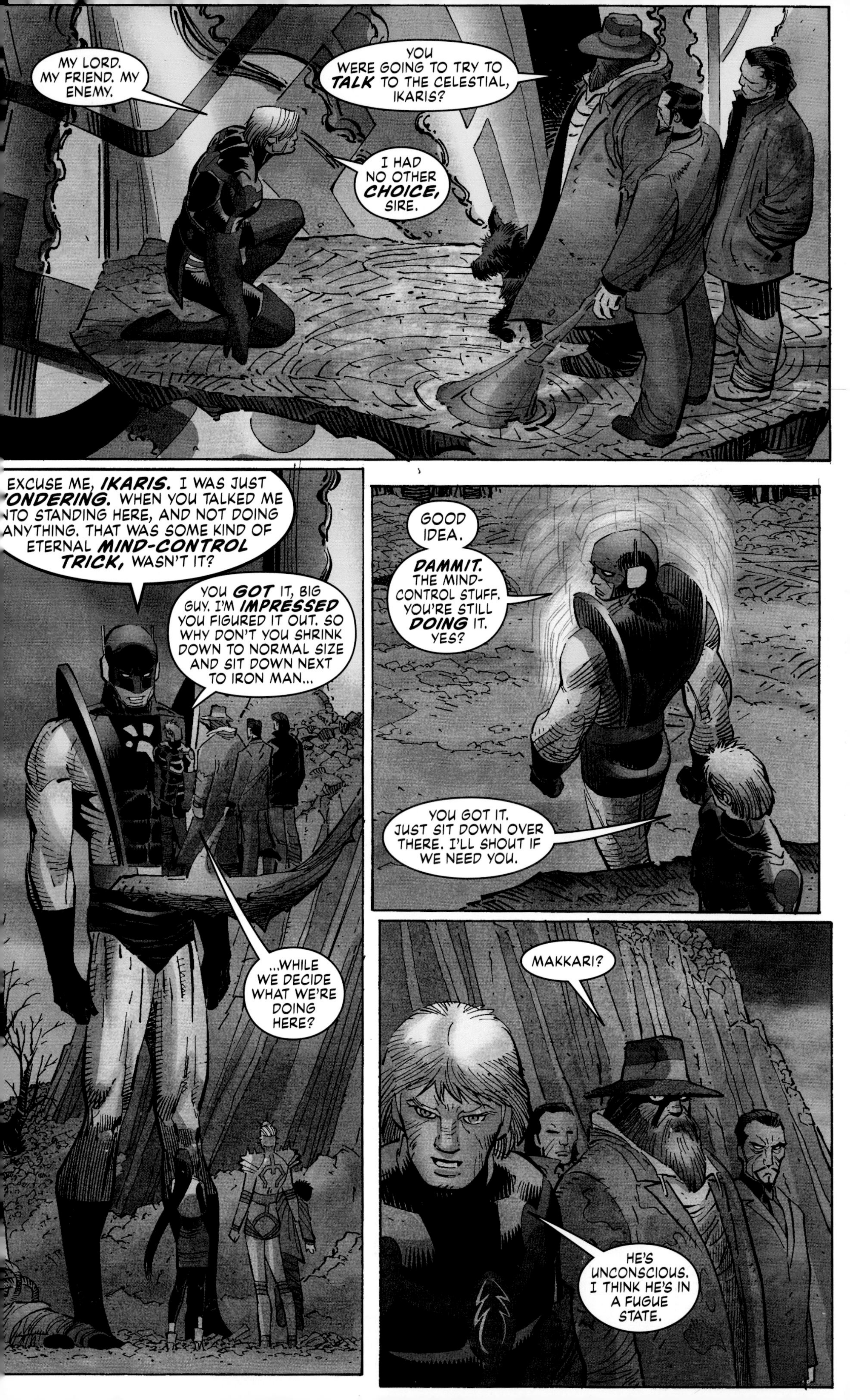
MY LORD. MY FRIEND. MY ENEMY.
YOU WERE GOING TO TRY TO TALK TO THE CELESTIAL, IKARIS?
I HAD NO OTHER CHOICE, SIRE.
EXCUSE ME, IKARIS. I WAS JUST WONDERING. WHEN YOU TALKED ME INTO STANDING HERE, AND NOT DOING ANYTHING. THAT WAS SOME KIND OF ETERNAL MIND-CONTROL TRICK, WASN'T IT?
YOU GOT IT, BIG GUY. I'M IMPRESSED YOU FIGURED IT OUT. SO WHY DON'T YOU SHRINK DOWN TO NORMAL SIZE AND SIT DOWN NEXT TO IRON MAN...
...WHILE WE DECIDE WHAT WE'RE DOING HERE?
GOOD IDEA.
DAMMIT. THE MIND-CONTROL STUFF. YOU'RE STILL DOING IT. YES?
YOU GOT IT. JUST SIT DOWN OVER THERE. I'LL SHOUT IF WE NEED YOU.
MAKKARI?
HE'S UNCONSCIOUS. I THINK HE'S IN A FUGUE STATE.

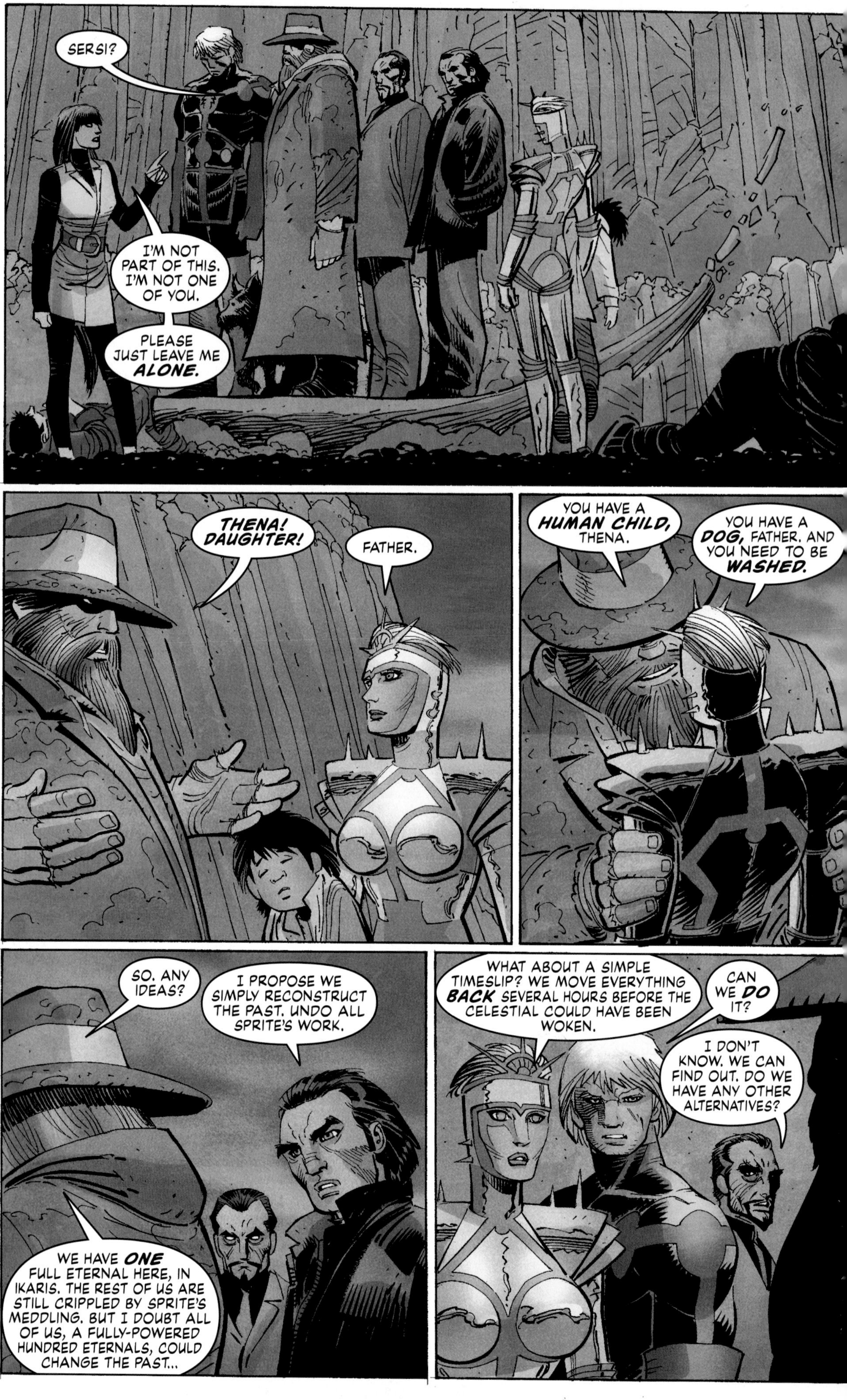
SERSI?
I'M NOT PART OF THIS. I'M NOT ONE OF YOU.
PLEASE JUST LEAVE ME ALONE.
THENA! DAUGHTER!
FATHER.
YOU HAVE A HUMAN CHILD, THENA.
YOU HAVE A DOG, FATHER. AND YOU NEED TO BE WASHED.
SO. ANY IDEAS?
I PROPOSE WE SIMPLY RECONSTRUCT THE PAST. UNDO ALL SPRITE'S WORK.
WE HAVE ONE FULL ETERNAL HERE, IN IKARIS. THE REST OF US ARE STILL CRIPPLED BY SPRITE'S MEDDLING. BUT I DOUBT ALL OF US, A FULLY-POWERED HUNDRED ETERNALS, COULD CHANGE THE PAST...
WHAT ABOUT A SIMPLE TIMESLIP? WE MOVE EVERYTHING BACK SEVERAL HOURS BEFORE THE CELESTIAL COULD HAVE BEEN WOKEN.
CAN WE DO IT?
I DON'T KNOW. WE CAN FIND OUT. DO WE HAVE ANY OTHER ALTERNATIVES?

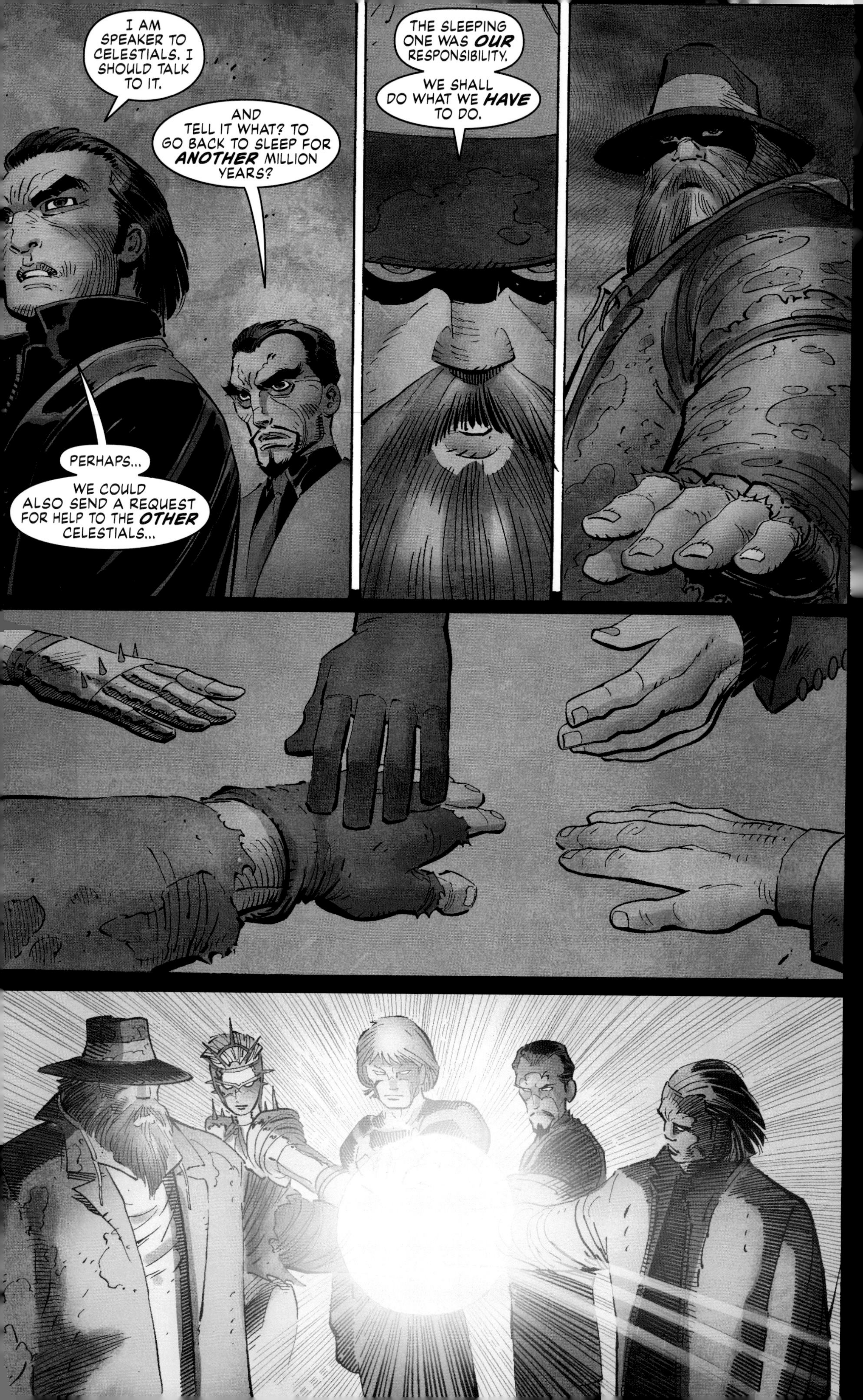
I AM SPEAKER TO CELESTIALS. I SHOULD TALK TO IT.
AND TELL IT WHAT? TO GO BACK TO SLEEP FOR ANOTHER MILLION YEARS?
PERHAPS...
WE COULD ALSO SEND A REQUEST FOR HELP TO THE OTHER CELESTIALS...
THE SLEEPING ONE WAS OUR RESPONSIBILITY.
WE SHALL DO WHAT WE HAVE TO DO.

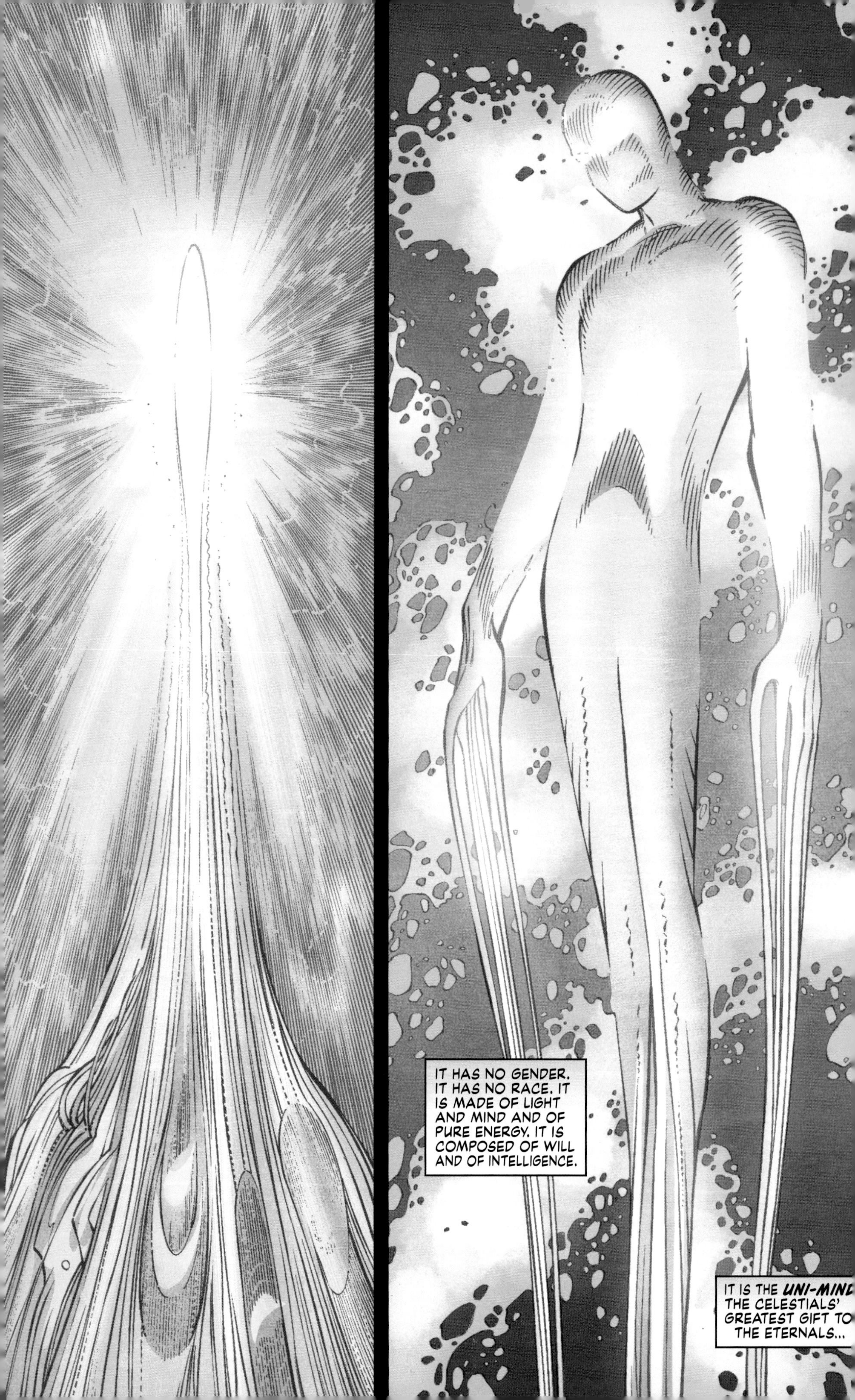
IT HAS NO GENDER. IT HAS NO RACE. IT IS MADE OF LIGHT AND MIND AND OF PURE ENERGY. IT IS COMPOSED OF WILL AND OF INTELLIGENCE.
IT IS THE ***UNI-MIN*** THE CELESTIALS' GREATEST GIFT TO THE ETERNALS...

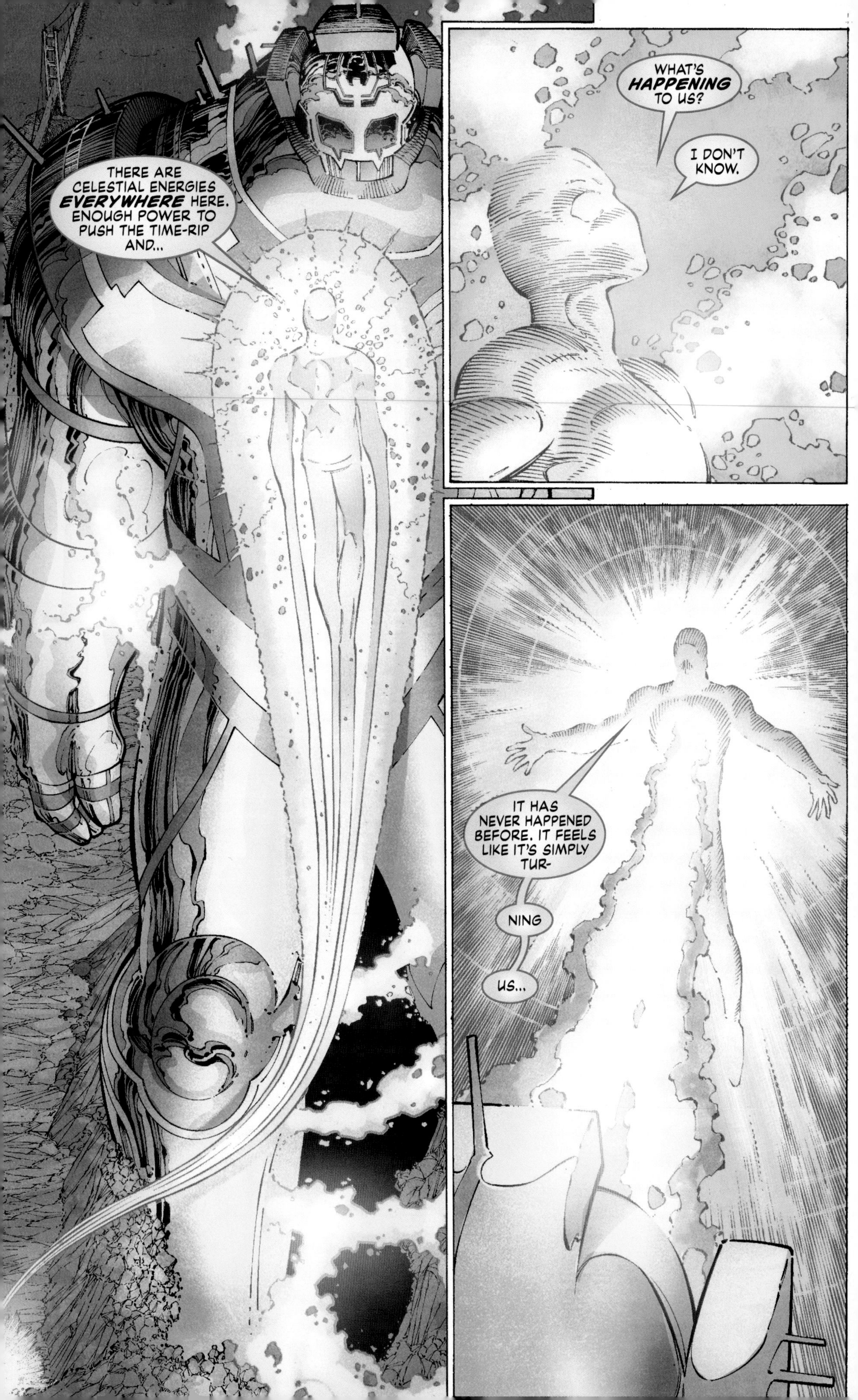
THERE ARE CELESTIAL ENERGIES EVERYWHERE HERE. ENOUGH POWER TO PUSH THE TIME-RIP AND...
WHAT'S HAPPENING TO US?
I DON'T KNOW.
IT HAS NEVER HAPPENED BEFORE. IT FEELS LIKE IT'S SIMPLY TUR-
NING
US...

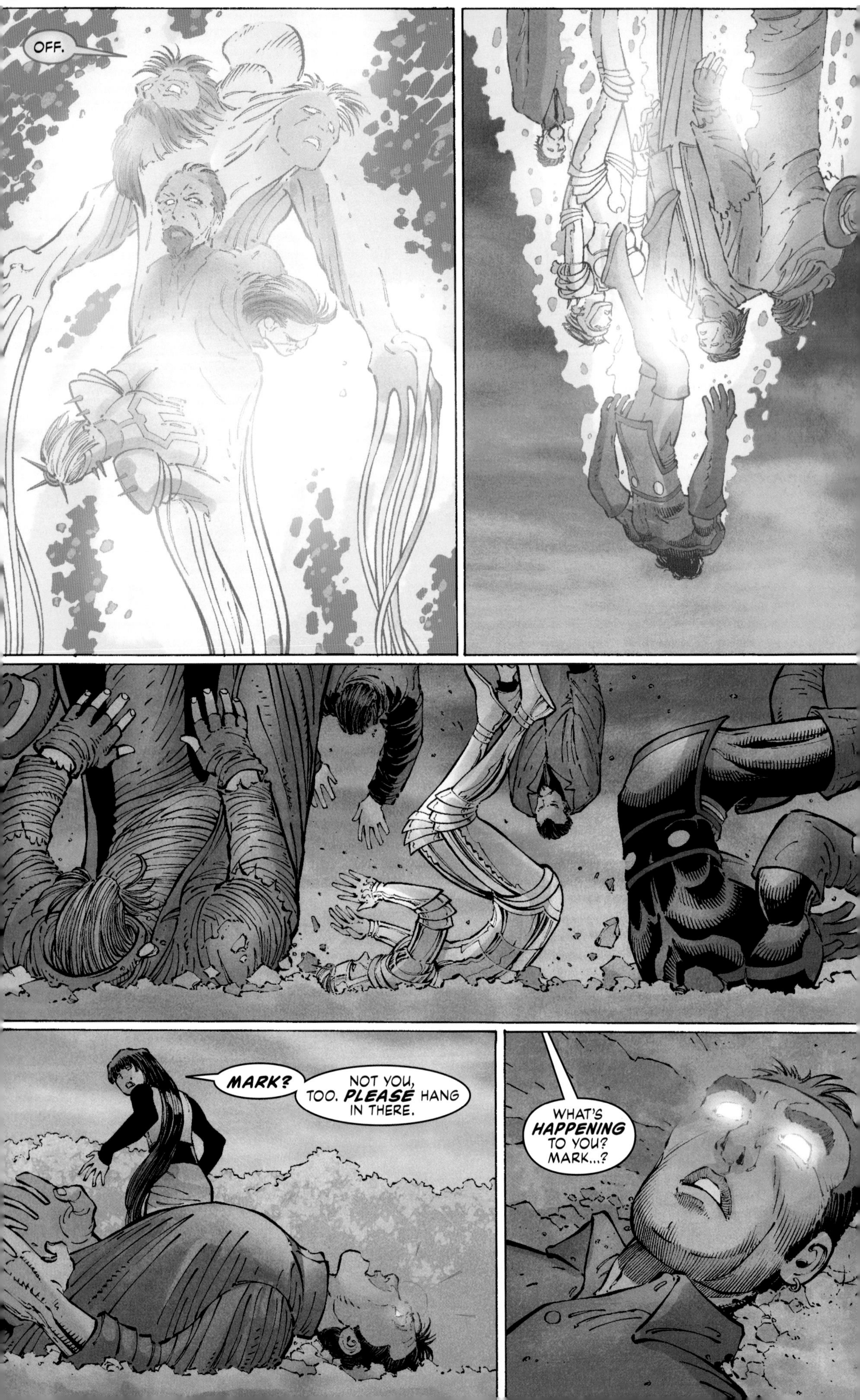

OFF.
MARK?
NOT YOU, TOO. PLEASE HANG IN THERE.
WHAT'S HAPPENING TO YOU? MARK...?

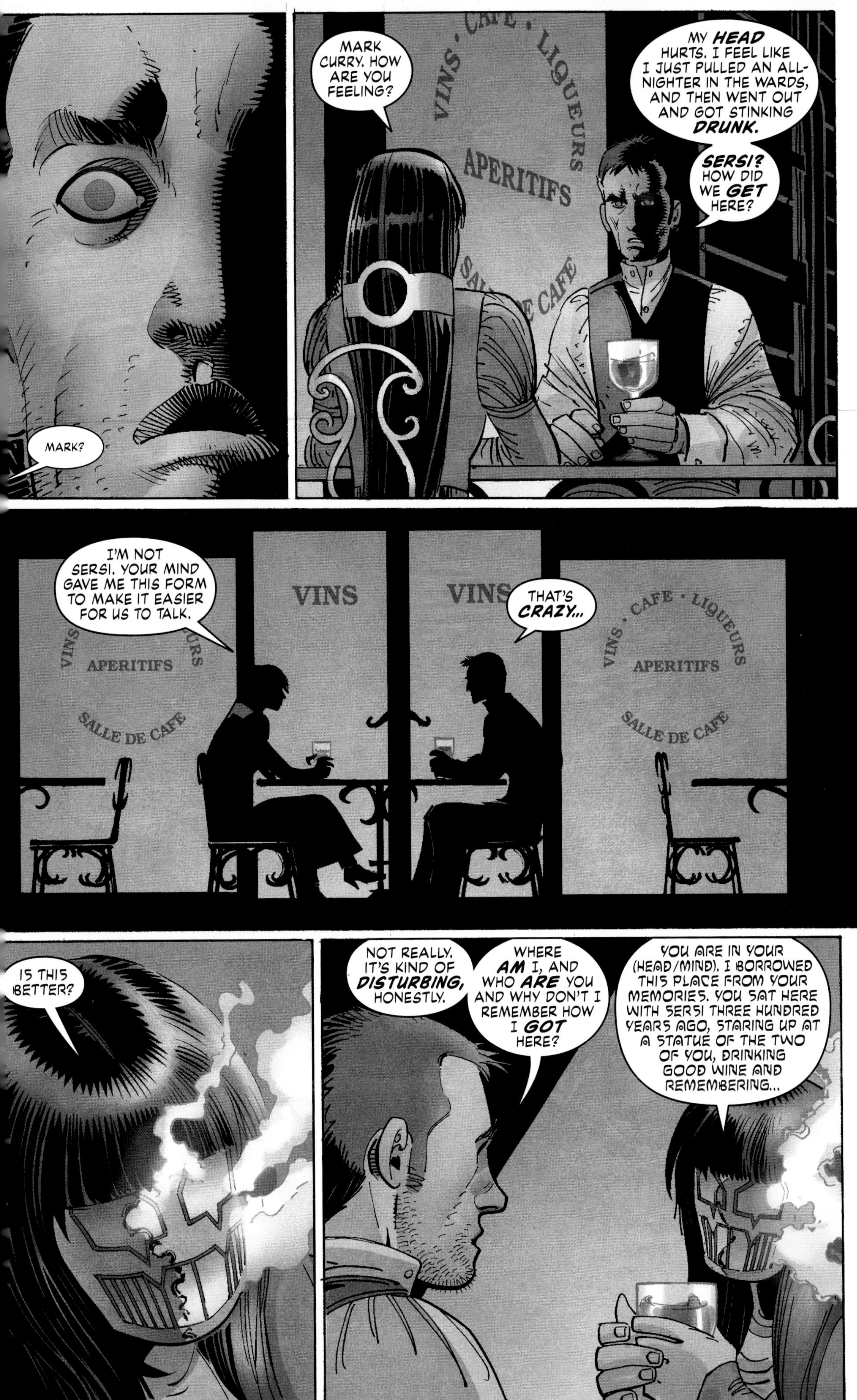
MARK?
MARK CURRY. HOW ARE YOU FEELING?
VINS · CAFE · LIQUEURS
APERITIFS
SALLE DE CAFE
MY HEAD HURTS. I FEEL LIKE I JUST PULLED AN ALL-NIGHTER IN THE WARDS, AND THEN WENT OUT AND GOT STINKING DRUNK.
SERSI? HOW DID WE GET HERE?
I'M NOT SERSI. YOUR MIND GAVE ME THIS FORM TO MAKE IT EASIER FOR US TO TALK.
VINS
VINS
THAT'S CRAZY...
IS THIS BETTER?
NOT REALLY. IT'S KIND OF DISTURBING, HONESTLY.
WHERE AM I, AND WHO ARE YOU AND WHY DON'T I REMEMBER HOW I GOT HERE?
YOU ARE IN YOUR (HEAD/MIND). I BORROWED THIS PLACE FROM YOUR MEMORIES. YOU SAT HERE WITH SERSI THREE HUNDRED YEARS AGO, STARING UP AT A STATUE OF THE TWO OF YOU, DRINKING GOOD WINE AND REMEMBERING...

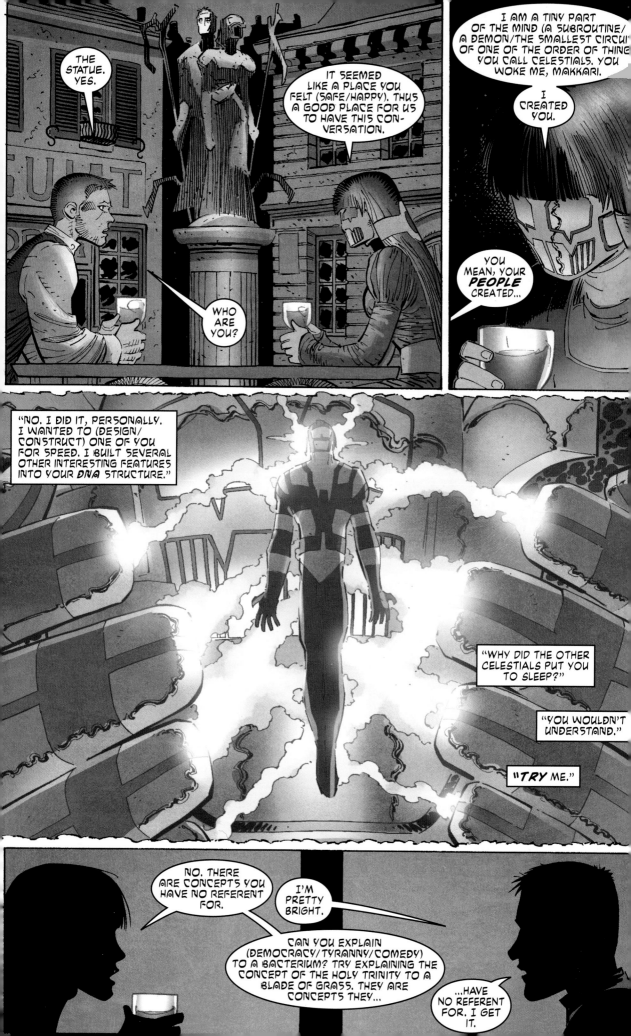

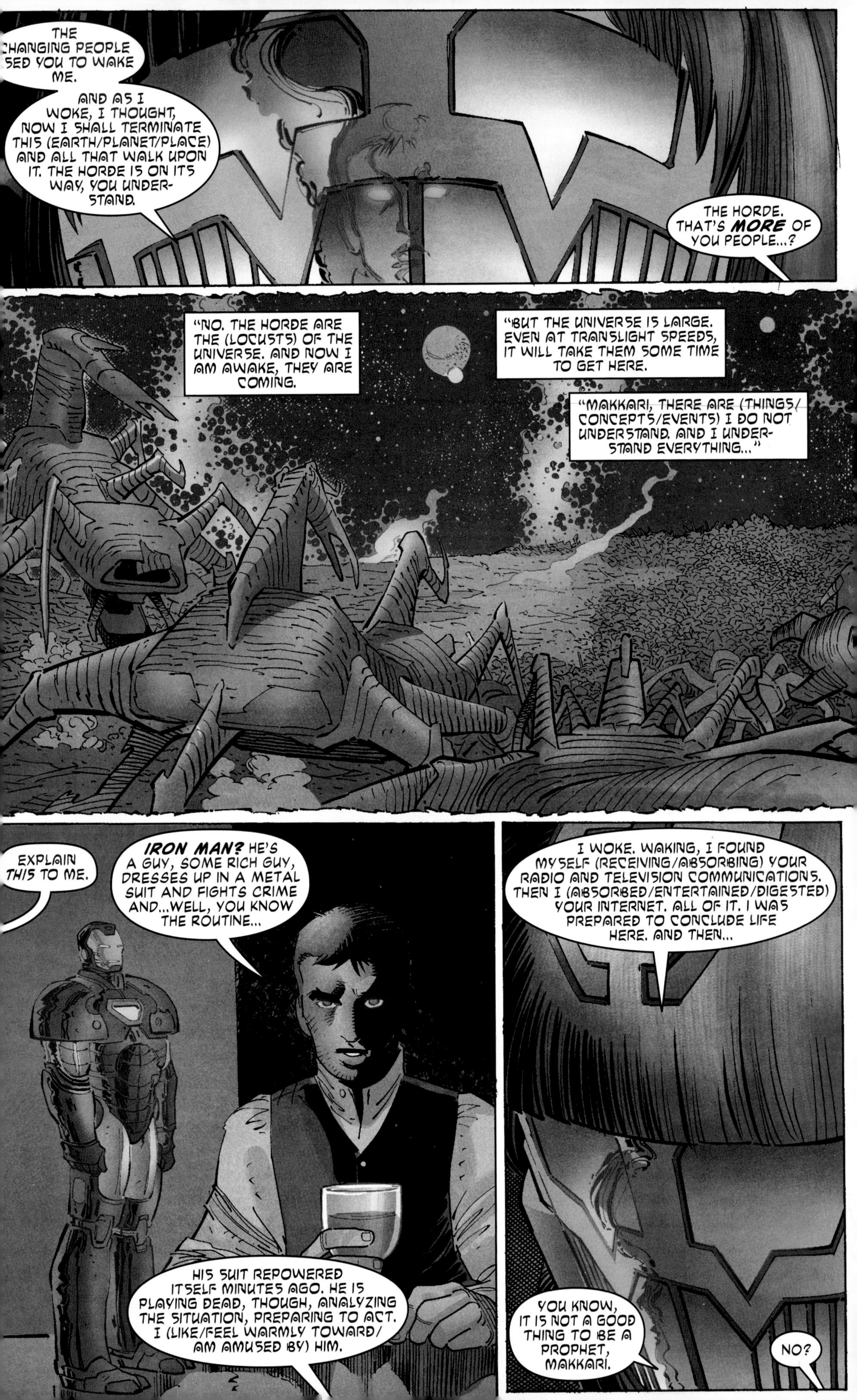
THE CHANGING PEOPLE SED YOU TO WAKE ME.
AND AS I WOKE, I THOUGHT, NOW I SHALL TERMINATE THIS (EARTH/PLANET/PLACE) AND ALL THAT WALK UPON IT. THE HORDE IS ON ITS WAY, YOU UNDERSTAND.
THE HORDE. THAT'S MORE OF YOU PEOPLE...?
"NO. THE HORDE ARE THE (LOCUSTS) OF THE UNIVERSE. AND NOW I AM AWAKE, THEY ARE COMING.
"BUT THE UNIVERSE IS LARGE. EVEN AT TRANSLIGHT SPEEDS, IT WILL TAKE THEM SOME TIME TO GET HERE.
"MAKKARI, THERE ARE (THINGS/CONCEPTS/EVENTS) I DO NOT UNDERSTAND, AND I UNDERSTAND EVERYTHING..."
EXPLAIN THIS TO ME.
IRON MAN? HE'S A GUY, SOME RICH GUY, DRESSES UP IN A METAL SUIT AND FIGHTS CRIME AND...WELL, YOU KNOW THE ROUTINE...
HIS SUIT REPOWERED ITSELF MINUTES AGO. HE IS PLAYING DEAD, THOUGH, ANALYZING THE SITUATION, PREPARING TO ACT. I (LIKE/FEEL WARMLY TOWARD/AM AMUSED BY) HIM.
I WOKE. WAKING, I FOUND MYSELF (RECEIVING/ABSORBING) YOUR RADIO AND TELEVISION COMMUNICATIONS. THEN I (ABSORBED/ENTERTAINED/DIGESTED) YOUR INTERNET. ALL OF IT. I WAS PREPARED TO CONCLUDE LIFE HERE. AND THEN...
YOU KNOW, IT IS NOT A GOOD THING TO BE A PROPHET, MAKKARI.
NO?

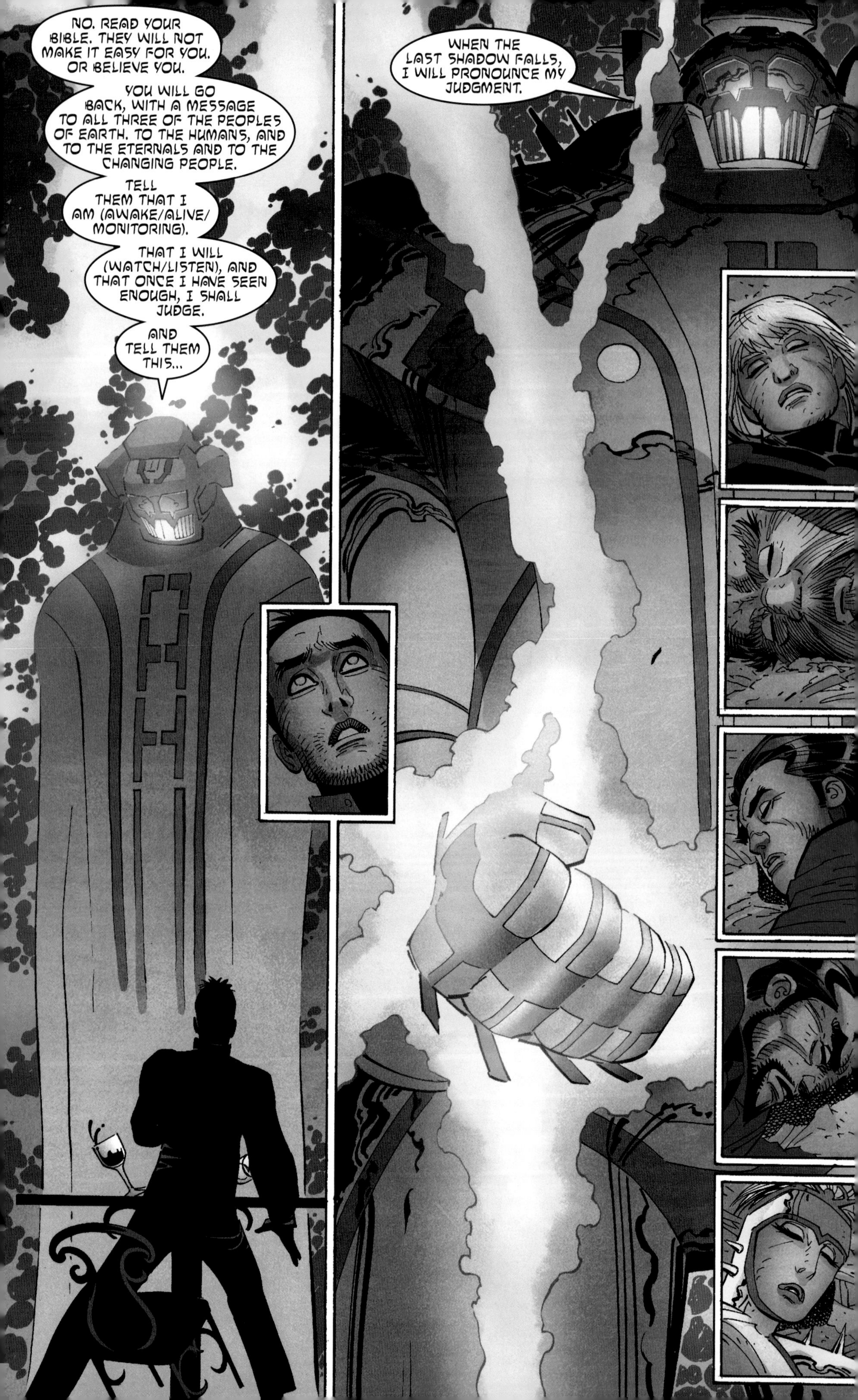

NO. READ YOUR BIBLE. THEY WILL NOT MAKE IT EASY FOR YOU. OR BELIEVE YOU.
YOU WILL GO BACK, WITH A MESSAGE TO ALL THREE OF THE PEOPLES OF EARTH. TO THE HUMANS, AND TO THE ETERNALS AND TO THE CHANGING PEOPLE.
TELL THEM THAT I AM (AWAKE/ALIVE/ MONITORING).
THAT I WILL (WATCH/LISTEN), AND THAT ONCE I HAVE SEEN ENOUGH, I SHALL JUDGE.
AND TELL THEM THIS...
WHEN THE LAST SHADOW FALLS, I WILL PRONOUNCE MY JUDGMENT.

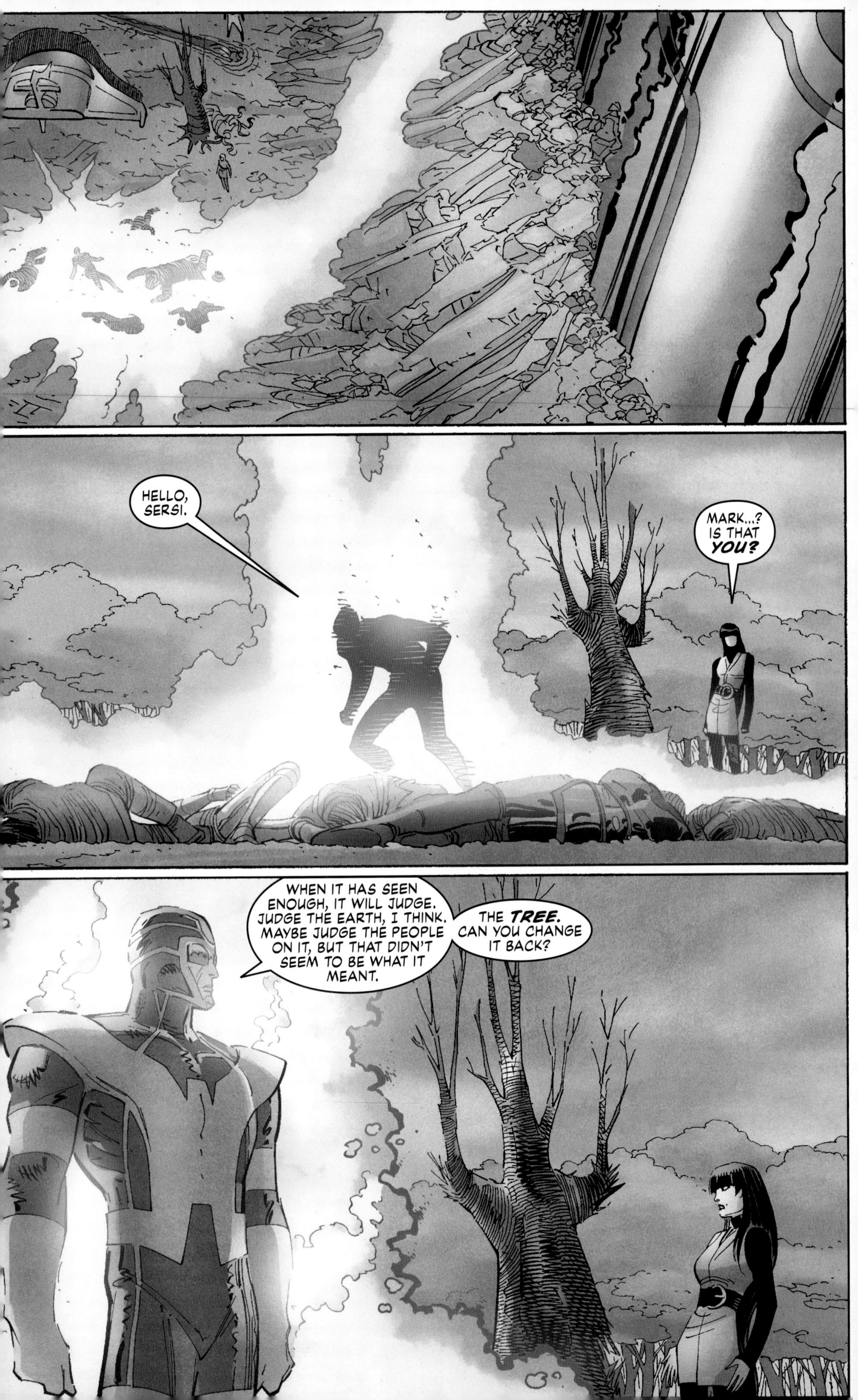
HELLO, SERSI.
MARK...? IS THAT YOU?
WHEN IT HAS SEEN ENOUGH, IT WILL JUDGE. JUDGE THE EARTH, I THINK. MAYBE JUDGE THE PEOPLE ON IT, BUT THAT DIDN'T SEEM TO BE WHAT IT MEANT.
THE TREE. CAN YOU CHANGE IT BACK?

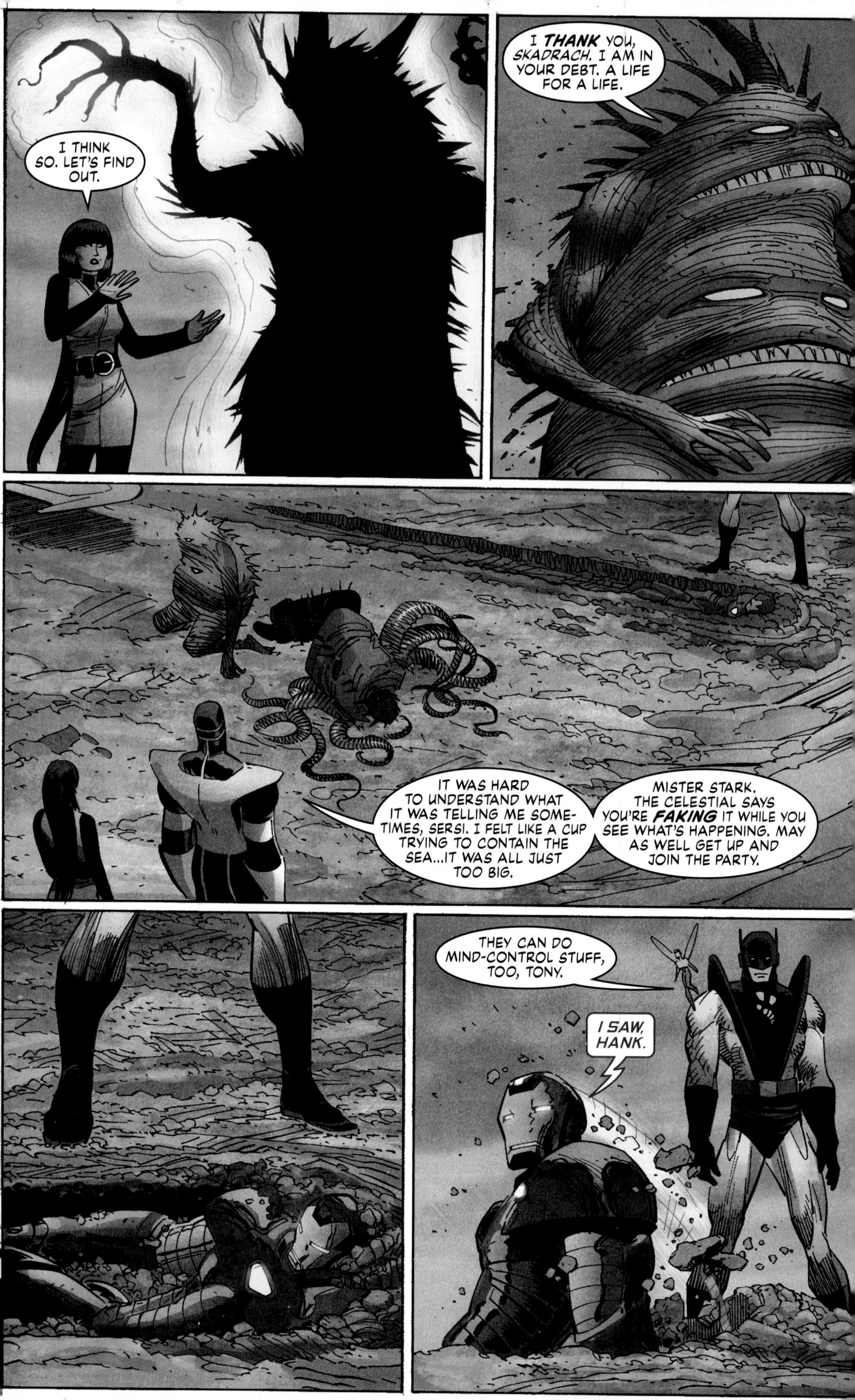
I THINK SO. LET'S FIND OUT.
I *THANK* YOU, SKADRACH. I AM IN YOUR DEBT. A LIFE FOR A LIFE.
IT WAS HARD TO UNDERSTAND WHAT IT WAS TELLING ME SOME-TIMES, SERSI. I FELT LIKE A CUP TRYING TO CONTAIN THE SEA...IT WAS ALL JUST TOO BIG.
MISTER STARK. THE CELESTIAL SAYS YOU'RE *FAKING* IT WHILE YOU SEE WHAT'S HAPPENING. MAY AS WELL GET UP AND JOIN THE PARTY.
THEY CAN DO MIND-CONTROL STUFF, TOO, TONY.
I SAW, HANK.

DO YOU THINK YOU CAN FIX HIM, SERSI?

I DON'T KNOW. HE TOOK AN EYE-BLAST FULL ON.

TRY. JUST TELL HIS CELLS TO REGENERATE THEMSELVES.

DOES THIS THING REALLY HAVE THE ABILITY TO DESTROY THE WORLD?

CERTAINLY.

WE HAVE TO FIGHT IT. WE HAVE TO REMOVE IT.

NO.

IT WILL REMAIN HERE, IN THE PARK.

IT WILL NOT BE DISTURBED. NOT BY YOU. NOT BY ANYONE.

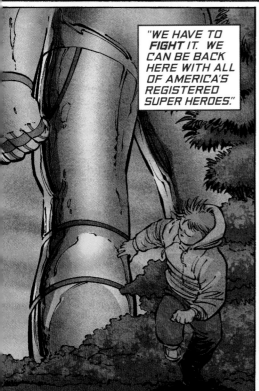

"WE HAVE TO FIGHT IT. WE CAN BE BACK HERE WITH ALL OF AMERICA'S REGISTERED SUPER HEROES."

IT CAN'T STOP ALL OF US.

WE'VE FOUGHT ALIENS BEFORE.

DOESN'T MATTER. YOU CAN'T HURT IT. YOU CAN'T EVEN AFFECT IT. YOU CAN'T DO ANYTHING TO IT IT DOESN'T WANT YOU TO DO.

LISTEN. IT'S JUST AN ALIEN SPACE ROBOT. IT'S NOT GOD.

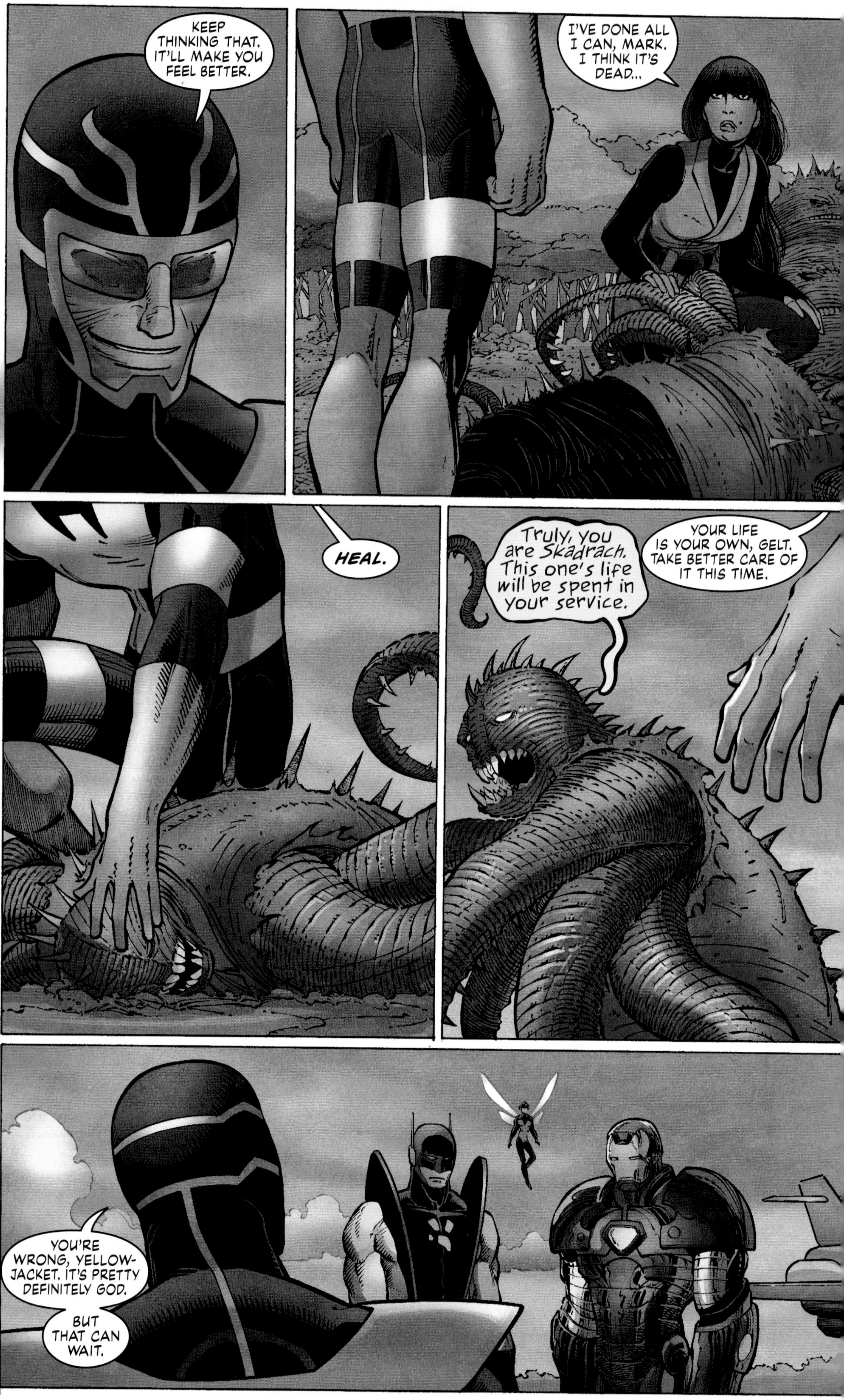
KEEP THINKING THAT. IT'LL MAKE YOU FEEL BETTER.
I'VE DONE ALL I CAN, MARK. I THINK IT'S DEAD...
HEAL.
Truly, you are Skadrach. This one's life will be spent in your service.
YOUR LIFE IS YOUR OWN, GELT. TAKE BETTER CARE OF IT THIS TIME.
YOU'RE WRONG, YELLOW-JACKET. IT'S PRETTY DEFINITELY GOD.
BUT THAT CAN WAIT.

AND BY THE WAY, IRON MAN...? IT *LIKES* YOU.

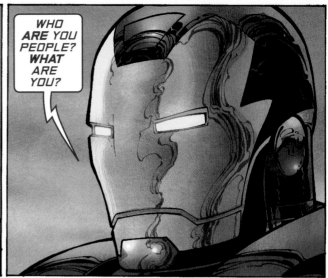

WHO *ARE* YOU PEOPLE? *WHAT* ARE YOU?

WE ARE THE ETERNALS. WE ARE THE COURT OF LAST RESORT FOR HUMANITY AND FOR ALL LIVING THINGS ON EARTH.

WHOSE SIDE ARE YOU ON?

WE DO NOT CHOOSE SIDES. COUNTRIES ARE LINES IN THE SAND. EMPIRES RISE AND FALL. WE ARE TIMELESS. WE WILL STILL BE HERE TOMORROW, AND A HUNDRED CENTURIES FROM NOW.

YOU *HAVE* TO CHOOSE SIDES. YOU HAVE TO *REGISTER*.

IF YOU SAW TWO GROUPS OF CHILDREN ARGUING OVER WHICH OF THEM COULD PLAY IN SOME WASTE GROUND, WOULD YOU CHOOSE SIDES?

CHAPTER SEVEN: JOURNEY'S END

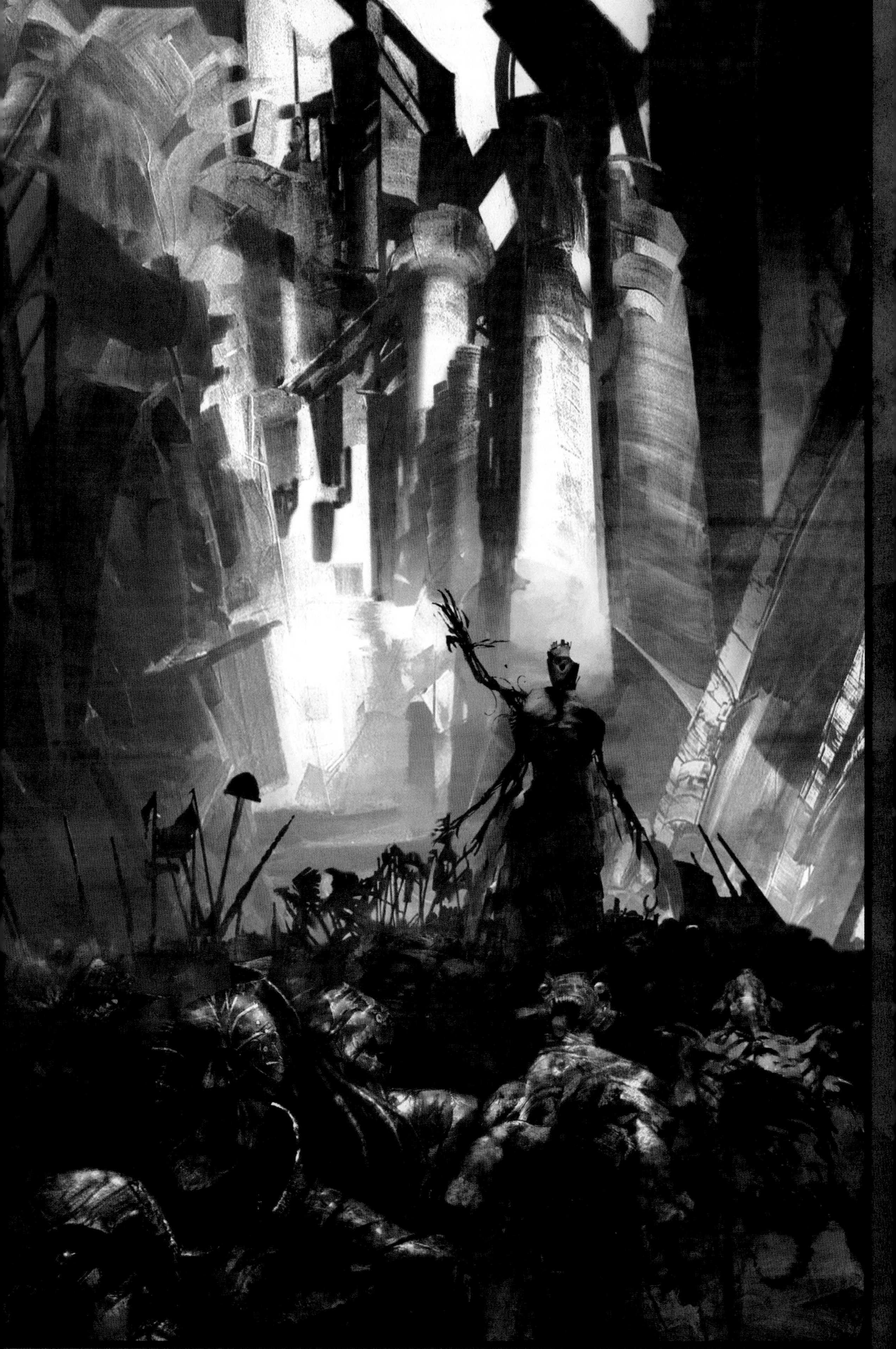

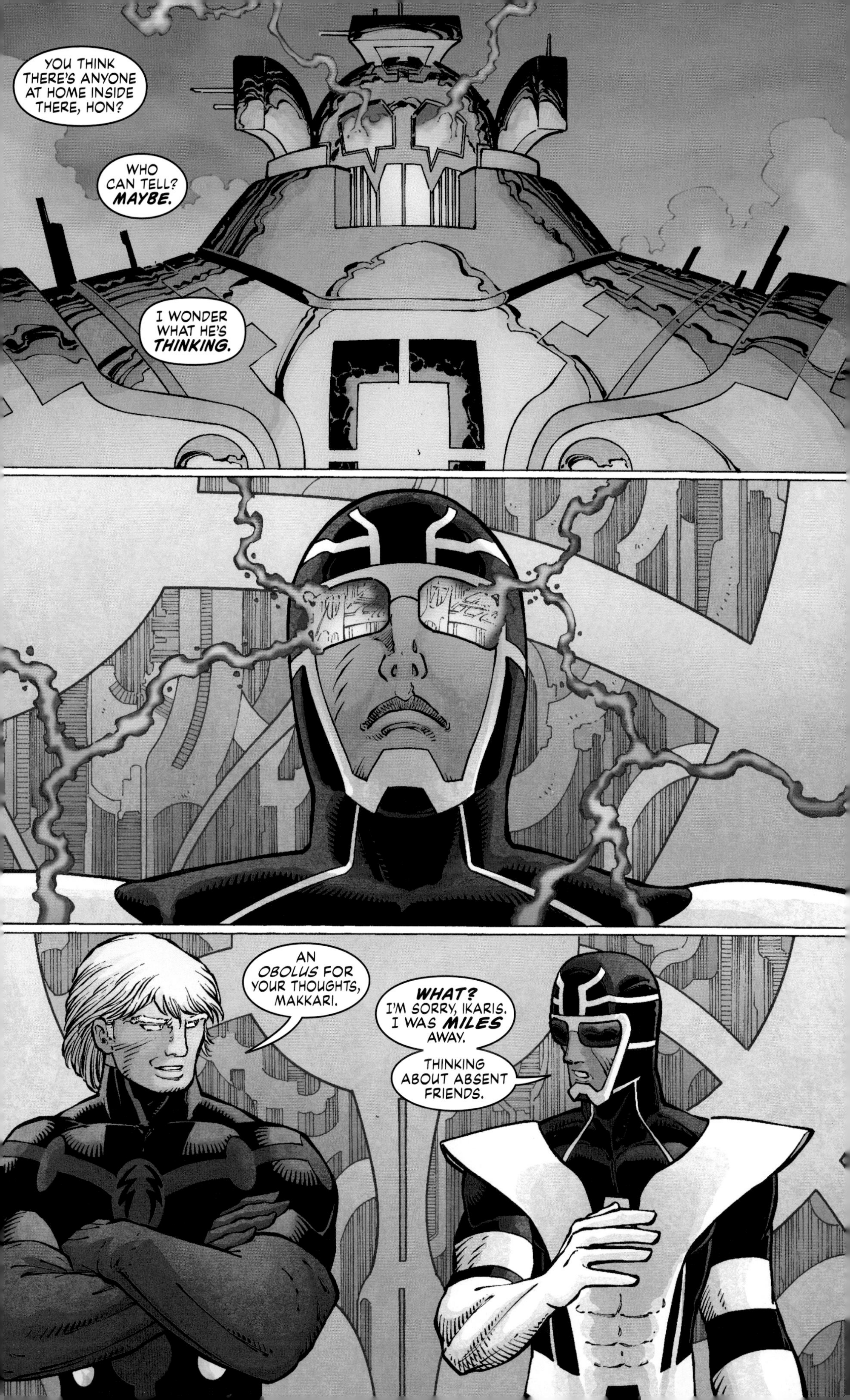
YOU THINK THERE'S ANYONE AT HOME INSIDE THERE, HON?
WHO CAN TELL? MAYBE.
I WONDER WHAT HE'S THINKING.
AN OBOLUS FOR YOUR THOUGHTS, MAKKARI.
WHAT? I'M SORRY, IKARIS. I WAS MILES AWAY.
THINKING ABOUT ABSENT FRIENDS.

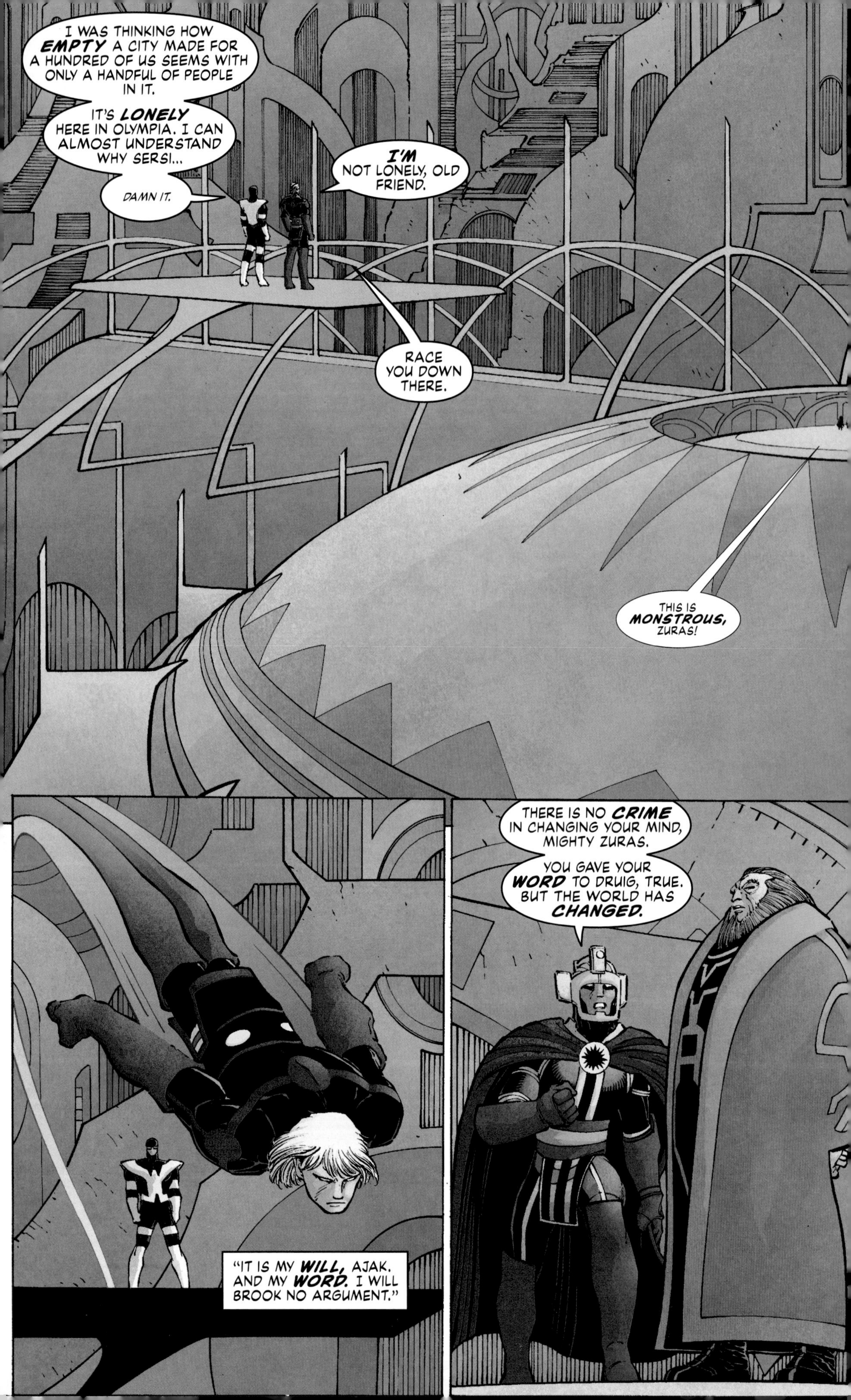
I WAS THINKING HOW EMPTY A CITY MADE FOR A HUNDRED OF US SEEMS WITH ONLY A HANDFUL OF PEOPLE IN IT.
IT'S LONELY HERE IN OLYMPIA. I CAN ALMOST UNDERSTAND WHY SERSI...
DAMN IT.
I'M NOT LONELY, OLD FRIEND.
RACE YOU DOWN THERE.
THIS IS MONSTROUS, ZURAS!
"IT IS MY WILL, AJAK. AND MY WORD. I WILL BROOK NO ARGUMENT."
THERE IS NO CRIME IN CHANGING YOUR MIND, MIGHTY ZURAS.
YOU GAVE YOUR WORD TO DRUIG, TRUE. BUT THE WORLD HAS CHANGED.

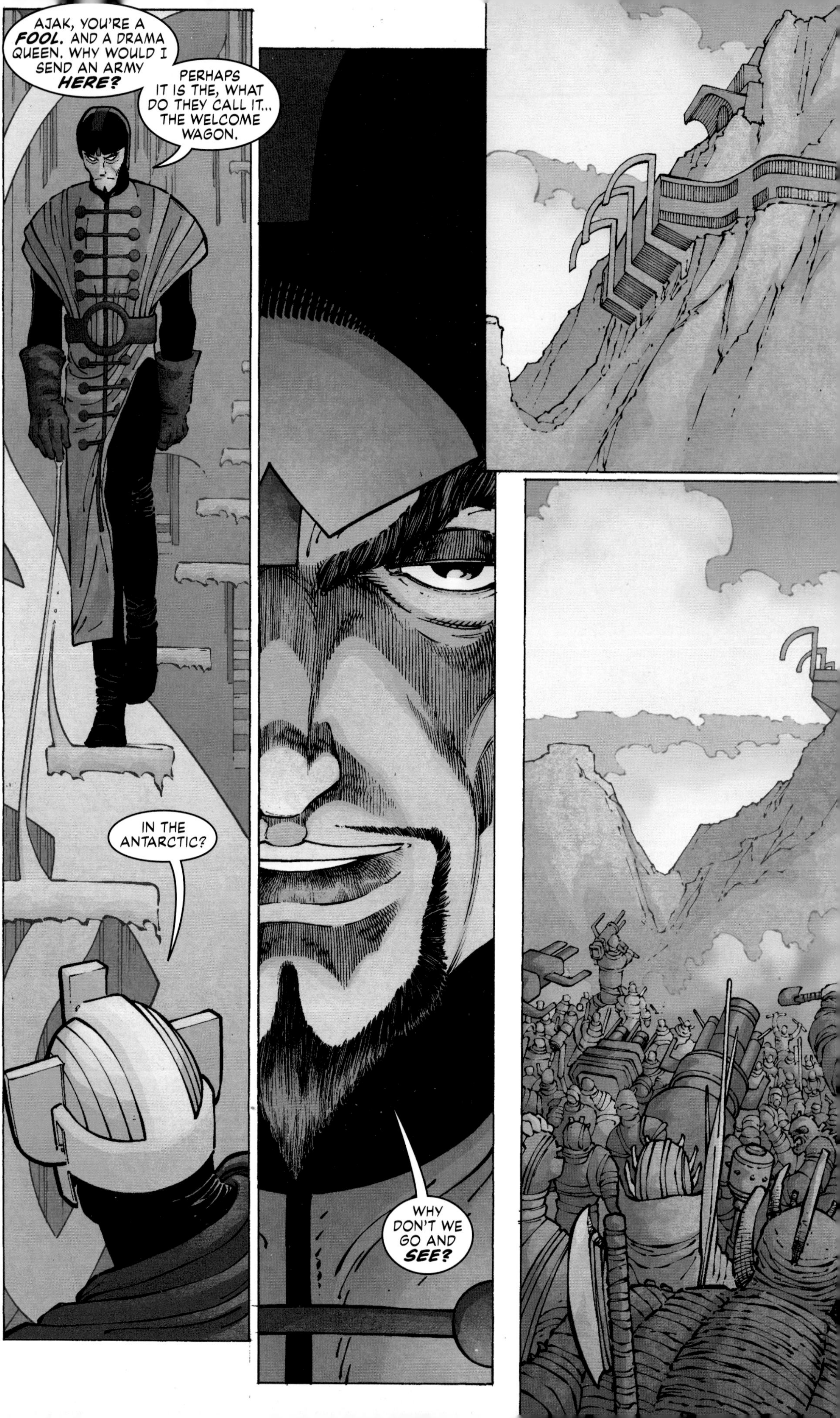
AJAK, YOU'RE A **FOOL.** AND A DRAMA QUEEN. WHY WOULD I SEND AN ARMY ***HERE?***
PERHAPS IT IS THE, WHAT DO THEY CALL IT... THE WELCOME WAGON.
IN THE ANTARCTIC?
WHY DON'T WE GO AND ***SEE?***

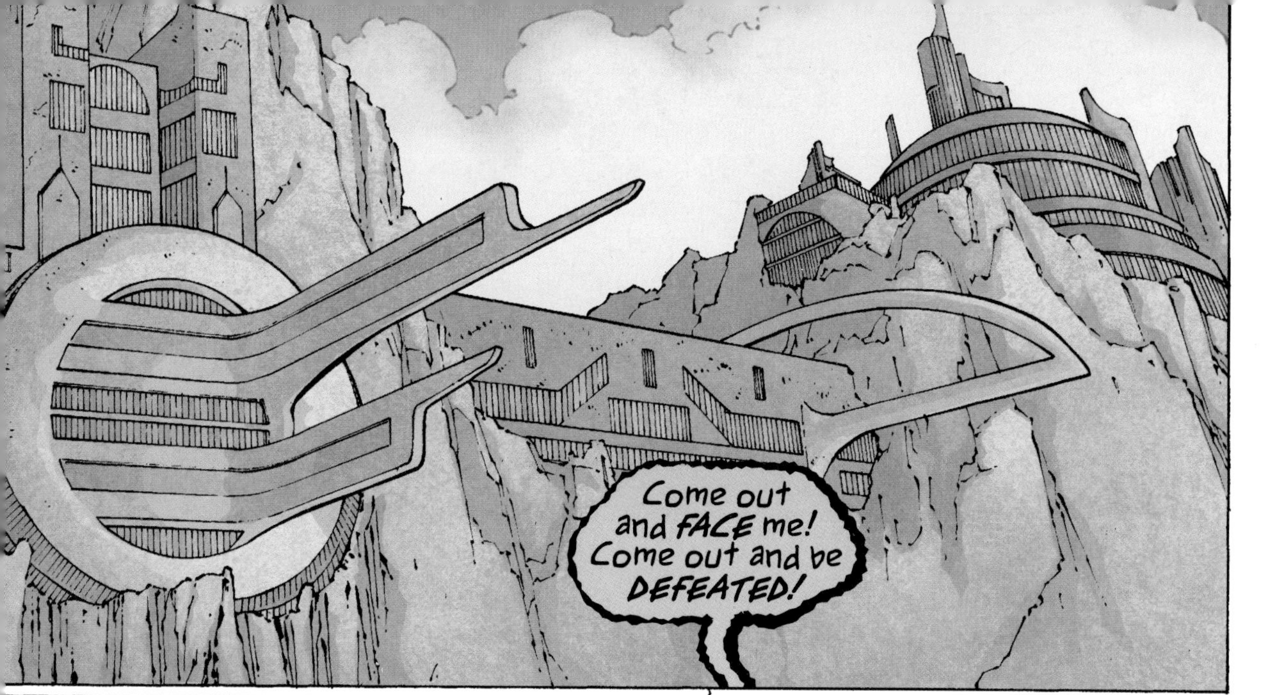
Come out and FACE me! Come out and be DEFEATED!

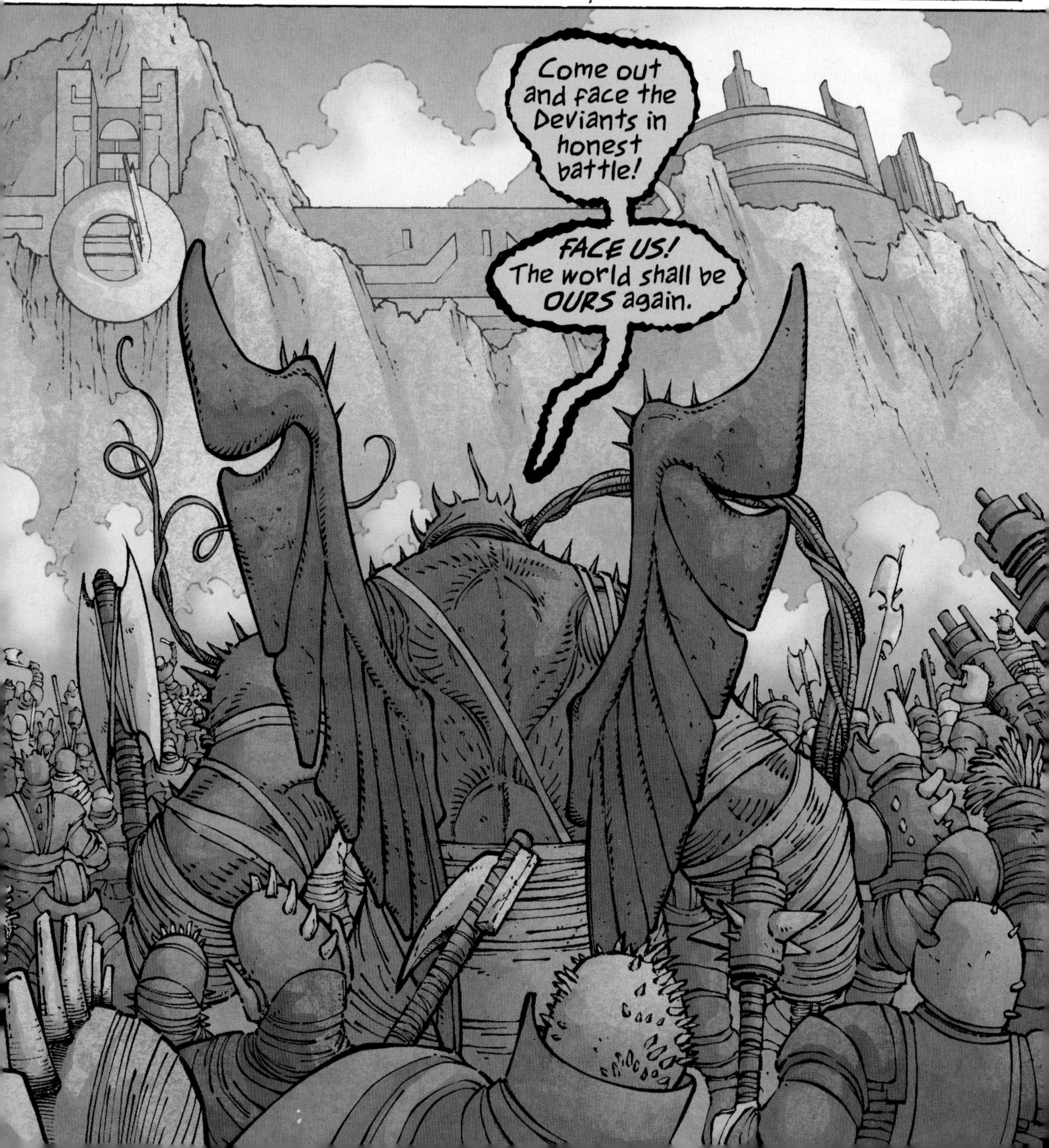
Come out and face the Deviants in honest battle!
FACE US! The world shall be OURS again.

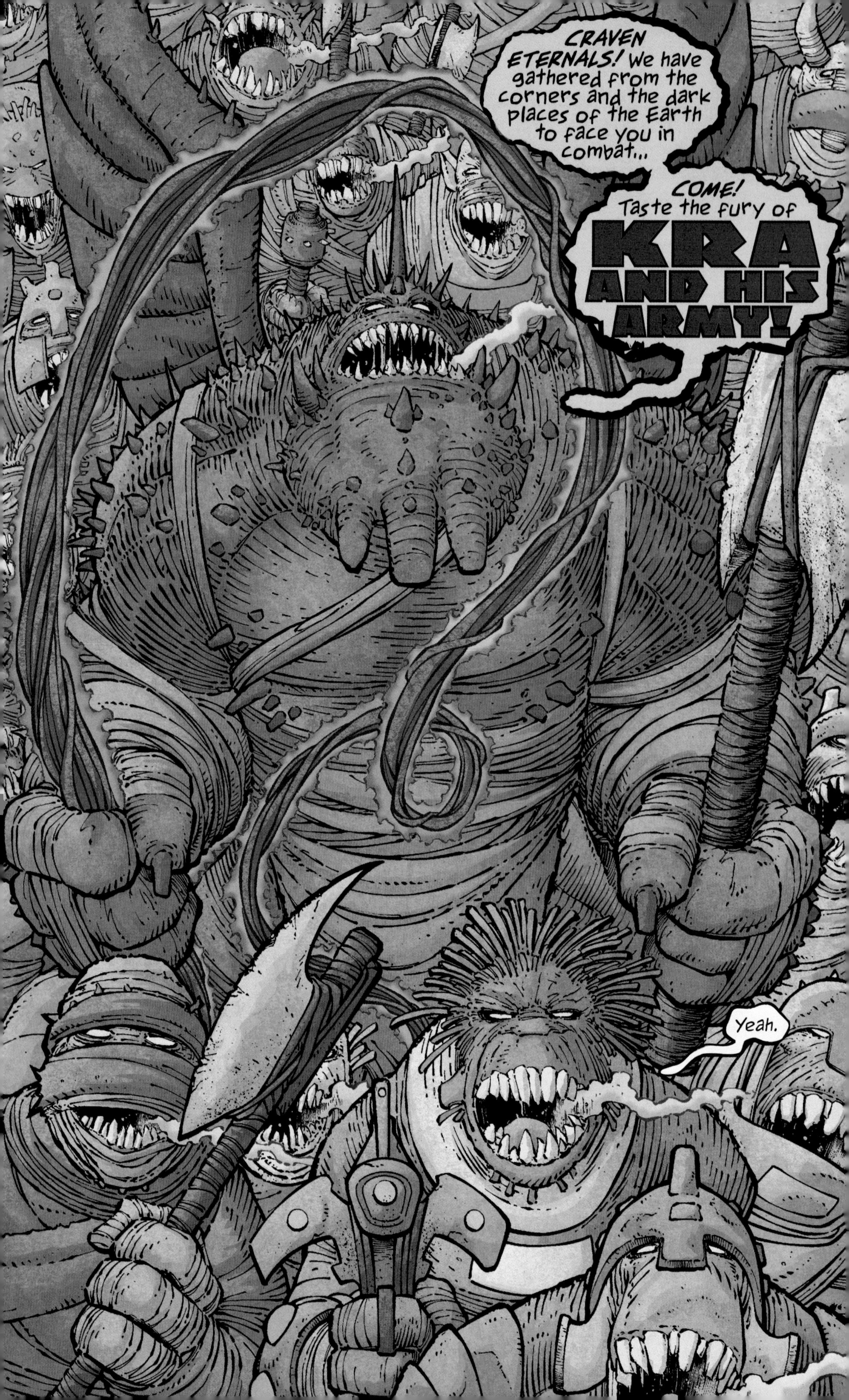
CRAVEN ETERNALS! We have gathered from the corners and the dark places of the Earth to face you in combat...
COME! Taste the fury of KRA AND HIS ARMY!
Yeah.

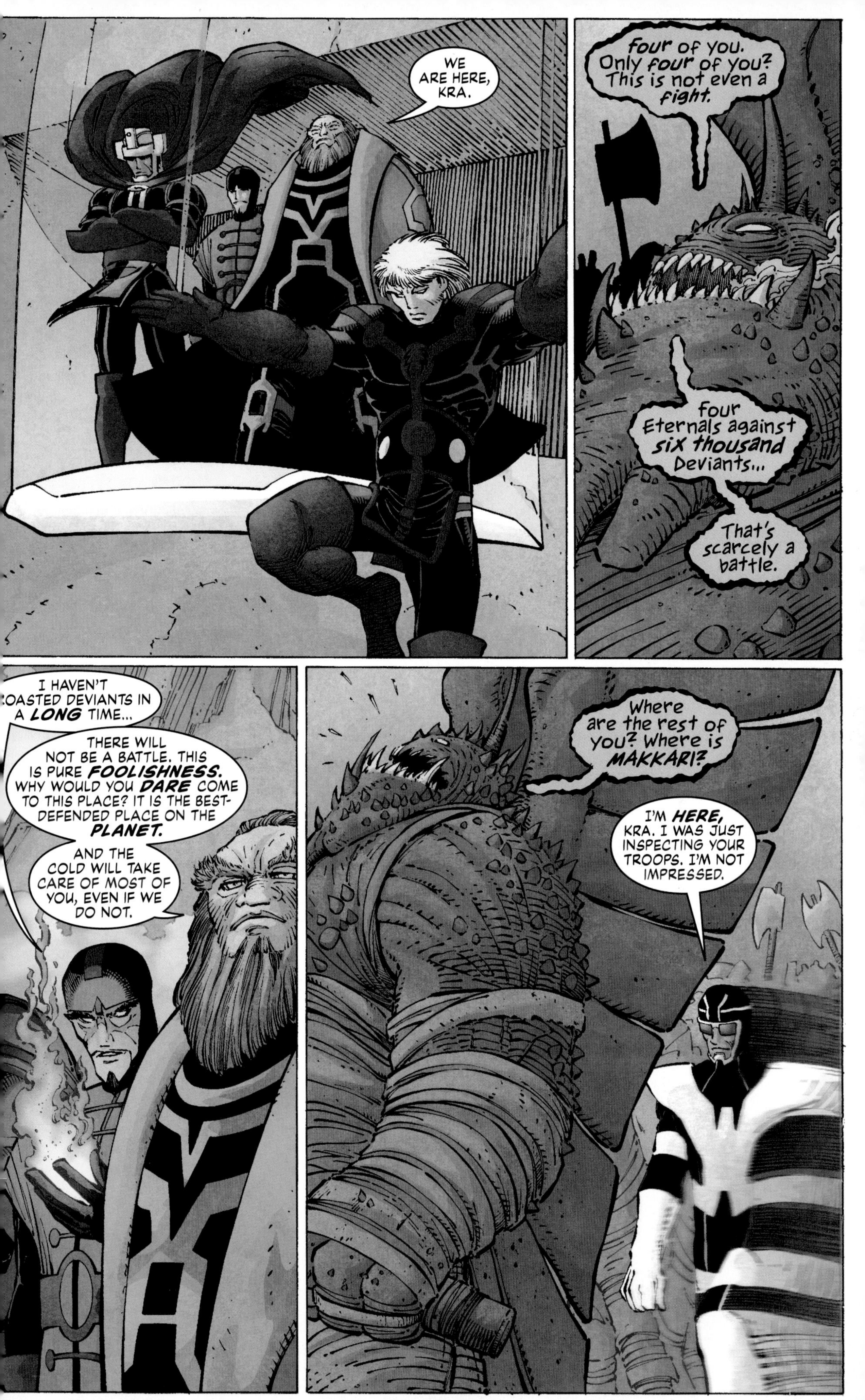
WE ARE HERE, KRA.
Four of you. Only four of you? This is not even a fight.
Four Eternals against six thousand Deviants...
That's scarcely a battle.
I HAVEN'T ROASTED DEVIANTS IN A LONG TIME...
THERE WILL NOT BE A BATTLE. THIS IS PURE FOOLISHNESS. WHY WOULD YOU DARE COME TO THIS PLACE? IT IS THE BEST-DEFENDED PLACE ON THE PLANET.
AND THE COLD WILL TAKE CARE OF MOST OF YOU, EVEN IF WE DO NOT.
Where are the rest of you? Where is MAKKARI?
I'M HERE, KRA. I WAS JUST INSPECTING YOUR TROOPS. I'M NOT IMPRESSED.

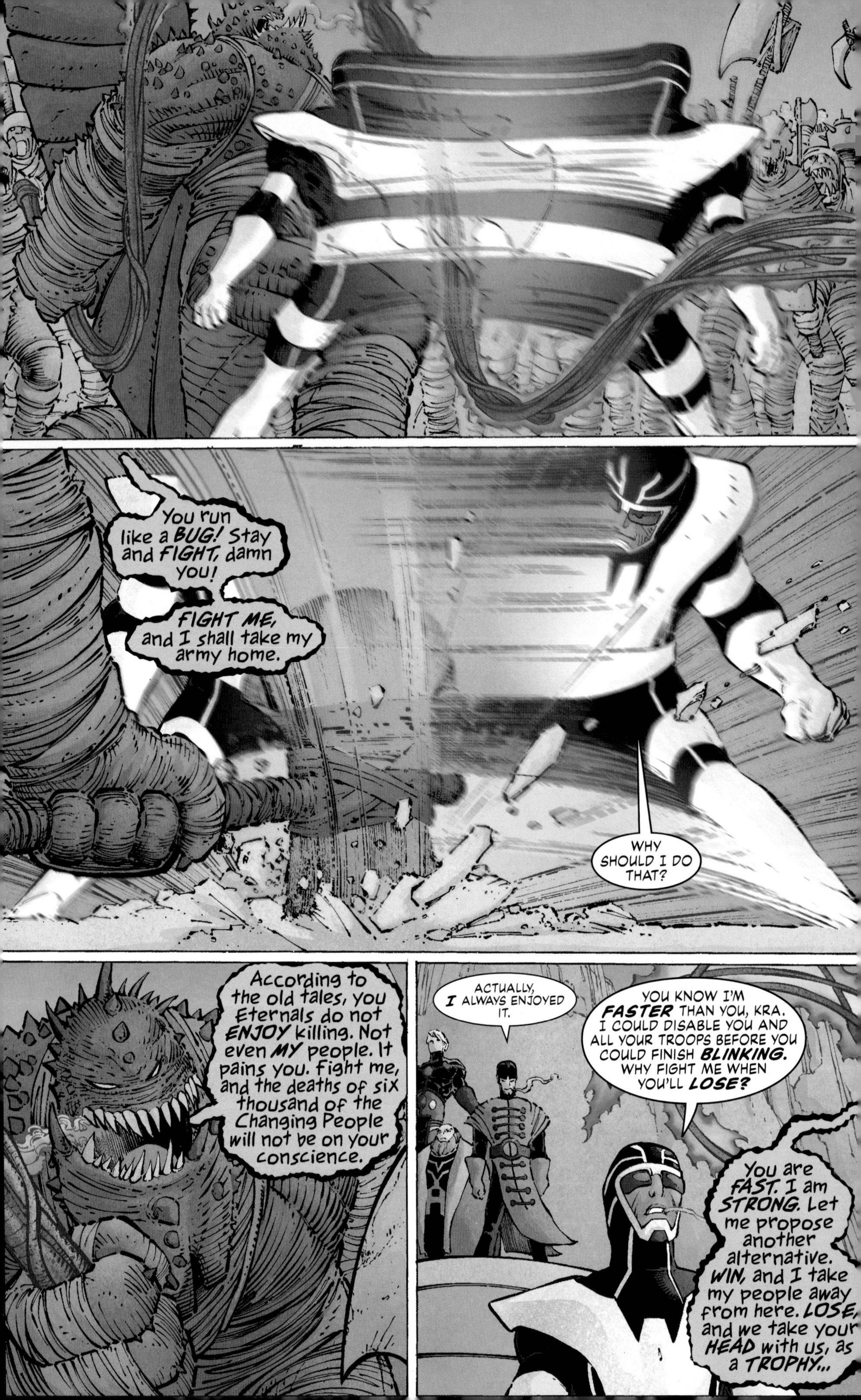

You run like a BUG! Stay and FIGHT, damn you!
FIGHT ME, and I shall take my army home.
WHY SHOULD I DO THAT?
According to the old tales, you Eternals do not ENJOY killing. Not even MY people. It pains you. Fight me, and the deaths of six thousand of the Changing People will not be on your conscience.
ACTUALLY, I ALWAYS ENJOYED IT.
YOU KNOW I'M FASTER THAN YOU, KRA. I COULD DISABLE YOU AND ALL YOUR TROOPS BEFORE YOU COULD FINISH BLINKING. WHY FIGHT ME WHEN YOU'LL LOSE?
You are FAST. I am STRONG. Let me propose another alternative. WIN, and I take my people away from here. LOSE, and we take your HEAD with us, as a TROPHY...

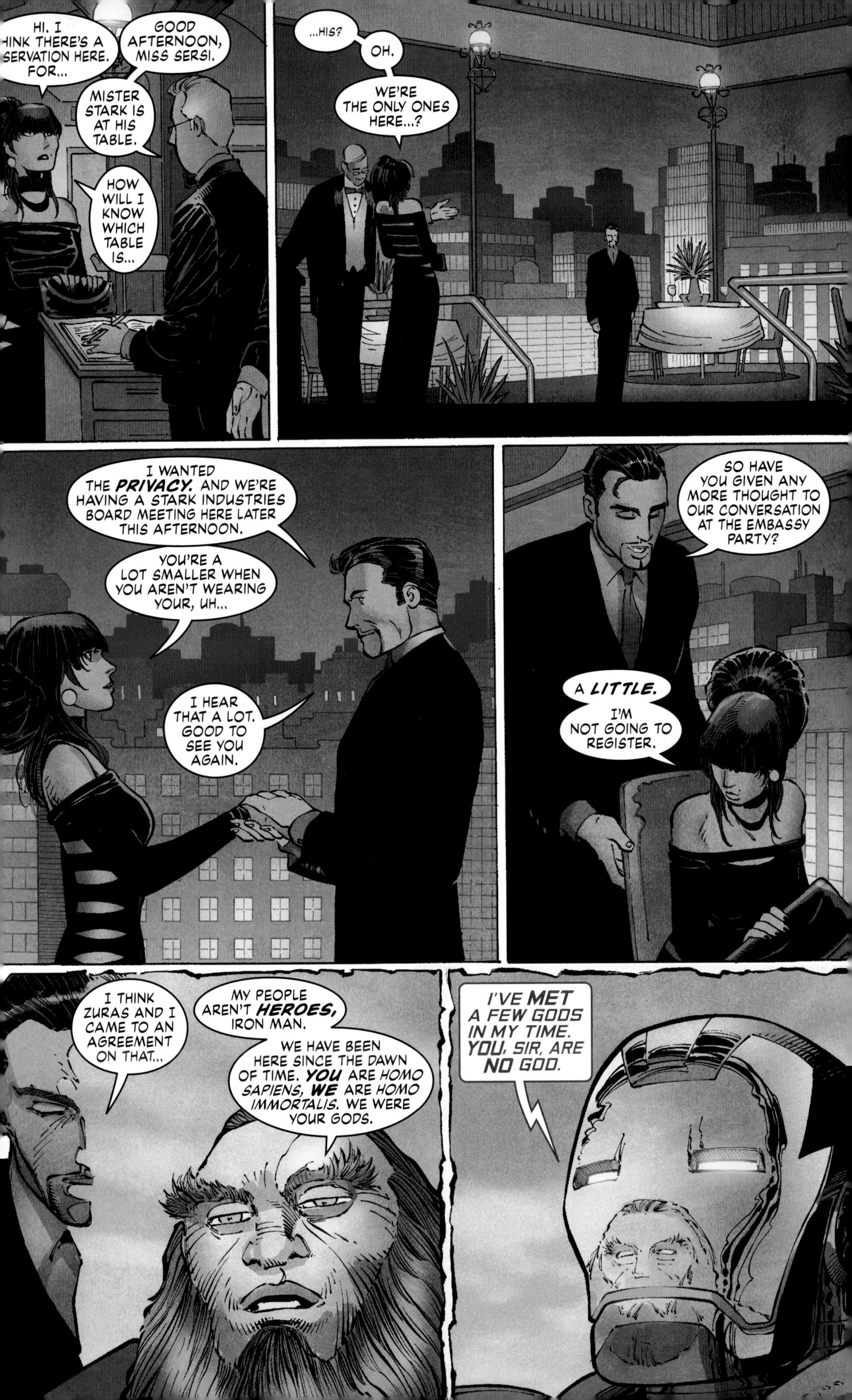
HI. I
HINK THERE'S A
SERVATION HERE.
FOR...
GOOD AFTERNOON, MISS SERSI.
MISTER STARK IS AT HIS TABLE.
HOW WILL I KNOW WHICH TABLE IS...
...HIS?
OH.
WE'RE THE ONLY ONES HERE...?
I WANTED THE PRIVACY. AND WE'RE HAVING A STARK INDUSTRIES BOARD MEETING HERE LATER THIS AFTERNOON.
YOU'RE A LOT SMALLER WHEN YOU AREN'T WEARING YOUR, UH...
I HEAR THAT A LOT. GOOD TO SEE YOU AGAIN.
SO HAVE YOU GIVEN ANY MORE THOUGHT TO OUR CONVERSATION AT THE EMBASSY PARTY?
A LITTLE.
I'M NOT GOING TO REGISTER.
I THINK ZURAS AND I CAME TO AN AGREEMENT ON THAT...
MY PEOPLE AREN'T HEROES, IRON MAN.
WE HAVE BEEN HERE SINCE THE DAWN OF TIME. YOU ARE HOMO SAPIENS, WE ARE HOMO IMMORTALIS. WE WERE YOUR GODS.
I'VE MET A FEW GODS IN MY TIME. YOU, SIR, ARE NO GOD.

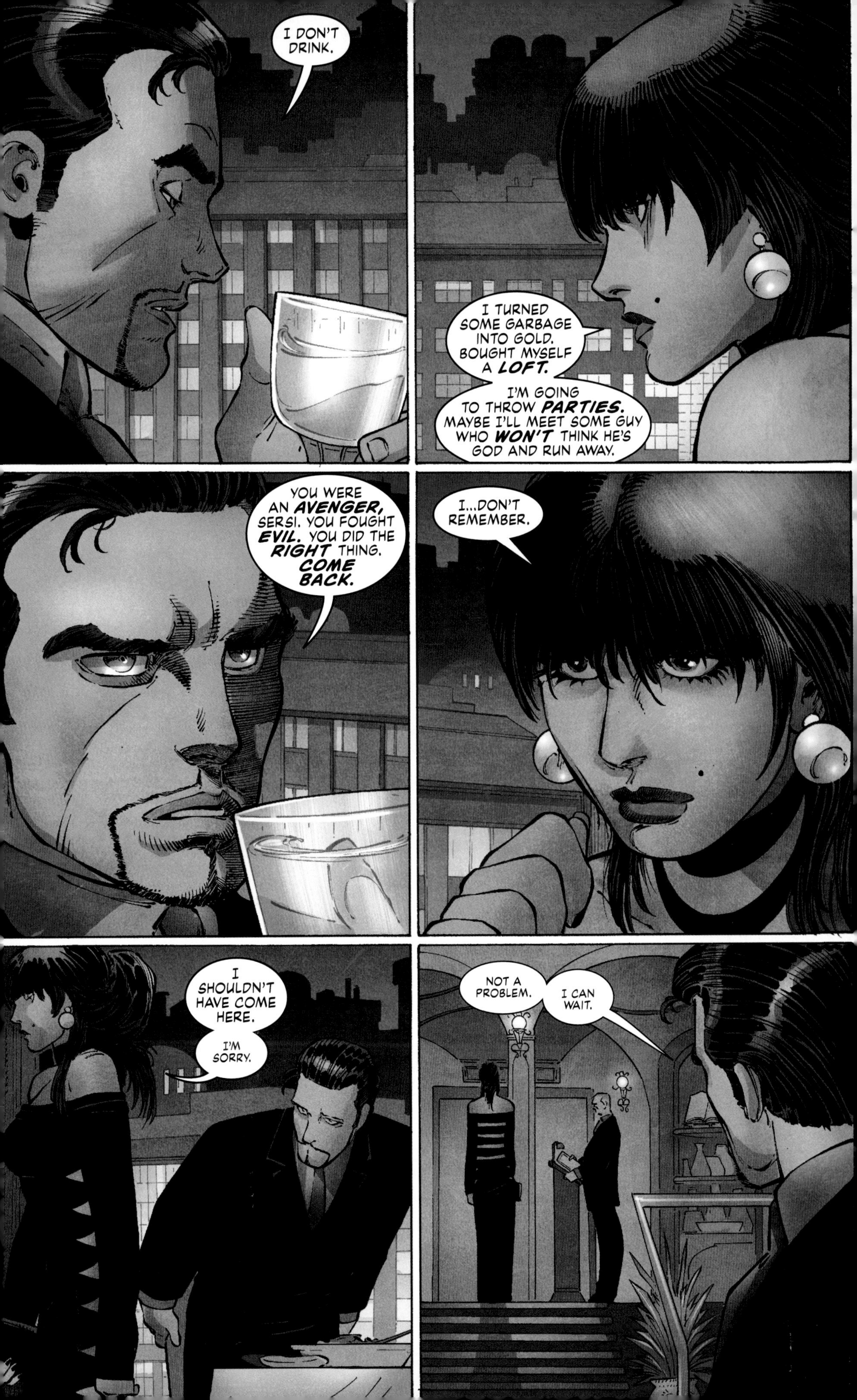
I DON'T DRINK.
I TURNED SOME GARBAGE INTO GOLD. BOUGHT MYSELF A LOFT.
I'M GOING TO THROW PARTIES. MAYBE I'LL MEET SOME GUY WHO WON'T THINK HE'S GOD AND RUN AWAY.
YOU WERE AN AVENGER, SERSI. YOU FOUGHT EVIL. YOU DID THE RIGHT THING. COME BACK.
I...DON'T REMEMBER.
I SHOULDN'T HAVE COME HERE.
I'M SORRY.
NOT A PROBLEM.
I CAN WAIT.

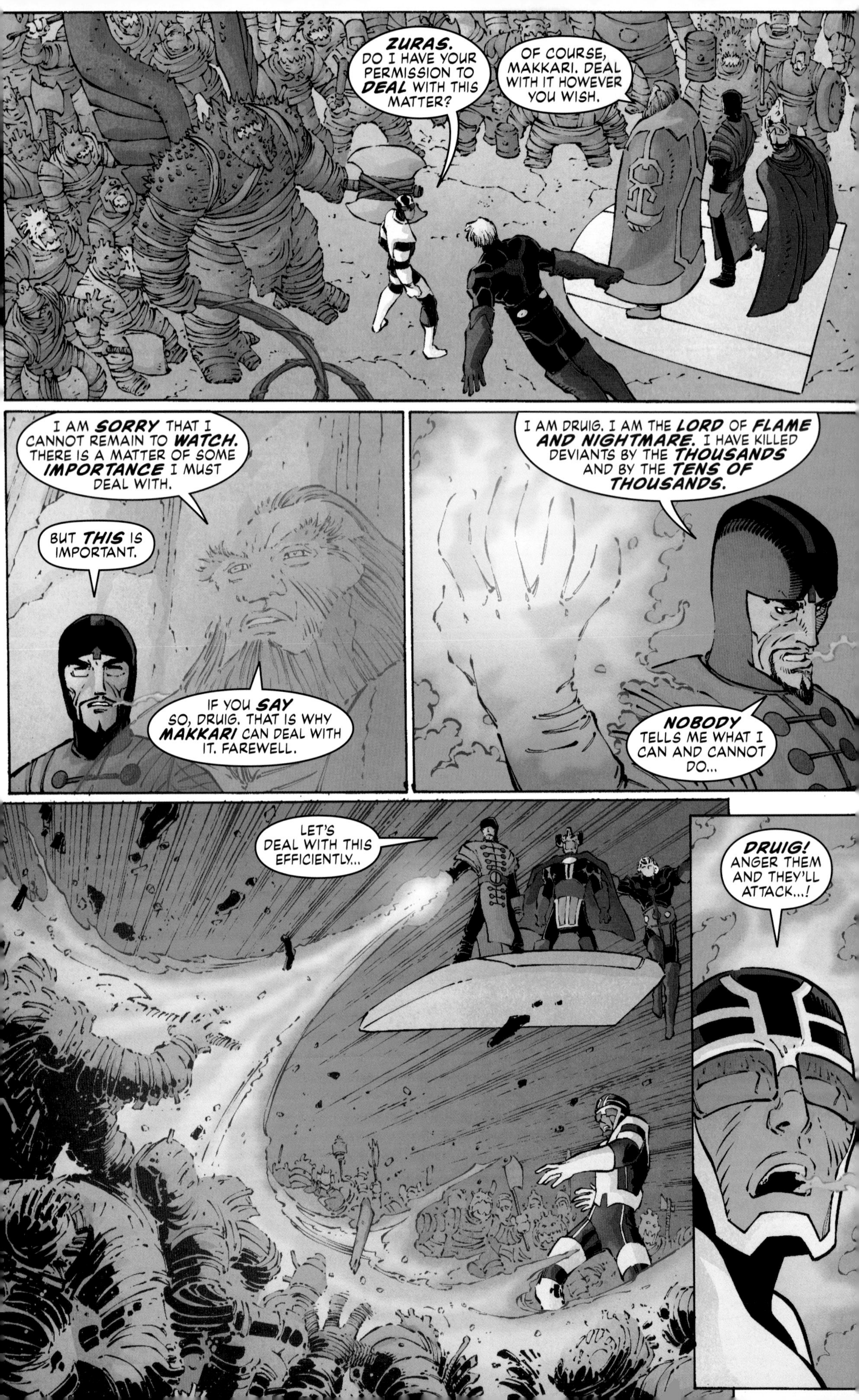
ZURAS. DO I HAVE YOUR PERMISSION TO DEAL WITH THIS MATTER?
OF COURSE, MAKKARI. DEAL WITH IT HOWEVER YOU WISH.
I AM SORRY THAT I CANNOT REMAIN TO WATCH. THERE IS A MATTER OF SOME IMPORTANCE I MUST DEAL WITH.
BUT THIS IS IMPORTANT.
IF YOU SAY SO, DRUIG. THAT IS WHY MAKKARI CAN DEAL WITH IT. FAREWELL.
I AM DRUIG. I AM THE LORD OF FLAME AND NIGHTMARE. I HAVE KILLED DEVIANTS BY THE THOUSANDS AND BY THE TENS OF THOUSANDS.
NOBODY TELLS ME WHAT I CAN AND CANNOT DO...
LET'S DEAL WITH THIS EFFICIENTLY...
DRUIG! ANGER THEM AND THEY'LL ATTACK...!

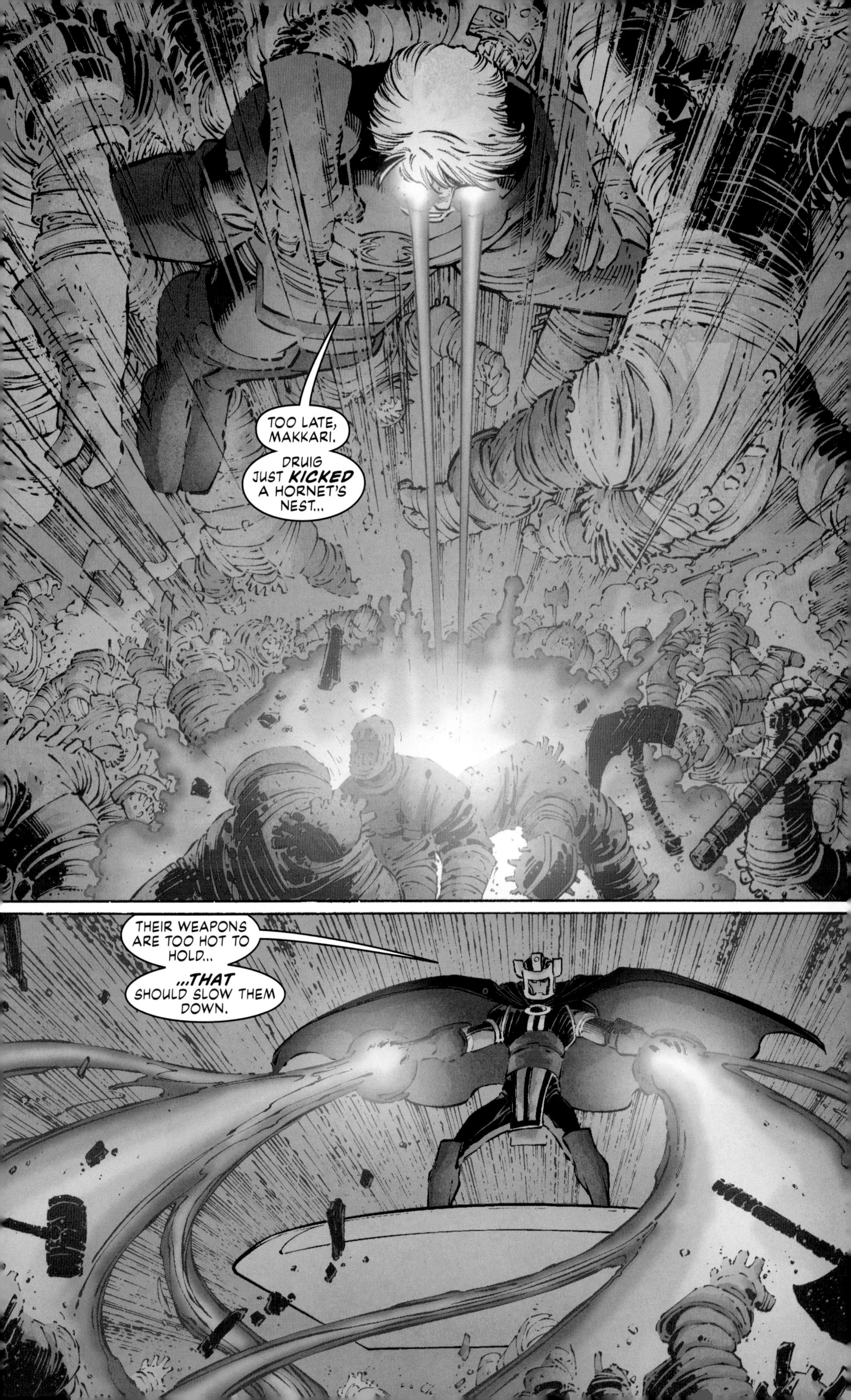
TOO LATE, MAKKARI.
DRUIG JUST **KICKED** A HORNET'S NEST...
THEIR WEAPONS ARE TOO HOT TO HOLD...
...THAT SHOULD SLOW THEM DOWN.

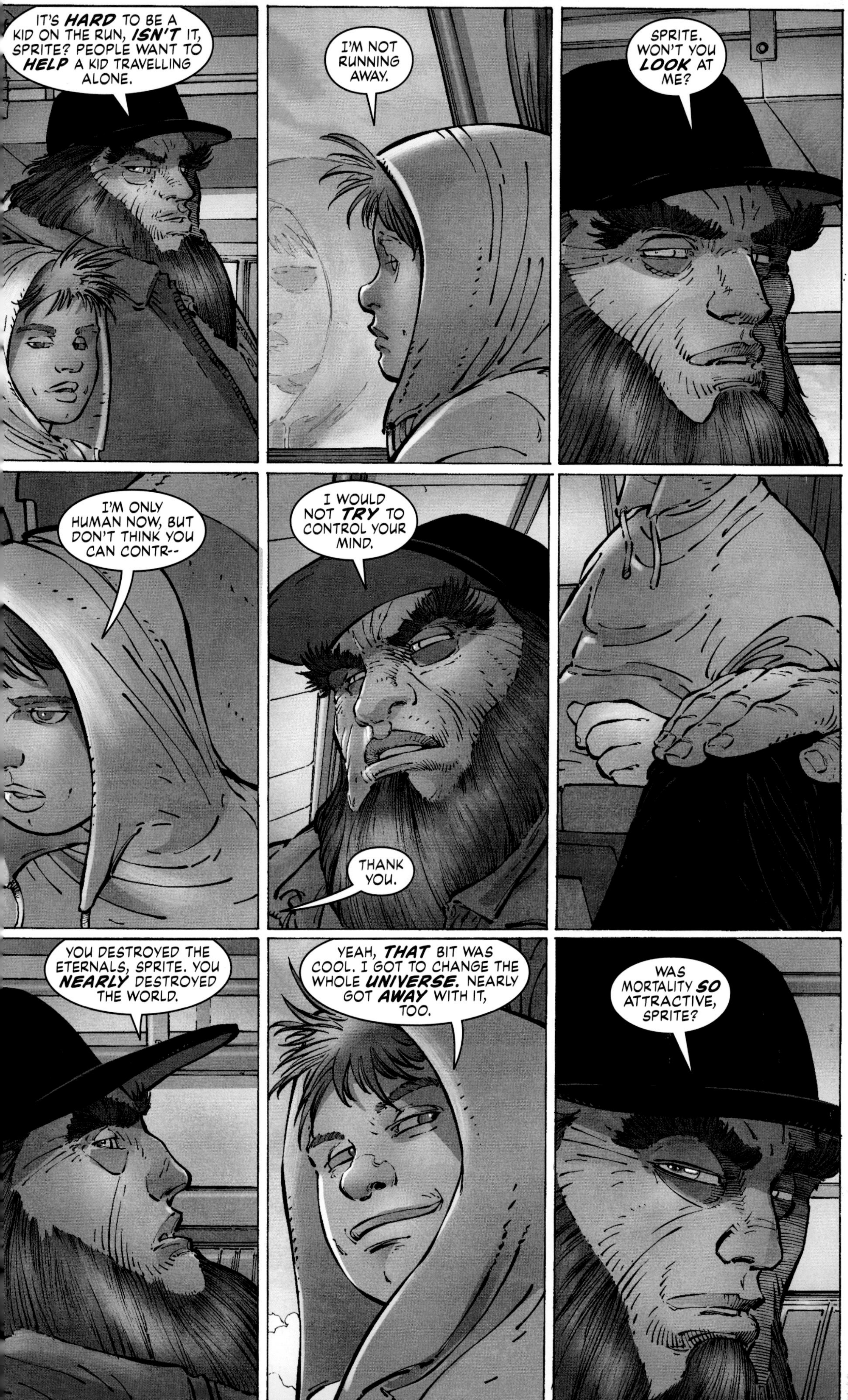
IT'S HARD TO BE A KID ON THE RUN, ISN'T IT, SPRITE? PEOPLE WANT TO HELP A KID TRAVELLING ALONE.
I'M NOT RUNNING AWAY.
SPRITE. WON'T YOU LOOK AT ME?
I'M ONLY HUMAN NOW, BUT DON'T THINK YOU CAN CONTR--
I WOULD NOT TRY TO CONTROL YOUR MIND.
THANK YOU.
YOU DESTROYED THE ETERNALS, SPRITE. YOU NEARLY DESTROYED THE WORLD.
YEAH, THAT BIT WAS COOL. I GOT TO CHANGE THE WHOLE UNIVERSE. NEARLY GOT AWAY WITH IT, TOO.
WAS MORTALITY SO ATTRACTIVE, SPRITE?

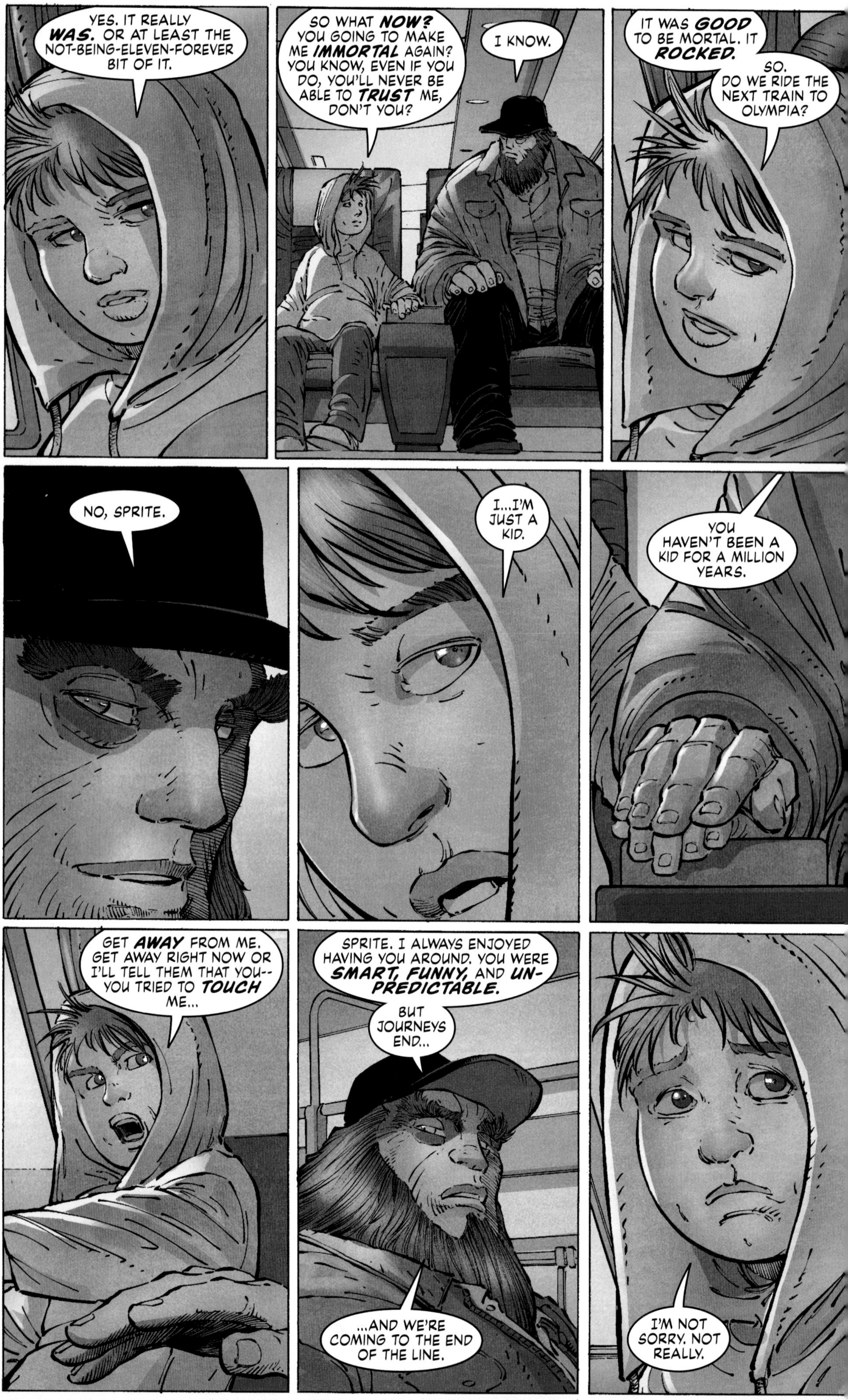
YES. IT REALLY WAS. OR AT LEAST THE NOT-BEING-ELEVEN-FOREVER BIT OF IT.
SO WHAT NOW? YOU GOING TO MAKE ME IMMORTAL AGAIN? YOU KNOW, EVEN IF YOU DO, YOU'LL NEVER BE ABLE TO TRUST ME, DON'T YOU?
I KNOW.
IT WAS GOOD TO BE MORTAL. IT ROCKED.
SO. DO WE RIDE THE NEXT TRAIN TO OLYMPIA?
NO, SPRITE.
I...I'M JUST A KID.
YOU HAVEN'T BEEN A KID FOR A MILLION YEARS.
GET AWAY FROM ME. GET AWAY RIGHT NOW OR I'LL TELL THEM THAT YOU-- YOU TRIED TO TOUCH ME...
SPRITE. I ALWAYS ENJOYED HAVING YOU AROUND. YOU WERE SMART, FUNNY, AND UN-PREDICTABLE.
BUT JOURNEYS END...
...AND WE'RE COMING TO THE END OF THE LINE.
I'M NOT SORRY. NOT REALLY.

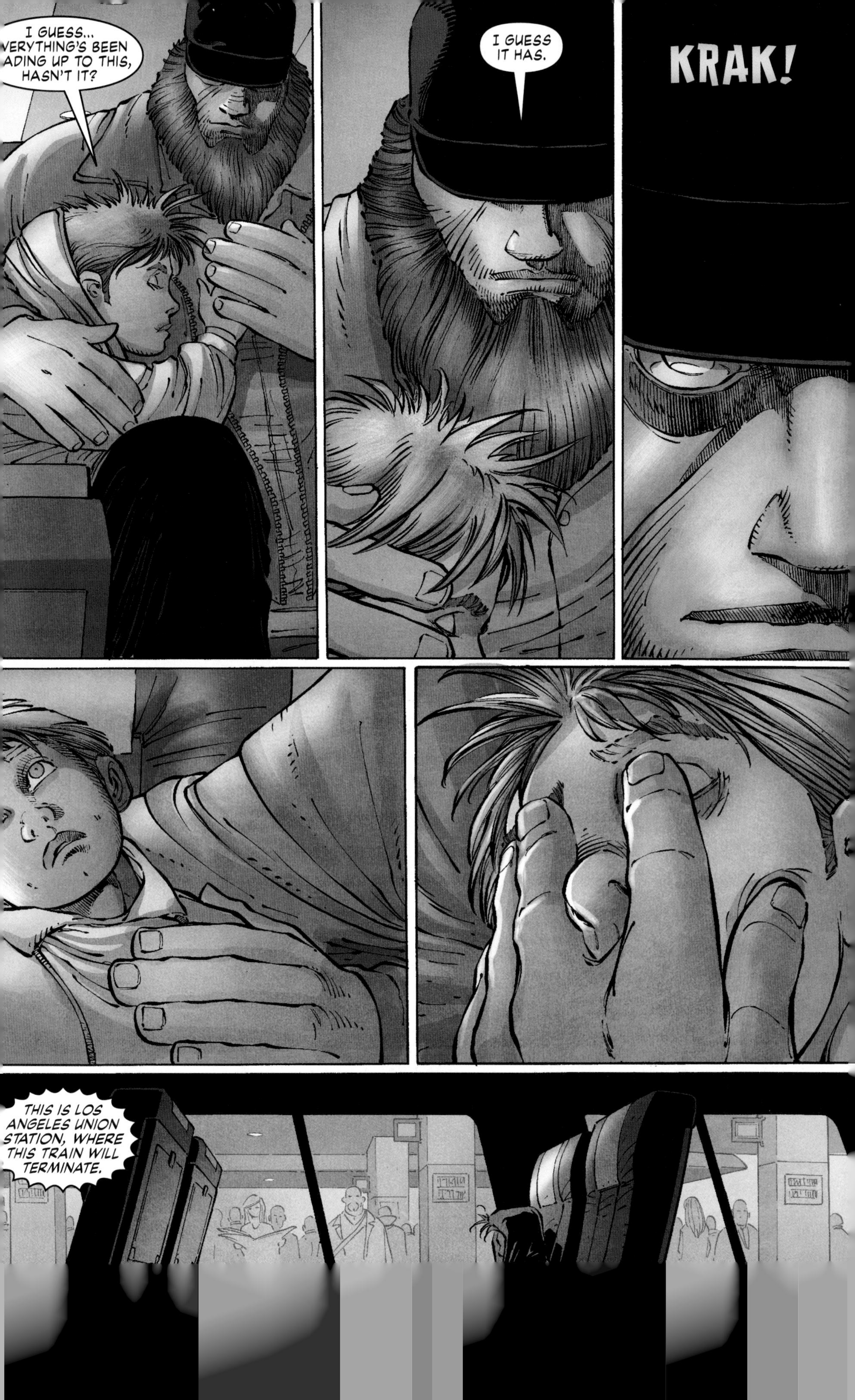
I GUESS... EVERYTHING'S BEEN LEADING UP TO THIS, HASN'T IT?
I GUESS IT HAS.
KRAK!
THIS IS LOS ANGELES UNION STATION, WHERE THIS TRAIN WILL TERMINATE.

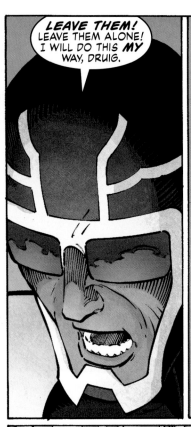

LEAVE THEM! LEAVE THEM ALONE! I WILL DO THIS *MY* WAY, DRUIG.

YOU ARE A *WEAKLING,* AND A *CRETIN.*

BUT YOU'LL LEARN YOUR LESSON SOON ENOUGH, MAKKARI.

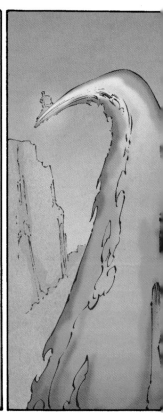

Are you going to *FIGHT* me, Eternal? Will you try your *SPEED* against my *STRENGTH?* With your head as my prize?

KRA, I AM ETERNAL. TAKE MY HEAD, AND I WILL STILL COME BACK, STRONGER, FASTER. *BUT* I *WILL* ACKNOWLEDGE YOU AS MY *MASTER* IF YOU CAN DEFEAT ME.

YOU CAN STRIKE ME THREE TIMES, IF *I* CAN STRIKE YOU ONCE.

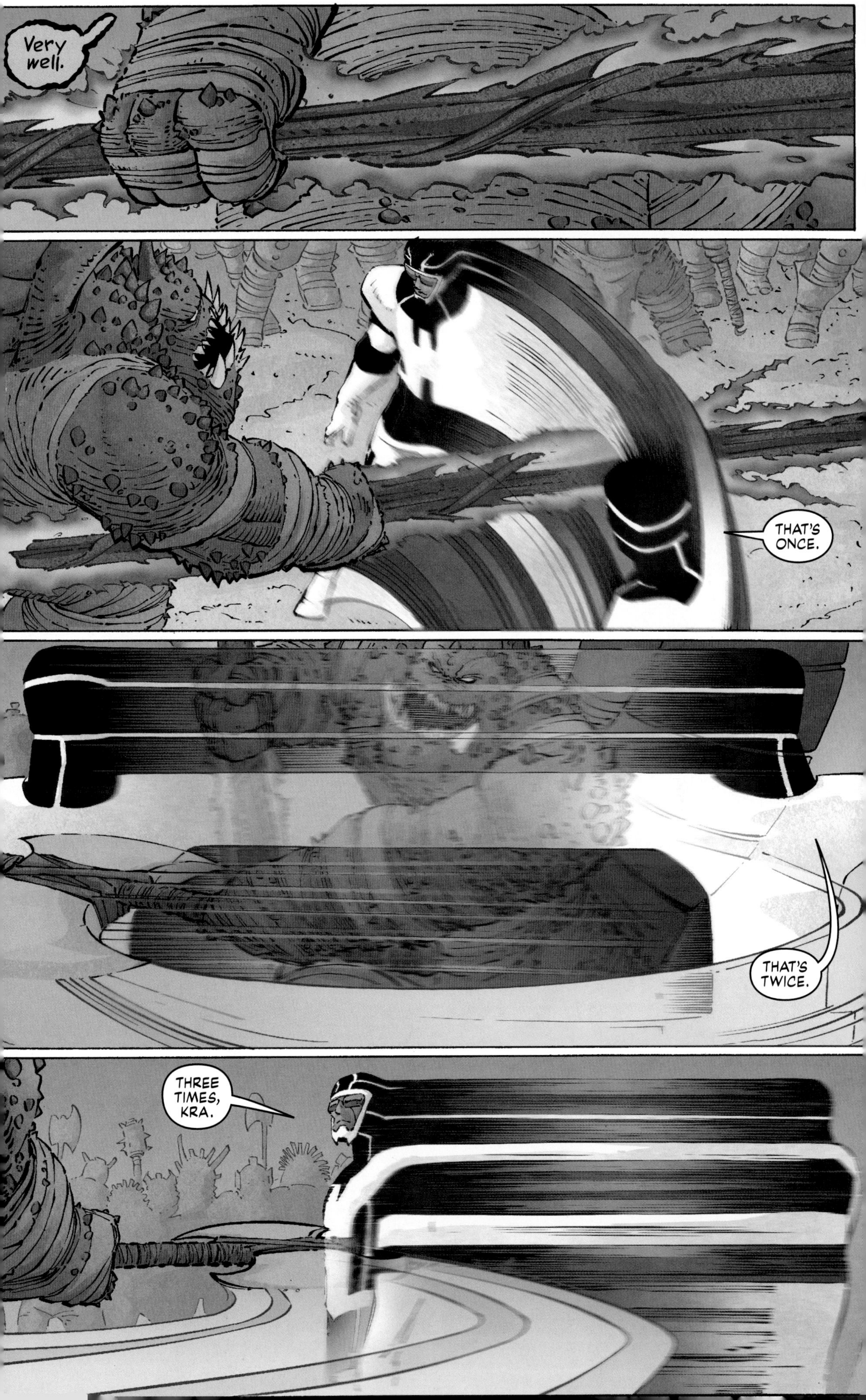
Very well.
THAT'S ONCE.
THAT'S TWICE.
THREE TIMES, KRA.

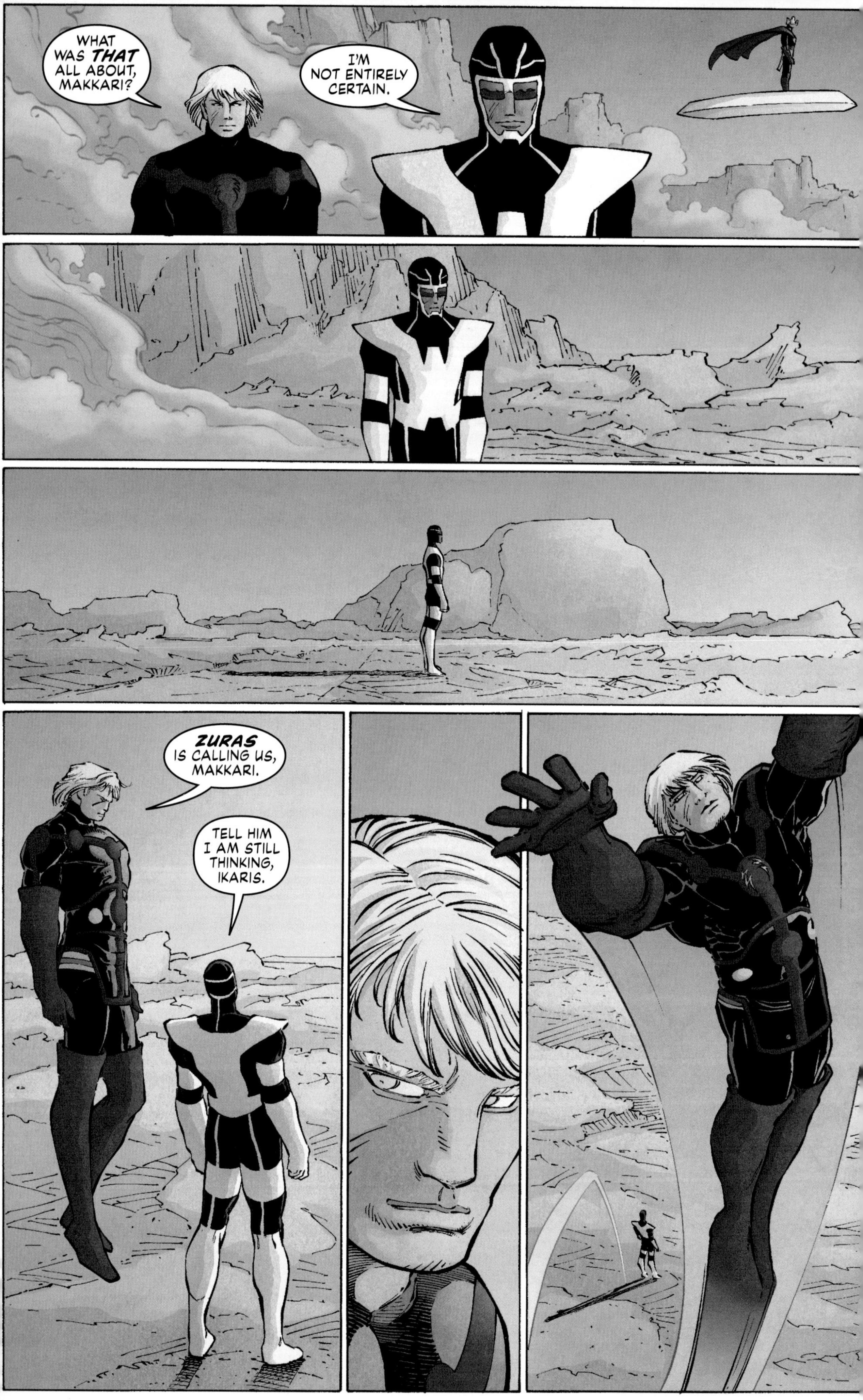
WHAT WAS THAT ALL ABOUT, MAKKARI?
I'M NOT ENTIRELY CERTAIN.
ZURAS IS CALLING US, MAKKARI.
TELL HIM I AM STILL THINKING, IKARIS.

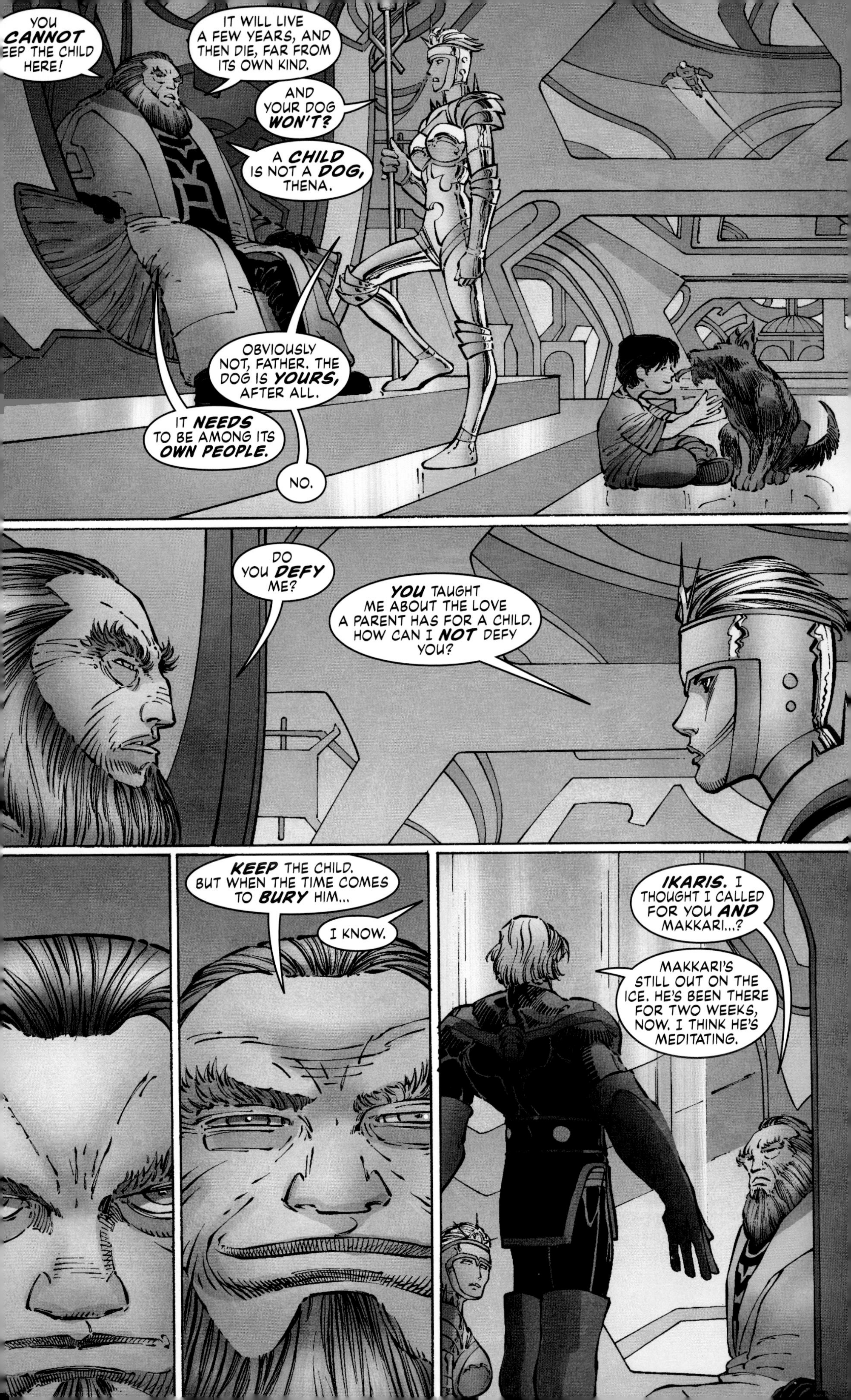

YOU CANNOT KEEP THE CHILD HERE!
IT WILL LIVE A FEW YEARS, AND THEN DIE, FAR FROM ITS OWN KIND.
AND YOUR DOG WON'T?
A CHILD IS NOT A DOG, THENA.
IT NEEDS TO BE AMONG ITS OWN PEOPLE.
OBVIOUSLY NOT, FATHER. THE DOG IS YOURS, AFTER ALL.
NO.
DO YOU DEFY ME?
YOU TAUGHT ME ABOUT THE LOVE A PARENT HAS FOR A CHILD. HOW CAN I NOT DEFY YOU?
KEEP THE CHILD. BUT WHEN THE TIME COMES TO BURY HIM...
I KNOW.
IKARIS. I THOUGHT I CALLED FOR YOU AND MAKKARI...?
MAKKARI'S STILL OUT ON THE ICE. HE'S BEEN THERE FOR TWO WEEKS, NOW. I THINK HE'S MEDITATING.

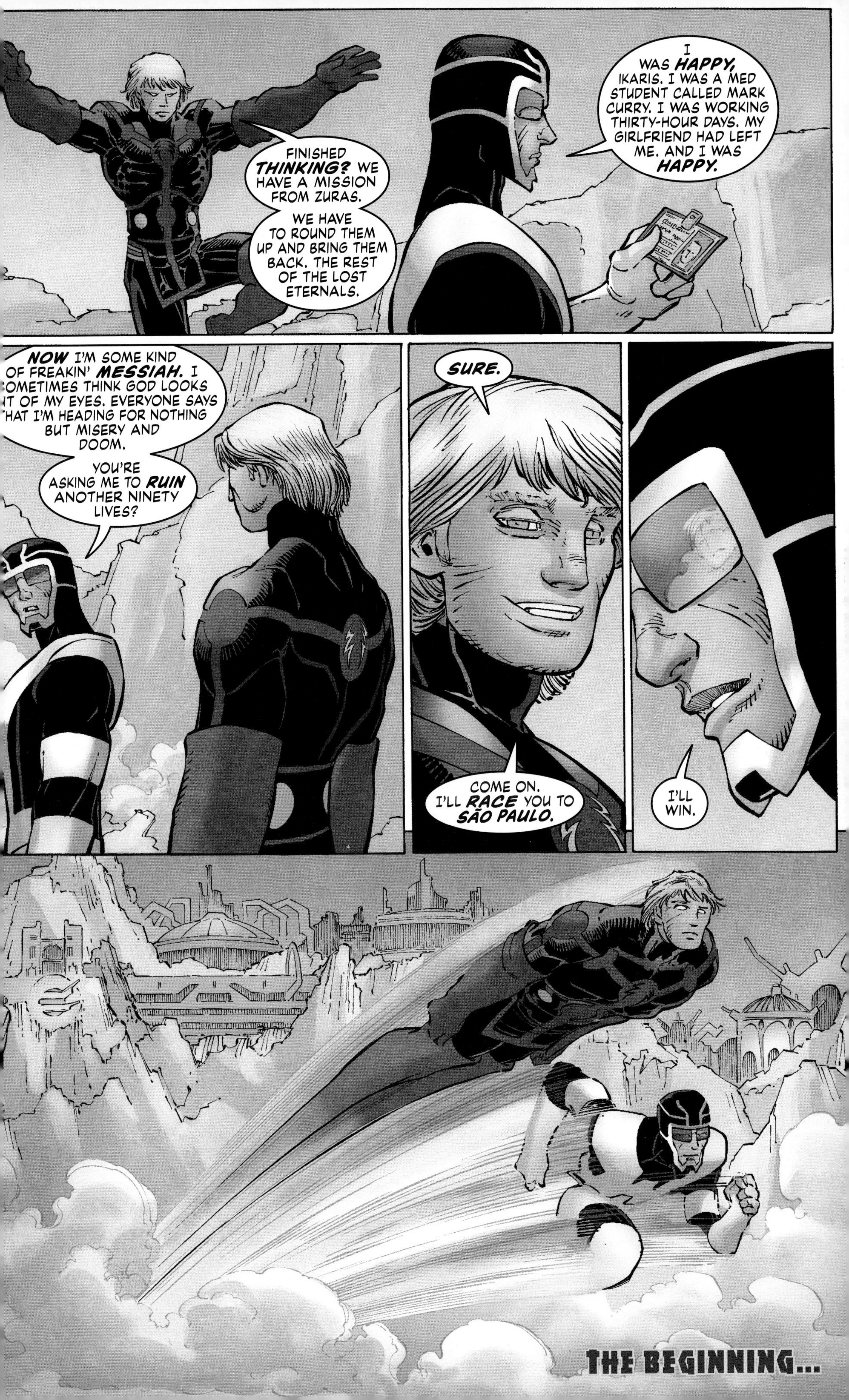
I WAS HAPPY, IKARIS. I WAS A MED STUDENT CALLED MARK CURRY. I WAS WORKING THIRTY-HOUR DAYS. MY GIRLFRIEND HAD LEFT ME. AND I WAS HAPPY.
FINISHED THINKING? WE HAVE A MISSION FROM ZURAS.
WE HAVE TO ROUND THEM UP AND BRING THEM BACK. THE REST OF THE LOST ETERNALS.
NOW I'M SOME KIND OF FREAKIN' MESSIAH. I SOMETIMES THINK GOD LOOKS OUT OF MY EYES. EVERYONE SAYS THAT I'M HEADING FOR NOTHING BUT MISERY AND DOOM.
YOU'RE ASKING ME TO RUIN ANOTHER NINETY LIVES?
SURE.
COME ON. I'LL RACE YOU TO SÃO PAULO.
I'LL WIN.
THE BEGINNING...

#1 VARIANT BY JOHN ROMITA JR.

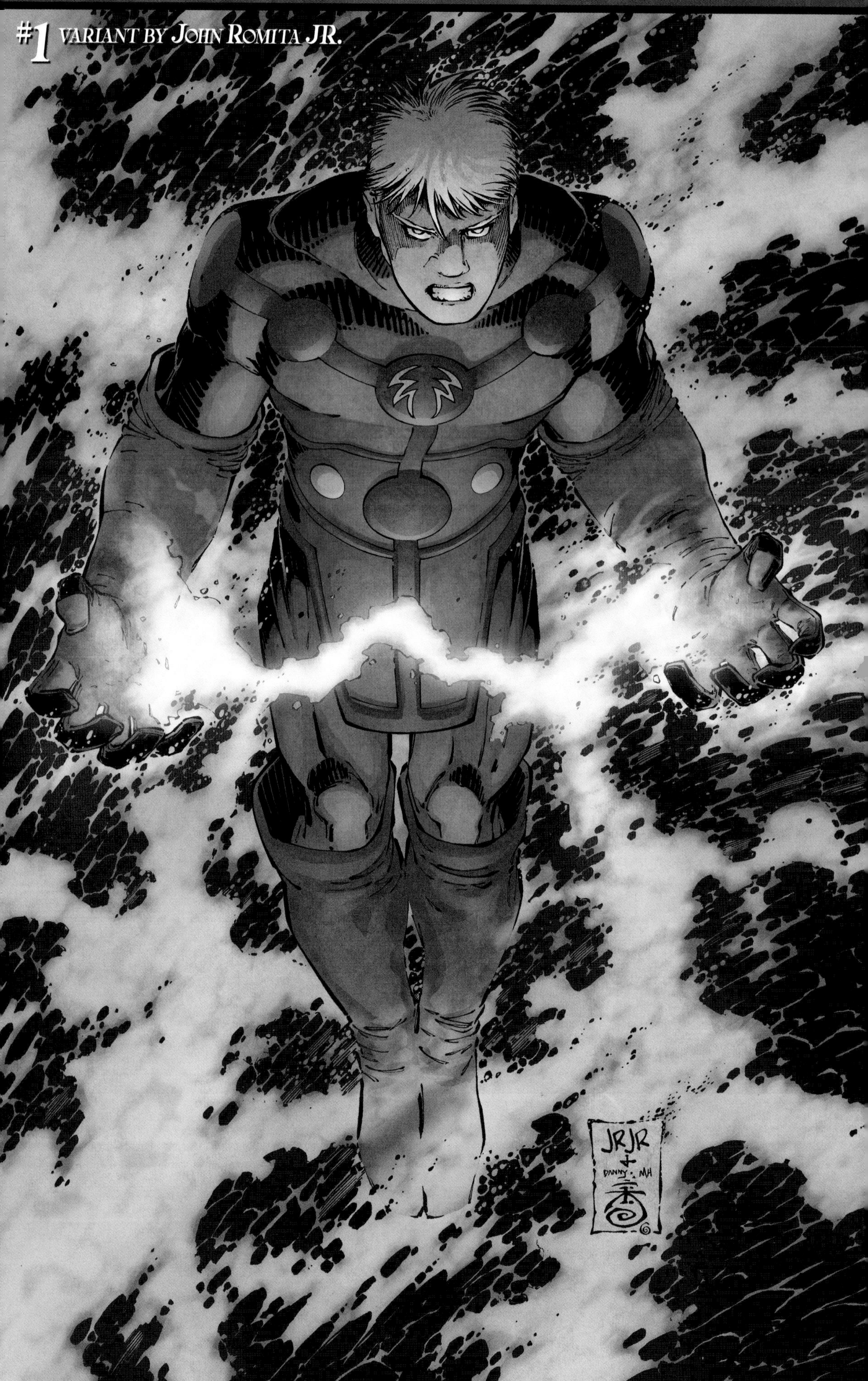
JRJR
+
DANNY MH

#2 VARIANT BY JOHN ROMITA JR.

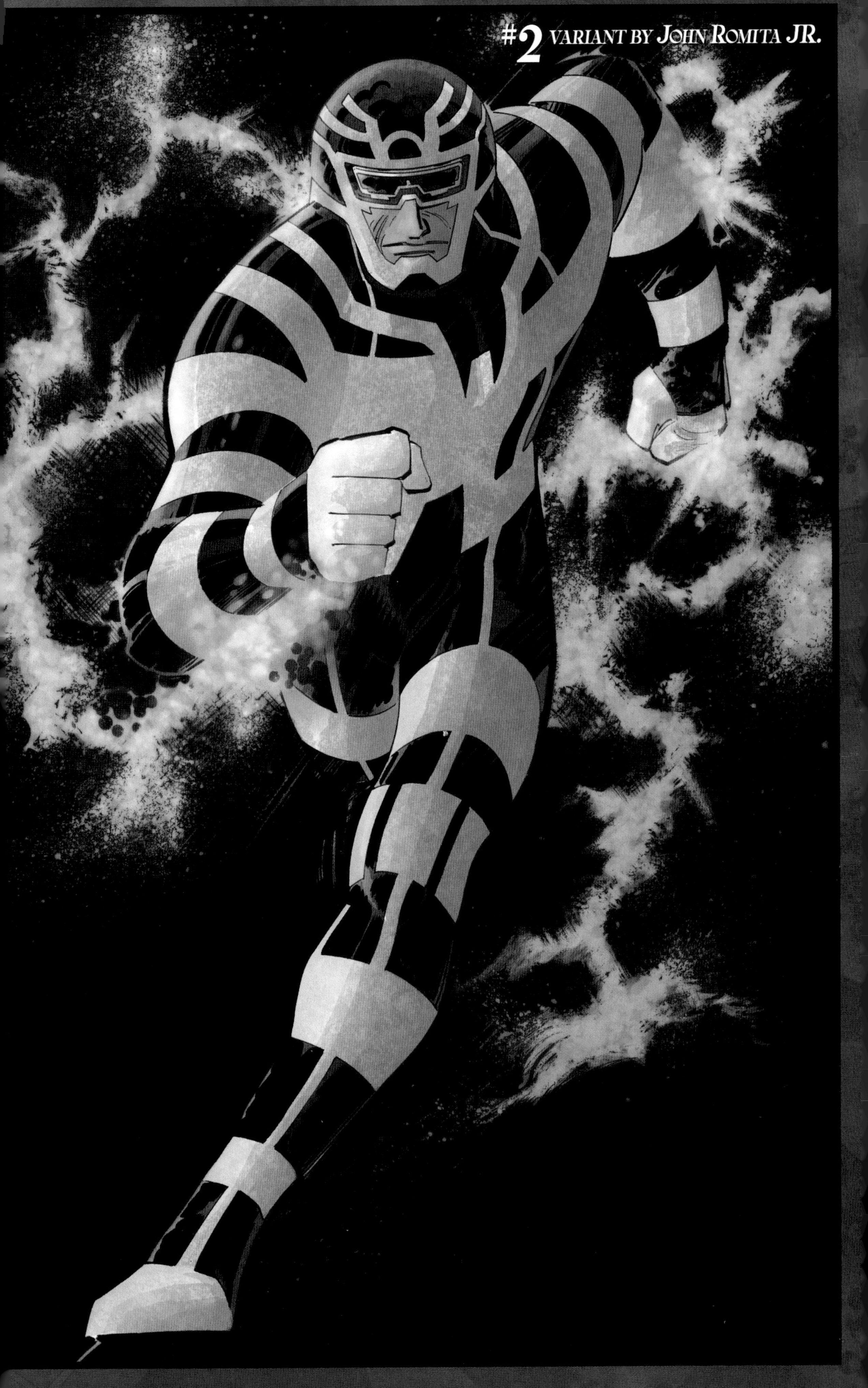

#3 VARIANT BY JOHN ROMITA JR.

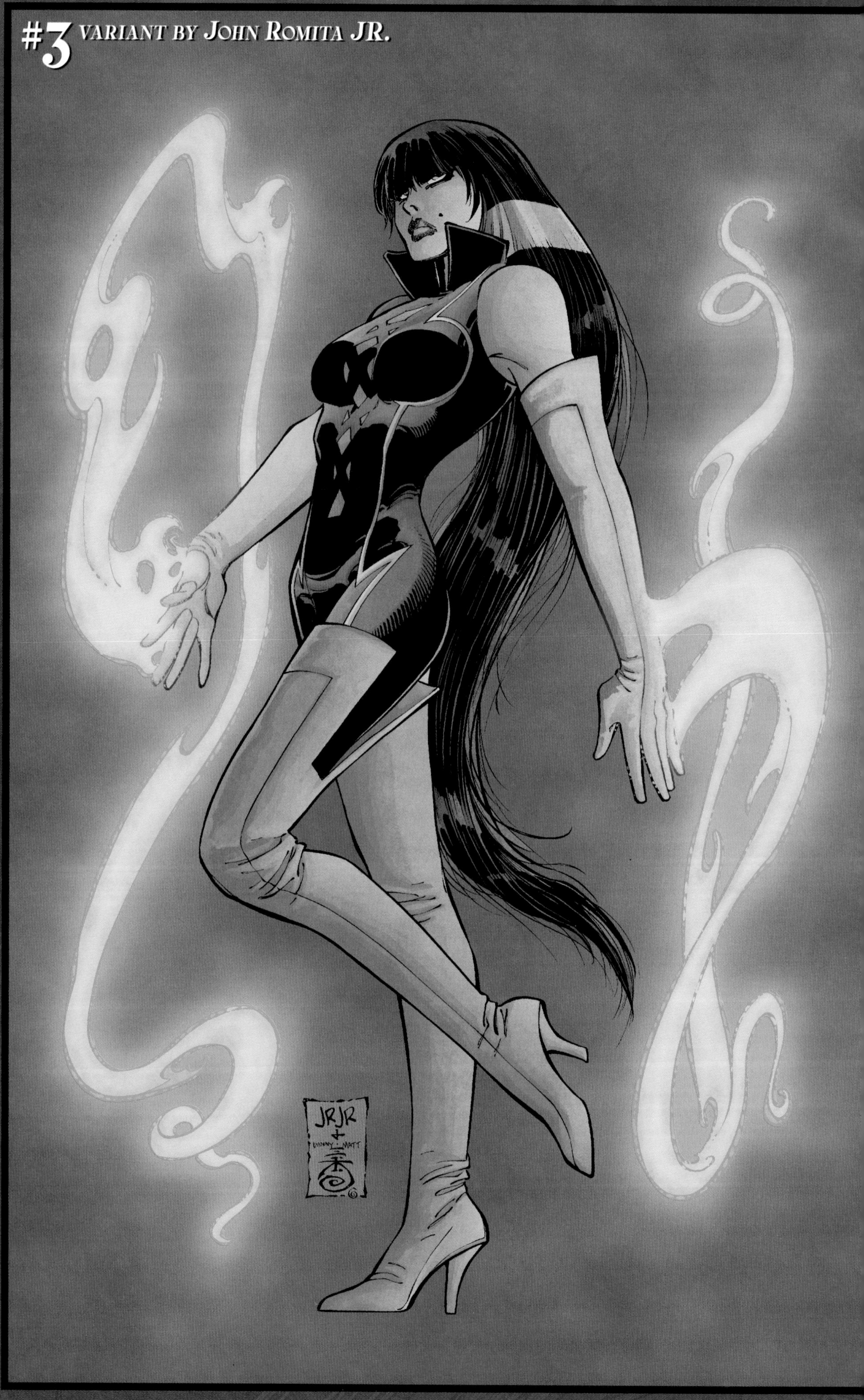
JRJR

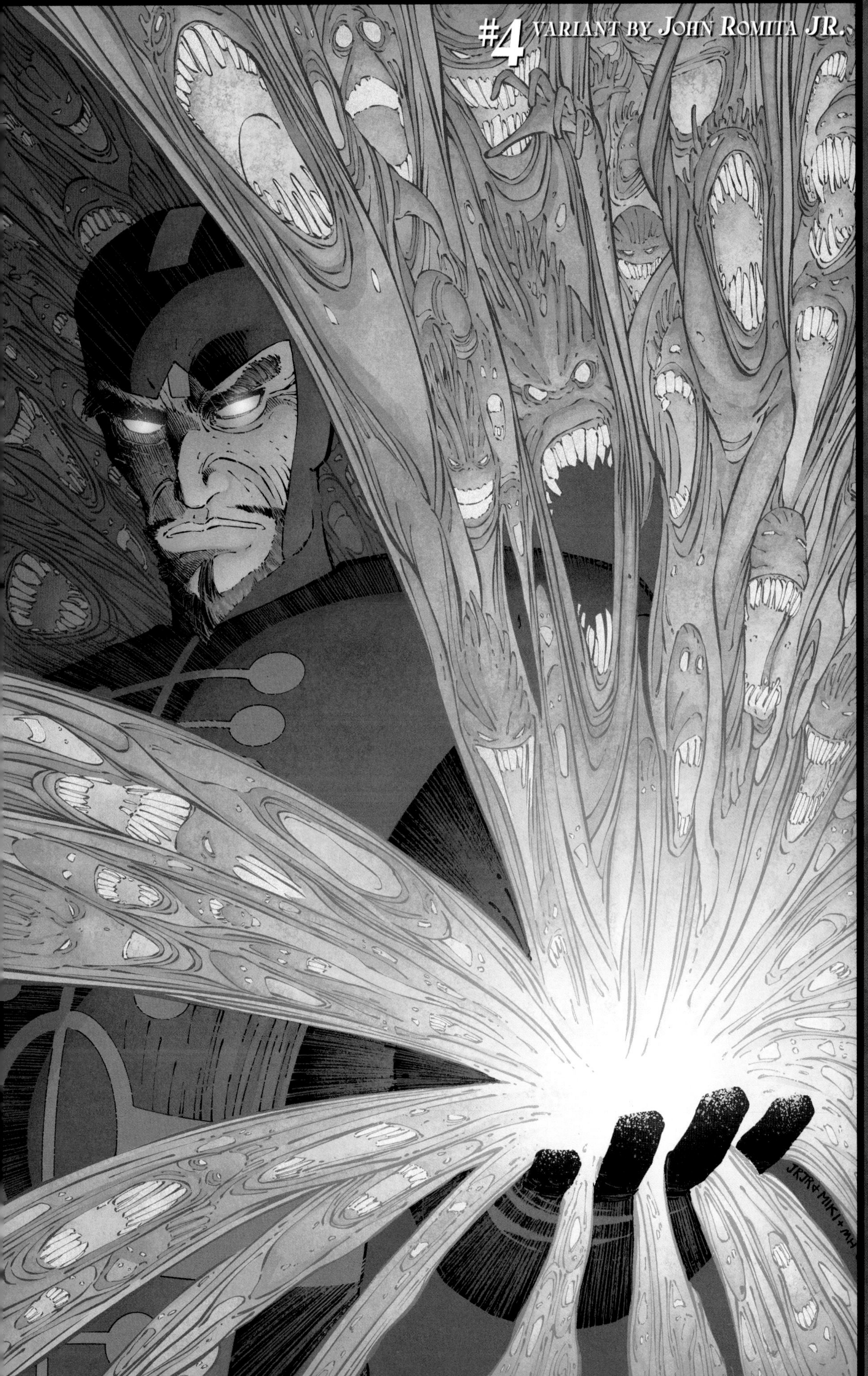
JRJR + MIKI + MH
#4 VARIANT BY JOHN ROMITA JR.

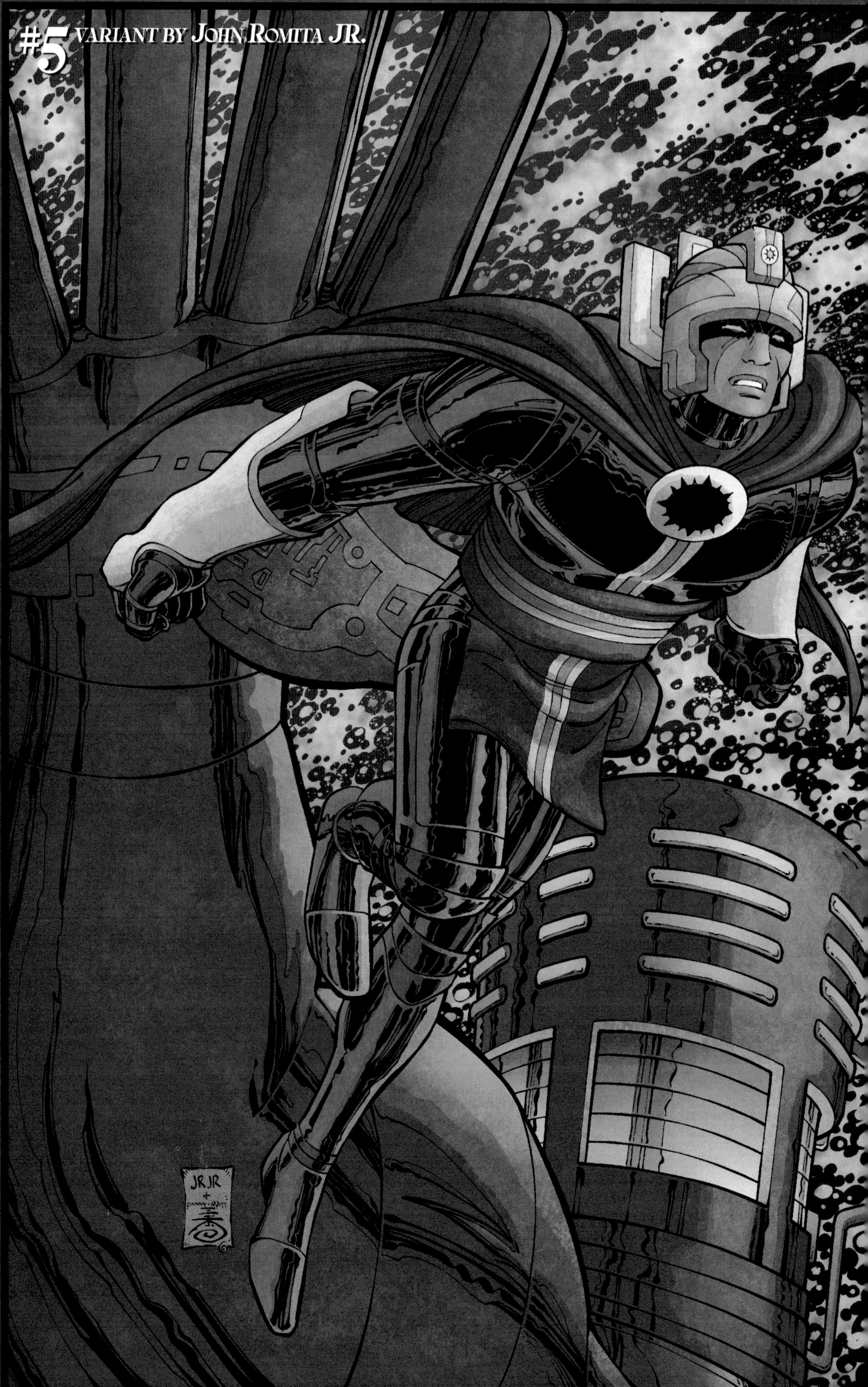

#5 VARIANT BY JOHN ROMITA JR.

#6 VARIANT BY JOHN ROMITA JR.

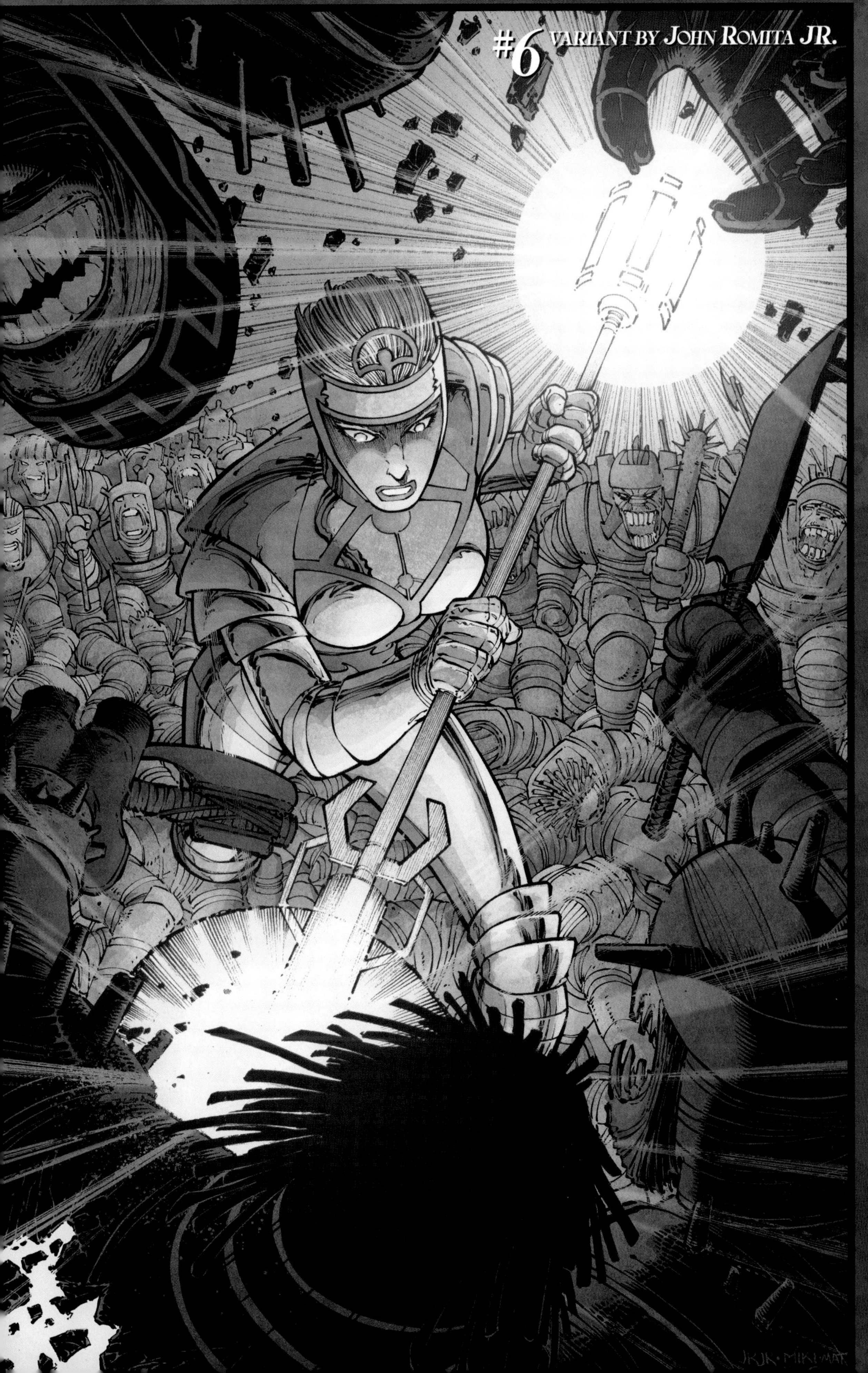

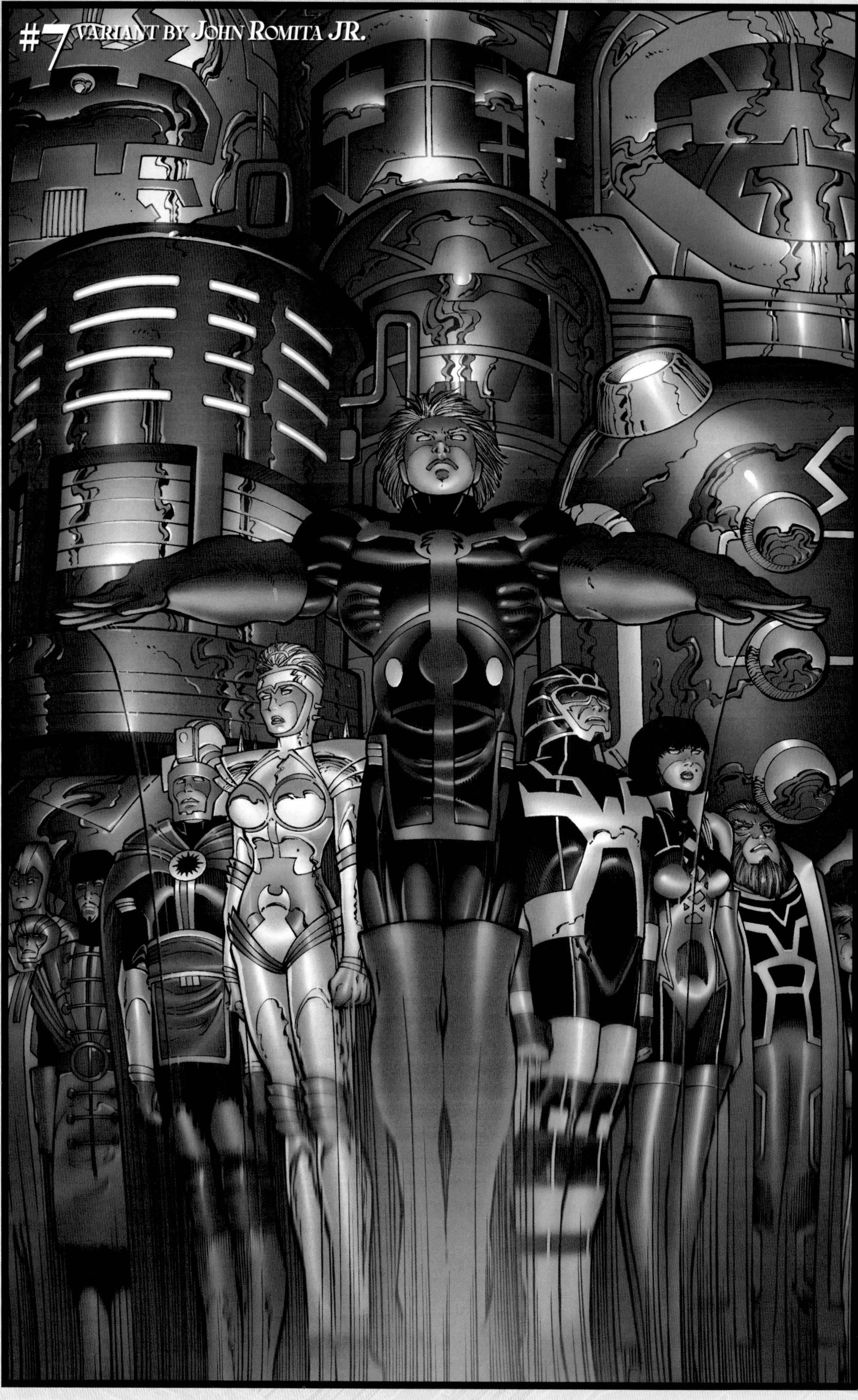
#7 VARIANT BY JOHN ROMITA JR.

#1 VARIANT BY OLIVIER COIPEL

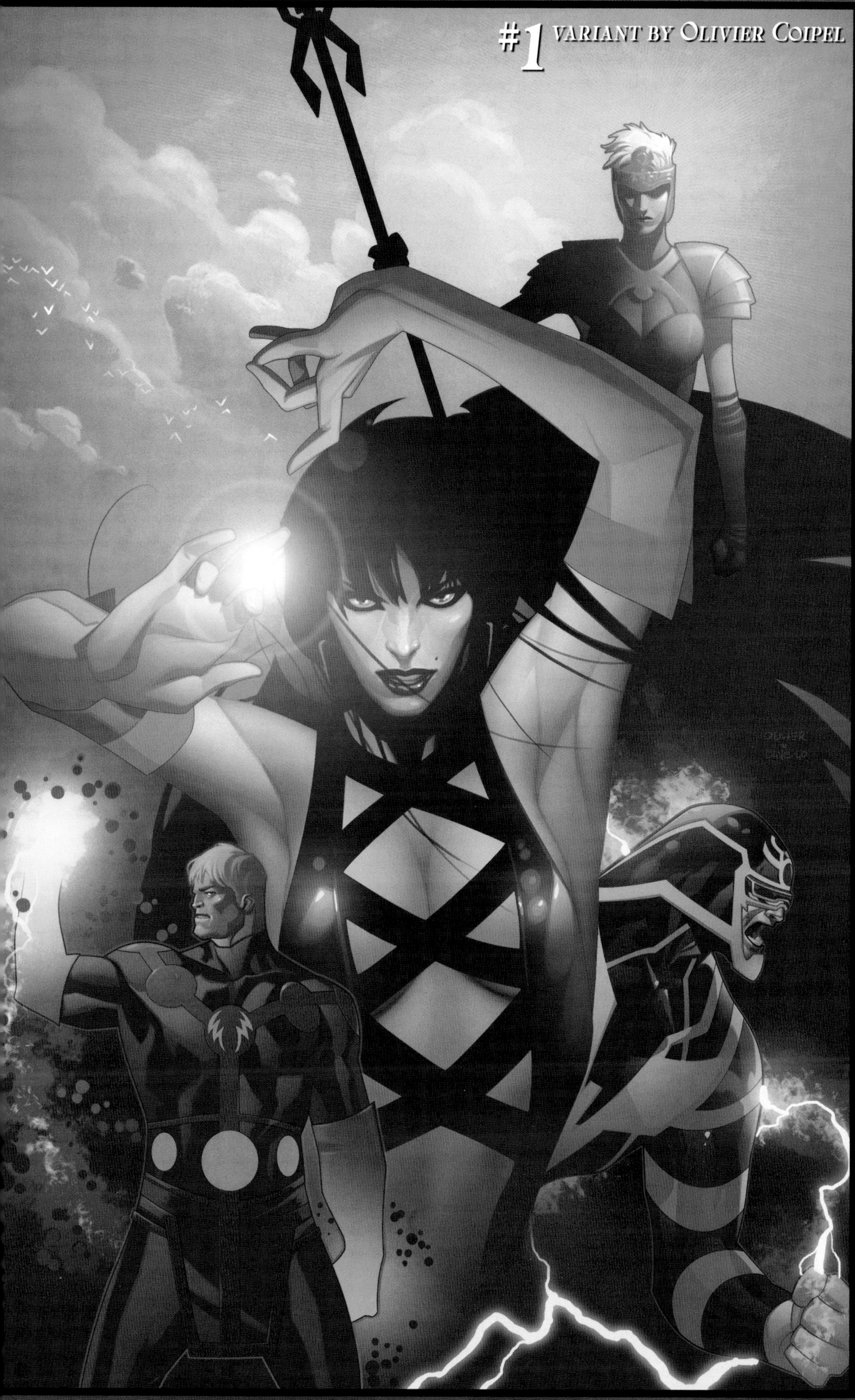

IN THE SHADOW OF THE CELESTIALS: Eternals escape from the Deviants under the ever-watchful eyes of the mysterious space gods. (From *Eternals #1*.)

THE SPOTLIGHT INTERVIEW WITH NEIL GAIMAN
By John Rhett Thomas

It's a *Marvel Spotlight* dream come true: share a phone call with Neil Gaiman and talk comics, *The Eternals*, and Jack Kirby! Tough work, brother! Tough work! Neil is a writer of longstanding reverence in this medium we love, and has the type of erudite resume one would assume might rightly include a fair bit of snobbishness towards four-color fandom. Not so! In this interview, Neil reveals his still abiding fascination with the comics he loved as a kid, and which still occupy much of his creative thoughts today, albeit in a more mature and evolved fashion.

SPOTLIGHT: Thank you so much for sharing some of your time with *Marvel Spotlight*. How are you doing today?

NEIL: Overworked, but well.

SPOTLIGHT: Overworked? Well, it has to be a good kind of overworked when you're talking about stuff like *The Eternals*, which looks to be a very exciting project, don't you think?

NEIL: Yes, it's rather fun and very, very, very strange.

SPOTLIGHT: Very strange? Well, that would be your fault, right?

NEIL: Yes, I guess! I got a lovely thing in from our colorist the other day. He sent me questions about the *Eternals* plot, which I thought was fun. Matt was getting so involved in the plot that he wanted to ask scientific questions, and then he finished by saying how amazingly "comic book" it was, which just made me amazingly happy!

SPOTLIGHT: I just had the thoroughly pleasurable experience of rereading the first *Eternals* series by Jack Kirby to prepare for our interview. Jack, and particularly his 70s work, is the reason I became a comics fan. *The Eternals* has always been one of my favorite books; it blew my mind when I was eight and nine years of age and reading this stuff on my school's playground. When I heard that you were involved in taking Jack's project up again, along with the amazing John Romita, Jr., I said to myself, "This is it!"

NEIL: Oh, and have you seen any of the art yet?

SPOTLIGHT: I've seen many of the pages as they've been trickling in. It's all explosively great stuff!

NEIL: It is great stuff, yes.

SPOTLIGHT: Did you have a similar history with *The Eternals*, of reading them when they were first published, of being entranced by their "Kirbyish" power, or are you coming to this project fresh without any previous exposure?

NEIL: I picked up *Eternals* when I was... how old? I suppose I would have been fifteen or sixteen when *Eternals* came out. I was a huge Kirby fan. He'd just gone back to Marvel after the Fourth World at DC Comics had sort of expired. He'd done a rather odd and unsatisfying *Captain America* run, which I had picked up simply because it was Kirby. And then, he did some *2001* stuff, and then *Eternals* came along, which seemed—at least at the beginning—to be Jack taking a lot of energy from his work on *2001* (you could tell that that was where his head had gone), and also, partly energy from some leftover Fourth Worldy stuff...and also that sort of Erich von Daniken spin. He took all that and started doing something with it. And even at the time, on one hand I really liked it, and on the other hand there seemed to be a few things that were very odd about it. Chiefly—and this is interesting because in some ways, it's something I've had to cope with—the *Eternals* obviously by definition were not meant to be part of the Marvel Universe, except even back then he was getting pressure to make them part of the Marvel Universe.

SPOTLIGHT: The letters pages for *The Eternals* back then were aflame with controversy over that particular point.

NEIL: And he got around it in interesting ways. He had some SHIELD agents come around in the early issues, and the Hulk comes in for a guest shot, but it's a mechanical Hulk! (*Laughter.*) A kid gets turned into the Thing for a panel but you genuinely can't tell if it's a comics character or not. But you know, I thought it was played very well, and then after it ended, and you could see the plug getting pulled on this thing just as it was really getting going, then you get various Marvel attempts to fold the Eternals into the Marvel Universe, which is right up there with trying to crossbreed a prize greyhound with Gibbon's *The Decline and Fall of the Roman Empire*. You know, you just sit there going, "Uhhhh ...nooooo...something is...how do they think...bleh..." (*Laughter.*) The attempts to do it sort of mucked things up a lot in terms of muddying the water of what made the Eternals interesting anyway.

The fun thing about *The Eternals* to me is that for about two years, ever since *1602* finished, Joe Quesada and I would meet in a variety of odd places, and we'd have lunch or breakfast or dinner, and while having lunch or breakfast or dinner, I'd say, "Ok, I've got an idea for whatever Marvel Project #2 is…" and I'd run something by him. And normally I'd get to the end and he'd say, "That's really good. Trouble is, Bendis just did something like that." Or, "Bendis is halfway through something like that." Or, "We just had a meeting and Bendis is going to do something like that."

We weren't able to figure out something that would be fun for me to do. I knew I wanted to do something very different from *1602*, in that *1602* was me getting to recreate 60s Marvel and do it in my own way, in my own time. (I suppose quite literally!) So I knew I wanted to do something in the present day, and I didn't want it to have quite the same hugeness of cast of characters, which seriously bit me in the ass by the time I got to the end of *1602*, where I was looking around and going, "Great! I've still got twenty-five major players and nobody is getting the time at the end that they ought to have!" That was very frustrating.

So I knew I wanted a smaller cast. I think it would have been after the publication of *Anansi Boys*, last September, when I popped in to the Marvel offices to say hello, and I just sort of wandered into Joe's office and we were chatting, and he said, "The Eternals. Do you remember *The Eternals*?" And I said, "You mean Ikaris, who went under the incredibly impossible to figure out pseudonym of Ike Harris?" (*Laughter.*) And he said, "Yeaaaaah!" He asked, "Would you like to do *The Eternals*? They're sort of sitting around the corners of the Marvel Universe, and they don't really relate to anything. There's nothing we can do with them." And I thought for about thirty seconds and I said, "Yeah, send me the comics again." (And as it turned out, I still had most of them downstairs, which was kinda cool!)

Mostly, what I'd never done with *The Eternals* was read them all as a giant batch. I had read them monthly as they were coming out. At the time, I just compared them to that rock solid burning madness that was Kirby's Fourth World at its height. And I thought, "Well, that's alright." I didn't think of *Eternals* as great Kirby. But going back and reading it again, I started thinking how much I really liked the concept there, and I really liked the characters and I really wished that…(*Reflective pause.*) I don't actually know anything about the editorial history, nor have I asked — I'm sure somebody around would only be too happy to fill me in — but it definitely reads like Kirby just wants to do Kirby, and there are other forces that are saying, "Hey can you get on to that stuff, and now can you get onto this?" and some of the stuff that would have made it wonderful, mad Kirby, isn't there as much as it should be.

SPOTLIGHT: *Eternals* was quite unlike any Marvel comic that was coming out in the late 70s. At the time of publication, you have to look at the Fourth World as precedent for something like *Eternals*, but even the Fourth World was doled out over several different titles. It seemed like Kirby wanted to jam all that good stuff

from all the different Fourth World series into one, streamlined title.

NEIL: Exactly.

SPOTLIGHT: As it was, it only lasted for nineteen issues and a double-sized Annual, but if given the chance to flourish under its own device, it might have gone on even longer.

NEIL: I like to think so. So what I did, then, was basically turn around to Marvel and basically say, "Okay, in terms of what Jack has done in *Eternals*, which bits of these can I use? What is actual canon in the Marvel Universe?" They mentioned that they were very concerned about Celestials creating humanity. They said, "Nope! Celestials *definitely didn't* create humanity, but they *did* create the Eternals and the Deviants!" And I said, "Oh, okay, well I can work with that!" And after that, it was really just, for me, a matter of coming in with a bunch of ideas that would allow me to go and play with the Eternals, play with some of the ideas that Jack had begun, change some things, fix some things, totally mess up some things. The joy of comics is, as I sit here doing my reboot or whatever it is, that if it doesn't work, in ten or fifteen years time someone will pick it up and go, "Ha! Gaiman! This one really sucked. We'll toss it out and have another go again." But I think that what I'm trying to do is remain bravely true to the Kirbyness of it all. And that includes things like trying to make the Celestials rather more unknowable than they have been. I love the idea that while we will actually find out a few cool things about the Celestials, there will be slightly more, as I say, "unknowables" as there have been before. (Although some of their motivations are kind of fun.)

SPOTLIGHT: The Celestials were an alien race of alleged space gods, who came to Earth on many occasions, broken into different groups called Hosts. Are you working with the full complement of Celestials that Jack conjured up? And is it still the Fourth Host that will be taking the lead?

NEIL: Yes and no. We get to cover the entirety of human history, three or four times, from different points of view. Which is kind of fun! This takes us from the First Host all the way to the Fourth Host. And we get to experience several events from several different points of view. I don't know that it's giving too much away to suggest that we are beginning in a world in which it would appear that all of the Eternals are here on Earth, and as far as we can tell they are regular human beings, but the only one who seems to have any inkling of what he is — or what he believes he is — is Ike Harris, or Ikaris…and he may well be barking mad. (*Laughter.*)

SPOTLIGHT: Well, that's nothing unusual for the Eternals! They have been many things over the years to many different people. Obviously, you have an abiding interest in mythology and how it has worked itself into the fabric of human understanding, and that is pretty much what Jack was after with Eternals, so this seems to be really simpatico with you.

NEIL: Oddly enough, I'm playing much less with that than I thought I would. Partly I think because I've done that, and partly because once Jack had set it up, he lost interest in it, too; you know, I think he was interested in it much more from a "Chariot of the Gods" point of view: "Look, Ikaris was the dove who led Noah's Ark to safety!" They turn up and people thought they were "the gods."

SPOTLIGHT: Ajak was thought to be Quetzalcoatl by the Mesoamerican cultures.

NEIL: Exactly, and that's all kind of fun. But it doesn't actually take you terribly far, especially in a universe in which you really *do* have gods. Not to mention superheroes, not to mention races like the Inhumans, and all sorts of other strange, affiliated, extra-curricular groups. So part of what I'm having enormous amounts of fun doing with this story, I'm just trying to find out what makes the Eternals special: Who are they? What do they do? How many of them are there? And then I started trying to figure out what Jack would sort of toss in and I sort of go, "How does that work on an evolutionary basis?" For example, the Eternals are pretty much perfect. They are unkillable. According to Jack at one point, when they were trying to hypothesize ways to kill one of the Eternals, they were thinking, maybe they could disperse him into a cloud of intelligent molecules. (*Laughter.*) And you're going, "Well that's kind of…"

They're completely unkillable, they're completely healthy, they are way, way above us. They apparently breed, because Thena is Zuras' daughter and stuff…and then you're wondering, "Why haven't they out bred us? We're just humanity! Why aren't there millions and billions of them? Why is it the ones that seem to reproduce incredibly fast and hard are the Deviants, and the Deviants are all members of different species, and they've been breeding like incredibly sexed-up rabbits?"

SPOTLIGHT: Yes, and the Deviants are also very judgmental about their own progeny!

NEIL: Yes, and that was all how I began to get into it. And I also just started to pick out the characters that I liked. I'd say, "Ok, you're in the story, you're in the story. I like you, so you're in the story. I like you, but you're dead. Ok, I'm bringing you back. You're in the story, but you've been completely mucked up; well, then I'm putting you back to the way you were when Kirby did you!" (*Laughter.*) You know, and moving on from there. One of my favorite things about this — which is kind of fun, but also takes advantage of the strange flexibility of the nature of time as perceived by the Eternals and the nature of time in the Marvel Universe — is that in my story, the Third Host did indeed arrive; Arishem came down to judge. In 1976.

SPOTLIGHT: Ahhh!

NEIL: About thirty years ago! Only nobody seems to — apart from Ikaris — nobody seems to know it ever happened. And as Makarri explains to him at one point, you really would think that if a mile high red alien had landed to judge the Earth, it would have been in the news.

SPOTLIGHT: (*Laughter.*) Yes, you would think! Did you ever read *Chariot of the Gods*? That book that alleged a connection between humanity and outer space aliens was quite the phenomenon in the mid-1970s, and it was obviously an inspiration for Jack on *The Eternals*. What do you make of that book and what it meant at the time, and what it means now?

NEIL: One of the things it is now is just noise. Now it's just part of the cultural wallpaper. It's more cultural baggage. At the time, I remember being fourteen or fifteen and that book being handed round in school. It was like, "No! No! The aliens came and here's the proof! How could they have built this? How could they have done that? Look! Here are guys in helmets!" (*Laughter.*)

What's fun in *The Eternals*, at least as we begin, is we see Mark Curry, alias Makarri, being incredibly doubtful about all of this kind of stuff and thinks it's silly, and when Ikaris explains to him that that is how he has the power that he has, Mark declares to him that, frankly, if Spider-Man turns up and said he got his powers from reading *Chariots of the Gods*, he'd think that he was mad. There's definitely a sort of feeling there of…you know, it was a lovely idea, and right now it's just one of thousands of lovely ideas. It also means less in the Marvel Universe. That's another way in which it made incredible sense to not put the Eternals into the Marvel Universe originally, because the Marvel Universe is filled with freaking space ships! They're landing all over the place! There's aliens left right and center. There's nothing special or exciting about the idea, "There are aliens! They might have had something to do with us!" So one of the things that is fun with this is trying to make these Celestials special in this story.

DREAM OR REALITY? Neil Gaiman sets Ike Harris on the path to self-discovery of his true nature in *Eternals #1*.

SPOTLIGHT: With their enormous size and their odd visages, Jack's visuals on the Celestials were literally out of this world. I suppose that John Romita, Jr. is doing the same thing while handling art chores on your *Eternals* series?

NEIL: The point I got excited is when the stuff from Johnny started coming my way. I just looked at this stuff and said, "Ooookay. All stops are out. This is gonna be such fun." And one of the things that's really fun in the first couple of issues is you're moving back and forth between these very human people and these very human stories, admittedly with all sorts of peculiar excitement and mysterious people and explosions and shootings and running around and kidnappings and attempted murders and stuff…but the first two or three issues are fairly normal. Except possibly the fact that we do keep cutting to a reality TV show called America's Newest Super-Heroes.

SPOTLIGHT: (*Laughter.*) Now, that sounds like an especially fruitful source of stories.

NEIL: Well, yes. Though none of the Eternals are in it, but it's a bunch of kids being run by the Wasp. You know, you've got the sort of "Marvel Civil Warry" stuff going on in the background, in a way that I hope won't bug anybody who has no idea what this is but will actually be kind of fun for anybody who does.

SPOTLIGHT: Do you expect that a lot of your fanbase, which may not be up on Marvel Comics, will be coming to this project and enjoying it? Do you write for that kind of person who is familiar with your wide expanse of work over the last twenty years, or when writing for Marvel, do you write for a Marvel type fan?

NEIL: I have no idea, just as I had no idea with *1602*. What I was doing with *1602*, was I thought, you know, it would be really fun to write something that feels like I am doing something in the Marvel Universe for the first time, I want to take all of the Marvel characters that I loved when I was seven or eight and I want to put them all in the story and have complete control over everything, including all continuity, and I'm going to set it four hundred years ago and it's going to be mine! I just wanted it to be a really fun Marvel Comic, but I wanted it to be mine! So that was my agenda with *1602*, which was not really having anything to do with anything else.

With *Eternals*, I wanted to do something that didn't feel at all like *1602*. I wanted to do something goofier, Marvellier, and with a kind of Kirbyish undertow to it. I love Kirby! I've always loved playing with Kirby ideas. As far back as *Sandman #5*, I got to do a three or four page sequence where I persuaded Sam Keith and Malcolm Jones to do pure Kirby.

SPOTLIGHT: I recall that scene vividly from when I was a kid: The Sandman in the dream world, chasing down the Skookie Bird! That was a beautiful sequence, by the way.

NEIL: Thank you! But this isn't a Kirby pastiche in the same way. This is us just going, "Okay! If you took that kind of energy, and if Jack was around now and I went to him and said, 'what do you think of me doing something like this?,'" and him going, 'Okay!'" That is sort of the kind of comic that I want to do. And to create a bunch of people that you care about, all of them are almost starting with no memory at all of the Eternals — the characters, that is, with the possible exception of Ikaris, and even he has some stuff that he's confused about. And I figure, what's nice about that is, everybody is starting out with a more or less blank sheet of paper. If you are completely up to date on everything that has ever happened to every member of the Eternals in the Marvel Universe ever, you may get more of a kick out of some of the things that happen. You may go, "Oh! Is that…? Okay! So…Ha ha! That's why so and so and whatever…!" But mostly, it's just something that I hope will work for somebody who has no idea what's going on, and I hope it'll work for somebody who *absolutely* knows what's going on! That's what I tried to get to happen with *1602*, something that would be just as satisfying for somebody who knew what was going on…

SPOTLIGHT: As a Marvel fan well steeped in Marvel history — and I love a big epic just like anyone — it was fun to read *1602* as it would unfold: the splendor of it all, the luxurious storytelling afforded by the big cast, all these characters that you know and love interacting with each other, out of the elements we understand them in and part of a different world that we don't intuitively understand. In comparison, unlike *1602*, I don't think a lot of people know a lot about *The Eternals*. Their history with Marvel has been rendered in a scattershot manner: once Jack's series ended, they sort of went away, then they came back for a supporting run on Thor, then they went away and came back for a mini-series in the mid-80s. Are you up on many of those stories?

NEIL: Some of those I've read, some I'm only familiar with through summaries.

SPOTLIGHT: Did any of that stuff grab you at all?

NEIL: Mostly as stuff that needed to be fixed. Mostly, just feeling like, this isn't what Jack would have done. This isn't where he was going. Now, I know that my thing isn't where Jack was going, but I hope that with my thing, at least by the end of it, we'll have the Eternals in a place that feels comfortable and usable. I don't feel like any of the previous stuff that wasn't Kirby increased their usability. Does that make any sense?

SPOTLIGHT: Absolutely. You've got your eye on their utility as Marvel characters while still keeping them in the Kirby ballpark.

NEIL: Yes, there would keep being these attempts to make a case for how they fold into the Marvel Universe, but by the end of which you'd go, "But they're just a bunch of super-powered people!" And that's one thing that the Marvel Universe simply does not need is a bunch more super-powered people. There are super-powered people all over the place!

SPOTLIGHT: It seems as if the main purpose of the stories was to fix them into the Marvel Universe rather than to simply tell a good Eternals story. Of course, there was a lot of good stuff there…

NEIL: Oh, and I'm not saying that it was all rubbish, because there was some very, very good stuff there. But I think what there also was was something very…(*Pause.*) I think I just felt like, you know, you didn't actually come away from any of that going, "Okay, *now* I get how they fit into the Marvel Universe and why they are cool!"

SPOTLIGHT: The front cover of Jack Kirby's *Eternals #1* has Ike Harris alerting his human friends saying, "We have found the space gods…and they're not dead!" Knowing that you are taking on this project, that statement reminds me of the Endless, the brethren who held court in your seminal *Sandman* comic all those years. I am wondering if there is any correlation in your mind between the Endless and the Eternals that you are bringing into the work?

NEIL: No…don't think that there is any correlation. Nor is it really…to be honest, if that was where it was going, I wouldn't bother. It would be kind of like somebody saying, "Neil, do Nightmare!" Ohhh…no…why would I want to do Nightmare? I already did Sandman! The joy in doing this for me is not doing gods, and it's not doing people as gods. The joy of this is trying to play with that Kirby madness.

SPOTLIGHT: Did you ever have the chance to meet him?

NEIL: I didn't. And I'm still kicking myself to this day. I was in San Diego in 1992, I guess, or maybe possibly even in 1993. I'm just trying to remember it properly. I had flown in to do something or other in San Diego, I came down on the lift and there was Jack talking to Paul Levitz, and…I was late for my plane! And I thought, "Shall I go over and get Paul to introduce me, shake his hand and tell him how important he is to me?" And then I thought, you know, there will be another convention. Then I got to the San Diego Airport — that little tiny airport they used to have — and I waited. For three hours. For a delayed plane. Kicking myself! And a few months later he was dead.

SPOTLIGHT: Talk about your comic book idolatry: Jack Kirby is number one for me, and I know I'm not alone. I had actually gotten out of reading comics in about 1990 — the only one I was keeping up with at the time was *Sandman*, ironically. I recall being out of the loop on comics news for the most part, but when I heard that Jack had died, it was devastating to me. His creative output was seminal in establishing the sense of wonder that I carry through this life. When you figure who's on the metaphorical Mt. Rushmore of the comic art medium, Jack Kirby is on there — without a doubt.

NEIL: I was very lucky recently. I was staying at the house of a friend, doing some work, and my friend had bought on ebay most of the first 100 issues of *Fantastic Four*, in rubbishy, reading condition. And, I actually got to do that thing of, you know, lie in the bath and read them through…(*Laughter.*)… with the ads and with that sense of wonderful Kirbyish excitement. Smart Stan dialogue, that Kirby energy, and you know, he's one of the people who's work I…(*Pause*)…the weird thing about Kirby is, especially when he moved to DC, there was this little period where I was eleven years old, maybe ten, and for a little bit it was *too weird* for me. And then it *wasn't* too weird for me any more. There was this point in there when I picked up *New Gods* and there would be these Kirby energy blasts, these black things surrounded by orangey flames and I'd say, "What the heck is that?" My little ten year old head would go, "Fire doesn't look like that!" and then you look at his women and go, "Women don't look like that!" And then after awhile, you just came to accept it. This is the Kirbyverse. This is what fire looks like in the Kirbyverse. This is what women look like in the Kirbeyverse.

SPOTLIGHT: How much of your *Eternals* series will be a strict homage to Jack and his legacy?

NEIL: There's no way that we are doing *The Eternals* as any kind of homage to Jack. It's not a pastiche, it's not any of those kinds of things. I thought about it…as I started writing, I thought that every ten pages I'd do a double page spread and call it a chapter heading or whatever. And I thought, you know what? That's not Jack, and that's not what we're doing.

My friend Roger Zelazny died very shortly before I finished *American Gods* and with that I guess my agenda was to write the kind of book that Roger would have liked. The happiest I got was about a year after *American Gods* came out and I got a note from Roger's girlfriend, when he died, and she said, "I think he would have really liked this book." That was who I wrote it for. And with this, I'm writing the kind of book that I think Jack would have liked. He would have read it and gone, "I wouldn't have done things like that. Ohhh, why are they doing that?!?! Ohhh why are they standing around talking! All these people standing around talking!" (*Laughter.*) But I think that I'd like to do a comic that he would have liked.

SPOTLIGHT: I definitely think you're on the right track so far. Your theme for Eternals is very similar in tone to Jack's, and the bombast brought to the artwork by John Romita, Jr…I'm sure he would have liked that element. The images that I've seen fit squarely into the realm of "Kirbyness." How far along are you right now?

NEIL: I'm halfway through issue #2, but most of it is in note form. Once I get off doing interviews, I have to go and type it up. The only thing that troubles me, though in some ways it kind of adds a wonderful sort of Kirbyish pressure to the whole thing, is that at the point where Johnny became free and I was ready to start, the message came from Marvel, "OK and we're putting this out in June!" (*Laughter.*) OK, when we did *1602*, we worked a year ahead so that we had six issues done before the first issue hit. And this one, we'll be lucky to have finished number three and if any of us get a cold, we're screwed. (*Laughter.*) You just have to hope that none of us get a cold.

SPOTLIGHT: Don't slip in the bath reading those FF comics!

NEIL: Yes, and be careful with what we eat.

SPOTLIGHT: Do those pushups, too!

Thanks to Neil for sitting with us and talking Eternals!

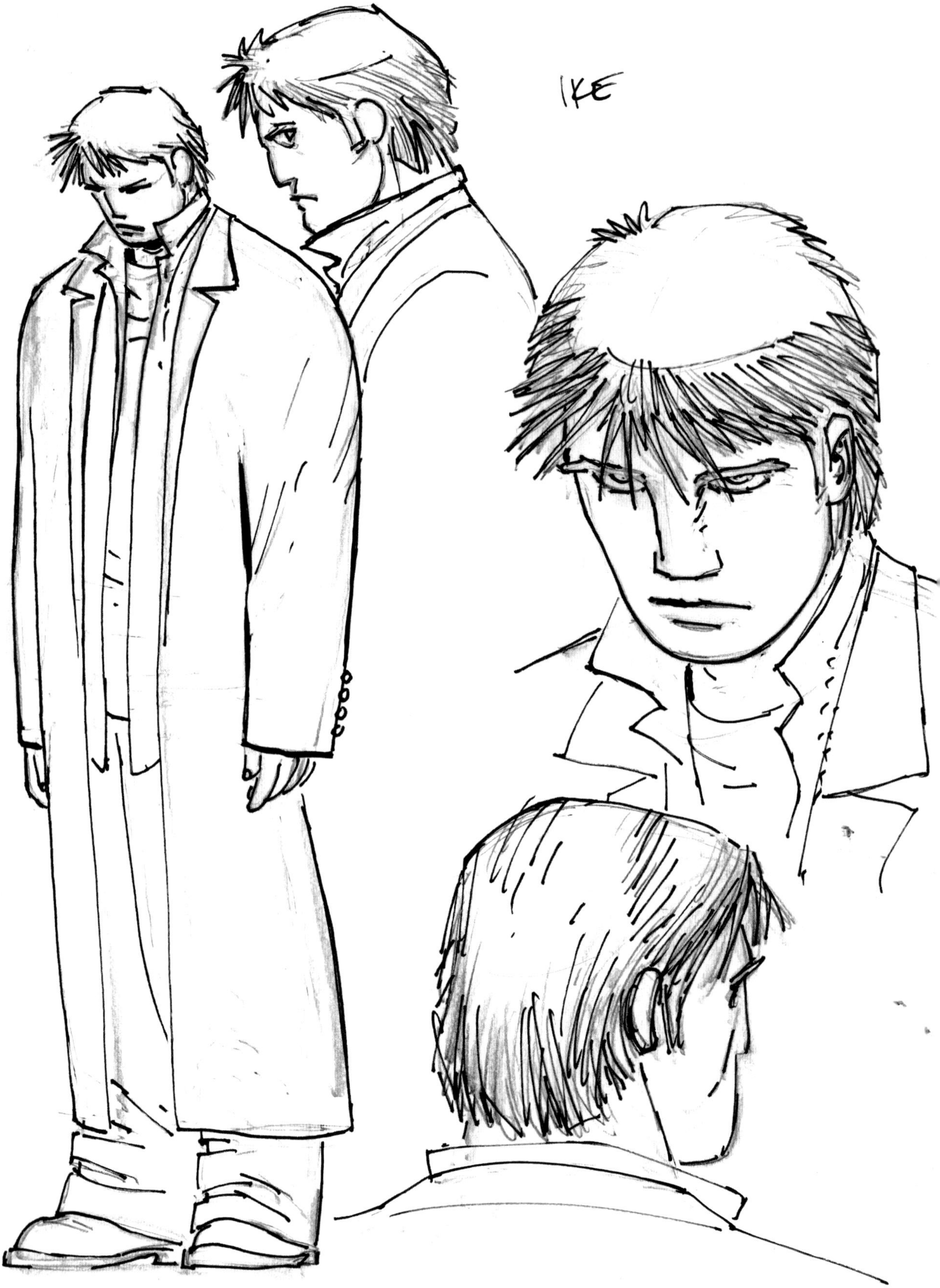
IKE

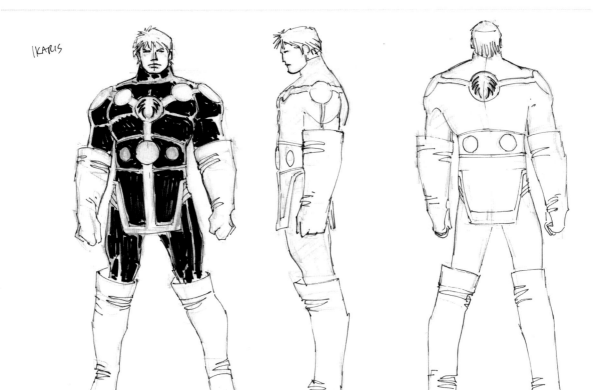

IKARIS

Original Design by Jack Kirby

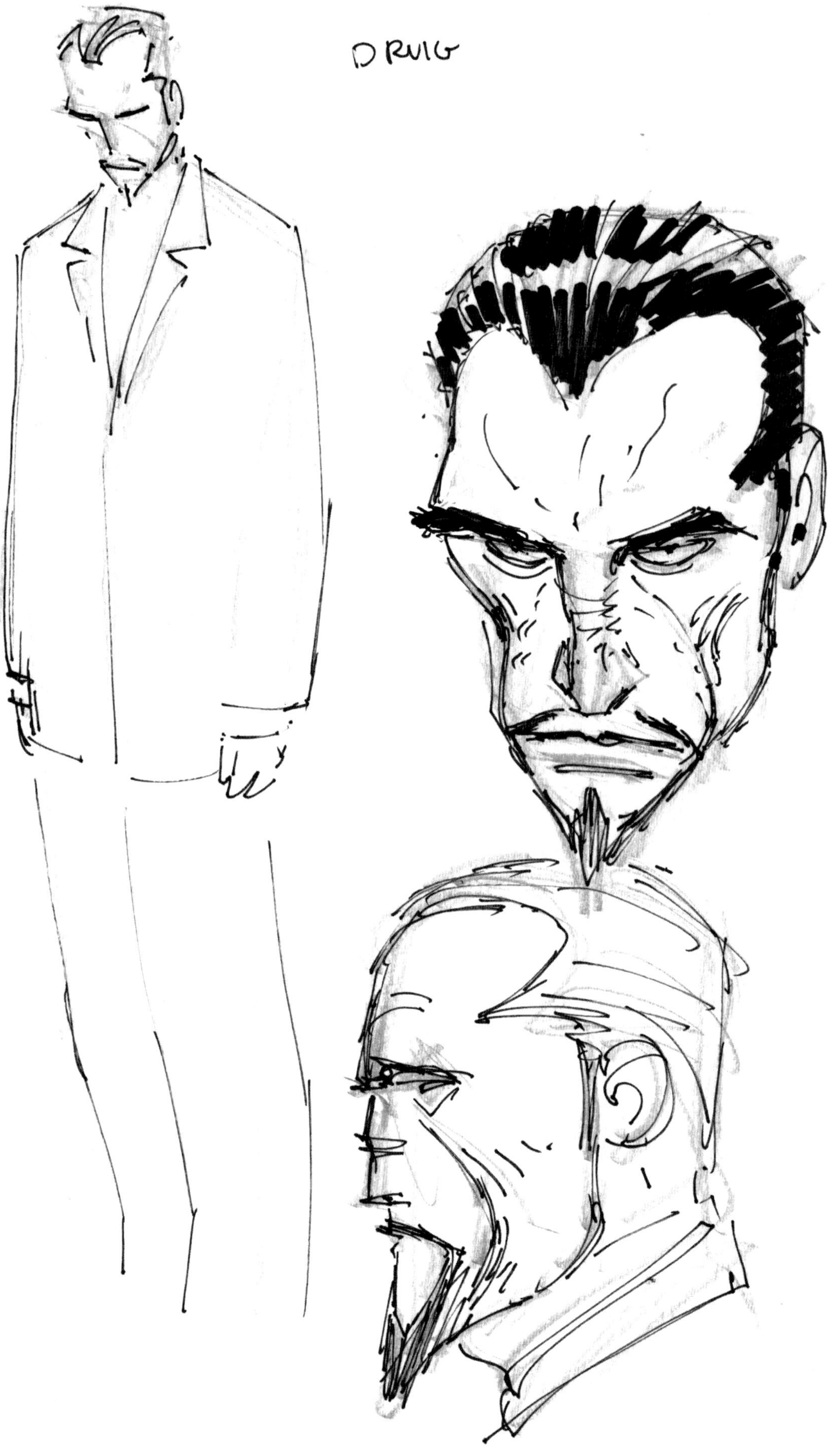
DRUIG

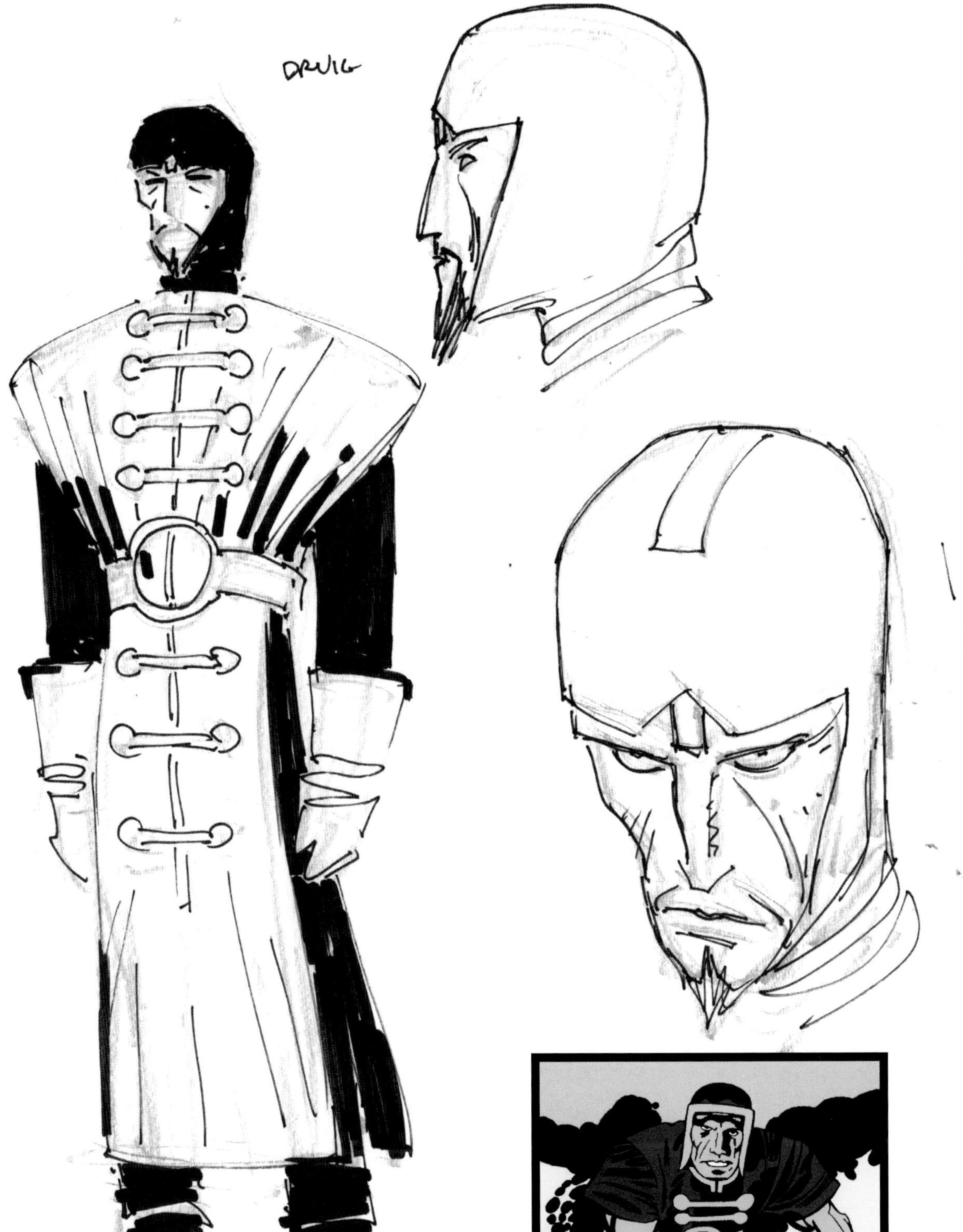
DRUIG

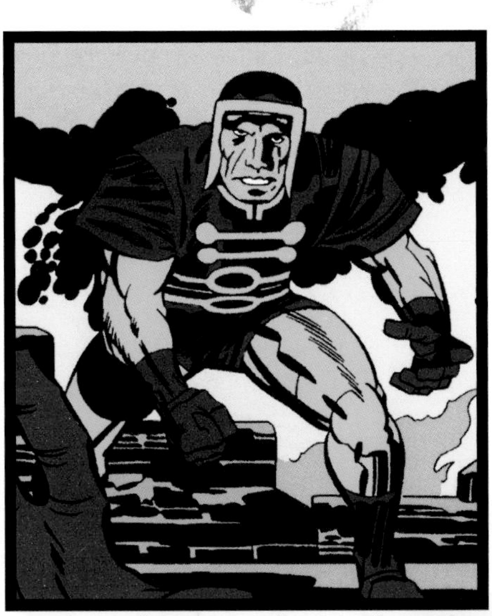

Original Design by Jack Kirby

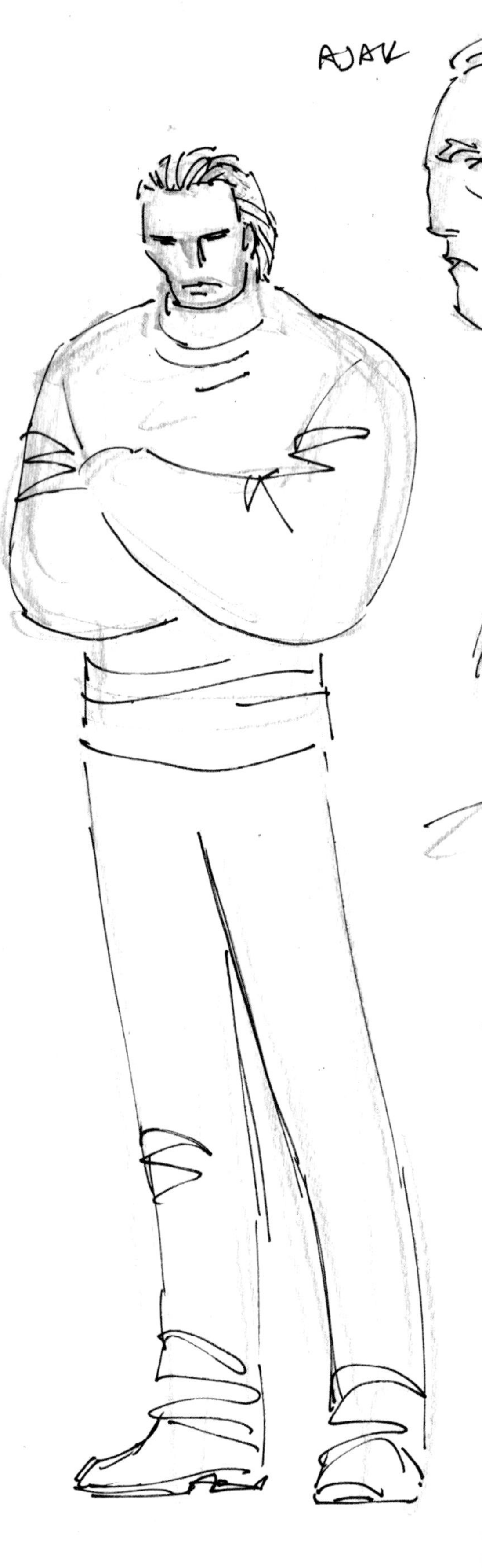
AJAK

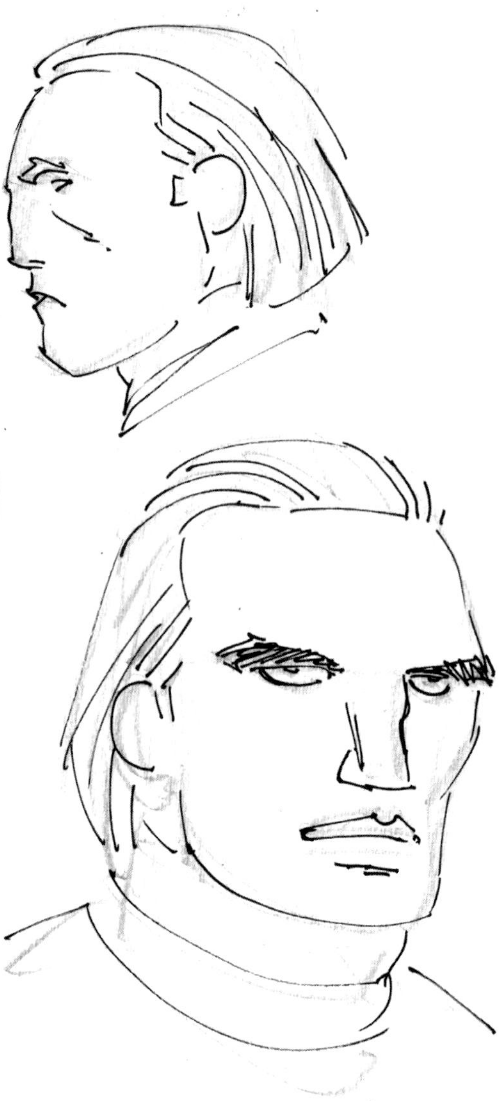

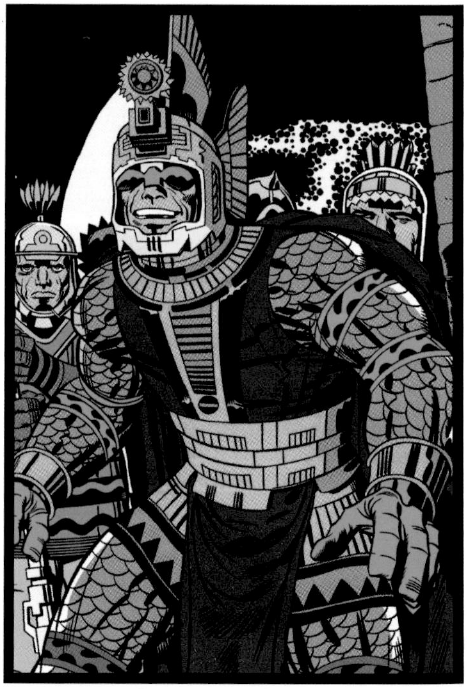

Original Design by Jack Kirby

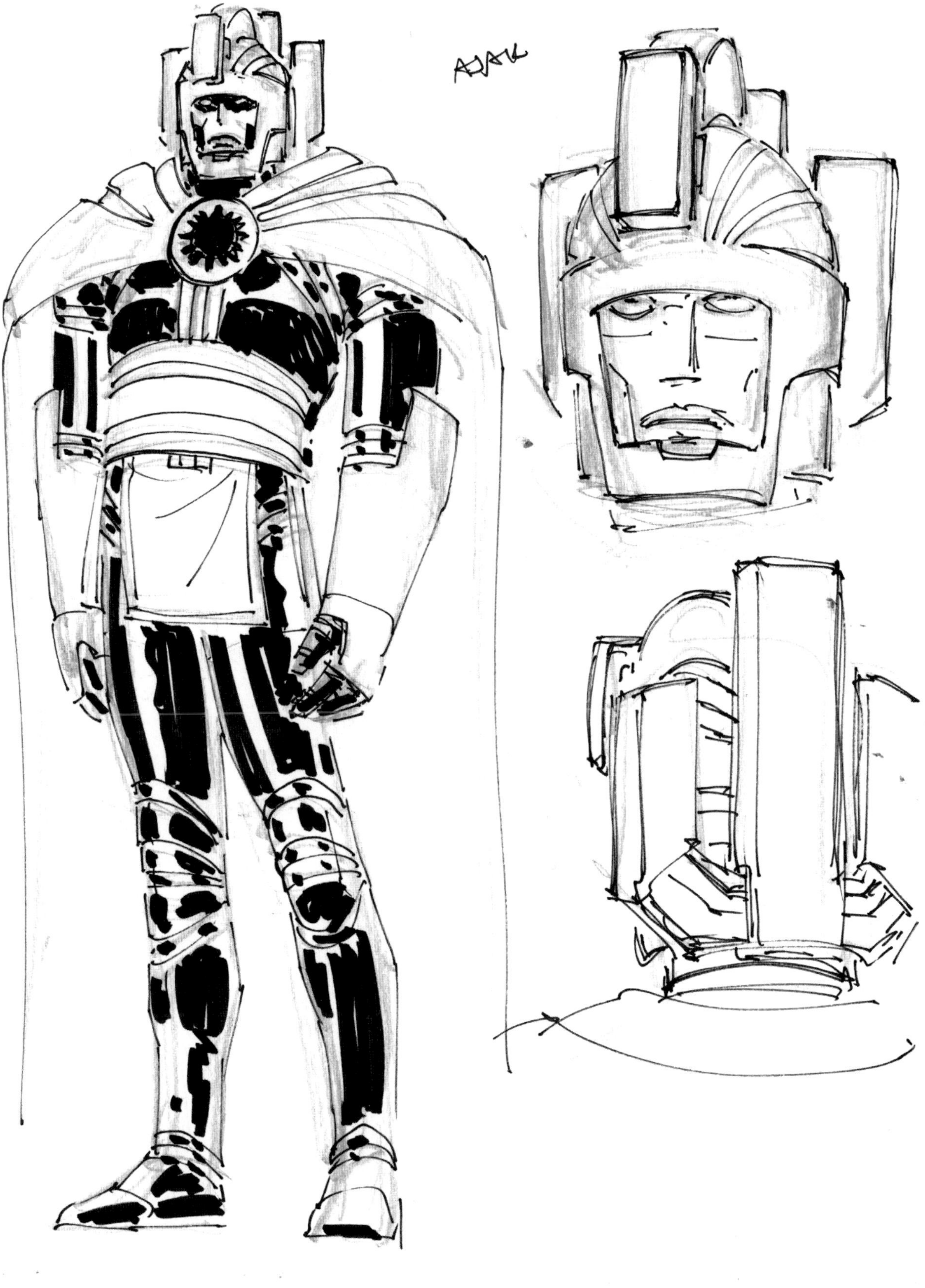
AJAK

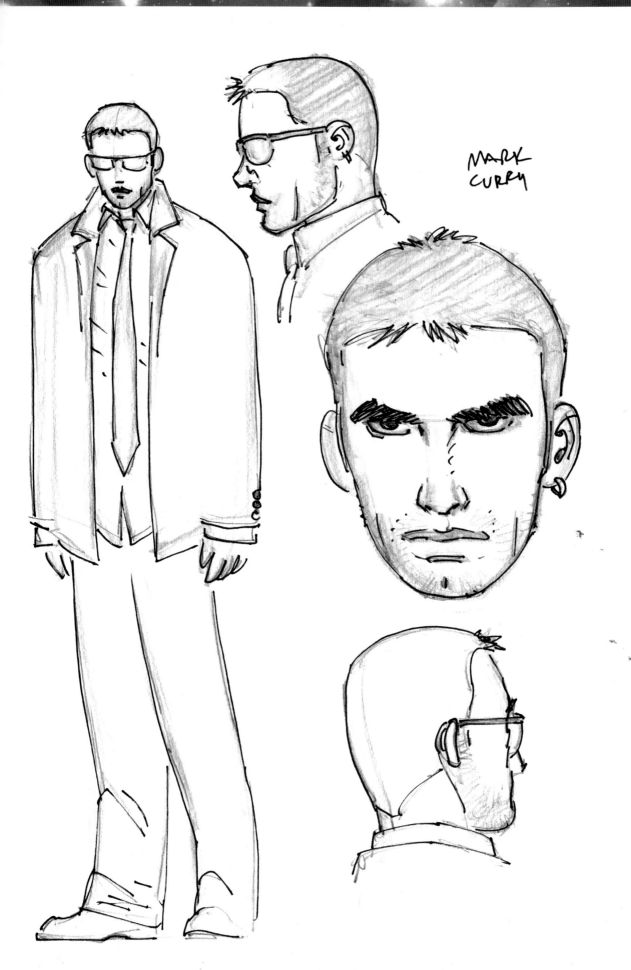

MARK
CURRY

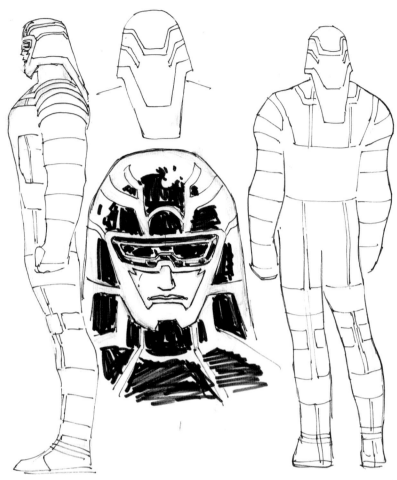

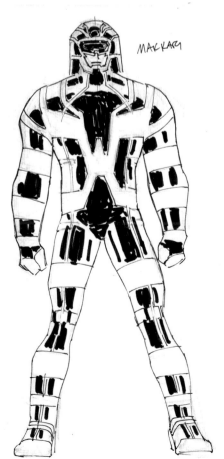

Original Design by Jack Kirby

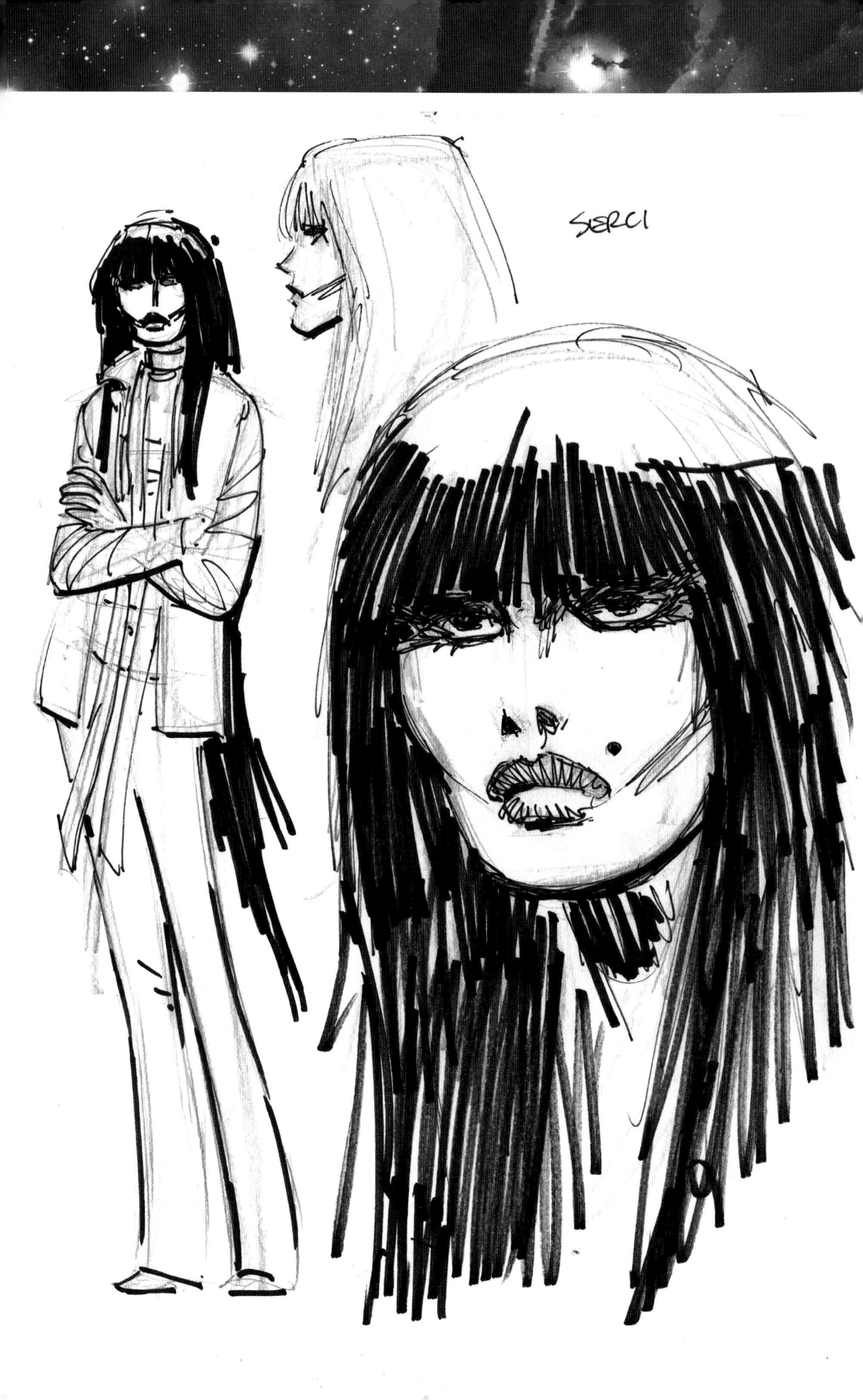
SERCI

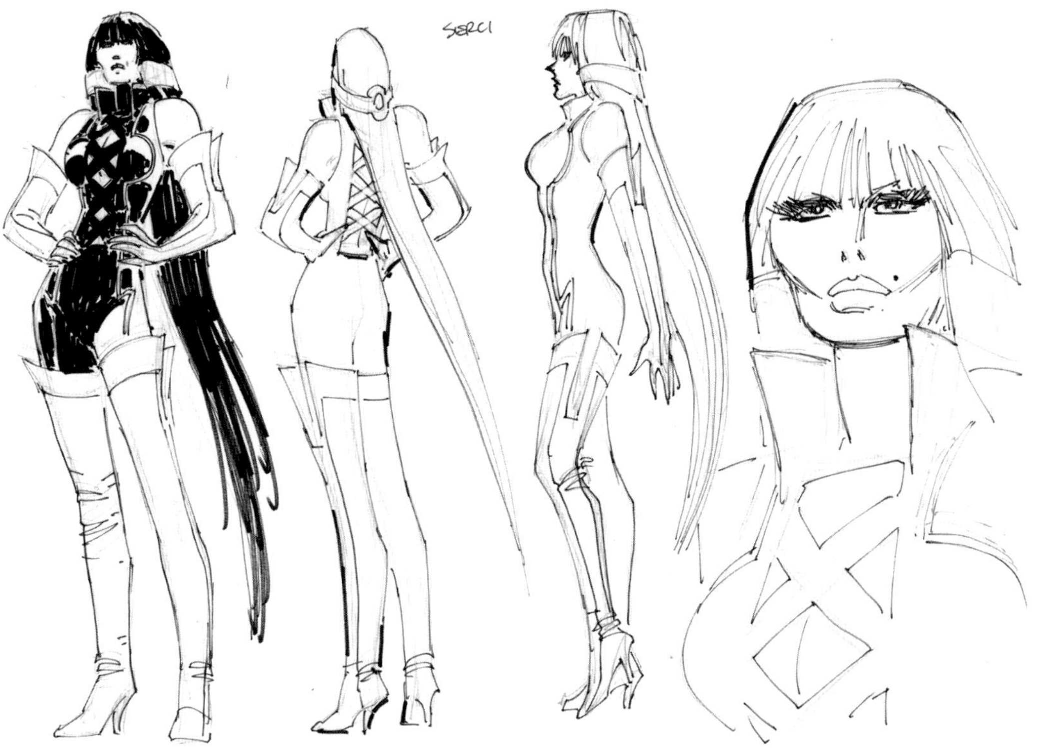

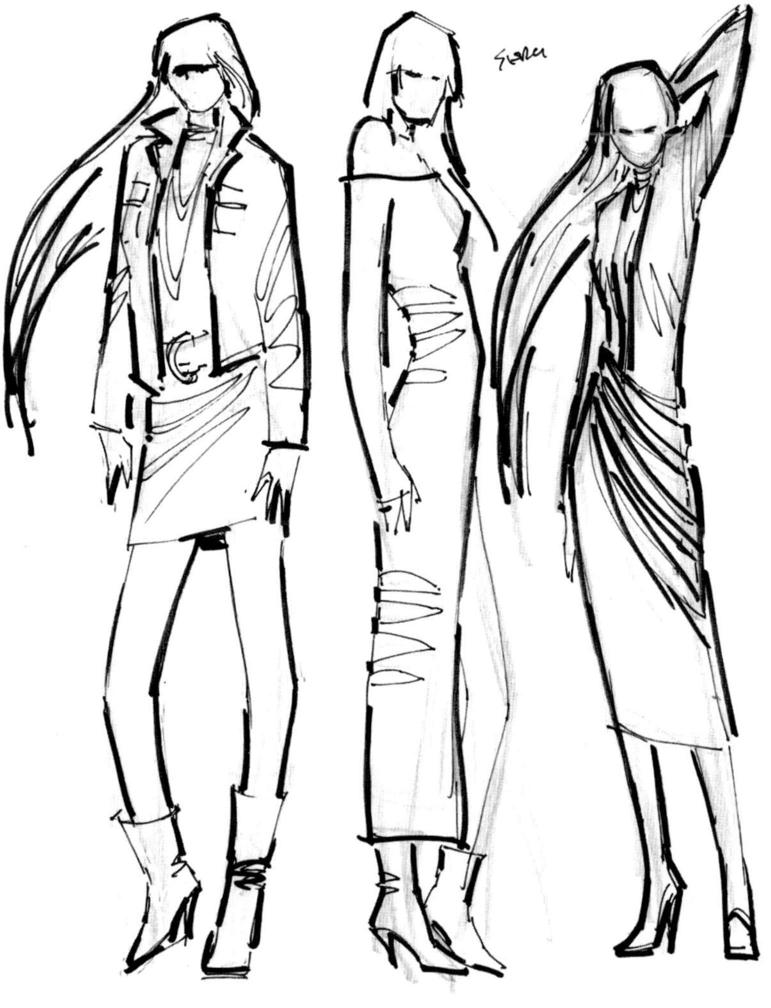

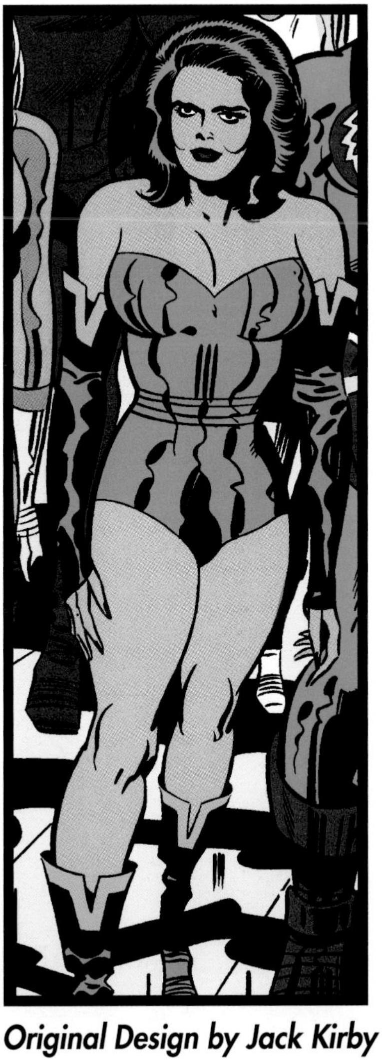

Original Design by Jack Kirby

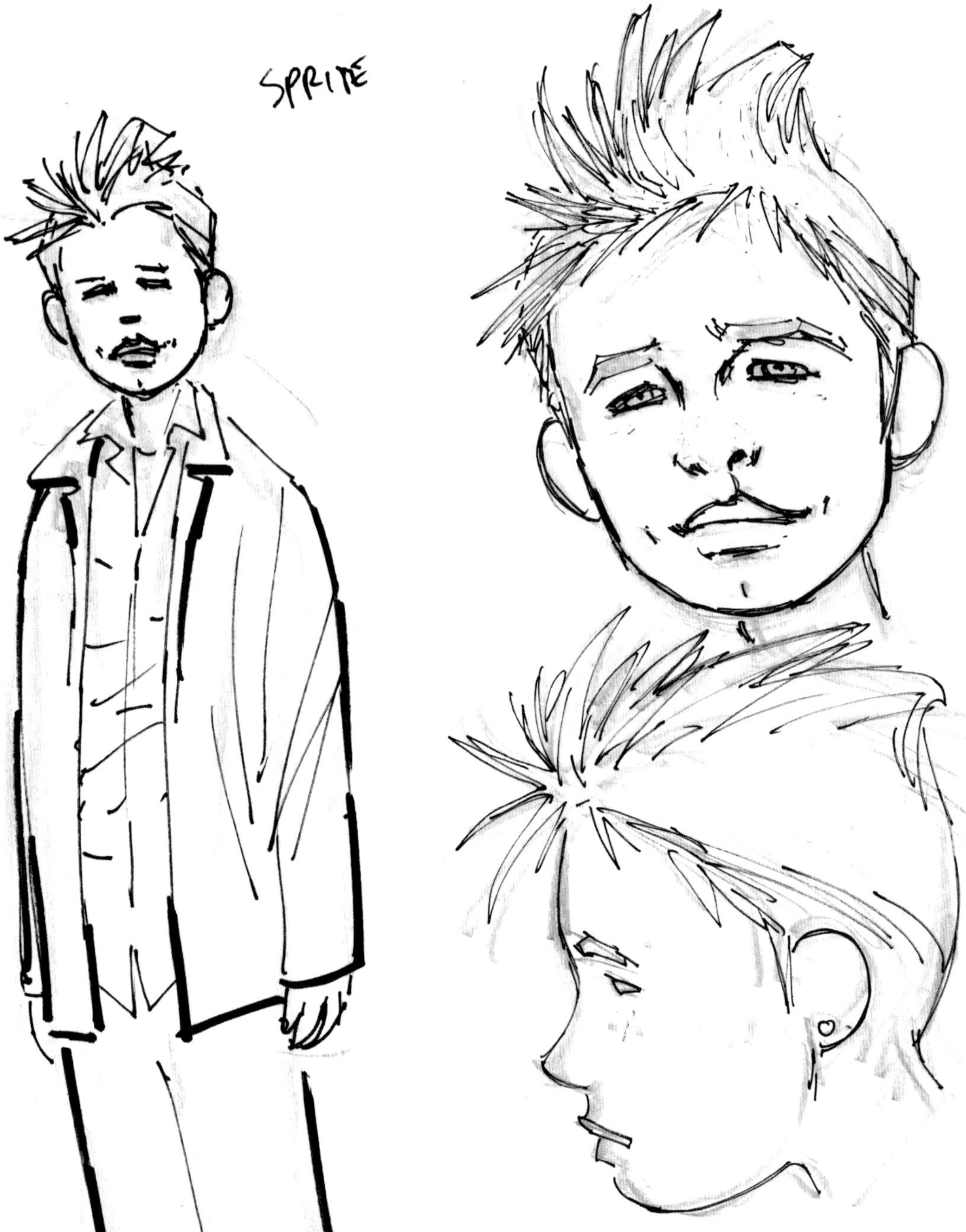
SPRITE

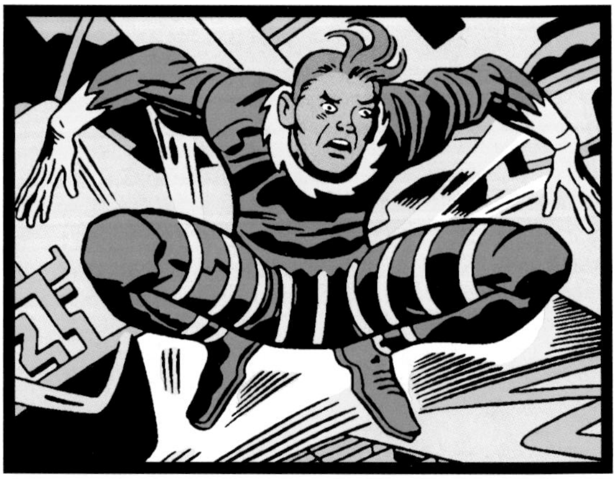

Original Design by Jack Kirby

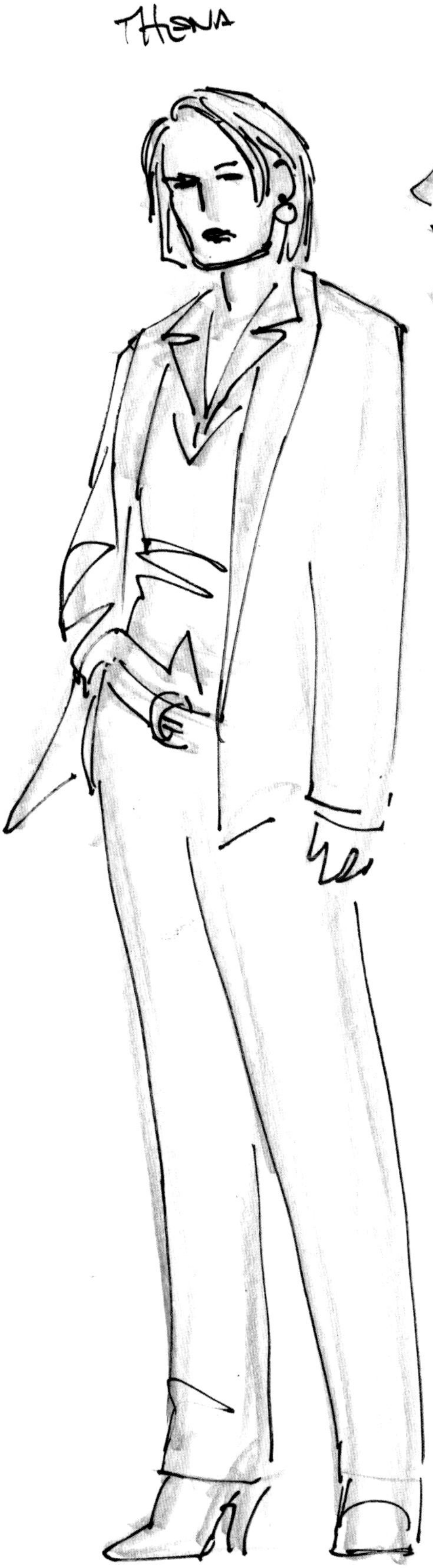
THENA

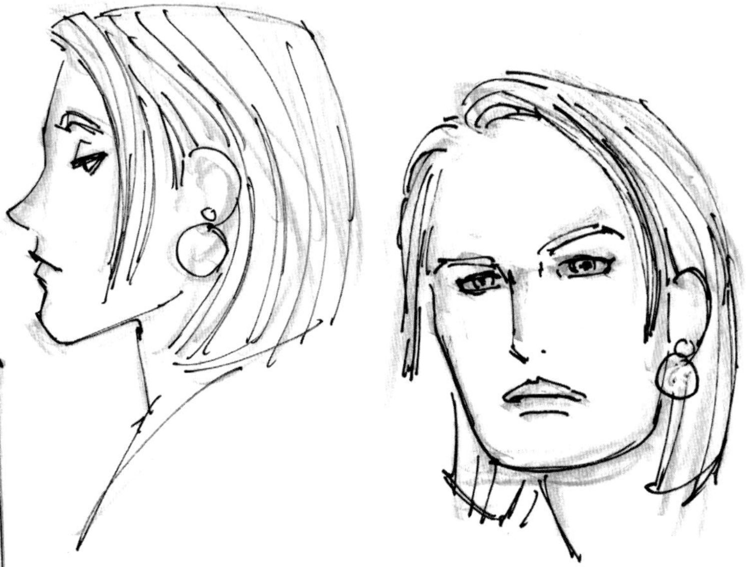

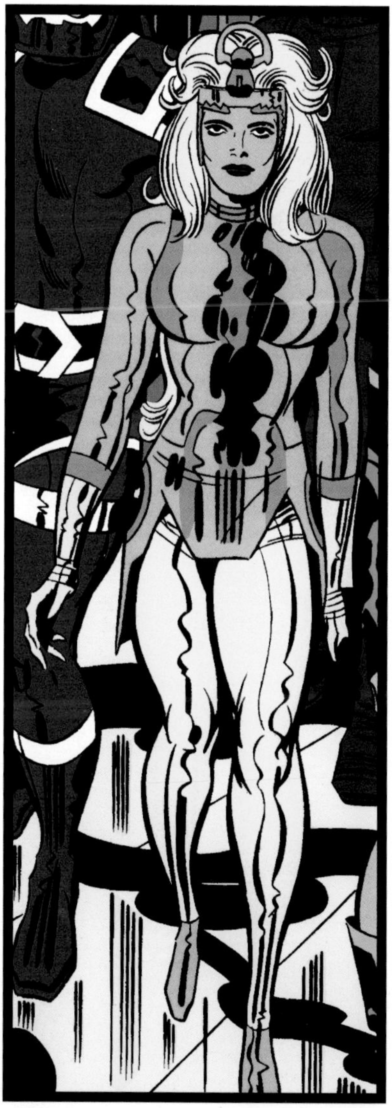

Original Design by Jack Kirby

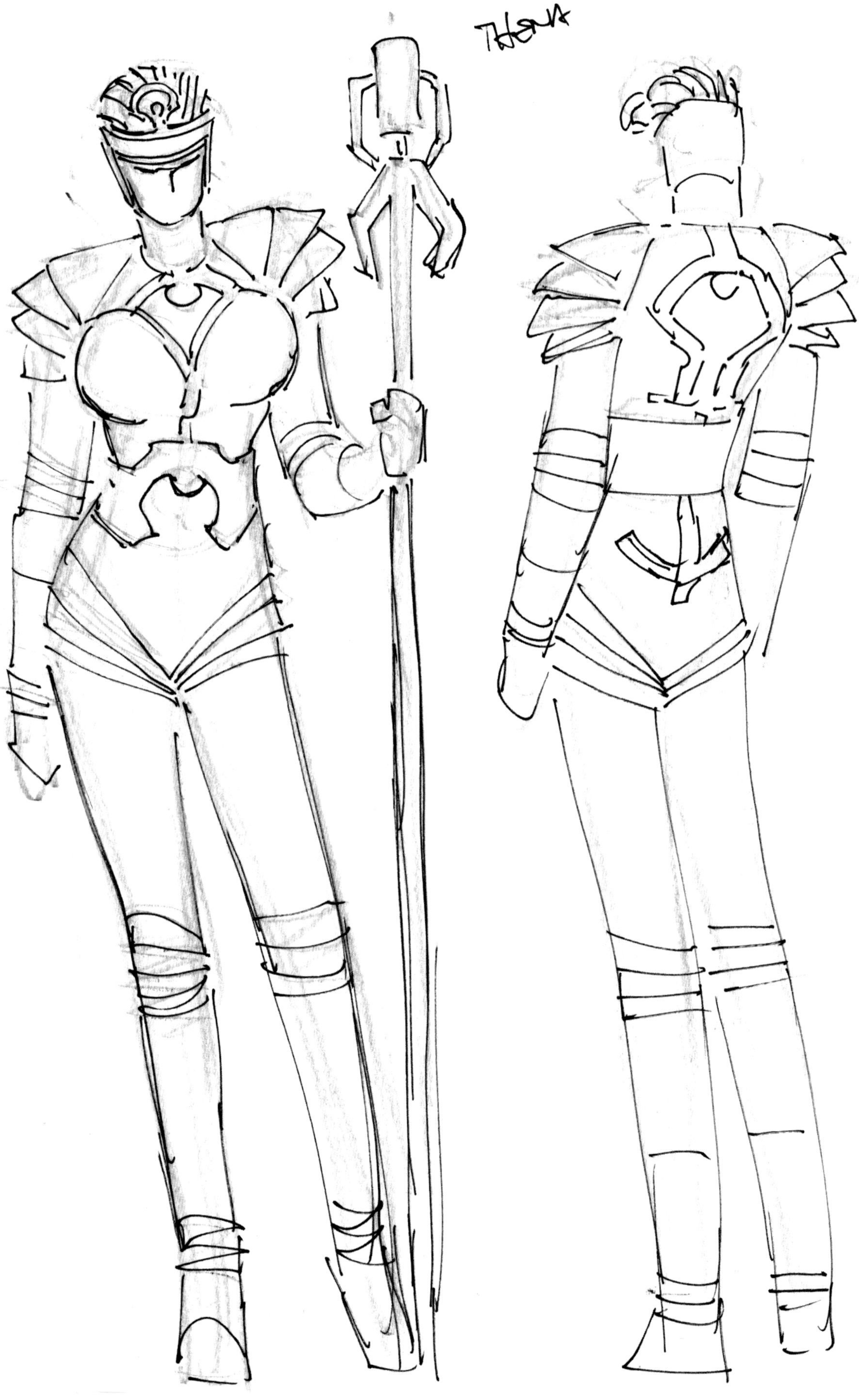
THENA

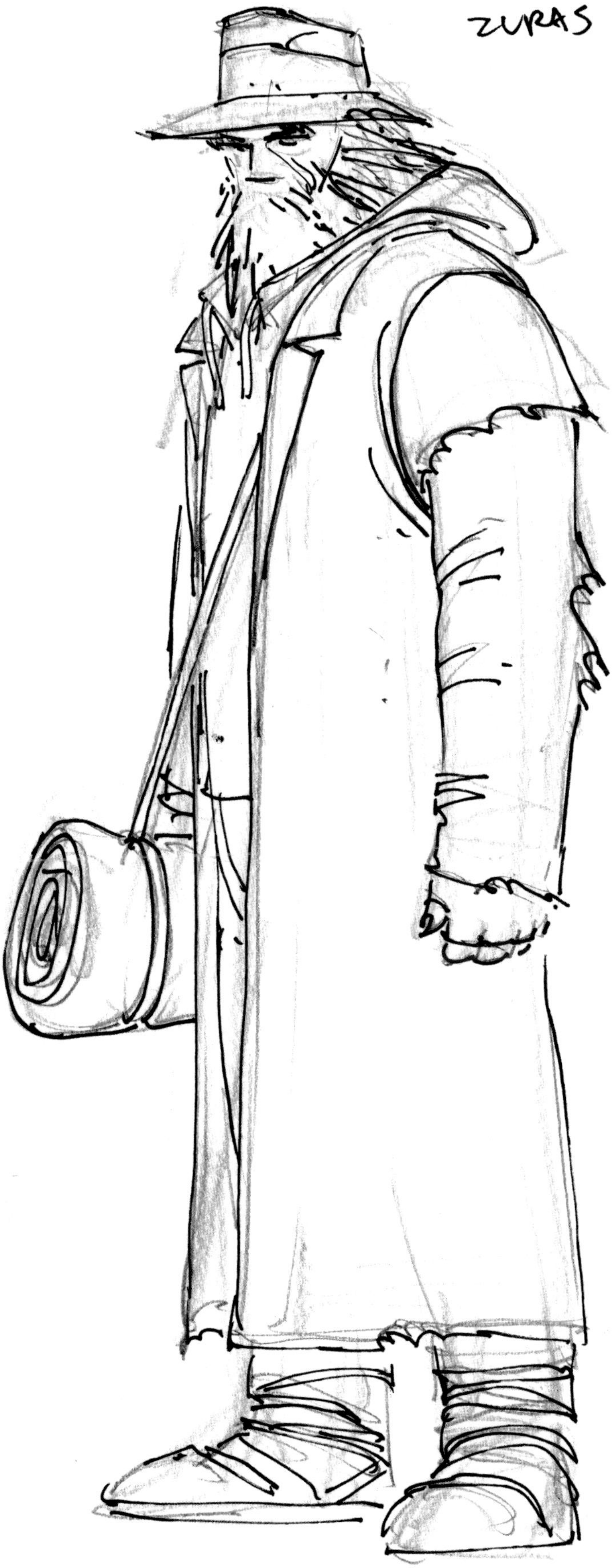
ZURAS

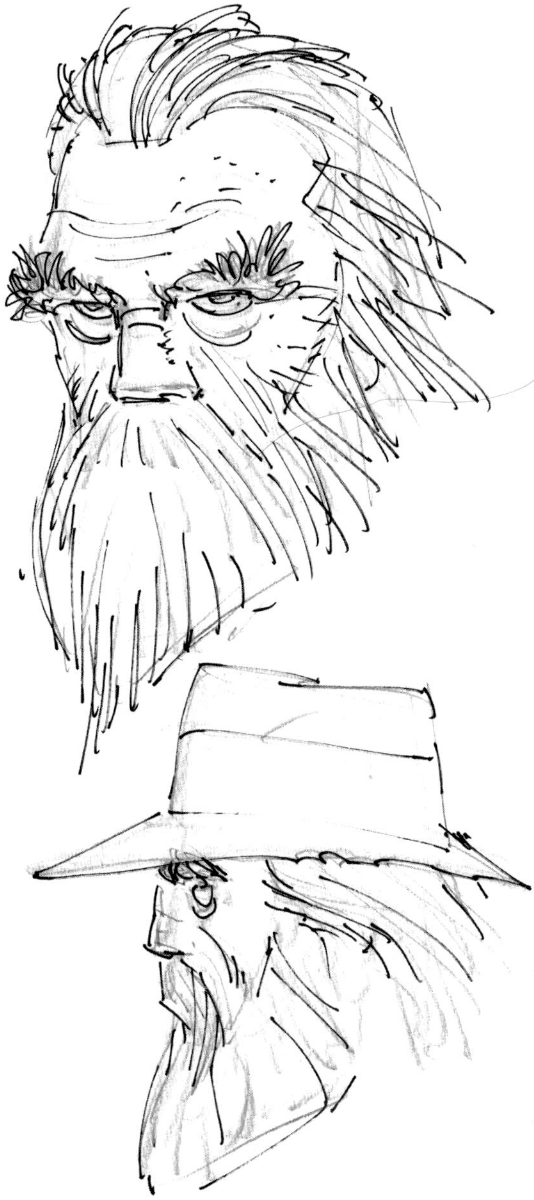

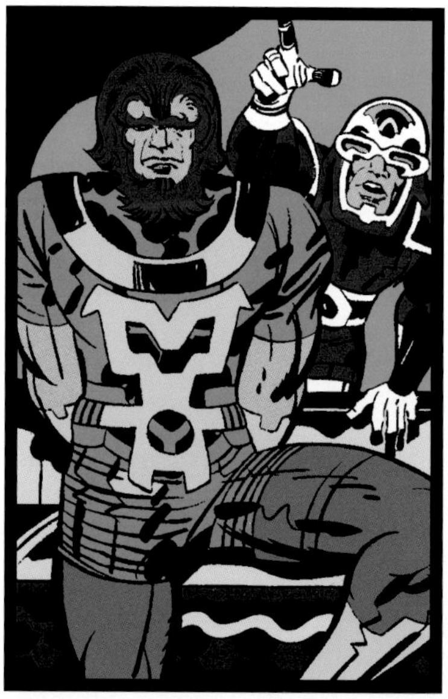

Original Design by Jack Kirby

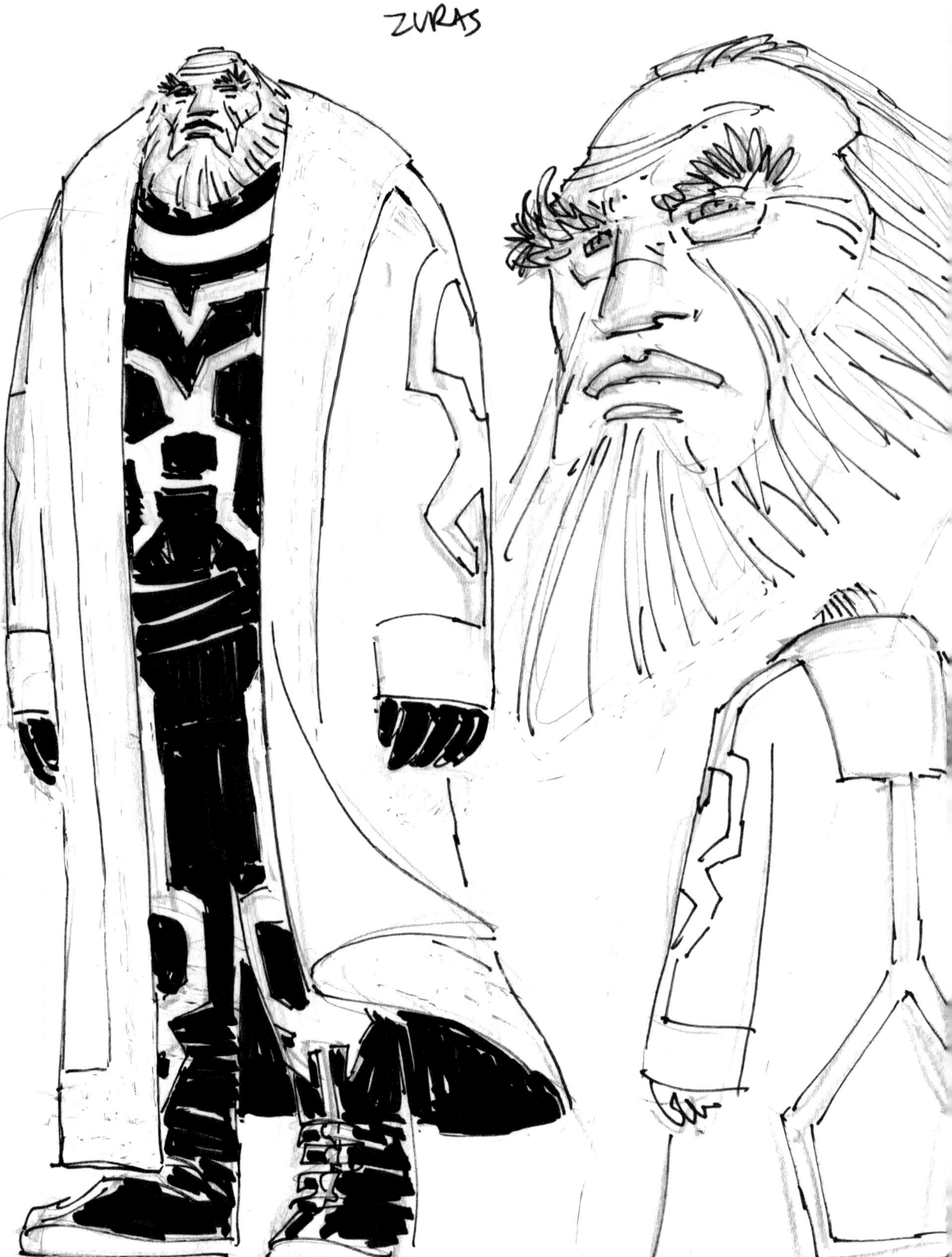
ZURAS

ISSUE #1, PAGE 23 PENCILS BY JOHN ROMITA JR.

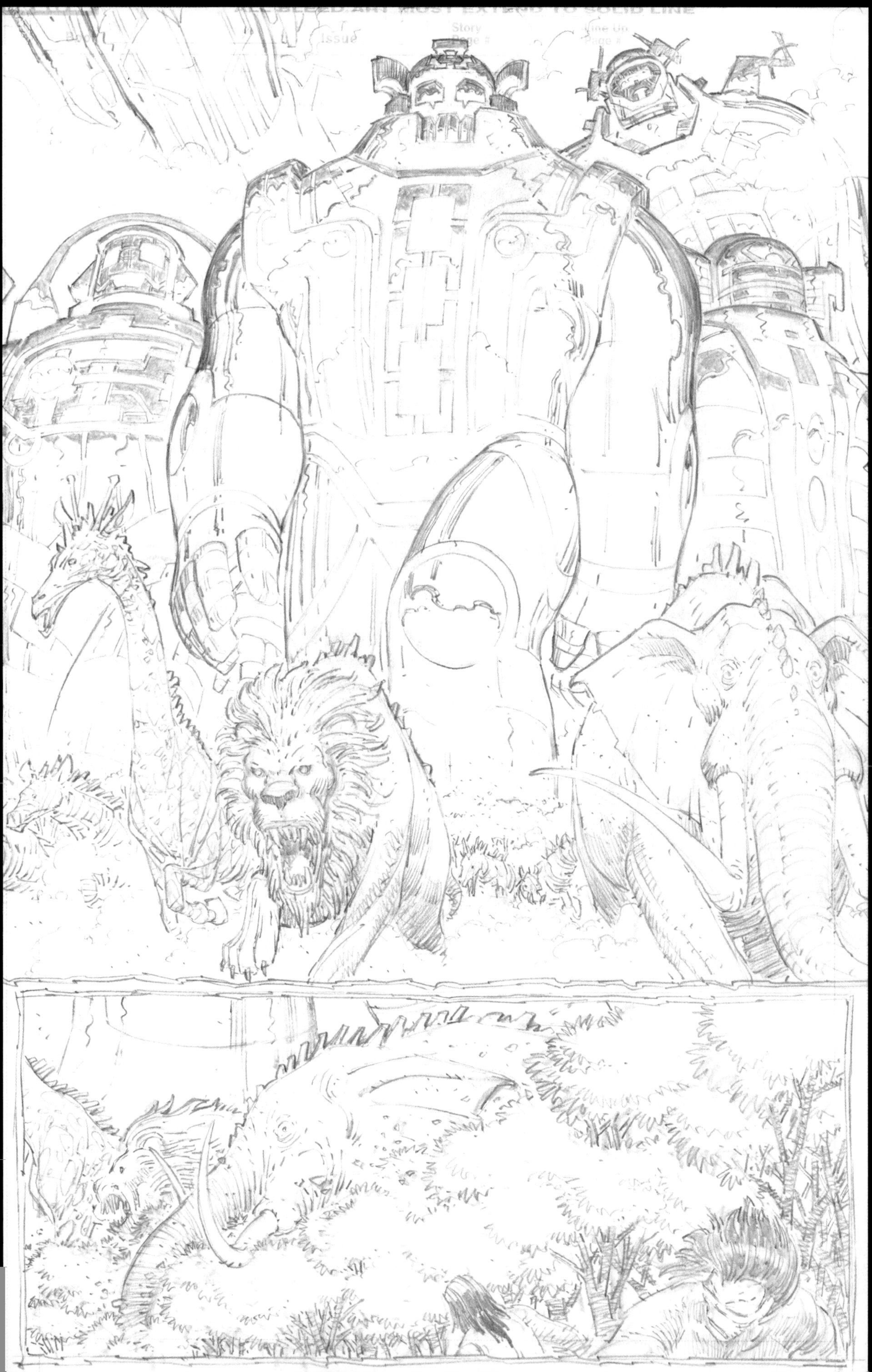

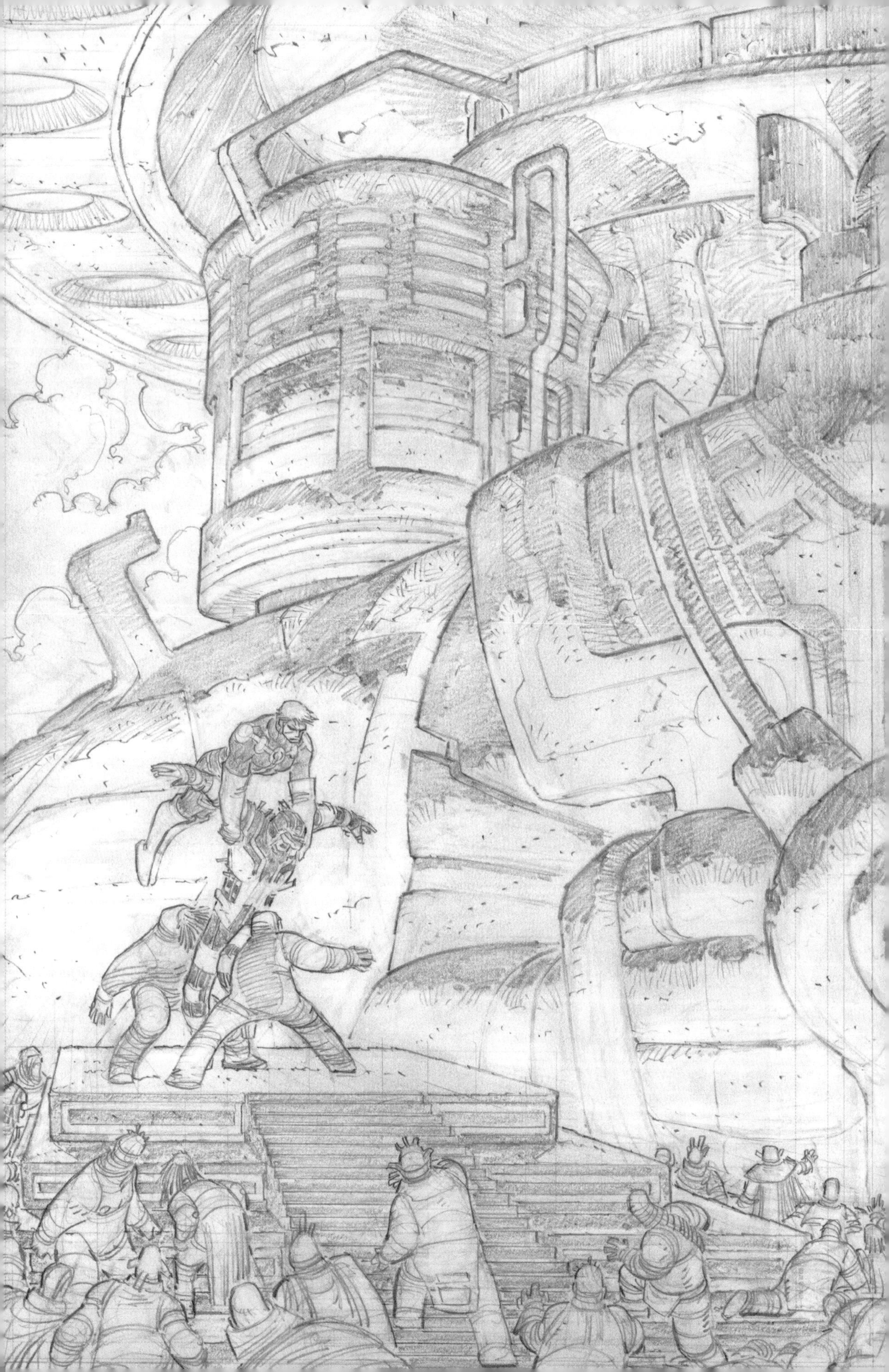

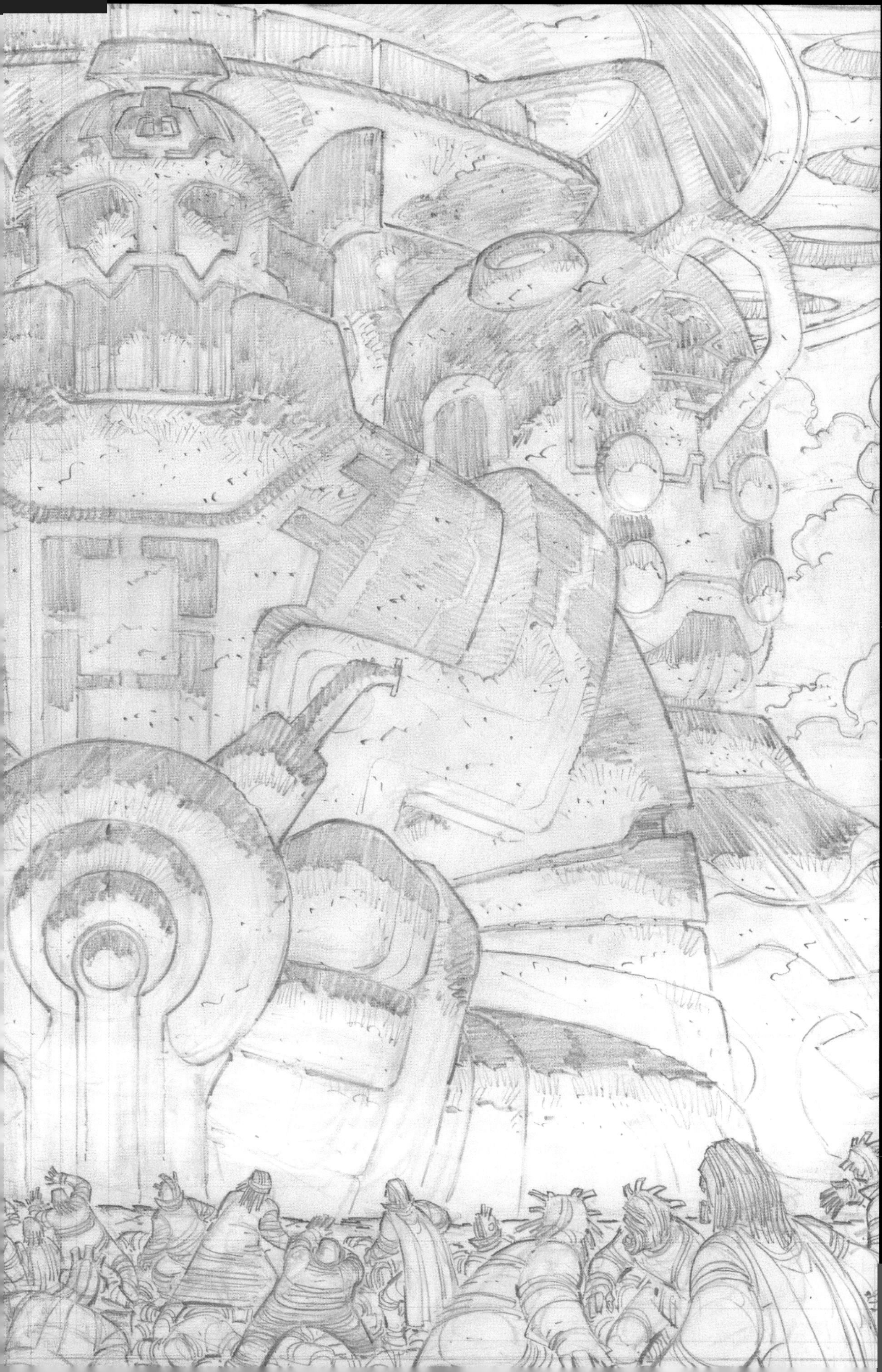

ISSUE #1, PAGE 30 ORIGINAL PENCILS BY JOHN ROMITA JR.

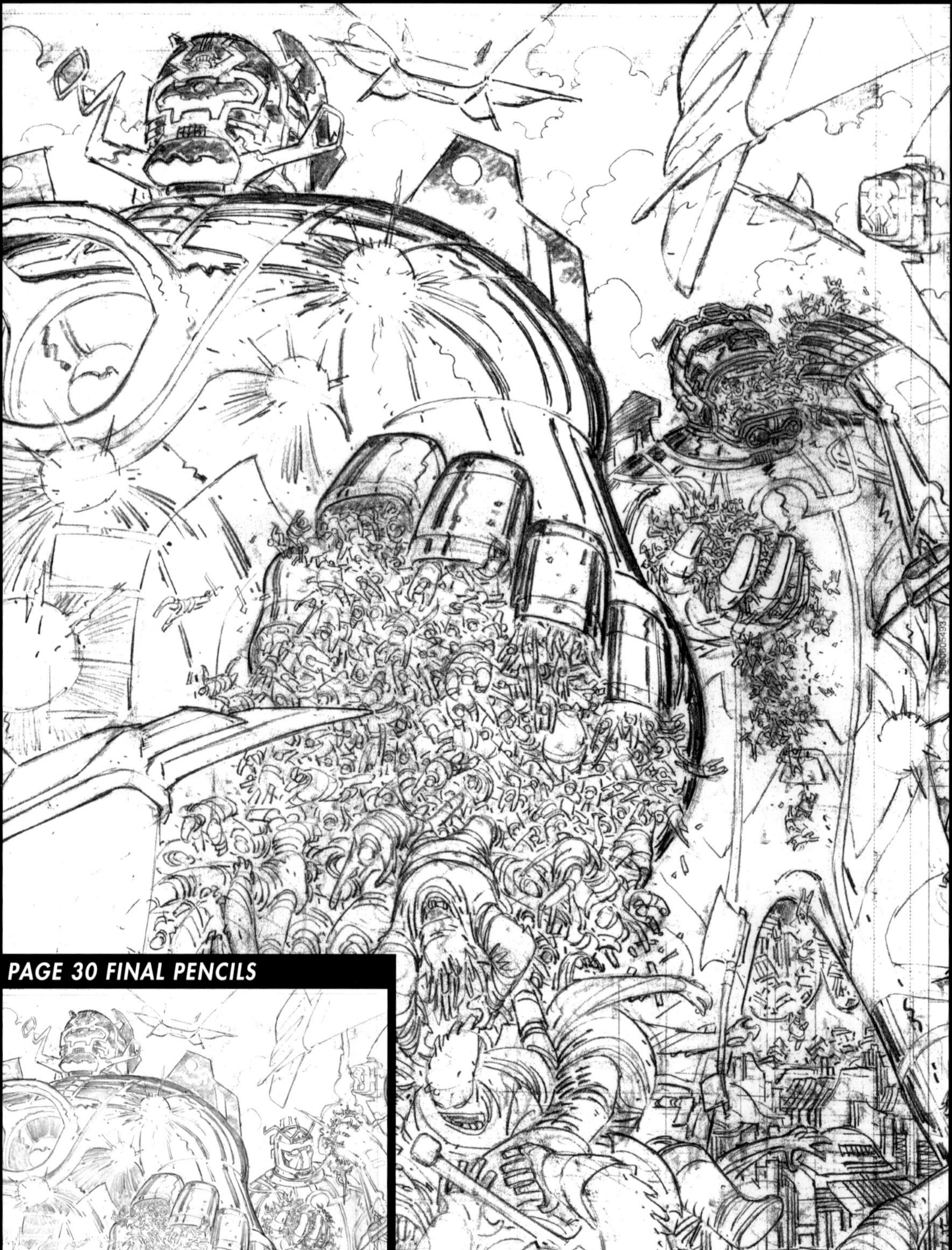

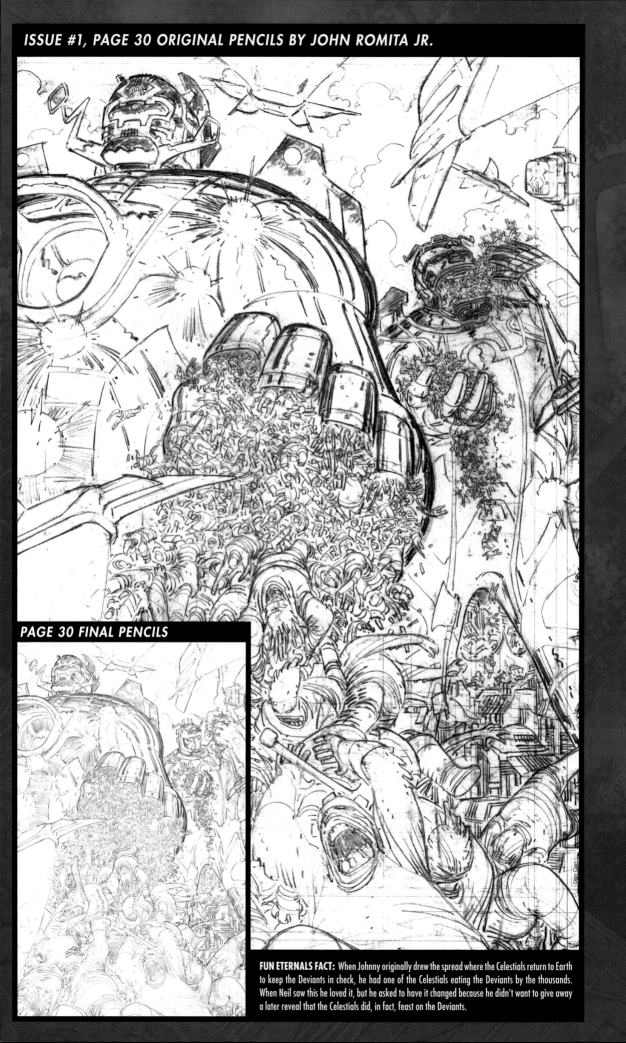

PAGE 30 FINAL PENCILS

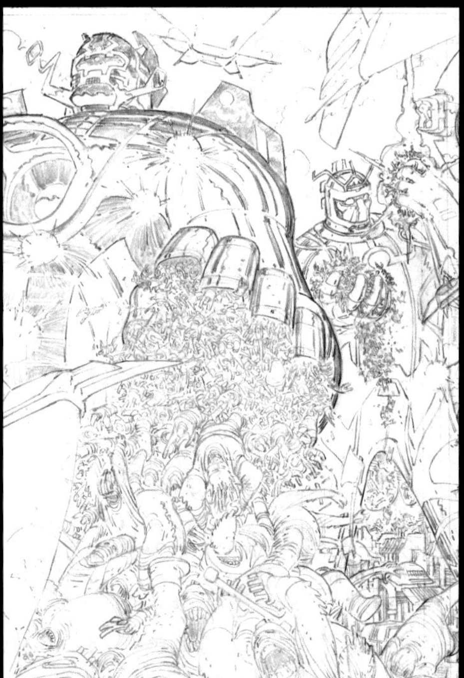

FUN ETERNALS FACT: When Johnny originally drew the spread where the Celestials return to Earth to keep the Deviants in check, he had one of the Celestials eating the Deviants by the thousands. When Neil saw this he loved it, but he asked to have it changed because he didn't want to give away a later reveal that the Celestials did, in fact, feast on the Deviants.

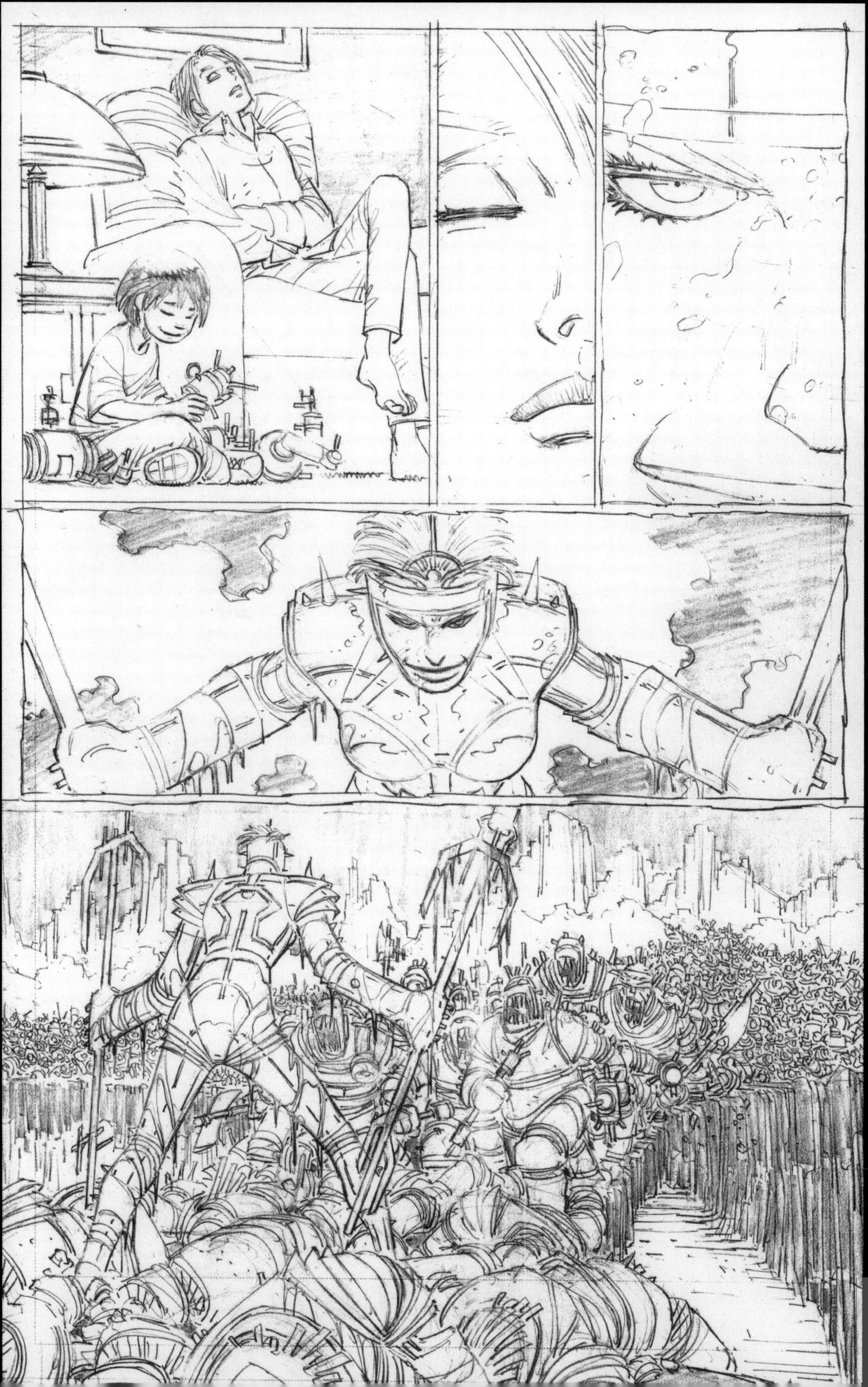

ETERNALS
PROPOSAL BY NEIL GAIMAN

In the beginning, the Celestials landed on Earth. They took a proto-human, ape-like creature and they dismantled it, stripping it back to its component DNA. They compared the results to other experimental subjects—a cave bear, an octopus, a dolphin, a panda. They built the proto-human back up, examined it in ways that we can barely imagine. And then they made their decision.

They destroyed the proto-human, and from its cellular information and genetic coding they produced two templates. One template was a genetic lucky dip and randomiser—the race that humans would come to know as "The Deviants": each member of which was unique and different, always in flux, always changing—a (mostly) short-lived race of monsters and freaks, unable to breed true. The other template was stranger. There were only two hundred of them made and they came off the production line with memories already in place. Built from Human Genetic Code, yet not human. Each of them unchanging, perfect, superhuman in every way. They did not age. They did not die.

The Celestials left. Time passed. The proto-humans became actual humans. Civilisations rose and fell. The Deviants evolved their own brutal civilisation—and at one point they enslaved the humans, and, despite the best efforts of the Eternals, they seemed unstoppable.

The Celestials returned at this point—whether to examine and correct their experiment or to change it, no-one knows. There was dissension amongst the Celestials themselves, and one of their number was imprisoned beneath a mountain-range on Earth, and left here to dream: The Dreaming Celestial.

No longer would the Deviants rule the humans—the age of the Deviants was over. They went, literally, underground, avoiding contact with humans. The Celestials left Earth, taking with them what they had come for. They would come again. They made certain adjustments to the Eternals at this time as well.

The Eternals mopped up, tidied up. They were the Celestials' caretakers on Earth, keeping the world going until the Celestials returned. Never aging, never changing as the years passed and the centuries and the millennia.

The people who saw them believed them to be gods.

…

The first thing he said to me was "What would you say if I told you that you were Eternal. You are a superhuman being who will live forever," and my heart sank. Like I need another nut trying to sell me religion.

Mark Curry is a medical student. He's working long hours in an inner city hospital.

He has strange dreams, of lives lived a long time ago.

The last thing he needs is a tall, blond, charismatic stranger named Harris, who starts following him around, telling him strange Seventies-style religious nonsense stories of an alien race on Earth, and how Mark needs to understand that he is Eternal. Stories he dismisses until Harris is beaten up beyond imagining and left for dead. And then, in a deep coma, he starts to heal…

Someone is taking Harris's stories seriously. And Mark wants to know how a man can do that, can heal.

He steals in at the dead of night. Harris comes out of his coma. He doesn't know who did this to him. But he's still babbling about his "Eternals." He's identified another five people who, he tells Mark, are like him.

A party organiser named Sersi.

A scientist named Tina.

The Ambassador to the UN from a small country, formerly part of the USSR named Druig.

A boy TV star called Sprite.

A Mexican gardener named Ajak.

Harris wants Curry to smuggle him out of the hospital, or discharge him. Something that Curry isn't going to do… until someone tries to blow up the wing of the hospital he's in. Curry freezes the explosion – somehow. And Harris is convinced. Something's going on.

Harris needs to return to his coma. To sleep and to heal.

Curry goes to talk to…

The people who aren't Eternals.

Harris claims that thirty years ago, the Celestials came back, but that when they left they took the knowledge of their visit with them.

He claims that they are not human—they do not have human DNA: the junk code is gone, as is anything that's coded for age or death.

He tells Curry that he was the leader of the Eternals, following the death of their leader, Zuras.

Harris goes to see the people on the list…

Sersi tries to seduce him.

Tina shows him that his DNA is as human as hers.

Sprite is a brat on his way to becoming a superstar. He's in California, not interested.

Ajak is also in California, impassive, not interested.

Curry is convinced, mostly, that his friend is nuts.

And then a old street man comes up to him and tells him he is Zuras, the leader of the Eternals. He's mad. Kidnaps Curry…

Ikaris takes the besotted Sersi with him to Avengers mansion.

It's obvious that nobody in the Marvel Universe knows anything about the Eternals. They aren't in the history books, or in the Avengers records. Some kind of superheroic Civil War seems to be going on in the background, so Ikaris will get no help there.

Ikaris comes up with one suggestion. The Uni-Mind. The blending of minds to form something greater and wiser than any of them…

Rounds them all up.

Curry has freed himself. Zuras knows more than any of them, but he is mad…

And, by Ikaris's memory, he should be dead. But then, so should Druig. And Ajak. Ikaris suspects Druig, his evil cousin, the Russian Oligarch.

It's almost impossible to get Sprite. He's a huge star, and getting huger. Curry and Ikaris managed to talk to him before, but he can't just go off with a bunch of adults…

Ikaris begins the Uni-Mind, and it starts to work…

They see the world from its conception… They start to recover their memories, start to become Eternals once again…

And someone tries to kill them.

Each of them is a wash of memories. They are starting to recover their powers.

But none of this makes sense…

Sprite.

Comes through the door with a gun. Kills Everyone except Curry and Ikaris.

You're going to ruin everything, he explains. You'll ruin the big plan.

The Big Plan…

Sprite has spent hundreds of thousands of years as an eleven year old boy. The Eternals do not age. They were not designed to age.

They do not breed.

They believe, mistakenly, that they have family relationships. They don't. They were all created at the same time, all two hundred of them. If they reproduced they would ruin the experiment, as they would outbreed anything else — disease-free, immortal, super-powered people that they are. On a Darwinian basis, they've won. So they were programmed to believe that they had family relationships, given artificial memories, programmed and not to question things.

Sprite was an error. Or perhaps it amused the Celestials to have a young eternal about. The only trouble was, he never aged. And slowly, he realised this. He wanted what the others had — adulthood, respect, sex.

So he investigated. He learned the Eternals secrets — he analyzed things that none of the others seemed curious about, poked and pried and read and listened…

And he learned things that no-one knew. And chief amongst those things he investigated was the Dreaming Celestial.

The one Celestial to remain on Earth, for reasons beyond our understanding. A rebel, perhaps, or insane. No-one knows. It was left here half a million years ago by the other Celestials — imprisoned forever beneath a mountain, an intelligence incomprehensible to humans… or to Eternals. It's unconscious, immobile. And it's the most powerful thing in this corner of the universe.

He also learned that Eternals don't die. There are only two hundred of them. If they get damaged or destroyed, they are rebuilt by Celestial circuitry, kept deep beneath Olympia until they are needed again.

Sprite laid his plans. And then he acted on them — he hijacked a Unimind, used it to tap into the Dreaming Celestial's power. The kind of power he could use…

…to become a real boy.

Human. Aging normally. With stardom, riches and — as soon as he's old enough to enjoy them — girls.

And if he was going to be human, they all were.

Now it's Ikaris, Makkari against Sprite. Who is still human, but with the power of the Dreaming Celestial at his disposal.

But Makkari has his speed back. And Ikaris has the incredible strength of will and sense of self that survived the rewriting of the universe.

But that may not be enough.

They take the battle back to the old Eternals Mountain to Olympia.

And when it seems like the world is lost, and that Ikaris and Makkari are going to get it…

With the aid of Mad Zuras, the other Eternals — Thena, Sersi, Druig, and Ajak — return, from beneath Olympus. Fully powered.

After all, Eternals don't die.

Sprite is captured and placed into stasis…

Even the Unimind cannot make everything be like it was.

But it can restore the powers to our Eternals.

And Zuras, now sane, reassumes his part as leader of the Eternals, gives Ikaris and Makkari their task. To track down the rest of the two hundred Eternals who don't know who or what they are…

They have a purpose. And a world that isn't going to be easy to rebuild…

JACK KIRBY AN

Kirby was coming…back!

After a five year hiatus, Jack Kirby was returning to Marvel Comics in 1975. Similar to his just-ended contract with DC Comics, the King would write, pencil and edit a line of comics from his California home. At this point in his illustrious career, Kirby had big ideas still waiting to make it onto the page and as a result, he didn't want to repeat himself. Still, publisher Stan Lee and then-Editor-in-Chief Roy Thomas wanted Kirby's energy to infuse some of the core titles. Reluctantly, Kirby returned to *Captain America* and helped relaunch the *Black Panther*. His imagination could not be earthbound so he agreed to adapt the movie *2001: A Space Odyssey* which led to an ongoing title, which begat the popular character Machine Man.

Kirby wasn't done, though.

Always captivated by the notion of legends, he thought heroic legends were created by people who needed something to look up to, to ease their suffering since so much of man's early history was a struggle. A Viking would come back from a battle, feeling tired and covered in blood, but he knew atop the mountain, Thor was still fighting the good fight. Such notions influenced much of his work dating back to Captain America, addressing a far more modern need.

Ever since his tenure on *Thor* in the 1960s, Kirby liked the notion of aliens being perceived by humans as gods. Now back at Marvel, he still wanted to explore the theme. The timing was fortuitous given Erich von Däniken's best-selling book *Chariot of the Gods?* which discussed the idea that aliens had visited Earth in the distant past, influencing ancient cultures, including the Mayans. Marvel thought the idea had merit, as they had already jumped on that bandwagon with the first issue of *Marvel Preview* in 1975.

Kirby was given the green light to produce The Celestials. As Kirby set to work, it was decided to rename the title Return of the Gods in order to cement the relationship in consumers' minds. A logo had been created which was even used in several house ads before the Legal Department stepped in and had it removed. They felt the type treatment was close to an infringement so the final title became The Eternals.

The first issue arrived cover-dated July 1976 and continued for nineteen issues and one annual, one of the longer runs for a Kirby creation that decade. In an introductory text piece, Kirby wrote, "How do we view the Eternals?

"That is the question. And it's a big question, because it involves us all in a great cosmic adventure which began when the dinosaurs split the scene and humanity was first pushed on the stage of that universal Gong Show we call History.

"Something happened back there, among the steaming ferns and moving continents of prehistoric Earth. And neither Walter Cronkite nor Howard Cosell nor your ever-lovin' current events teacher was there to take notes on the events we must nowadays sift from the myths, the mummies, and the skeletons that lay buried beneath tons of soil.

"So what happened there, in that unreported, unwritten, mystifying beginning of all things? How many mammoth events provided the oil which still spins the wheels of this plastic pickle-works we hail as modern civilization?

"I feel that playing around with this sort of conjecture is highly entertaining, and that we should aim our gun sights at this giant puzzle we've inherited more often. We can't leave it all to the professors, pundits, and paperback prophets. The puzzle belongs to you and me as well."

In the telling, Kirby postulated that a race known as the Celestials had come to Earth during the early days of life. These titanic, armored figures came from the far reaches of the cosmos to various planets to weigh and measure life as it was developing. Their studies occur over countless years in four visits with different delegations, known as Hosts. The First Host arrived on Earth about one million years ago and began their experiments with the humanoids found at that time. As a result, two new species were created: Eternal and Deviant.

The Eternals were given superior genetics, imbued with cosmic energies that took centuries to discover and master. The Deviants, on the other hand, were given an unstable genetic code which caused them to mutate over the years.

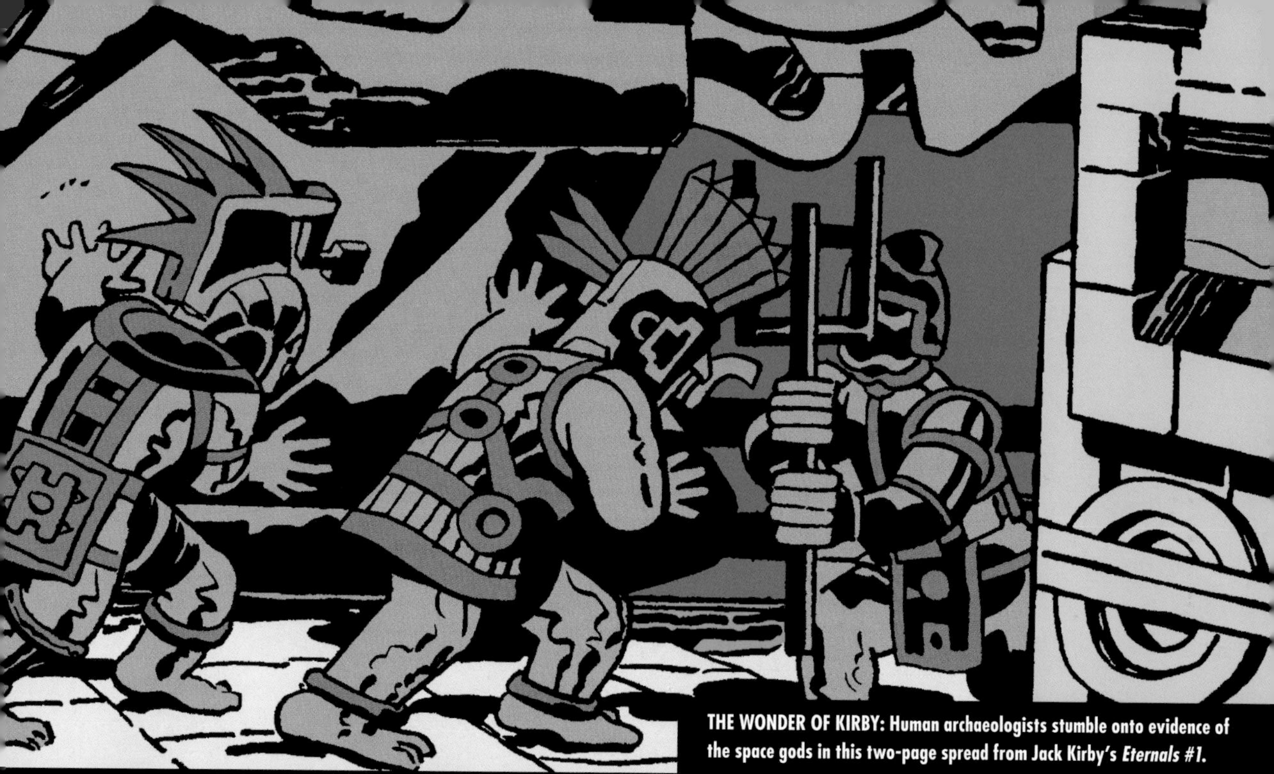

THE WONDER OF KIRBY: Human archaeologists stumble onto evidence of the space gods in this two-page spread from Jack Kirby's *Eternals #1*.

D THE ETERNALS

By ROBERT GREENBERGER

The Second Host arrived some 20,000 years back when the Deviants had managed to forge a worldwide government—based in Lemuria—crushing any human resistance. During one such attack, the city of Atlantis sank. In their hubris, they thought to challenge their creators. The Celestials had other ideas and much of the Deviant civilization was eradicated during the Great Cataclysm, including the sinking of the continent of Mu, and man was left to evolve on his own.

The Eternals kept to themselves in their polar retreat, recognizing their advanced abilities would frighten the humans. Among them, one stood out, having fought brave battles but then was shunned by man and even Eternal, earning the title the Forgotten One. There were other periodic exchanges between Eternal and human, such as the Eternal later named Ikaris marrying a human woman and having a son, Icarus. When the son died, Ikaris adopted the name in tribute. Best known are the exploits of Sersi, the bombastic woman who enjoyed dealing with man and his culture. She frequently walked through man's world, savoring hedonistic pleasures, notably dancing.

They were nobly led by Kronos until his death when the son, Zuras, succeeded him. Zuras was the Prime Eternal until the arrival of the Fourth Host and is noted for being the first to combine all the Eternals into the Uni-Mind. Zuras perfected the Ritual that brings just about all Eternals together so their cosmic energy can be merged into a brain-like construct. Much remains to be learned about the Uni-Mind but it has been formed only during times of great crisis, requiring a unified effort. The records indicate humans and Deviants have also been tapped to help form the Uni-Mind which showed its adaptability.

About 1000 B.C. heralded the Third Host, their duties described by the Eternal Ajak as "inspection and cultivation." The Incas worshipped the visiting Host as gods while instilling fear in others around the globe. The Eternal Ajak spoke directly with the Celestials, protecting their base, and then placed himself in suspended animation, awaiting the Fourth Host.

THENA AND MAKARRI: Two of Kirby's Eternals who were built for action, on the hunt for Deviants terrorizing New York City! (From Jack Kirby's Eternals #6.)

In the nineteenth century, the Eternal Ikaris sensed it was time to prepare Earth for the Host's arrival and left his home to interact with man. Using the name Ike Harris, Ikaris dealt with humans for the first time since the Third Host and marveled at the changes.

The Fourth Host came to Earth in the recent past, ready to render judgment—the setting for Kirby's run. They witness what man had wrought, as well as the resumption of the ages-old conflict between Eternal and Deviant. The Deviants sought to either gain favor with the Host or see to it no one benefited. The Eternals, meanwhile, sought to preserve not only their lives but that of the noble, less powerful humans, whom they saw as having great potential. A small group, known as the Young Gods, made a gift of themselves to the Celestials to show how well the experiment had worked. Arishem, leader of the Fourth Host, accepted them and gave Earth his verdict: a thumbs-up.

Sales were solid but never spectacular. Looking back, historians Gerry Jones & Will Jacobs called it "great fun" while Peter Sanderson in *Marvel*

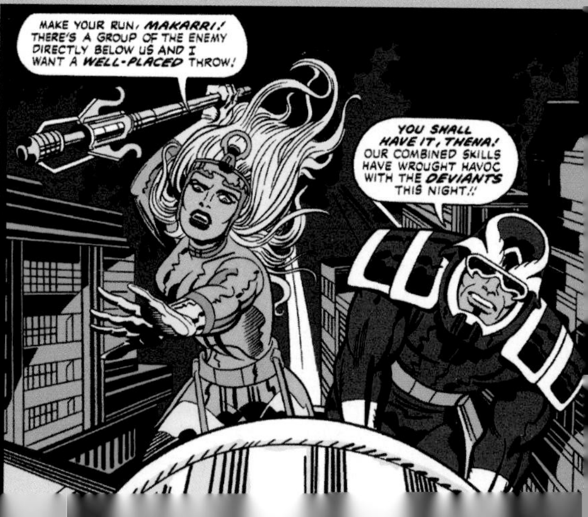
MAKE YOUR RUN, MAKARRI! THERE'S A GROUP OF THE ENEMY DIRECTLY BELOW US AND I WANT A WELL-PLACED THROW!
YOU SHALL HAVE IT, THENA! OUR COMBINED SKILLS HAVE WROUGHT HAVOC WITH THE DEVIANTS THIS NIGHT!!

HE'S OUT OF CONTROL!

Ray Wyman Jr., in *The Art of Jack Kirby*, suggested, "Although the story writing in *Eternals* was fragmented and distracting, Kirby's pseudo-techno designs were as fascinating as ever."

In Kirby's mind, his space saga was in its own reality, divorced from the Marvel Universe. By 1977, though, editors back in New York wanted to play with his concepts and thought the book would benefit from the familiar super heroes and super-villains making appearances. Kirby, by then, was already battling with editors over the way his dialogue had been altered without approval in his various titles. In an effort to be one of the gang, he made a few attempts to acknowledge the Marvel Universe in his cosmic series. S.H.I.E.L.D. agents began to show up followed by one of his earliest hits, The Thing — however, the blue-eyed adventurer proved to be a regular Joe whose features were momentarily transformed into a likeness of the Fantastic Four hero by Sersi. Another attempt had an appearance by The Hulk, but this too proved to be a falsity — this one was a cosmically-enhanced robot.

After 1978 Kirby stopped the title, and the characters were fair game to the next generation of editors, writers and artists, many of whom were strongly influenced by Kirby's creations and were eager to play with them.

But none of the series featuring these entities has proven successful, a track record likely to change with 2006's miniseries from Neil Gaiman and John Romita, Jr. When the announcement was made, Gaiman said, "What drew me to it was not the god side of things, but the incredibly long-lived nature of things. I just loved the idea of seeing two people standing in a town square looking at a statue of themselves that was erected 1,000 years before.

"It was kind of the opportunity to create a mythology. In *1602* I re-created everything that had happened in the Marvel Universe because they'd got it right. *The Eternals* still had that amazing Jack Kirby outpouring of ideas, and there were some amazing things. But he didn't get it right. It's sort of weird and lumpy."

Universe called it Kirby's last great creative achievement. He wrote: "Like much of Kirby's work for Marvel and DC in the 1960s and 1970s, *The Eternals* is an inquiry into the nature of God. Working with Lee, Kirby had created the Stranger *(in X-Men)*, Odin and the High Evolutionary *(in Thor)*, the Source *(in New Gods)*, the Watcher and Galactus (in *The Fantastic Four)*; now, working on his own in *The Eternals*, he presented us with 'space gods,' the Celestials.

"The Eternals is as memorable for its characters as it is for Kirby's epic feats of visualization. There was the shadowy, brooding figure of the Forgotten One, the Eternal who was known to ancient civilizations as Gilgamesh, Samson, and Hercules. There was Kro, the demonic military leaders of the Deviants, who despite his ruthlessness was still gripped by passion for his former lover, Thena, the fiery warrior daughter of Zuras, monarch of the Eternals. And there was Sersi, perhaps the most fascinating of all, an Eternal with many sides to her personality. She was known to the Deviants as Sersi the Terrible for her temper and her ability to alter the shapes of persons or objects at will, as when she transformed Ulysses' men to pigs in ancient times. (Sersi explained that Homer had misspelled her name in *The Odyssey*.)

"Despite its considerable merits, the original *Eternals* series was not a commercial success, perhaps because Kirby dealt with his large cast of characters as a true ensemble, continually shifting the focus from one group in one issue to another set in the next; there was no central heroic figure who appeared in every story line."

While most comics of the day focused on one or two main characters, even the team books such as The *Avengers* and *X-Men* kept the focus tight on a handful of protagonists and gently shifting that focus over the course of issues. Not Kirby, whose kinetic storytelling meant readers were treated to a rush of concepts, one coming after the after with little time spent fully exploring any one character or concept. As a result, his titles tended to either be embraced by fans who loved the art and energy or shunned by those who were left breathless.

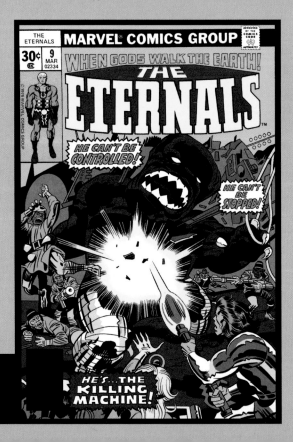

THE ETERNALS • MARVEL COMICS GROUP • 30¢ • 9 • MAR 02334 • WHEN GODS WALK THE EARTH! • THE ETERNALS • HE CAN'T BE CONTROLLED! • HE CAN'T BE STOPPED! • HE'S...THE KILLING MACHINE!

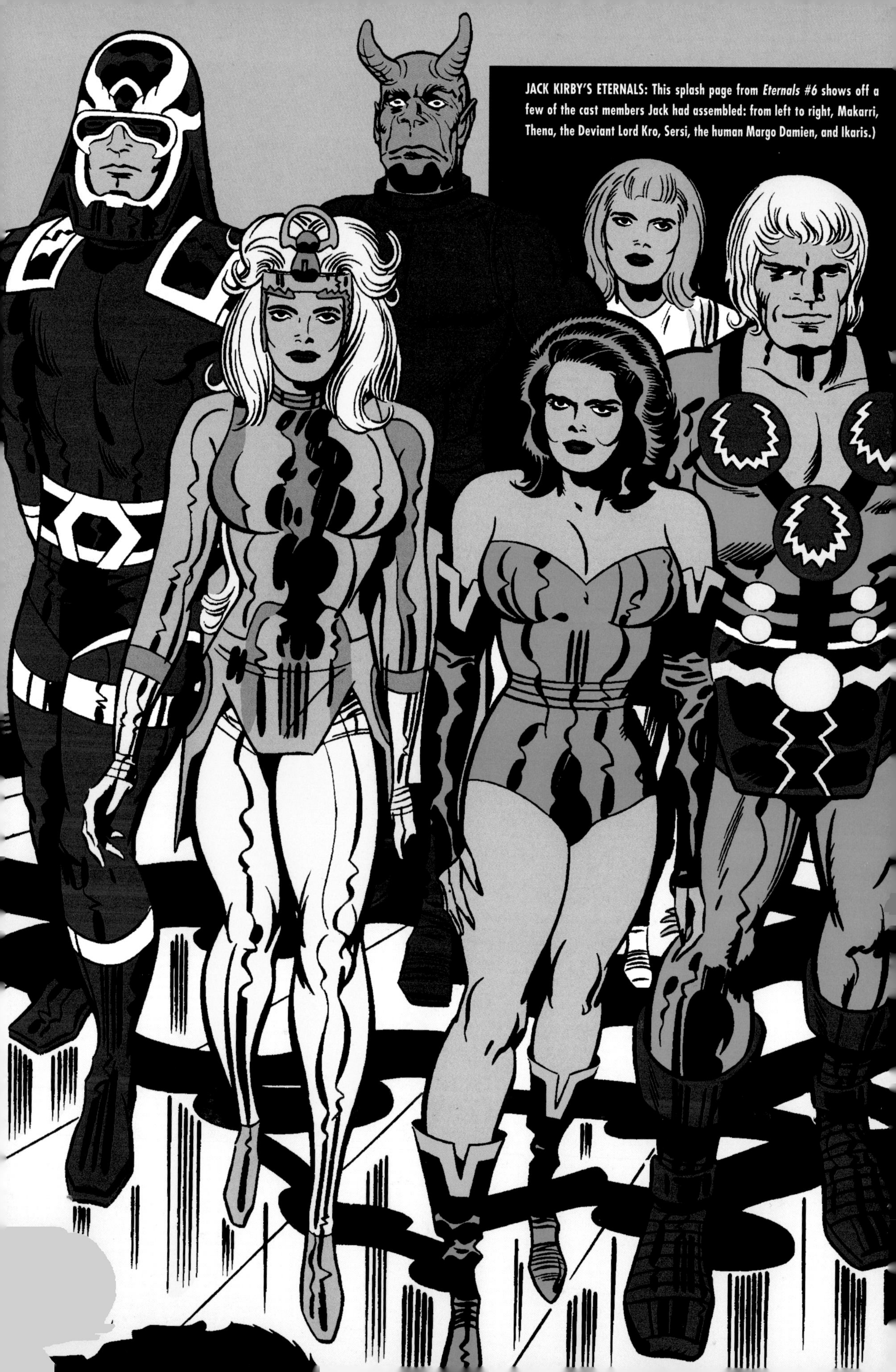

JACK KIRBY'S ETERNALS: This splash page from *Eternals #6* shows off a few of the cast members Jack had assembled: from left to right, Makarri, Thena, the Deviant Lord Kro, Sersi, the human Margo Damien, and Ikaris.)

Unused Eternals Pin-up by John Romita JR.

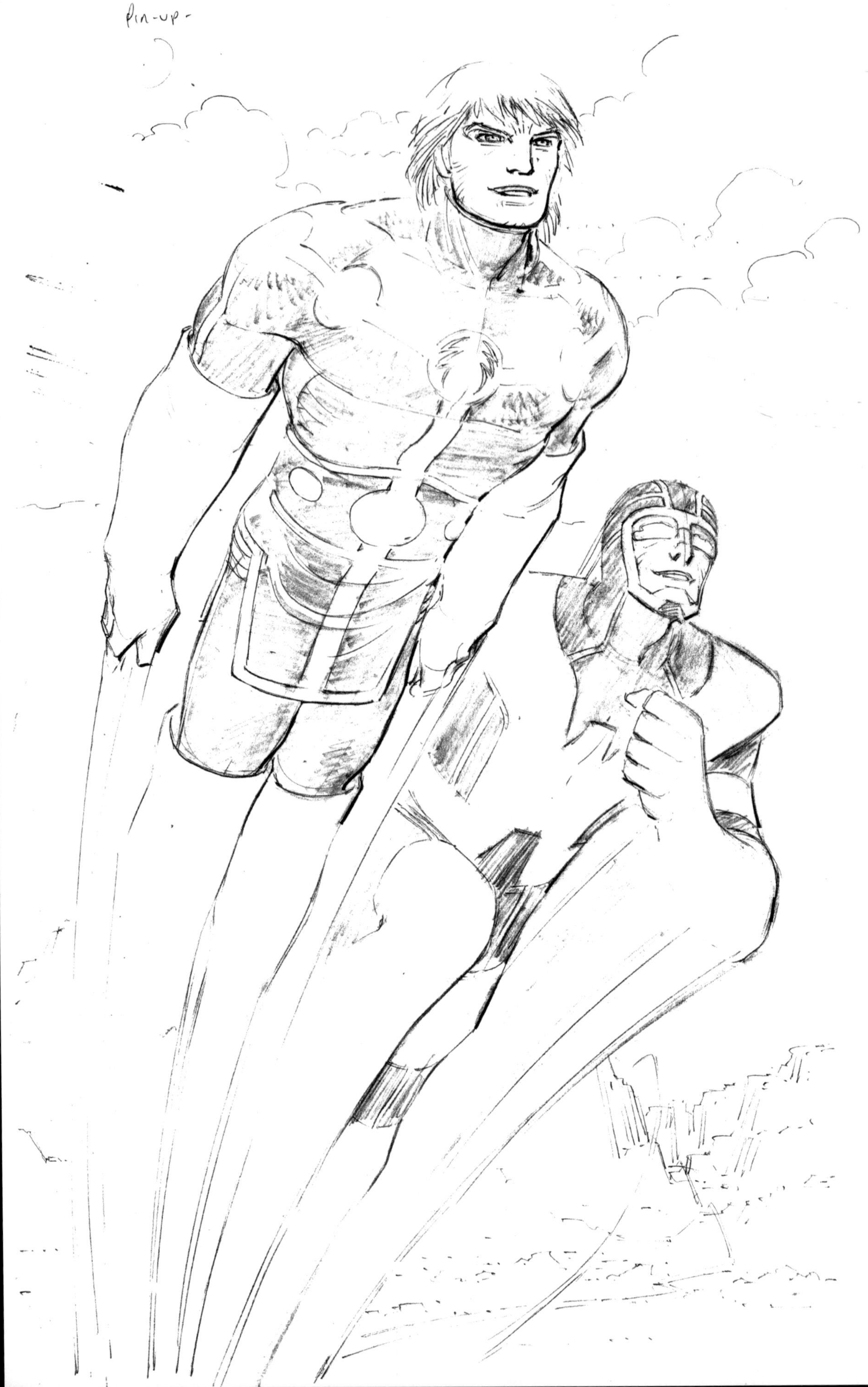
Pin-up -